# APPLES AND ORANGES

# APPLES AND ORANGES

## EXPLORATIONS IN, ON, AND WITH COMPARISON

### BRUCE LINCOLN

*The University of Chicago Press*
*Chicago and London*

The University of Chicago Press, Chicago 60637
The University of Chicago Press, Ltd., London
© 2018 by The University of Chicago.
All rights reserved. No part of this book may be used or
reproduced in any manner whatsoever without written
permission, except in the case of brief quotations in critical
articles and reviews. For more information, contact the
University of Chicago Press,
1427 East 60th Street, Chicago, IL 60637.
Published 2018

27 26 25 24 23 22 21 20 19 18    1 2 3 4 5

ISBN-13: 978-0-226-56391-6 (cloth)
ISBN-13: 978-0-226-56407-4 (paper)
ISBN-13: 978-0-226-56410-4 (e-book)
DOI: https://doi.org/10.7208/chicago
/9780226564104.001.0001

Library of Congress Cataloging-in-Publication Data

Names: Lincoln, Bruce, author.
Title: Apples and oranges : explorations in, on, and with
    comparison / Bruce Lincoln.
Description: Chicago ; London : The University of Chicago
    Press, 2018. | Includes bibliographical references and index.
Identifiers: LCCN 2017055603 | ISBN 9780226563916 (cloth :
    alk. paper) | ISBN 9780226564074 (pbk. : alk. paper) |
    ISBN 9780226564104 (e-book)
Subjects: LCSH: Religions—Study and teaching—Methodology. |
    Religions—History—To 1500. | Myth—Cross-cultural
    studies. | Social sciences—Comparative method.
Classification: LCC BL41 .L55 2018 | DDC 200.72—dc23
LC record available at https://lccn.loc.gov/2017055603

To the Memory of Dear Friends
and Esteemed Colleagues

*Marilyn Robinson Waldman (1943–1996)*
*Mark Krupnick (1939–2003)*
*Carsten Colpe (1929–2009)*
*Cristiano Grottanelli (1948–2010)*
*Juanita Garciagodoy (1952–2012)*
*Braulio Montalvo (1934–2014)*
*Martin Riesebrodt (1948–2014)*
*Anthony C. Yu (1938–2015)*
*Paul Friedrich (1927–2016)*
*Saba Mahmood (1962–2018)*

# CONTENTS

# FIGURES AND TABLES

# ACKNOWLEDGMENTS

Chapter 2 was presented at the University of Minnesota's Center for Humanistic Studies in fall 1984 and was coauthored with Cristiano Grottanelli during the time he served as James J. Hill Visiting Professor at Minnesota. It was first published as Occasional Paper #4 of the Center (1984–85) and republished as an article in *Method and Theory in the Study of Religion* 10 (1998): 311–25.

Chapter 3 was presented at a special meeting of the Atelier Chicago-Paris pour l'étude des religions anciennes in December 2010. It was subsequently published in the proceedings of that meeting, Claude Calame and Bruce Lincoln, eds., *Comparer en historie des religions antiques* (Liège: Presses Universitaires de Liège, 2012), 99–110. Chapter 4 was presented as the Hayes Robinson Distinguished Lecture in History at Royal Holloway College, University of London in March 2015 upon the invitation of Evrim Binbas. It is published here for the first time. Chapter 5 was presented at meetings of the Sawyer Seminar on "The Comparative History of Comparatism" held at Cambridge University in September 2015 upon the invitation of Simon Goldhill, Geoffrey Lloyd, and Reynaud Gagné. It is published here for the first time. Chapter 6 was presented at Oxford University, Corpus Christi College in June 2014 upon the invitation of Jaš Elsner. It is published here for the first time. Chapter 7 was written in conjunction with chapters 6 and 8 and was published in Per Pippin Aspaas, Sigrid Albert, and Fredrik Nilsen, eds., *Rara avis in Ultima Thule: Libellus festivus Sunnivae des Bouvrie dedicatus/Festschrift for Synnøve des Bouvrie* (Tromsø, Norway: Septentrio Academic, 2014), 19–34. Chapter 8 was presented at meetings of the Sawyer Seminar on "The Comparative History of Comparatism" held at Cambridge University in April 2015 upon the invitation of Simon Goldhill, Geoffrey Lloyd, and Reynaud Gagné. It is published here for the first time. Chapter 9 was written as a follow-up to chapter 3 and was published in *History of Religions* 54 (2014): 323–40. Chapter 10 was first presented at a conference on "Sacrifices humains: Discours et réalités" at the University of Geneva in May 2011 and subsequently as a lecture at the University of Bayreuth in May 2012. It was published in Agnes A. Nagy and Francesca Prescendi, eds., *Sacrifice humain: Dossiers, discours, comparaison* (Turnhout, Belgium: Brepols, 2013), 177–94. Chapter 11 was presented at Stanford University (May 2013), the University of Lausanne (September 2013), and Carleton University (October 2013). The original English version is published here for the first time. The French text presented at Lausanne was published in *Asdiwal* 10 (2015): 111–36.

In addition to those who gave me the opportunity to write and present the pieces listed above, there are many others to whom I owe thanks for stimulating conversation, probing questions, useful references, principled challenges, and the kind of kibbitzing good colleagues offer one another. In addition to those already named, these include Cliff Ando, John Archer, Stefan Arvidsson, Daniel Barbu, Lauren Berlant, Ulrich Berner, Maurizio Bettini, Philippe Bourgeaud, Synnøve de Bouvrie, Gabriele Cappai, Justin Champion, Eugen Ciurtin, Pietro Clemente, Zeba Crook, Touraj Daryaee, Marcel Detienne, Wendy Doniger, Prasenjit Duara, Page DuBois, Chris Faraone, David Frankfurter, Carlo Ginzburg, Fritz Graf, Helen Graham, Dominique Jaillard, Sarah Johnston, Tom Kasulis, Richard Leppert, Martha Lincoln, John Ma, Philippe Mathey, Aglaia McClintock, Bernard McGinn, Nicolas Meylan, Kenneth Northcott, Richard Payne, Marshall Sahlins, Erik Sand, John Scheid, Stefanie von Schnurbein, Jim Scott, Pier Giorgio Solinas, Jørgen Podemann Sørensen, Matt Stolper, Guy Stroumsa, Gary Thomas, Mihaela Timuş, Aaron Tugendhaft, Hugh Urban, Yuhan Vevaina, Marilyn Waldman, Margit Warberg, Morten Warmind, Christian Wedemeyer, and Stephanie West. Deepest thanks of all go to Louise Lincoln, who read and offered critical commentary on every chapter, after listening to rambling discussions of the material over the dinner table.

# I
# GENERAL OBSERVATIONS

# I: INTRODUCTION

### I

This is a book about comparison; more specifically, about the practice of comparison in the study of history, religion, discourse, and society. It does not claim to be comprehensive or systematic. Rather, it reflects my decades-long engagement with the problem, during which I have come to see comparison as an indispensable instrument of human thought that most often goes seriously astray. Specialization surely seems safer, but only in comparison to comparison, which is thus revealed to be inescapable even in the moment one (thinks one) rejects it.

### II

My views, like everyone else's, took shape in and reflect the course of an idiosyncratic trajectory. That being the case, some autobiographical background is probably in order.

*I never aspired to do specialized research. Never was fascinated by or fell in love with any particular time, place, culture, or tradition. As an impressionable undergraduate, I was sufficiently dazzled by T. S. Eliot's reorchestration of world mythologies in "The Wasteland" that I tried to understand how it was done. Not knowing Eliot added footnotes to his poem mostly to justify its publication in monograph form, I pored over them as if they held the key to some hidden kingdom.*

*The results were decidedly mixed. Eliot's notes led me to Ovid, the Upaniṣads, and the Grail romances via Jessie Weston's* From Ritual to Romance *and Frazer's* Golden Bough, *both severely outdated texts by the time I got to them. Even so, Frazer dazzled me even more than Eliot and led to Balder, Adonis, the Rex Nemorensis, and countless others. How was it possible, I wondered, for one human being to know so many things and bring them together in such magisterial synthesis? Not for years would I realize that like most other comparatists, Eliot, Weston, and Frazer knew a few things well and the others badly. What is more, their relative ignorance proved useful, since the more superficial their knowledge of a given datum might be, the easier it was to impose their theories on it: theories that, like all others, reflected the desires, values, fantasies, era, and milieu of the theorist.*

## III

Proverbs to the contrary notwithstanding, there is no problem in comparing apples and oranges. The result is "fruit," a category that operates at a higher level of abstraction.[1] The things apples and oranges have in common (seeds, sweetness, a process of ripening until they become available for consumption, etc.) provide the basis for the concept "fruit," while the qualities distinctive to one fruit but not others (specifics of color, flavor, shape, etc.) disappear from the general category. To the extent that "fruit" permits one to think beyond specifics and helps place "apples" and "oranges" in a broader field of relations, it enhances our understanding. Where it erases their unique features, our understanding is impoverished. Ideally, if the specific properties of oranges and apples could retain their significance without dissolving into the generalities of fruit the comparison would achieve its full utility, i.e., when the Many are complemented and complicated, rather than simplified and displaced by the One.

## IV

*I arrived at the University of Chicago in fall 1971 intending to study history of religions with Mircea Eliade, whom I naively (but probably correctly) took to be the closest contemporary equivalent of Frazer. Eliade, however, had suffered a cardiac "event" the preceding year, and the institution was protecting him against unnecessary demands, including new students like me. Accordingly, I was directed to Jonathan Z. Smith, incoming chair of the department. Having recently completed a dissertation demolishing Frazer, Smith was turning his critical energies to Eliade's methods and theories.[2]*

*Asked about my projected course of studies, I voiced interest in comparative work. "Comparison is over," Smith responded bluntly. "You need to get serious and specialize." Undaunted, I persisted. Rather than ask the reasons for his pronouncement, I sought an exception to his verdict. Surely, there must be some way to do comparison that would meet whatever objections he harbored? "One only," he replied and pointed me toward Indo-European linguistics.*

*I have replayed this conversation many times, for it shaped my studies and early work. It is possible Smith's advice reflected trends of the place and moment. In the years just before, two giants in the study of Indo-European religions had presented Haskell Lectures at Chicago: Stig Wikander in 1967 and Georges*

*Dumézil in 1969.*[3] *Both used philological analysis, close reading of texts, and a* Stammbaum *model of linguistic/cultural relations to compare Indic, Iranian, Greek, Roman, Celtic, and Germanic materials, justifying this by limiting their comparative purview to peoples who were part of the same language family and were thus understood to share a common cultural inheritance. Those who heard these lectures found them enormously impressive. Conceivably, Smith felt they displayed a methodological rigor previously lacking at Chicago: something he was willing to encourage as an alternative to Eliade's wider-ranging, more intuitive style.*

*Alternatively, his advice may have been disingenuous, designed to produce frustration and failure, followed by acceptance of the need to specialize. The price of doing the only legitimate and defensible form of comparison, Smith explained, was to learn a dozen or more very difficult ancient languages. Any reasonable person might be expected to balk, but I quickly fell in line. Within a year, I was doing Sanskrit, Avestan, and coursework in the methods of historical linguistics. Greek, Latin, Old Persian, and Old Norse followed, along with a smattering of Irish, Russian, and Hittite (Pahlavi and a few others would come some years later). When I finally approached Eliade, he welcomed me warmly and supported my efforts, encouraging me to learn more languages, read more broadly, and expand my comparative horizons. Finding his enthusiasm more inviting than Smith's skepticism, I moved in his direction.*

V

Like all categories, the one named "fruit" can be misleading, particularly if mistaken for something extant in nature, rather than an artificial construct generated through acts of comparison. To continue the inquiry—which gets ever more interesting, complicated, and productive as it leads further afield—one might ask what the idea of "fruit" includes, where it comes from, and how it develops.

There are many ways one might proceed, but my training and habits lead me to start with two philological observations. First, attestations in English date from the twelfth century, with considerable orthographic variation (inter alia, *frught, fruct(e), fruict, fruyt(e), frute, fruth,* and *fruit*), but all forms derive from Latin *frūctus.*[4] Second, the term encompasses two semantic domains. One is narrower and more concrete. The *Oxford English Dictionary* lists it first, since it is attested slightly earlier (from 1175 on).[5]

1. Vegetable products in general, that are fit to be used as food by men and animals.
   Example circa 1325: "The power of man is like the field / that much fruit is wont to yield."[6]

2. The edible product of a plant or tree, consisting of the seed and its
   envelope, as in the apple, orange, plum, etc.
   Example circa 1380: "The fairest fruit that may grow in the earth /
   Like the orange and other fruit."[7]

The second semantic domain is more abstract and considerably broader
(attested since 1230).

3. Anything accruing, produced, or resulting from an action or effort, the
   operation of a cause, etc.
   a. Material produce, outgrowth, increase; products, revenues.
      Example circa 1450: "The fruit and profit of that land and of beasts
      in this time."[8]
   b. An immaterial product, a result, issue, consequence.
      Example from 1413: "All the wide world is filled full with the fruit
      of their good labor."[9]
   c. Advantage, benefit, enjoyment, profit.
      Example circa 1230: "Thus God's friend has all the fruit of this
      world that he had forsaken."[10]

Surprisingly, Latin *frūctus* is used with the general sense much more
often than the narrowly botanical, which is not included in the three definitions that appear in the standard reference dictionary.[11]

1. an enjoying, enjoyment.
   Example: "I consider your singular kindness to be an enormous enjoyment and delight (*fructum atque laetitiam*) to my soul."[12]
2. the enjoyment that proceeds from a thing; proceeds, produce, product,
   profit, income (very frequent).
   Example: "In a short time, they became known for their wealth,
   whether from products (*fructibus*) of the sea or the earth."[13]
3. consequence, effect, result, return, reward, success.
   Example: "It is my greatest wish that Publius Sulla . . . could have
   obtained some beneficial result (*fructum*) from his moderation."[14]

This range of meanings reflects the verb from which *frūctus* derives:
Latin *frūor*, "to derive enjoyment from a thing, to enjoy, delight in." In legal
contexts, its semantics are quite precise: "to have the use and enjoyment
of a thing, to have the usufruct."[15] English *usufruct*, moreover, is itself a
compound of two complementary words and ideas: *usus*, "the right to make
productive use of something (e.g., a plot of land)," and *frūctus*, "enjoyment

of the good things that follow."[16] To put it differently, use (*usus*) is the process of transformative labor, and fruit (*frūctus*) is the ultimate product of that labor: not just a material item, but the benefit, profit, and pleasure it yields.

To make "fruit" the category that encompasses apples, oranges, and like comestibles thus represents a narrowing of the Latin concept consistent with the interests of a society where the products that had greatest value and brought greatest satisfaction were agricultural.[17] English shows the same semantic narrowing, although the older, broader, and more abstract sense still peeks through in expressions like "fruits of their labors" and "fruit of their loins." Careful comparison permits a fuller, more nuanced understanding of both the Latin and the English terms, as well as the history that connects them and the kind of society, culture, and economy in which these words assumed, exercised, and changed meaning. It also lets us refine our understanding of apples and oranges. Insofar as we see them as "fruit," we identify them as products cultivated by someone's labor, and things to be enjoyed, quite possibly by others.

## VI

*My earliest works were broadly comparative, most often within an "Indo-European" paradigm, but occasionally not.*[18] *But opinion was turning decisively against comparatism in those years, and this was not an idle change of fashion or swing of some pendulum. The transition from structuralism to poststructuralism, for instance, came not because Lévi-Strauss's ideas lost their novelty and cachet. Rather, their shortcomings became apparent in the course of sharp challenges by Foucault, Bourdieu, Deleuze, and others, who focused critical attention on structuralism's ahistorical and apolitical nature, its preference for the mind over the body, its relative disinterest in and inadequacy for addressing urgent problems of the here and now.*

*The critique was sharper and even more damaging with regard to other influential styles of comparison and their foremost practitioners. Eliade's involvement with the Romanian Legionary Movement came back to haunt him,*[19] *as did Dumézil's enthusiasm for Charles Maurras and the Action Française.*[20] *In both cases, critics perceived connections between these scholars' past political commitments (never acknowledged, let alone repudiated) and aspects of their scholarship. Particularly troubling was the privileged status Indo-European (a.k.a. "Aryan") examples enjoyed in the work of both men and the way some of their core themes—e.g., Eliade's disdain for secular modernity or Dumézil's interest in warrior fraternities and the sacred nature of sovereign authority—showed continuity with the fascist beliefs of their youth.*

*Persuaded—albeit with profound regret—that most of the critiques were justified, I became uncertain how to proceed, as the enterprise in which I'd invested heavily had proven appallingly tainted. The problem was not just whether the competences I'd acquired could be redeployed, but whether there was anything to salvage from comparatism's recurrent train wrecks.*

## VII

Italian has several words derived from *frūctus* that anglophones find surprising. Most important is the verb *sfruttare*, where the prefix *s-* functions like *dis-* in English. Literally, the word thus denotes "de-fruiting." The question is whether the fruits in question are agricultural (Apples + Oranges) or more abstract (the enjoyment and profit derived from the products of labor). Modern dictionaries show both possibilities.

1. (literal) to obtain the maximum possible return from a given piece of land; to exhaust its vigor.
2. (figurative) to extract illicit profit from the labor of another; to remunerate inadequately those who work.[21]

However tempting it might be to imagine a historic development whereby the second sense developed from the first as agriculture yielded to industrial production, earlier dictionaries show both well before industrialization, as in the *Vocabolario degli Accademici della Crusca* of 1741.

1. With reference to plots of land, to make them unfruitful, sterile, and less productive (*meno atti al frutto*); to weaken them.
2. With reference to other things, to seek to extract from them more profit (*più frutto*) than can be done with regard for proper maintenance.[22]

The same dictionary distinguishes between *frutta* (feminine) and *frutto* (masculine), both derived from Latin *frūctus*. The first denoted the edible produce of trees and plants.[23] In contrast, the primary sense of the second was "annual income, proceeds, profits."[24] The verb *sfruttare* relates equally to both nouns and the de-fruiting action it describes can apply to comestibles (*frutta*) or surplus values (*frutto*).

If comparing apples and oranges leads to the idea of "fruit". . . and comparison of English *fruit* to Latin *frūctus* leads to the idea of profit . . . the comparison of *fruit* and *frūctus* to Italian *sfruttare* leads to the idea of exploitation.

## VIII

*Trying to understand why comparatism has repeatedly—and rightly—fallen into discredit, I'd begin with processes of decontextualization and exploitation. When scholars treat the complex products of another society's imaginative labors as the raw materials from which they confect their theories, and when they regard their theories as an intellectual product of a higher order than that of the materials they extracted, grievous abuses have been committed.*

- *Valuable goods have been appropriated, often by those who have little claim to or investment in them.*
- *The makers of those goods have been recognized and compensated, if at all, in very inadequate fashion.*
- *Sign-values have displaced use-values as items of discourse and practice that actively shaped people's lives are transformed into "comparanda" and "examples."*
- *As examples accumulate, they are treated with increasing superficiality and inattention to whatever aspects (all of which had import in their original context) fail to support the comparatist's point.*

*All too often, comparative reprocessing makes different fruits look and taste alike, while none of them tastes very good. In effect, they have been de-fruited: distanced from the soil in which they grew, deprived of the specifics that gave them flavor, converted into cheap, homogenized goods for undiscriminating consumers, yielding profit that comparatists call theoretical gain, but which usually amounts to little more than a transient spike in their reputation.*

## IX

Although the idea of exploitation has become ubiquitous (much like its practice), the word acquired its modern sense only recently. From the fifteenth to the middle of the eighteenth century, the verb *exploit* had a variety of senses, all of which became obsolete.[25] In 1838, however, an anonymous author redeployed the word to describe something for which English previously had no terminology. Surprisingly, the first acts of exploitation named as such were not industrial, but academic.

This was reported in a satirical article describing lessons its author learned from "the great Professor von Humbughausen," whose expertise included "transcendental philosophy, homœopathic medicine, the unknown tongues, and the more abstruse branches of oudenology."[26] This last term, itself a neologism, denotes the "science of nothing,"[27] but to the extent the professor had something like a discipline, it was the comparative study of religion.

From the gymnosophists, my guide, philosopher, and friend derived his lineage through the magi of Persia, the mystagogs of Egypt, the Etruscan augurs, the wise men of the Dom Daniel, and the long line of German sages from Paracelsus and Vanhelmont to Mesmer and Hahnemann.[28]

Von Humbughausen is reported to have taught that beyond the division of humanity into male and female, there is a binary opposition "of a far more transcendental importance, upon which the whole frame of civilized society reposes."[29]

To define this distinction in so many words, might offend the susceptible ears of the squeamish; you will guess what I mean, when I tell you that it bears some relation to the difference between lawyers and their clients, between the wolves and the sheep. But keep that to yourself. To the adepts it is known that in all civilized societies, mankind spontaneously divide and range themselves into two classes, of which the one is led by an instinctive desire to be ridden, while the other is as instinctively domineered by a desire to ride; and in beautiful harmony with this arrangement, the one is created with an inexhaustible appetite for what they cannot understand, the other with a corresponding disposition to supply them with the materials.[30]

Apparently, the great scholar knew something about the dynamics of knowledge/power, cultural capital, and the reproduction of asymmetric relations. As he went on to explain, "riding" types like himself found it easy to extract profit from the "ridden" via claims to vaporous forms of pseudo-knowledge. Best of all is the mystic nonsense for which "the horses, asses, and mules of the species" have high regard and insatiable appetites. That established, the author deploys his new word.

From the beginning of time, the Humbughausens have addicted themselves to mysticism, have nauseated demonstration, and have *exploited* the obscure (to use a French phrase where we have no proper equivalent) with equal delectation and profit; making a great name for themselves, and equally great fools of all that believed and followed them.[31]

X

*Up to this point, we have considered production-side exploitation, i.e., the process of expropriating cultural goods from their makers as grist for comparatists' mills. In contrast, von Humbughausen worked the consumption side, extracting cash and deference from those to whom he hawked his dubious wares. Whether the man actually knew anything was inconsequential, for his stock-in-trade was*

*not learning, but the authority effect his performance cultivated in a clientele
equally hungry and uncritical.*

*In the awe the great professor excited in his students, I recognize my own
youthful reactions to Eliot, Frazer, Eliade, Dumézil, and other comparatists.
Unlike von Humbughausen, none of them was a vulgar charlatan in cynical
pursuit of profit and fame, but all studies of religion run the risk of remystifying
the mystificatory, while preying on the credulous. Comparison compounds the
problem, especially when practiced on a grand scale. All too often, comparatists
dazzle audiences with their ability to keep lots of oudenological balls in motion.*

## XI

Experience suggests that comparatists go wrong in many ways, and no principles or protocols guard against every pitfall. Nonetheless, we are obliged
to continue, for even the most circumscribed inquiry has its comparative
aspects, as when a geographer compares two neighborhoods in "the same"
city, a historian connects moments in time (whether as continuity or rup-
ture), and editors ponder variant readings of a text.

If comparison is to have a viable future, we can begin by identifying and
reining in its most exploitative tendencies. Inter alia, we need to resist the
impulse to subordinate the particular to the general, to privilege similarity
over difference, and to construe favored examples as the standard against
which others are measured and interpreted. We also need to avoid superficial engagement with any of the materials we treat, giving serious attention
to their full content, not just such aspects as strike our fancy, serve our
interests, and make our point. Finally, we need to avoid striking pretentious
postures, claiming to know more than we do, while hiding behind a host of
examples we juggle fast and dirty.

In recent years, I have come to favor what I call "weak comparisons,"
i.e., inquiries that are modest in scope, but intensive in scrutiny, treating a
small number of examples in depth and detail, setting each in its full and
proper context. In such endeavors, apples and oranges provide no more than
a starting point, beyond which one is obliged to reflect on the trees that
produce them, the environments in which these grow, the people who cultivate and consume them, and what exactly we mean by "fruit." Often, one
ends up working harder on a few choice items than grand comparatists do
on the far greater number they treat, with the result that one's conclusions
prove more probative, reliable, and surprising.

## XII

The chapters of this book were written at various times, frequently in
response to one invitation or another, and I have organized them in four

parts depending on the way they engage the issue of comparison. Part 1 includes programmatic responses to the question of why comparative studies are necessary, why they regularly run into trouble, and how they might be done better. This includes some of my earliest work on the topic (chapter 2, written in 1984 in collaboration with the late Cristiano Grottanelli) and my most recent (the present chapter, finished in September 2016), as well as the most systematic (chapter 3). Part 2 contains critical reflections on the two most serious attempts of recent years to undertake comparison on the scale of a Max Müller, Tylor, or Lévi-Strauss. In both instances, I should make clear my admiration for the learning, ambition, and seriousness of the colleagues whose work I consider: Carlo Ginzburg (chapter 4) and Michael Witzel (chapter 5). That I take their projects to replicate many of their predecessors' flaws is not meant to highlight their failings, but to suggest that not even scholars so gifted as these can make comparison work on so ambitious a scale.

Part 3 takes up a classic case—that of the ancient Scythians—which has invited comparative studies of a more focused and restricted sort than those considered in part 2. What makes this a particularly intriguing site of experimentation is that the available evidence (textual and archaeological) is enough to be tantalizing, but not conclusive on any points. Facing that situation, some scholars (particularly François Hartog, discussed in chapter 6) have reacted with caution, arguing that the Greek sources on which we depend tell us more about Greeks than Scythians. Others (particularly Karl Meuli, discussed in chapter 8) thought that comparison of the Greek accounts to anthropological reports of other steppe peoples not only confirms Herodotus and others, but lets one see the way Scythian influence transformed Greek culture. Again, I take Hartog and Meuli to be exceptionally gifted scholars, whose style of comparison led them to exaggerated results of a negative sort (in the case of Hartog, who made Greek culture the prime comparandum) or conclusions that were seductive, but misleading (in the case of Meuli, who privileged ethnographic accounts of Siberia). In chapters 6 (which is concerned with royal oaths), 7 (with origin myths), and 8 (with priests and shamans), I argue that a more rigorous, measured, and systematic comparison lets us augment the available evidence in ways that permit a deeper, richer, and sounder understanding.

Part 4 includes five studies that make use of "weak" comparison and demonstrate its potential. Each of these brings together two or three examples that are not connected to one another in any direct (i.e., historic, geographic, or linguistic) way, but resemble one another in form, content, and detail. Close study shows how these resemblances reflect and result from the various peoples' engagement with similar issues and problems, which may be ethical and economic (chapter 9, which treats materials from Anglo-Saxon England and Zoroastrian Iran), ethical and political (chapter 10, Old Norse and West African), social and political (chapter 11, the North American Plains, South Africa, and the Spanish Republic), or all the above (chapters 12 and 13, Achaemenid Iran and the American Southwest). I would like to think each chapter makes important points about large issues, including inequity, resentment, ambition, the way unstable institutions seek to stabilize, legitimate, and perpetuate themselves, and the ways shrewdly crafted acts of discourse and practice help reproduce or attempt to modify the maldistributions of wealth, power, and privilege that countless other such acts have naturalized as the norm. None of these chapters aspires to identify universal (or near-universal) patterns, structures, or truths, being more concerned with the agency of actors, narrators, and others who adapt the patterns and structures of their time, place, and culture to engage issues arising in that context and do so in ways similar—but never identical—to others who find themselves in like circumstances. Read collectively, these chapters show how potent and revealing "weak" comparisons can be.

# 2: THE FUTURE OF HISTORY OF RELIGIONS

## (with Cristiano Grottanelli)

## I. INTRODUCTION

Although the academic study of religion (as a general category and in its specific historic forms) is a relatively recent phenomenon, the variety of motivations that have prompted scholars to undertake this study is considerable, and the methods and data that have been employed by students of religion are also manifold. Yet for all of this, there are relatively few scholarly works on the topic that have shown themselves to be of any lasting significance, and fewer still such works that have appeared in the last half century. As Clifford Geertz lamented some years ago, "[We are] living off the conceptual capital of [our] ancestors, adding very little, save a certain empirical enrichment to it. . . . There is Durkheim, Weber, Freud, or Malinowski, and in any particular work the approach of one or two of these transcendent figures is followed, with but a few marginal corrections."[1] One could discuss the precise list of names—we would add Marx and Engels, while deleting Freud—but the situation has not changed appreciably since Geertz wrote, although his own name and that of Claude Lévi-Strauss might now be added to the list.

Such a state of affairs raises numerous questions, to be sure. Why is it that theoreticians working prior to 1925 or thereabouts were able to meet with such success and continue to exert such influence? Why is it that prior to this time the study of religion was a central concern for scholars of such varied interests? And why is it that so little significant work has been done since their pioneer researches? One particularly striking datum must be noted at the outset: of those individuals whose contributions have had enduring influence, not one was or would have considered himself a specialized student of religion, nor were any of them—in principle—particularly interested in "religion" per se. Rather, they tended to be people of varied professional callings—sociologists, anthropologists, political activists, and the like—who came to study the nature of *society*, and in so doing were forced to confront the powerful role of religion in shaping, maintaining, and also at times changing the nature, structure, and functioning of those societies with which they were concerned. As a result, for all their differences—and they are many—classic theoreticians of the nineteenth and early twentieth centuries, whose writings continue to inform the great majority of current studies, explored religion not as a denatured and isolated *Ding an sich*, but as one part, albeit an extremely important part, of a broader sociopolitical and historic field.

## II. MYTHIC ANCESTORS

One can recognize this, for instance, in Marx's treatment of religion in his writings of the 1840s, the earliest works that we will consider.[2] Here, moving beyond Feuerbach's purely philosophical discussion of the essence of religion, Marx (1818–83) set this problematic within a specific context, connecting the religious thought and institutions with which he was familiar to their correlated social and economic structures, i.e., the capitalism of Europe and America of his day. Beyond this, in the last major work where he explicitly treated religion, Marx offered a rich and suggestive treatment of religion as a mode of ideology, indeed as a particularly (historically) influential and (critically) instructive mode of ideology, although one might well quarrel with his restricted sense of this latter term and the somewhat rigid model he posited for the relation of socioeconomic structure and ideological superstructure.[3]

Although the criticism of religion was an important theme in Marx's early works, he nowhere pursued it systematically, and his contributions to the study of specifically religious phenomena and of the historic complexities of specific religions were, in fact, less than those of his patron and collaborator, Friedrich Engels (1820–95). In several studies, Engels explored the way in which religious differences were caught up in social (i.e., class) conflicts, as, for instance, in his analysis of the revolutionary aspects of Anabaptist thought, which he contrasted to the positions—religious and sociopolitical—taken by Luther.[4] What is important here is less the question of whether Engels's view of the Reformation and the Peasants' War is correct (it remains controversial), but rather his recognition of the tensions and competition between the religious tendencies and groupings, along with their complex dialectic possibilities. For, in contrast to Marx, who dismissed religion as false consciousness tout court, Engels perceived that within any society and any historical moment, there may be multiple competing religious attitudes and movements, which express, maintain, and even (at times) exacerbate the other tensions and conflicts within that society.

A similar focus on the complex interrelations of social and religious forms is characteristic of Max Weber (1864–1920), whose vast work on the sociology of religions remains classic, as does his discussion of the religio-political category of "charisma."[5] Yet his most enduring contribution of a theoretical nature is found (in our opinion) in *The Protestant Ethic and the Spirit of Capitalism*, where he argued—*pace* Marx and Engels—that far from being secondary or epiphenomenal to socio-material formations, religion could be highly influential, even causal for the latter. And as his central case in point, Weber sought to demonstrate how Calvinist theology and ethics—that is to say, religious ideology—had forcefully contributed to the emergence of a new class of merchants and manufacturers in early modern Europe.[6]

Yet another view of the relations between religion and society was offered by Émile Durkheim (1858–1917), who consecrated his chef d'oeuvre to the topic, a book prompted by a much broader concern still, which lay at the heart of the most projects undertaken by Durkheim's *école sociologique*.[7] That problematic, briefly stated, is the question of what sorts of things provide the bonds that join people together in social aggregates of any size (e.g., families, lineages, communities, states), and what holds those aggregates intact over time. Given this overriding concern, it was inevitably the ways in which religion furthers the integration of society that most fascinated Durkheim and his disciples. One need not unduly stress Durkheim's famous, but ill-founded attempt to see in religion merely the worship of some projected image of society itself in order to recognize this point. For in their development of such eminently useful concepts as the collective representation or the total social fact, Durkheim and his school consistently focused on the ways in which religious phenomena—funerary and sacrificial rituals, sacred calendars, totemic systems, taxonomic orders, etc.—fostered both a common worldview and powerful sentiments of solidarity among those who shared them.[8]

For all that Bronislaw Malinowski (1884–1942)—the last major figure cited by Geertz and the last whom we will consider—shared Durkheim's view of the social locus and utility of religion, there are significant differences of emphasis between them: differences that go beyond the simple fact that Malinowski eschewed armchair comparatism in favor of intensive firsthand observation in the field. Chief of these differences is that whereas the Durkheimians tended to study religions as global systems of thought and sentiment, stressing particularly the sentiments of group solidarity aroused by religious phenomena, Malinowski was more concerned with the detailed ways in which religion functions to inform, model, and/or legitimate concrete patterns of action and organization, as, for instance, in his classic discussions of how myth provides a charter for clan or tribal hierarchies, and how magic supplements techniques of economic production.[9]

To be sure, there are strong objections that could be—and have been—raised regarding Malinowski's insistence on the purely and immediately practical, even pedestrian value of myth and magic, which has as its partial corollary an underestimation of the speculative and intellectual aspects of "primitive" thought. Lévi-Strauss has voiced this point most aggressively, in stating that "Malinowski claimed that primitive peoples' interest in totemic plants was inspired by nothing but the rumbling of their stomachs."[10] There is truth in this criticism, as in the complementary observation that Lévi-Strauss's own writings tilt too heavily toward abstract and ahistorical intellectualism. But our goal here is not a detailed critique of the various approaches to religious phenomena that we have quoted. Rather, it is a general assessment of the contributions of those classic theoreticians who first established the scientific study of religion, and whose works continue to have utility for the construction of proper and productive research methods.

It is not enough, however, to continue employing the methods of one or another past master out of comfortable habit or in slavish devotion. Rather, we think it helpful to consider the scholars discussed above as a set, and to search out certain similarities within their works. Of these, first and most important was their insistence on treating religion within a broad social context. Rather than isolating religion as a pristine object of itself, they consistently saw it in relation to other dimensions of society such as law, politics, kinship, economy, and the like. Second, with the exception of Malinowski, all made skillful use of comparative method within the limits of the data available to them. The nature of their interests required this, for they hoped to achieve an understanding of general categories: class struggle, social cohesion, charismatic authority, or the like. In order to do this, it was—and is—necessary to consider disparate data. Finally, with the exception of Durkheim, all the figures we have considered were sensitive to historic process. In their eyes, neither society nor religion was a static system, perfect and unchanging in its construction. Rather, they recognized that tensions are present always, and that contradictions within a social field find expression in religion, and vice versa. To do justice to the dynamics of religion and society alike, it is thus necessary to study them processually, paying careful attention to the critical moments at which conflicts erupt into the open, as well as to more subtle changes and mechanisms for the management of stress over long periods of time.

These three tendencies—attention to social context, comparatism, and awareness of conflict and historic process—are, of course, present to greater and lesser degrees in the work of the scholars we have discussed. Durkheim, as we noted, was not particularly concerned with conflict and process; Malinowski, not particularly comparative. No one of them managed to blend perfectly all three tendencies, although Engels and Weber perhaps came closest. But at least two, and sometimes all three, of these theoretical and methodological propensities are quite pronounced in the work of all, and in our view, it was these very propensities that gave their work its lasting value.

## III. THE FALL

It is thus with a sense of profound disappointment and regret that we come to the next chapter of our story: the formation of a specific academic discipline devoted to the study of religion, a discipline variously known as history of religions, comparative religion, religious studies, or *Religionswissenschaft*— a field that effectively took shape in the period between the two world wars.[11] For, despite its initial promise, this field never inherited the critical and methodological legacy of the figures we have mentioned, and consequently remained relatively fruitless and isolated.

Perhaps the central figure in the creation of this discipline was Raffaele Pettazzoni (1883–1959), professor of history of religions at the University of Rome and first president of the International Association for the History of Religions (IAHR), for whom the constitution of an autonomous discipline devoted to the critical, secular study of religion was nothing less than a mission. A liberal with strong socialist sympathies, Pettazzoni was acutely aware from an early age of the church's power in Italian politics and intellectual life. His insistence on the need for an autonomous discipline was largely an attempt to secure an institutional framework in which scholarly independence and objectivity in the analysis of religious issues and data might be preserved, insulation being provided against pressures and/or reservations of a confessional nature. In order to win his case, however, Pettazzoni came to argue for a very different autonomy: the autonomy of the subject matter itself. That is to say, in order to justify a disciplinary autonomy he considered politically and institutionally advantageous, indeed indispensable, Pettazzoni felt constrained to speak of the unique ontological status of religion—its autonomy or irreducibility—something that had (and among many still has) a certain rhetorical appeal, but was (and is) difficult, if not impossible, to justify in strictly logical terms.[12]

To his credit, Pettazzoni always maintained an openness to problems of context and process, while practicing a disciplined and erudite comparatism.[13] Yet others of a very different spirit—less critical and more pious— rallied to his call for an autonomous discipline, embracing warmly his ill-considered arguments concerning the autonomy of religion. What emerged, then, in the work of such individuals as Rudolf Otto (1869–1937), Nathan Söderblom (1866–1931), Wilhelm Schmidt (1868–1954), Friedrich Heiler (1892–1967), Gerardus van der Leeuw (1890–1950), Joachim Wach (1898–

1955), and others whose works were even more severely biased, was the radical decontextualization and deprocessualization of religious data.[14] For these scholars managed to establish as the dominant orientation for the new field a recognition—little more than a leap of faith—that an autonomous aspect of the human spirit (and for many, something more than merely the human spirit!) exists, which may be referred to as "the sacred." Moreover, from "the sacred" were seen to stem all religious phenomena, the term *phenomenon* being used in its precise etymological and philosophical sense as a "manifestation" or "epiphany" of some underlying *noumenon*. All religious forms were thus taken as the specific historico-cultural manifestations or expressions of some transcendent, transhistoric, and transcultural reality. Attempts to contextualize religious data were and often still are denounced as species of "reductionism," a reductionism thought to impugn the autonomy and dignity of a mythic species these scholars dubbed *homo religiosus*. What resulted was a comparatism, but an undisciplined and uncritical comparatism that is not only ahistorical, but even antihistorical, seeking to discover within the variety of religious forms and representations some perennial sacred truth.

If Pettazzoni opened the door for the phenomenologists, the phenomenologists pushed it wide open for others: Jungians, theosophists, and *homines religiosi* of one stripe or another all gravitated to the field in which "the sacred" had been exalted and detached from every other dimension of human activity and experience. Ironically, the very state of affairs that Pettazzoni had hoped to avoid—the powerful intrusion of religious belief into the academic study of religion—was the end result of his life's labor.[15] There can be no shrinking away from the painful fact: the establishment of an autonomous field has, paradoxically, damaged the study of religion (and of religions) immensely, for it has removed that study from its proper grounding.

The consequences of this situation may be summed up by stating that the discipline history of religions managed to marginalize itself in the name of autonomy. Its connections with history, anthropology, sociology, political science, and other relevant fields are scarce, while its ties with theology—however much they are denied—remain strong, if implicit, covert, and distorted. Nor is the field only self-marginalized at present, for historians, anthropologists, and those in other disciplines have often come rightly to distrust or ignore the products of *Religionswissenschaft* and *Religionswissenschaftlern*.

The marginalization of this field, of course, has not resulted in any disaster for the study of religious ideas, institutions, and behaviors elsewhere. Rather, constructive research has continued under other disciplinary banners and has produced some noteworthy results, although little that can claim the breadth or influence of the nineteenth- and early twentieth-century theoreticians. Thus, for many years it was anthropologists who contributed the most useful, perceptive, and original studies of religious data, focusing either on their symbolic dimensions[16] or on their relation to social structures and conflicts.[17]

As anthropologists have gradually become more attentive to issues of diachrony and process—that is, as they have gained a more astute historical consciousness—so also have historians broadened their sense of context and social totality, moving away from the traditional *histoire événementielle* to a more anthropologically informed history, which incorporates social, economic, intellectual, and religious issues, as well as the structures and forms of everyday life. Considerations of space permit little more than a listing of names of some historians who have significantly enriched our understanding of certain religious phenomena in recent years, names such as those of Jacques Le Goff (1924–2014), Eric Hobsbawm (1917–2012), Christopher Hill (1912–2003), Natalie Zemon Davis (1928–), and Carlo Ginzburg (1939–).[18]

Beyond their specific accomplishments—largely in areas of medieval and early modern European history—what these scholars have offered is an approach to religious data more fruitful than any that have emerged from the specialists devoted to the study of religion per se. What they lack, however, is the broadly comparative approach characteristic of a Marx or a Durkheim, as they themselves have occasionally recognized.

Witness, for instance, the editor's introduction to the fiftieth volume of the journal *Past and Present*, one of the leading organs (with *Annales ESC* and *Comparative Studies in Society and History*) for this new style of historical investigation.

> Our present range is still far from satisfactory. For all our efforts, European history articles, and especially British history articles, predominate far more than we would wish. Of the two hundred and forty or so articles we have published, only about thirty have been on non-European history. . . . There have been disappointingly few of those articles and debates on frontiers between conventional history and allied disciplines which are one of our special fields of interest. If, fifty issues from now, the statistics are similar [Note: they are, CG & BL], we will have failed in a very important part of our aims.[19]

To sum up and generalize: the study of religion has survived the negative influence of the specialized field supposedly devoted to that very study, a field that wandered into a dangerous blind alley while pursuing autonomy. The survival of meaningful research in this area has been due, then, primarily to the work of anthropologists, historians, and others outside the field (one thinks, for instance, of classicists like Jean-Pierre Vernant [1914–2007] or orientalists like Marshall Hodgson [1922–68] and Joseph Needham [1900–1995]) who combined a strong sense of social context and historical process in their analyses of religious data.[20]

## IV. PARADISE REGAINED?

Religions, then, should be studied as these scholars study them: as social and historical entities, within their proper cultural context. They must be studied not only as phenomena that change over time as the result of their own internal dynamic, but more importantly as expressions of broader conflicts and tensions within specific social and historical configurations and, what is more, as vehicles of change and conflict. But if historians, anthropologists, and others have retained the concern with context and process that was characteristic of the classic theoreticians, they have not, for the most part, continued to pursue the same kinds of broad, comparative inquiries that characterized their predecessors. Consequently, their results—while rich and provocative—have regularly been more particularistic and less at the level of general theoretical constructs. In truth, it is the historians of religion, whatever their other failings, who managed to keep comparatism alive, as in the works of such disparate figures as Pettazzoni, Geo Widengren (1907–96), Mircea Eliade (1907–86), and Georges Dumézil (1898–1986).[21]

One need not be a prophet to understand that a return to comparatism in all the human sciences lies in the very near future, and that comparatism will be a central issue once more in the decades ahead. For whatever the errors of past comparatists—and they are legion, as is well known—it is only comparative research that can yield generalizations of a truly probative nature. The problem is not *whether* to compare, but *how*.

The methodology of comparatism deserves a far fuller discussion than is possible in the present context. Nevertheless, the nature of our general position should be clear from the preceding discussion. That is to say, we maintain that the modes of comparison that have most often been attempted—evolutionist, diffusionist, genetic, phenomenological, morphological, structuralist, and so forth—are inadequate insofar as they have been insufficiently attentive to issues of context and process. It is not enough, for instance, simply to assemble a set of myths that display certain common themes and/or structures, although that might provide a convenient starting point for a comparative endeavor. For such an endeavor to bear fruit, however, there would have to follow a massive task of placing each myth within its total social environment and identifying its connections to other relevant dimensions of culture. Then, each of these contextualized myths would have to be considered within their proper historic moment, as part of an ongoing diachronic process marked by conflicts, contradictions, and dynamism.

Comparison, attention to context and process, concern with issues of power and conflict: all these are fundamental for the study of religious phenomena, yet they are not exclusive to it and thus they do not define that study. What defines it is the very quality of its object. But if, on the one hand, religion is a specific phenomenon, and if, on the other hand, religion is *not* humanity's ongoing dialogue with some eternal "sacred," then what is the study of religion really about?

It has often been observed that religions are systems for conferring value and meaning upon human existence, offering answers to the fundamental questions of life, death, and suffering, while orienting human activity within a coherent view of the cosmos. While perfectly valid and unexceptional, such a formulation stops short of having really probative force. For inasmuch as religions *are* systems for the provision of meaning, they are systems of ideology.

In using the term and category of ideology, we must quickly reject any view that takes ideology to be nothing more than false consciousness and that contrasts it with some secure and verifiable knowledge, science, or philosophy. We are particularly concerned to avoid a position in which ideology, and a fortiori religious ideology, is taken to be a system of persuasion and deception employed more or less consciously by ruling (or hegemonic) classes against the other members of society. First, one must note that while a strong connection between class interests and beliefs is regularly apparent, that relationship is never simple, and seldom fully conscious in individuals or in groups.

Moreover, ideologies—especially religious ideologies—are powerful largely because they are *shared* systems of belief, and because those classes and groups who benefit from them profess them as wholeheartedly as do the others.

Further, one must stress that there are no alternatives to ideology for dissident groups, merely alternative ideologies that they may marshal against dominant groups and the ideologies propagated by the latter. The normal state of affairs within any social field will be the existence of multiple competing ideologies, one of them dominant or official, and the others oppositional (also articulated and influential) in widely varying degrees. None of these, moreover, are to be understood as being intentionally deceptive or seductive. Rather, they are global views of reality shaped and informed by experience, tradition, and material (i.e., class) interests, while in turn they shape the hopes, expectations, and behaviors of those who come to espouse them. To be sure, without ideology the perpetuation of social structures and dispositions of power would be impossible; but without ideology, challenges to such structures would be equally impossible.

If one is willing to entertain our notion that religion is best understood as a mode or style of ideology, it is useful to ask what, precisely, are its specific features: that is, how does it differ from other, non-religious modes of ideology?

First, religions appear to be the most ancient form of ideology, as indicated by archaeological evidence and—indirectly—by the study of the most insulated and technologically conservative cultures of the modern world. Conversely, non-religious ideologies are a fairly recent and restricted phenomenon, for although some criticism of religion has always existed, philosophical and scientific constructs of reality devoid of (or, better yet, self-proclaimedly devoid of) religious traits first appeared only in the early modern era, coincident with the rise of industrial production, the nation-state, and other correlated factors. And while non-religious ideologies have proliferated since, religious ideologies have also persisted and continue to flourish, although they no longer enjoy a relative monopoly. One may thus observe that religions are the most ancient, widespread, and enduring ideological systems attested over the course of human history to date.

Second, religions are the ideologies that are most rich in symbolic discourse, both in certain linguistic forms (myths) and behavioral patterns (rituals). The useful ambiguity and polyphony of symbolic discourse accounts in part for the powerful appeal of religious systems, also for their resilience and adaptability, which permit them to exert influence over long periods of time.

Third, religious ideologies are those that are most audaciously totalistic in their contents. They address issues from the most personal to the most cosmic, which the vast majority of non-religious ideologies dismiss as moot. They deal with disease, death, injustice, primeval beginnings, and ultimate ends, providing answers at both practical and speculative levels. Moreover, all levels of discourse—personal, social, and cosmic—come to be interrelated within religious ideologies, such that they are all mutually implicative and mutually reinforcing. It is, moreover, precisely this linkage of different levels that gives religions their tremendous persuasive power, insofar as sociopolitical formations and the normative attitudes and behaviors (ethics) that sustain such formations are regularly correlated to some perceived universal and natural (or supernatural) order.

This leads us to our last point: religion must be understood as the most extreme form of ideology, for religions provide arbitrary social formations and habituated patterns not merely with persuasive rationalizations of an abstract conceptual nature, as do non-religious ideologies, but with nothing less (so they claim) than sacred warrants and ultimate legitimation. It is only in religion that social structures and dispositions of scarce resources (wealth, power, prestige, etc.) can be represented in such a way as to make them appear absolutely incontrovertible: sacred givens and/or revealed truths. For within the religious perspective, cultural and historic contingencies or contradictions are regularly expressed as eternal, absolute, and transcendent verities, and thus—by definition—placed beyond debate.

To study religions with due attention to context and process, as we have repeatedly urged, is thus—in part—to deconstruct the ideological work of religion: to focus on the world in which religions operate (i.e., the world of society and history), as well as the world they describe; to focus on what religions do, as well as what they claim to be. And if the study of the most ancient, widespread, and extreme form of ideology is undertaken in this manner, we are persuaded that the results of such a study might be of no little interest and importance.

# 3: THESES ON COMPARISON

I

Let us begin with a few schematic observations concerning the goals, logic, and continuing appeal of comparatism, the very formidable obstacles it faces, its sorry historic record, and the reasons for its many failures.

1. As both Heraclitus and Saussure observed, meaning is constructed through contrast. All knowledge, indeed all intelligibility, thus derives from consideration of data whose differences become instructive and revealing when set against the similarities that render them comparable.

2. It is also the case that the same exercise supports errors and misconstructions of every sort, there being no guarantees. At best, comparison yields not knowledge, but that which provisionally passes for knowledge, while inviting falsification or revision as further examples are considered and familiar examples receive fuller study. This process of testing, amplification, and rectification is interminable.

3. All generalization depends on comparison, although the latter is usually pursued in ways inadequate to the task. Still, the only alternatives are (a) a discourse whose generalizations remain intuitive, unreflective, and commonsensical, i.e., without basis, rigor, or merit; and (b) a parochialism that dares speak nothing beyond the petty and the particular.

4. Comparison is never innocent, but is always interested, and the interests of the researcher (which are never arbitrary, exclusively intellectual, or fully conscious) inevitably condition (a) definition of the issues and categories to be considered, (b) selection of the examples judged relevant, (c) evaluation of these data (including the relative dignity and importance accorded to each), and (d) the ultimate conclusions.

5. Whether acknowledged or not, the researcher's world (nation, culture, religion, politics, e.g.) and his/her attitudes toward it enter and inflect all comparative projects, most often providing the implicit point of reference against which other data are measured. The only check on this tendency is collegial criticism.

6. Wide-ranging comparison—comparatism of the strong sort—has

consistently disappointed. The books of Lévi-Strauss, Dumézil, and Eliade now sit beside those of Max Müller and Frazer as cautionary examples. Although one can admire the energy, intelligence, and dedication of all these scholars, they consistently misrecognized products of their own imagination and desire ("the human mind," "tripartite ideology," "homo religiosus") for objects having historic, prehistoric, and/or transhistoric actuality. Others made the same mistake regarding such fictive entities as "totemism," "Urmonotheismus," "la mentalité primitive," and "the collective unconscious."

7. The more examples compared, the more superficial and peremptory is the analysis of each. In such cases, researchers regularly turn their understanding of a few key data into a template for treating less familiar examples. The deception and self-deception involved in such ventures is of the same sort that typifies all ideology: misrepresenting a part for the whole.

8. Comparative endeavors of the strong sort fall into one of three types, based on the horizon of their ambitions: (a) those that claim to reveal universal patterns (Tylor, Jung, Lévi-Strauss, Lévy-Bruhl, Eliade, Girard, e.g.); (b) those that claim to demonstrate a genetic relation among specific peoples and phenomena (Jacob Grimm, Max Müller, Robertson Smith, Dumézil, Gimbutas, e.g.); (c) those that claim to trace diffusion of certain traits from one group to others over the course of history (Reitzenstein, Widengren, Burkert, Bernal, e.g.). All three types constitute similarity as the fact of primary interest and regard difference as a complicating development of considerably lesser importance.

9. With regard to the universalizing type: there are no true universals, save at a level of generalization so high as to yield only banalities. Thus, while it is true that all humans have bodies, the way they theorize their bodies, also the ways they use and experience them, vary with history, class, and culture (as Mauss was first to observe). Real interest emerges only as one pays attention to these differences.

10. With regard to the genetic type: use of comparison to reconstruct (i.e., hypothesize) a remote past era for which no direct evidence survives is an invitation to project one's favored fantasies onto a relatively blank screen. That screen, moreover, is distorting and prejudicial, as it invests such projections with the prestige of "origins" (e.g., "our most ancient traditions," "the world of our ancestors," "the archaic," "the primordial").

11. With regard to the diffusionist type: the attempt to show transmission of culture traits always advances—if only subtextually—a tendentious ranking of the peoples involved, constituting temporal primacy ("originality," "invention," "authenticity") as the sign of superior status, while conversely treating reception as a mark of relative backwardness, need, and submission.

12. These strong forms of comparatism having failed, it is time we enter-

tained comparatism of weaker and more modest sorts that (a) focus on a relatively small number of comparanda that the researcher can study closely; (b) are equally attentive to relations of similarity and those of difference; (c) grant equal dignity and intelligence to all parties considered; and (d) are attentive to the social, historical, and political contexts and subtexts of religious and literary texts. As precedents, one might invoke the examples of Fustel de Coulanges (1830–89), Eric Havelock (1903–88), and Geoffrey Lloyd (1933–), or—should one stray beyond classical antiquity—those of Marc Bloch (1886–1944), Norbert Elias (1897–1990), Max Gluckman (1911–75), and Marshall Sahlins (1930–).

## II

As an example of weak comparatism in this mode, let us offer a case involving two data only: a classic scene from Middle Persian myth and one from Anglo-Saxon epic. The first is taken from the *Greater Bundahišn*, a priestly compendium committed to writing in the ninth century CE.[1]

Chapter 1 of that text opens with two antithetical beings: the Wise Lord (Ohrmazd), possessed of omniscience and benevolence, and the Evil Spirit (Ahreman), characterized by a spiteful, destructive stupidity. Neither is omnipotent, and each has to confront the other's power. Still, their initial situation is a stability born of separation, with Ohrmazd dwelling in endless light above, Ahreman in infinite darkness below.[2] Still, the Wise Lord anticipates conflict, understanding that Ahreman's innate disposition to envy (Pahlavi *arešk*) will make him turn aggressive.[3] In contrast, the Evil Spirit understands nothing. Wandering idly, he encounters light for the first time and his reaction—one of aggression, prompted by envy, just as the Wise Lord foresaw—sets all subsequent history in motion.

> Because he possessed (only) knowledge-after-the-fact, the Foul Spirit was unaware of the Wise Lord's existence. Then he rose from the depth and he came to the boundary of the visible lights. When he saw the Wise Lord and the light of ungraspable brightness, because of his aggressivity and his envious nature (*arešk-gōhrīh*), he launched an attack in order to destroy it.[4]

Most broadly, the text identifies Ohrmazd as a plenum, characterized by the possession of goodness, wisdom, and light, while Ahreman is an absence of these same qualities. Zoroastrian theory associates him with non-being in general, as recent research has shown, and the primordial assault represents his attempt to replace Ohrmazd's something with nothing.[5] Another Zoroastrian text develops this point, once again stressing Ahreman's envy of creation.

The Creator of the world made the spiritual creation pure and undefiled. He made the material creation immortal, unaging, without hunger, without bondage, without sorrow, and without pain. . . . In envy (*pad areš̌k*), full of vengeance, perfect in deceit, [the Evil Spirit] rushed to seize, destroy, smash, and ruin this well-made creation of the gods.[6]

Ahreman's envy thus involves bitterness at his absolute deprivation, an anguished sense of emptiness, and wild indignation at his deficiencies vis-à-vis Ohrmazd. Jealousy, resentment, and wounded pride are all involved, as are frustration, self-pity, and a self-righteous sense of cosmic injustice. All these give rise to an infantile destructive rage, motivating his assault.[7] Zoroastrian theology understands the world's woes as having originated with that assault and looks forward to the day when Ahreman will be overcome, at which point history will end and the world's perfection will be established.[8]

In its treatment of Ahreman, the *Bundahišn* passage is not concerned to provide nuance, sympathy, or psychological depth in the mode of a modern novel. Rather, as a religious text it integrates ethics and cosmology, tracing all violence and destructivity to that which it identifies as the primordial vice of envy, which will manifest itself in humans throughout history, and against which moral agents must constantly struggle, as the fate of the cosmos hangs in the balance.

### III

Similar themes and images are found in a passage from *Beowulf* (a text whose dating remains controversial), where Grendel shows intriguing similarities to Ahreman, as well as important differences.[9] To appreciate the significance of the monster, it is useful to start with his lineage and descent.

| | In the abode of the race of monsters |
| An unhappy man | long dwelt |
| Since the Creator | had banished him. |
| The eternal Lord | avenged that murder |
| On the race of Cain, | the one who slew Abel. |
| The Judge did not rejoice at that feud, | but for that crime, |
| He banished Cain far | from the race of man. |
| | |
| From him all | misbegotten creatures arose: |
| Giants and elves, | and infernal beasts, |
| Likewise giants | who have struggled against God |
| For a long time.[10] | |

This passage works with traditions well attested in Anglo-Saxon literature, in which Cain—who committed the first homicide and did so out of envy—was theorized as primordial ancestor to a race of miscreants, spawned in the barrens, who became ever more bestial with each generation.[11] Cursed by God, cast out from human society, they sank ever further into a state of sin and savagery, becoming monsters (*fifel-cyn*), misbegotten things (*untȳdras*), infernal creatures (*orcnēas*), and giants (*eotenas, gigantas*), constantly battling against the deity (*wið Gode wunnon*).

This passage says nothing explicit about the emotions and motives that prompt such aggression, for all that it suggests a bitterness cultivated over many generations. The immediately preceding lines, which introduced Grendel as he lurks outside Hrothgar's mead-hall, are less coy on this question.[12]

| | |
|---|---|
| Then a powerful spirit | suffered |
| Miserably while | lingering in the shadows, |
| As every day | he heard rejoicing |
| Resound through the hall. | There was the sound of the harp |
| And the sweet song of the poet, | who told |
| The well-known ancient story | of mankind's creation. |
| He said that the Almighty | made the earth |
| A magnificent plain | ringed by water. |
| Triumphant, he established | sun and moon, |
| Luminaries to provide light | for land-dwellers |
| And he adorned | the quarters of the earth |
| With limbs and leaves. | Also life he created |
| For each type | of living beings who move about. |
| So then Hrothgar's retainers | lived in rejoicing, |
| Happily, until | that one began |
| | |
| To commit terrible sins, | a fiend from hell. |
| He was a grim spirit | named Grendel, |
| Famed waste-wanderer, | he who occupied the moors, |
| Fens and fastnesses.[13] | |

Grendel's sins and crimes (*fyrene*) thus originate in his suffering, more precisely in the pain he experiences upon perceiving the pleasure (*drēam*) enjoyed by the hall's inhabitants. Above all, he is anguished to hear the sweet song of the poet (*swutol sang scopes*) recounting how God Almighty— the ancestral enemy of Cain's race—created heaven and earth, bringing light, life, and splendor into material existence.[14] To this, Grendel reacts first with agony, then with rage, for the song conjures up everything he is

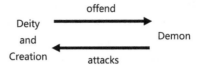

Figure 3.1. Dyadic structure of *Greater Bundahišn* 1.14–15.

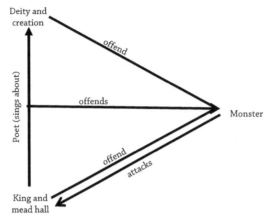

Figure 3.2. Triadic structure of *Beowulf*, lines 86–114.

not and has not: beauty, grace, harmony, sociability, and goodness, but above all the creative power enjoyed by God, the poet, and the king, but which he is utterly lacking.

This scene thus resembles the episode from the *Bundahišn* in many ways, as both identify envy—and more precisely, envy at creation—as the motive behind a malevolent being's violent attacks, which sets all subsequent action in motion. There are, however, significant differences between the two narratives. Whereas Ahreman is a demon (and the archdemon at that), Grendel is a monster or, more precisely, the last, most degenerate descendant in the line of the most sinful human. And whereas Ahreman's envy sets him against Ohrmazd and creation, Grendel's assault is not directed against God, but against King Hrothgar and his mead-hall.

The two narratives thus differ in structure. That of the *Bundahišn* is dyadic and is set at the level of the supernatural (figure 3.1).

In contrast, the episode in *Beowulf* has a triadic structure, connecting human and divine levels via the mediation of the monstrous (figure 3.2).

## IV

There is, however, more to this story. Immediately before introducing Grendel, the epic describes how Hrothgar's mead-hall was built.

| | |
|---|---|
| Then was success in war | granted to Hrothgar, |
| Glory in battle, | so that his friends and kinsmen |
| | |
| Eagerly obeyed him, | until the youths around him increased |
| To form a mighty band. | It came into his mind |
| That he wanted to order | the building of a hall, |
| A great mead-hall | for men to make |
| So that men and children | would ever hear of it. |
| And inside there | to young and old |
| He would distribute all things | such as God gave him, |
| Except for the land itself | and peoples' lives. |
| Then I heard from all over: | many men |
| Were ordered to work | throughout this middle earth, |
| | |
| To adorn the place of the folk. | In due time |
| The work was done quickly | and it was all ready, |
| The greatest of halls. . . . | |
| Not leaving his boast unfulfilled, | Hrothgar distributed rings |
| And treasure at banquets.[15] | |

The hall is thus the material manifestation of Hrothgar's political, military, and economic success. His victories and control over labor made possible the construction of a structure whose magnificence announces his wealth and power, while serving as a theater for displays of royal generosity.[16] Alternatively, one might describe this as the site where the king defined his troop-won booty as the product (and proof) of God's grace (*eall . . . swylc him God sealde*), a portion of which he redistributed to secure the loyalty of those troops, doing so in a way designed to win the admiration of all who witnessed—or heard about—these transactions.

Beyond God's creation and the poet's song, Grendel's envy is thus occasioned by the more immediate—and more human—fact of Hrothgar's hall. Huddled outside its warmth and splendor, he resents the wealth, power, and prestige that find expression in the hall's grandeur and adornments, also the ceremonies and festivities staged therein. Surely, if he understood how the hall functions as an apparatus for the legitimation, naturalization, reproduction, and enhancement of royal privilege—something the text lets readers perceive—he would resent that also. One way or another, his envy is bitter and violent, but not demonic or anti-cosmic. It is a human— all-too-human—envy: the kind those with far too little harbor toward those with far too much.

The triadic structure of *Beowulf* sutures together different types, causes, and objects of envy, creating the impression that when outcastes envy kings, they also resent God and threaten the cosmos. As a priestly, rather than a

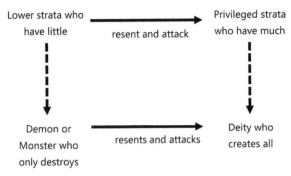

Figure 3.3. Implicit quadratic structure underlying both *Bundahišn* 1.14–15 and *Beowulf*, lines 86–114.

courtly work, the *Bundahišn* is less concerned to protect the position of kings per se, but it does defend privilege in general by construing human envy as a local manifestation of Ahremanian evil.

Although the two narratives differ in their details and structure, they treat the same themes, advance similar projects of persuasion, and protect the interests of similar social institutions and strata. Ultimately, both are concerned to stigmatize certain kinds of feelings and action, although they do this indirectly, speaking more of gods, demons, and monsters than of fully human subjects. If one restores the primacy of the human, what emerges is a quadratic structure (figure 3.3).

The weak form of comparison refrains from imagining that universal themes, a shared prehistory, or a process of diffusion is responsible for the similarities between mythic narratives, nor does it constitute their similarities as evidence for same. Rather, we take these stories to have arisen independently of each other in very different times, places, and cultural milieux. Such common features as they share are not accidental, however. Rather, they reflect similar points of tension in the social structure of the peoples among whom these stories circulated. The stories address these problems and seek to resolve them, not by modifying social structure itself, but by reshaping the consciousness of the audiences they reach and influence.

Most immediately, our two examples are concerned with something commonly called "envy," and they show the point of departure for this discourse to be a situation in which certain desirable goods (light, wisdom, goodness itself in the first case; wealth, power, prestige in the second) are inequitably distributed. Seen from below, such inequality appears as injustice and maldistribution; in pointed—and far from innocent—contrast, from above inequity seems the just and proper result of meritocratic distribution. Have-nots then charge those who have most with greed, and the latter reciprocate by accusing their critics of envy (also "jealousy," "*ressentiment*," "ingratitude," and "Communism," for the surplus enjoyed by the rich extends to the lexicography of invective).

The texts we have considered intervene in this dispute in multiple ways, but always to the same purpose. Thus, they treat the possessions of Ohrmazd and Hrothgar as unproblematic expressions of their innate excellence and nobility: something they have created and something they richly deserve. Accordingly, they ignore the issue of greed, while amplifying the charge of envy by (a) attributing it to demons and monsters, (b) making it culminate in mindless destructive violence without exploring any other means of redress, and (c) representing it in its most extreme form: envy at creation, which casts it as a cardinal sin, an offense against God, and a threat to the order of the cosmos itself.

Although apparently simple, recoding of this sort involves three correlated operations. First, there is an ethical inversion, as moral condemnation shifts its object from the disproportionate assets of the dominant to the "envy" of subalterns. Second is a political reversal, as a call for change is transmuted into a defense of the status quo. Third is an ontological displacement, as a critique of social, political, and property relations is relocated from the human to the divine level, where the order of things is no longer contingent or negotiable.

These three levels do not always co-vary precisely as they do in the texts we have studied. Deprivileged strata can frame their critique as an expression of God's judgment on the arrogant, for instance, as often happens in millenarian movements, apocalyptic texts, and prophetic discourses. The alignment we have observed, however, is probably the most common, not because "God" favors kings and big battalions—however much it may seem that way—but because a religious coding offers the best protection for systems, structures, privileges, and inequities that are otherwise very difficult to defend.

In closing, I cannot take sole credit for the above discussion, least of all the initial theses. Most of my views on comparison took shape in prolonged exchanges with Cristiano Grottanelli.[17] On most points, it is difficult, if not impossible, to separate my ideas from his, for they are the product not of a person, but of a friendship and a sustained conversation. I remain deeply indebted to Grottanelli, and his untimely death was a terrible loss. This chapter is dedicated to his memory.

# II
# RECENT ATTEMPTS AT GRAND COMPARISON

# 4: THE WEREWOLF, THE SHAMAN, AND THE HISTORIAN

I

In April 1691, the trial of an accused thief in Swedish-dominated Livonia took an unexpected turn when a witness smiled as he was sworn in.[1] Concerned to maintain order, the Royal Judges of the District Court of Wenden (today's Cēsis, 88 km northeast of Riga)[2] asked the man why he smiled. He explained that he saw his neighbor, Old Thiess (a nickname for Matthias), was waiting to testify, and this greatly amused him. "Everyone knows that he goes around with the Devil and was a werewolf," he told the court. "How could Old Thiess swear, since he would not lie about such things, and he had pursued them for many years?"[3]

With that, attention shifted to Thiess, a man of eighty-some years, who freely acknowledged his werewolf past and recounted how he had earlier told this to the District Court of Nitau (today's Nitaure), where the judges laughed and dismissed him without sentence.[4] Hearing this, one of the judges at Wenden asked whether the old man was in his right mind, but all those who knew him—including the other judge, who had earlier been Thiess's employer—vouched for his physical and mental health, his probity, and the accuracy of his account.[5]

The judges then asked Thiess a series of questions, trying to ascertain how he became a werewolf, what he did in that state, the number and identity of his fellow werewolves, his status as a Christian, and the nature of his dealings with the Devil. On most points, his answers conformed to stereotypes that circulated widely. Along these lines, he told them he had gained the power of lycanthropic transformation when a stranger gave him a charmed drink, after which he was able to put off his human form and assume that of a wolf. Several times each year on ritual occasions, he gathered with other werewolves to steal livestock, dismember the animals, and feast on their meat.[6]

On the most important point, however, Thiess's testimony differed from the judges' expectations. Contrary to the court's repeated attempt to find diabolic associations, he insisted that werewolves oppose the Devil and regularly battle the "sorcerers" (*Zauberer*) and "witches" (*Hexen*) who serve him. True, the werewolves entered Hell each year, but they did so as "hounds of God,"[7] seeking to recover the *Seegen*—most literally the blessing that finds expression in prosperity, well-being, abundance of crops and livestock[8]— that sorcerers had previously stolen. When the werewolves succeeded, the harvest was good; when they failed, there was hardship and famine.[9]

At several points, the judges introduced theological niceties to show Thiess the error of his ways. Did werewolves not defy God, they asked, by abandoning the human form the Lord created in His image?[10] And since it was impossible for humans to undo God's creation in this way, did it not follow that their supposed lupine transformation was really "a devilish deceit and delusion"?[11] Unable to persuade the old man on these points, they called in reinforcements.

> The Herr Pastor of this place, Magister Bucholtz, was summoned and asked to attend the proceedings. He sought to urge this self-professed *Seegenspre-cher*,[12] a sinner caught in the Devil's snares, to take to heart his grievous sins, by which he was led astray and in which he persisted for so many years, and to stir his conscience that he might convert and repent by a rightful repentance and he might make an abjuration of these devilish beings.[13]

Going further, the pastor pronounced Thiess a grievous and wanton sinner facing harsh punishment in this world and worse in the next should he not confess and repent his sins.[14] Stunningly, Thiess insisted he understood these things better than the pastor, who was just a young fellow.[15] Angered at what he considered unjust and ill-founded accusations, Thiess rejected any characterization of his deeds as diabolic or evil.

> He showed himself truly obstinate and remained insistent that all he had done was no sin against God. Rather, he had done God much service thereby in fulfillment of His will that they recover the prosperity (*seegen*) from the Devil that the sorcerers had carried to him, and he did good thereby for the whole land.[16]

Such defiance placed the judges in a difficult position, as they had neither a confession nor any direct evidence of Thiess's compact with the Devil, the normal requisites for conviction. In this situation, they decided they could "not reach a definitive verdict on so difficult and complex a case."[17] Making use of a legal procedure known as *leuteratio*, the judges appealed the case and referred it to higher authorities.[18] A year and a half later, judgment was finally pronounced by the Assessor of the Royal High Court, who stressed all the stereotypes in his finding: "As the accused has made clear by his own testimony, for many years he showed himself to be a werewolf. He ran about with others, was also in Hell, and in such groups he stole livestock from others and helped commit more acts of the same sort."[19] By rejecting the pastor's accusations, Thiess had also "powerfully sinned against himself and others, whom he led into superstition."[20] For "his truly weighty and vexatious offenses," he was sentenced to public flogging.[21]

## II

Roughly a half century ago, reading the transcript of this trial prompted the Italian historian Carlo Ginzburg to undertake an extraordinary methodological experiment, involving a shift from micro- to macrohistory and from specialized to comparative research.[22] In 1964, Ginzburg submitted his dissertation, studying certain Friulian peasants who faced charges of witchcraft in 1575–1645. At first, they rejected this characterization of their activities, insisting they were not witches (*streghe*) or sorcerers (*stregoni*), but *Benandanti* ("well-goers"), who undertook ecstatic journeys each year on the Ember Days to battle witches for the coming year's harvest. Agents of the Inquisition dismissed such testimony as the lies and evasions of people engaged in maleficent activity, using occult powers obtained through a diabolic pact. This reflected orthodox views on demonology, which informed the questions they compelled the Benandanti to answer, often under torture. Over time, the process not only produced the desired confessions, but led later Benandanti to reshape their self-understanding, consistent with the assumptions of their inquisitors.[23]

Initially, Ginzburg took the Benandanti to be an isolated datum, and he suggested that focusing on the gap between inquisitors' questions and defendants' answers provides unique insight into a deep archaeological stratum of pre-Christian religious beliefs the Friulian peasants preserved. Shortly after delivering his dissertation for publication, however, he stumbled across the transcript of Thiess's trial, which resembled the Benandanti closely enough that he added several pages and introduced it as a comparandum: the only one he had found to date.[24] Speculating about the relation between the two cases, he argued that their resemblances were not random, but sweeping and systemic; second, that their morphological similarities suggested common descent from "a single agrarian cult . . . that must have been diffused in an earlier period over a much vaster area"; finally, that this ancient cult was shamanic in nature.[25]

Twenty years later, Ginzburg returned to these materials in *Storia notturna* (1989), a very different sort of book.[26] Here, Thiess and the Benandanti still occupy prominent positions, but the text introduces many subsequently adduced examples that resemble the two original cases in one fashion or another. Some fill in the geography between northern Italy and Livonia, while others expand the picture in space and/or time. Ultimately, the field of comparison extends from western and southern Europe to central Asia and the Arctic, leading Ginzburg to posit that shamanism[27] spread from Asia across virtually all Europe in the course of an indeterminate but deep prehistory, with Scythians, Celts, and Slavs mediating the process of diffusion. Further, he now took the ecstatic journeys and otherworldly battles of shamans, werewolves, Benandanti, and their confreres to constitute the folkloric roots of the witches' Sabbath.

Although the two books are intimately related, their reception was rather different. Along with *The Cheese and the Worms* (1976),[28] *I Benandanti* was hailed as a brilliant success and helped make Ginzburg's reputation,[29] while *Storia notturna* elicited enthusiasm from some, and sharp criticism from others.[30] Notwithstanding Ginzburg's formidable erudition, ingenuity, and tenacity, the latter book shows the same problems that plagued the great comparative projects of the past. Regrettably, the ambition and scale of such projects lead even the best scholars to venture beyond their competence; to read texts superficially; to ignore nuance, details, and particularities of context; to select and stress the importance of those data that fit their preconceptions, while downplaying details that are inconvenient; to emphasize similarities, rather than difference; and to construct an imaginary—but unattested—prehistory that ties the loose ends together.

Considering the difference between the two books in which Ginzburg moved from the Friuli to Livonia and then far beyond tempts one to conclude that specialized research yields success, while comparison leads to failure. This, however, is surely wrong, for even in the dissertation version of *I Benandanti*, Ginzburg's inquiry depended on astute comparison of inquisitors' questions to the accused's responses; early trials to later ones; Christian orthodoxy to traces of pre-Christian religiosity; and popular to elite culture. The project went wrong, not when Thiess entered the discussion, but when Ginzburg exchanged a modest, carefully delimited, and highly successful comparative method for a looser, riskier, more open-ended style whose ambitions were more grandiose.

In chapter 3 and elsewhere, I argued for the practice of "weak" comparison, i.e., one that focuses sustained attention on a small number of examples and entertains the possibility that they share the features they have in common, not because of a historic connection involving diffusion, influence, or genetic descent, but because these features are the product of similar forces and conditions. In the present chapter, I would like to reconsider Old Thiess's case and suggest that his testimony resembles that of the

Benandanti, not because they share a (shamanic) prehistory, but because they responded to similar socioreligious and judiciary pressures, and did so in similar ways.

III

Let us begin by taking stock of the dramatis personae who figured in Thiess's trial. The transcript identifies the following as officers of the court and religious authorities cooperating with them.

Herr Assessor Bengt Johan Ackerstaff, substitute Judge of the District Court of Wenden, who lives in Castle Klingenberg outside Lemburg (Mālpils)
Herr Assessor Gabriel Berger, Judge of the District Court of Wenden
Herr Baron Crohnstern, Judge of the District Court of Nitau (Nitaure)
Herr Rosenthal, Judge of the District Court of Nitau
Herr Caulich, Judge of the District Court of Nitau
Herr Richter, who has an estate in the vicinity of Sunszel (Suntaži)
Herr Pastor of Lemburg
Herr Pastor of Jürgensburg (Jaunpils), Magister Bucholtz
Herr Chief Deputy Clodt
Herr Assessor Martini
The illustrious, praiseworthy Assessor of the Royal High Court, Herr Herman Georg von Trautvetter

All these worthies receive the honorific title *Herr* and with the exception of Herr Assessor Martini, all have German surnames. They are, transparently, members of the German elite who constituted the upper stratum of Livonian society ever since the Teutonic Knights (specifically, the Livonian Brothers of the Sword) conquered the territory early in the thirteenth century. Under Swedish rule (1629–1721), ethnic Germans continued to own the bulk of the land, control most of the wealth, and monopolize the offices (political and clerical) through which power was exercised over the indigenous peasantry. The latter group included both Latvians and Estonians, who were classed together and referred to as *Undeutsche*, literally "non-Germans." Thiess, the other witnesses, and almost everyone mentioned in their testimony fell in this group. The transcript identifies them as follows:

The church-thief of Jürgensburg, Pirsen Tönnis
An inhabitant of Kaltenbrunn (Kniediņu mulža) named Old Thiess, "in most obvious ways . . . a poor man and thoroughly powerless"[31]
The Kaltenbrunn innkeeper Peter

Skeistan, a peasant from Lemburg, who broke Thiess's nose

A peasant from Marienburg (Alūksne), who gave a wolf pelt to a peasant from Allasch (Allaži)

Skeistan Rein, son of the above-mentioned Skeistan

A scoundrel from Marienburg who tricked Thiess into becoming a werewolf

Tirummen, a peasant from Seegewold (Sigulda), a werewolf who was particularly skilled at stealing livestock

A peasant of Rodenpeisch (Ropaži) who accompanied Thiess to a tavern

A fellow from Jürgensburg, Gricke Jahnen, stepson of the blessed Herr Pastor, whose leg Thiess healed

Ilgasch, a peasant from Nitau, who obtained a (magical?) net from Thiess

Gurrian, a peasant of Jürgensburg = the old innkeeper Gurrian Steppe, who had his grain blessed by Thiess

All these men came from villages within a very small area in eastern Latvia, about 15 kilometers in radius (figure 4.1).[32] Most are identified as peasants (*baur*, 9/13, assuming this description fits the younger Skeistan, whose father is so identified), the others as innkeepers (*krüger*, 2/13), thieves (*dieb*, 1/13), or scoundrels (*schelm*, 1/13). Most have only a first name, usually non-German (Pirsen, Skeistan, Tirummen, Gricke, Ilgasch, Gurrian). None is accorded the title *Herr* or shown courtesy of any sort.[33]

The same social divide is evident in the seventeen other Livonian werewolf trials for which we have records, where officials were consistently *Deutsche* and defendants *Undeutsche*.[34] This was, in fact, the most important line of cleavage in the early modern Baltic, separating elite from popular classes. As Stefan Donecker and others have shown, religious difference played an important role in legitimating and maintaining this hierarchic divide.[35] Thus, notwithstanding the fact that the last Baltic pagans accepted Christianity in 1386, the descendants of the Teutonic Knights justified their dominant position by stressing their religious difference from the indig-

Figure 4.1. Map of the territory in central Livonia named in Thiess's trial. Photograph: Courtesy of the Public Library of Cincinnati and Hamilton County.

enous population, whose conversion—so they insisted—was superficial, incomplete, and potentially reversible.

The Non-German peasants were commonly depicted as primitive, untrust-worthy and superstitious folk, in particular their Christian conviction was regularly doubted, and both Protestant and Catholic observers agreed that many Estonians and Latvians continued to worship pagan gods, even though they had been officially converted to Christianity. They were particularly notorious for their willingness to enter into pacts with the devil and for the magic abilities that they received from such an unholy alliance.[36]

Producing a steady stream of *Undeutsche* defendants whom they could successfully prosecute as witches and werewolves thus permitted the elite to understand and represent themselves as continuing the noble—but interminable—work of advancing civilization, morality, and the True Faith, thereby legitimating their position and power. Institutions of church and state collaborated in providing a moral character to the discriminatory contrast of *Deutsche* and *Undeutsche* by recoding this opposition in religious terms, rather than ethnic, national, or socioeconomic. Witch and werewolf trials were a primary theater in which this recoding was renewed and ren-dered credible, but after the Swedish king issued a royal decree abolishing the use of torture—in 1686, five years before Thiess's trial—it became more difficult to produce the confessions on which these proceedings depended.[37]

## IV

Having already once been acquitted, Thiess faced the court with more confidence than did most of his predecessors.[38] His remarks constitute an atypical, but fascinating brief for the defense that accepts the charge of werewolfery, then disputes the court's construction of key terms, including "Hell," "Devil," and "werewolf." With regard to the first, the court imag-ined Hell as a realm antithetical to God, the church, morality, faith, good Christians, and their hopes of salvation. Any contact with a Hell of this sort was prima facie evidence that a person was infected with sin and posed a serious danger to others. The judges articulated this most fully when rebuking Thiess as follows.

He broke the oath he had sworn to his savior Christ as part of his holy baptism, in which he had renounced the Devil, all his creatures and works. Having forgotten God's way, he committed other highly forbidden sins of similar sort, consistently turning to abomination and scandal, not to

God's house where he formerly could come to knowledge and service of God through preaching and Christian instruction. Instead, he preferred to run to Hell.[39]

Here, Thiess is portrayed as not just a sinner, but a backsliding reprobate. Having received care, instruction, and sacraments from a kind and generous church, he abandoned "God's house" (*Gottes hause*) to resume his old ways, which the authorities define as sinful and describe through the metaphor of "running to Hell" (*höllen zulauffe*). They held out hope, however, that the old man might avoid eternal torment, if only he would accept their construction of morality, admit his errors and ignorance, acknowledge their authority, and thereby reaffirm not just the proper moral order of the cosmos, but the sociopolitical order of Livonia. The old man declined to cooperate.

Q: Was it not his intention, before his death, to convert to God, to let himself be instructed regarding His nature and will, to renounce such Devilish excesses, to repent his sins and thereby to save his soul from eternal damnation and the pains of Hell?
A: Hereupon, he would not answer properly. He said, who knows where his soul would remain? He was now very old, what more could he grasp of such things?[40]

In significant measure, Thiess's understanding of "Hell" differed from the court's. Evil it was, to be sure, but its evil extended only to the owner of this realm, his guests and servants, even though its space could be entered by certain others. In particular, the fact that werewolves visited Hell each year did not mark them as evil, nor did it condemn them to return after death,[41] since they came there as enemy invaders. Raiding Hell was relatively easy, moreover, since it was not distant from their homes, either spatially or metaphysically.

Q: How did the witness come to Hell, and where is that located?
A: The werewolves go thither on foot in wolf form, to the place at the end of the lake called *Puer Esser*, in a swamp below Lemburg about a half mile from the Castle Klingenberg of the Herr substitute President. There were lordly chambers and commissioned doorkeepers, whom the werewolves knocked aside as they wanted to take back some of the seed corn and the grain itself that the sorcerers had brought there. The seed corn was guarded in a special container and the grain in another.[42]

Hell was thus part of the local topography (see figure 4.1), situated about 6 kilometers from Thiess's home in Kaltenbrunn by a lake outside Lemburg (today's Mālpils), near the estate of Assessor Bengt Johan Ackerstaff: the judge who heard Thiess's case.[43] For Hell to be close at hand was consistent with Latvian constructions of the otherworld,[44] but to place it in the judge's backyard might be understood to imply that the infernal associations of the court were closer, stronger, and more enduring than the defendant's. As Thiess further explained, this Hell's entrance lay a bit beneath the earth's surface, hard to find unless one "belongs inside,"[45] like the sorcerers who regularly feast with the Devil.[46] Most importantly, perhaps, Hell includes the storehouse of a great manor, whose lord stockpiles the precious goods— grain and seed corn—his minions stole and brought him.[47]

As for the Devil, the judges and pastor construed him as the enemy of God and of all righteous Christians, whom he seeks to corrupt and delude. Those who succumb to his snares are branded with his mark[48] and enter a formal pact[49] that leads them to sin and damnation. By deceiving the weak, ignorant, and gullible, the Devil leads them away from the religious instruction and moral grounding supplied by the church and robs them of their soul.[50]

Thiess agreed that the Devil was a thief of souls, but understood this differently than did the judges and pastor. Although he nowhere spelled out his views or integrated them in a coherent system, three points emerge from his testimony. First, in response to questions about his healing of live-stock, Thiess explained how the Devil, acting through witches (*Hexen*), can take the souls of people and animals, causing illness and death. To recover souls, Thiess engaged in healing practices employing sacred substances and formulae.

Q: Where did he learn to prophesy, since many people came to him and asked him what would happen to them?
A: He could not prophesy; rather, he was a horse doctor and if other sinners had done harm to someone's horses, he counteracted that and removed it from them. Toward that end he used a few words, only about three, and he administered bread or salt to them, which he had blessed with these words.
Q: What did he know about the sinners who do harm to horses?
A: They were the same witches or agents of the Devil, who do nothing but evil.
Q: What then were the words he used in this way?
A: The sun and the moon go over the sea, bring back the soul that the Devil brought to Hell and give back to the animal the life and health that was taken from it—and that helps other animals besides horses.[51]

Thiess also maintained that the Devil's servants—a group that included "sorcerers" (*Zauberer*) and "witches" (*Hexe*), but emphatically not werewolves—forfeited their souls to him, as a result of which, they carried out thefts on his behalf,[52] won the right to banquet with him,[53] and became his after death.[54] Although clergy and court focused on the theft of souls, Thiess voiced greater concern with the Devil's thefts of a material nature that the authorities ignored, for he repeatedly charged the Devil and his henchmen with stealing crops, seed, animals, and the community's prosperity every winter.[55]

Q: How could the witness say that on last St. Lucia's Eve (December 13) they had already brought back this year's prosperity from Hell, which the sorcerers had taken there, since the sowing and blossoming time was now just approaching (i.e., on April 28, the date of the trial) and thus nothing could yet be harvested?

A: The sorcerers had their own special time and the Devil had already sowed long before. Thereafter, the sorcerers took something from that and brought it to Hell and this was the prosperity the werewolves carried back out of Hell and subsequently much growth followed from our seed, just as rich fruit was obtained from the trees, which was also taken from Hell, as was good fishing. Already since Christmas there was perfectly verdant grain of all sorts and trees, whose growth similarly came from Hell.[56]

The fact that the Devil employs servants, has storerooms filled with surplus produce, gives banquets, and lives in dwellings described as *herrlich* identifies him as a noble, and Thiess consistently depicted the source of his wealth as theft from the peasantry. In a trial of 1651, another accused werewolf ventured a bit further, testifying that "the Evil One appeared in person, *in black German clothing*,"[57] and in witchcraft trials such depictions were common. Here, as in the Baltic folklore studied by Udo Valk, "images of demonic evil acquired a concrete embodiment in the figure of the German landlord."[58]

V

While the authorities aligned werewolves with sin, damnation, Hell, and the Devil, Thiess disarticulated them from this set and repositioned them in opposition to all evils, which also included sorcerers and witches.[59] In his account, the struggle of werewolves against malevolent forces found its most salient expression in competition over livestock, produce, and fertility, in which a three-act drama unfolded each year. Initially, these assets were the rightful possessions of the peasant community, being the material manifestation of the blessed prosperity (*Seegen*) they obtained by God's grace and their own labor. During the winter, sorcerers stole this wealth and carried it just beneath the earth's surface, doing so on behalf of the Devil, greatest thief of them all.[60] Finally, werewolves raided the Devil's storeroom, battled his servants, and took back the stolen goods. In doing so, they did not act as thieves, but as agents of restorative justice, returning property, blessings, profits, and the means of production to their rightful owners.

Most often, Thiess described the material stake of this battle in agricultural terms, but he acknowledged that the werewolves also seized animals, usually in response to the judges, who focused on livestock more than grain, consistent with their stereotype of werewolves as cattle rustlers.[61] The following exchange is particularly revealing.[62]

Q: When you were transformed into wolves, why didn't you eat meat raw, as wolves do?

A: That wasn't the way. Rather, they eat it like men, roasted.

Q: How could they be animals with hands, if according to his testimony they had wolf's heads and paws? With what could they hold knives, prepare the food, or use other tools to accomplish their work?

A: They used no knives, but tore pieces off with their teeth and with their paws they stuck the pieces on spits that they found, and when they consumed the meat, they had already turned back into men, but they made no use of bread. They took salt with them from the farm as they departed.[63]

Here, both parties implicitly theorize "werewolf" as mediating the categorical divide between human and animal, but do so in different fashion. Thus, the judges maximize the werewolves' bestial nature by imagining they eat their meat raw and run on all fours. In response, Thiess parries as best he can (not without contradiction), describing how the werewolves employ technology (fire and spits) to roast their meat, season it with salt, use their paws as hands, and slip back into human form over the course of their eating.

A sharp contrast existed between the werewolf of the court's imaginary and that of Thiess's narration. In the first instance: a savage beast, ensnared by the Devil and lost in sin, driven to commit brutal violence against lesser creatures to satisfy its rapacious appetites. In the second: a fierce and courageous champion of justice, committed to recovering the abundance rightfully belonging to the peasants, which greedy lords and their thieving lackeys regularly steal. Here, as elsewhere, werewolves proper are not at issue; rather, in the discourse of both contesting parties, they figure as a trope for the situation of *Undeutsche* Livonians in relation to the *Deutsche* elite.

Court officials spoke the interests and perspective of the elite in thinly veiled fashion by construing werewolves as extreme, but instructive examples of the paganism, aggression, and bestial violence present as a potential in all *Undeutsche*. The latter group, like subalterns everywhere, had to be more guarded in their attempts to invert the werewolf sign and turn it to their advantage. Only once in the transcript does Thiess explicitly say anything about the *Deutsche* elite. The passage is brief and ambiguous, but fascinating.

Q: Weren't there women and maidens among the werewolves? Also were Germans (*Deutsche*) found among them?
A: Women were certainly among the werewolves, but maidens were not. Rather, they were of use to the flying sprites or dragons and were sent out to take away the yield of milk and butter. The *Deutsche* don't join their company; rather, they have a special Hell of their own.[64]

Neither of the issues raised here was pursued further,[65] and the question of "the Germans" (*die Deutsche*) enters almost as an afterthought, which Thiess skillfully deflected. Apparently, the judges were satisfied with his statement that "The *Deutsche* . . . have a special Hell of their own," and saw no need to pursue the issue. Yet we might ask what exactly the old man meant. Did he mean to suggest that the *Deutsche* fight sorcerers and demons, but do so in a "special" (*sonderliche*) Hell, separate from that visited by their *Undeutsche* inferiors? Perhaps, although this would contrast with the way Thiess described Russians and those of other villages as having their own werewolf bands, but visiting the same Hell that he did.[66] Alternatively, did he mean to suggest that there is a "special" Hell the *Deutsche* own and inhabit? Both interpretations are available, and it is possible that Thiess framed his response so that different fractions of his audience could understand it consistent with their interests and inclination. Still, one must note that he never used the verb "to have" when describing the *Undeutsche* relation to Hell, which was invasive, and not proprietary.[67]

## VI

Close analysis of Thiess's trial permits us to recognize the struggle between the *Deutsche* elite and the *Undeutsche* peasantry for control over werewolf discourse and to understand that such skirmishes were not just reflections of, but interventions in, their larger struggle over the maldistribution of wealth, power, prestige, dignity, and justice. In this way, I find the situation comparable to that of the Benandanti and countless other groups who appropriate and redefine the potent terms through which their social superiors disparage and classify them. As I see it, that which connects the two cases and accounts for the similarities between them is not an underlying prehistory of shamanism diffused from central Asia across Europe, but similar socioeconomic, political, and discursive dynamics.

Rather than imagining that a shaman stands behind the werewolf in some real historical sense, it is more useful to replace the notion that Thiess "was a werewolf" with a more nuanced understanding of "werewolf" as a tendentious item of discourse through which the *Deutsche* elite demeaned and devalued the *Undeutsche* peasantry. Most of the latter accepted the term, while denying its applicability to them. Thiess, in contrast, accepted the nomenclature, but attempted to redefine it by inverting its moral valence. "Yes, I am a werewolf," he affirmed with pride, "and we werewolves are *good*. We fight the forces of evil and secure our people's welfare." Such a stance is unparalleled in the Livonian court records, but this is the point where Old Thiess is most precisely comparable to the Benandanti.[68]

Recognizing the similarity of the two cases, Ginzburg erred in thinking that behind the "morphological" features they had in common, there must be real historical connections, apparently believing that the only alternative was an appeal to Jungian archetypes or structuralist universals.[69] I hope to have shown that a sociocultural explanation permits one to see how similar circumstances—specifically, what Ginzburg described as "the cultural and psychological violence exercised by the inquisitors"[70]—produced similar adaptive responses in Thiess and the Benandanti.

## VII

I would like to carry the discussion a bit further in a direction that is only seemingly tangential, by shifting attention from Thiess to Ginzburg and others who studied the old werewolf. The first to do so was Hermann von Bruiningk (1849–1927), a distinguished Latvian archivist, who published the trial transcript as the centerpiece of a landmark article in which he assembled the documentary evidence regarding Livonian werewolves.[71] Writing in the first flush of Baltic independence, he felt this material offered access to the history, experience, and worldview of the indigenous Livonian population, distinct from—and occasionally in opposition to—that of their foreign overlords (German, Polish, Swedish, and most recently Russian). His article generated considerable excitement among nationalist scholars, who continued this line of research in the pre- and post-Soviet eras.[72]

Von Bruiningk's article did reach a few scholars outside the Baltic, most importantly the Austrian philologist Otto Höfler (1901–87), who—like Ginzburg—came across Thiess's case just after completing his dissertation, "Kultische Geheimbünde der Germanen" (1934).[73] Here, Höfler argued that groups of martial males who cultivated strong solidarity (including solidarity with the dead), consecrated themselves to a deity identified with ecstasy and inspiration (of berserkers, as of poets), and imposed their will as law (using force and fear as necessary) were core institutions of ancient Germanic society. Further, he saw these *Männerbünde* as having provided the Aryans of northern Europe with a unique capacity to found states, and conquer and rule over others.[74] Such groups cultivated ritual states of ecstasy in which they understood themselves transformed into bears, wolves, and other savage beasts, unleashing a physical force that made them virtually unstoppable. Images of berserks and werewolves are attested in Germanic prehistory, and Höfler cited Thiess's trial as evidence that such *Männerbünde* persisted into the early modern era.[75] Indeed, he subtextually suggested even stronger continuity, for his book effectively imagined a deep Aryan prehistory behind Hitler's Stormtroopers, Mussolini's Blackshirts, and the paramilitary organizations of other fascist movements. Such, moreover, was consistent with the extra-academic commitments of its author, for in 1922, upon first hearing Adolf Hitler speak, Höfler was inspired to help found the National Socialist *Ordnertruppe* (the Austrian precursor of the SA), in which he served through the 1920s, even though the organization was illegal. When his dissertation came to the attention of Heinrich Himmler, the SS Reichsführer was sufficiently impressed that he secured university chairs for Höfler first in Kiel (1934), then in Munich (1937). In the latter year, Höfler joined the Nazi Party, and shortly thereafter Himmler recruited him to serve in the Ahnenerbe, the ideological and "research" branch of the SS, where he continued to the end of the war.[76]

Höfler was so excited by the transcript of Thiess's trial that he republished the first half of it, along with his commentary, as an appendix to the published version of his dissertation.[77] The book gained a wide readership in the 1930s and remained a favorite of right-leaning scholars committed to the study of "Indo-European" religion, including Georges Dumézil (1898–1986), Stig Wikander (1908–83), Jan de Vries (1890–1964), and Mircea Eliade (1907–86), and it was via Höfler that Ginzburg first encountered Old Thiess.[78]

Where von Bruiningk treated Thiess in the context of the early modern Baltic, Höfler resituated him in a deeper history and a broader cultural geography, stressing the way his case and other Livonian werewolf narratives resembled accounts of berserkers and Vikings, the warrior bands described by Tacitus, legends of the *Wilde Jagd*, and *Wütende Heer*, as well as mythological figures like Oðinn and his Einherjar. Expanding the discussion further still, Ginzburg recognized other features that led him to connect Thiess to the Benandanti and the religious specialists of other, relatively pacific agricultural communities outside Germanic territory. In so doing, he became convinced that far from confirming Höfler's theories, the old werewolf's testimony actually undermined them. In an article published five years before *Storia notturna*, he made this point in emphatic fashion.

> In the commentary that accompanied the republication of [Thiess's] trial records in an appendix, an obvious embarrassment makes itself felt: the stories told by the old werewolf were full of fabulous details that are difficult to interpret as literal descriptions of rites; moreover, they were based explicitly on the theme of battles fought periodically for prosperity against witches and sorcerers; and, finally, they actually mentioned the participation of female werewolves in these battles. Höfler extricated himself by saying that the werewolf was a braggart, and a Balt besides. The Germanic warrior groups, in contrast, were strictly male and did not concern themselves with questions of fertility—to sum up, they were something entirely different.[79]

This is an overstatement. The occasional presence of women in Thiess's band posed no great difficulty for Höfler, as female figures (real or mythic) also appeared in several other examples he treated. Concern for fertility also arose in some of those data, and Höfler devoted reasonable attention to them.[80] He did find Thiess's werewolves insufficiently martial, but treated this as a minor discrepancy, not a paradigm-challenging anomaly, and he accounted for it with relative ease (if racist disdain) by observing that Thiess's band was Baltic, not German.[81]

In *Storia notturna*, Ginzburg tempered his argument and relegated it to a footnote. No longer charging Höfler with having "turned interpretive somersaults" to hide the fact that Germanic and Livonian werewolves were "entirely different" (*tutt' altra cosa*), he more accurately described him as having drawn a "distinction between a warrior nucleus (properly Germanic) and marginal elements linked to fertility and witchly eroticism."[82] Even in this more modest form, the point had crucial importance, for it was Thiess's description of himself as fighting to recover the *Seegen* stolen by the Devil's sorcerers that let Ginzburg associate him with the Benandanti and dissociate him from the proto-Nazi *Männerbunde*. Armed with this datum and argument, he pried Thiess from Höfler's hands, redescribing the Livonian werewolf as concerned with the well-being of an agrarian community, not violence and state building; an ecstatic shaman, not a frenzied warrior;[83] part of a cultural complex originating in central Asia, not in the Nordic-Aryan *Urheimat*. Much as Höfler appropriated Old Thiess from von Bruiningk, recasting him to suit his own ideals and interests, Ginzburg turned the same trick on Höfler and did so in more self-conscious fashion, with a stronger sense of the scholar's—and more particularly, the historian's—commitment to justice.

## VIII

I began by noting that *Storia notturna* started with the same core content and issues as *I Benandanti* and that it sought to confirm the hypotheses of the latter by incorporating more material and employing different methods. A similarity of spirit and goals also connects these books to *The Cheese and the Worms* (1976) and *The Judge and the Historian* (1991),[84] works where Ginzburg read court records against the grain to achieve a more accurate— and more humane—understanding of people whom judicial authorities had consigned to death and oblivion (in the case of Menocchio) or jail and ignominy (in the case of Adriano Sofri). Historical research and hermeneutical skill here served to rescue the reputation of people who had been abusively misperceived and misconstrued by their captors. The same spirit informs his treatment of Thiess, who had to be saved twice over: once from Livonian judges, then again from a Nazi scholar.

One problem in associating Livonian werewolves with shamans is that the latter typically make their cosmic journeys, mobilize their helping spirits, and battle monsters and demons *in order to rescue the souls of their patients*. However similar they might be in other ways, the werewolves Thiess describes had a different goal: the recovery of stolen wealth, in the form of animals and grain. This is, at most, a decidedly materialist revision of the shamanic scenario. Closer to the shaman's practice—not just morphologically, but ethically—is the work of a historian concerned to rescue the departed from oblivion or worse, consistent with Walter Benjamin's messianic dictum.

> The only historian capable of fanning the spark of hope in the past is the one who is firmly convinced that *even the dead* will not be safe from the enemy if he is victorious. And this enemy has never ceased to be victorious.[85]

Ginzburg was well aware of Benjamin, as he showed in a number of crucial passages.[86] In an oft-quoted, highly revealing aside, he also observed: "The attempt to attain knowledge of the past is also a journey into the world of the dead,"[87] suggesting that his professional labors are not only informed by political and ethical commitments, but manifest something on the order of soteriological aspirations, albeit of a secular sort. One is also justified in observing that shamanic careers typically begin with a crisis, interpreted as a calling—a vocation in the literal sense—whereby the spirits stake their claim to a young person. One masters that crisis by descending into other realms, heeding the spirits, and establishing productive relations with them, after which one is not only healed, but gains the power to heal others. Here, it is tempting to connect the history Carlo Ginzburg writes to the history he experienced and, most specifically, to the memory of his father, Leone Ginzburg (1909–44), who taught Slavic languages and Russian literature at the University of Turin, co-founded the Einaudi publishing house, and was active in numerous antifascist groups. Stripped of his teaching post in 1934, when he refused to swear loyalty to the Fascist regime, he subsequently lost his citizenship when Mussolini introduced racial laws (1938). In the same year, he married Natalia Levi, who would become one of Italy's foremost authors. The next year, their son Carlo was born, and shortly thereafter the family was transferred to Pizzoli, a small village of the Abruzzi, where they were sentenced to political confinement. After Mussolini's fall in 1943, the Ginzburgs made their way to Rome, where Leone was active in the partisan group Giustizia e Libertà, helped found the antifascist Partito d'Azione, and edited the newspaper *L'Italia Libera*. On November 20, 1943, however, he was arrested by the Italian police and shortly thereafter turned over to German forces, who imprisoned and tortured him, leading to his death in February 1944.[88]

If there is a shaman in this story, one who undertakes journeys to the underworld, communes with spirits of the dead, battles against demonic forces, and gains the power to heal self and others, I am inclined to think it is not Old Thiess, but Carlo Ginzburg, an extraordinary historian, whose personal situation and professional practice both manifest and shed light on the intricate, sometimes hidden, but always potent relations connecting the past and the present.

# 5: THE LINGERING PREHISTORY OF LAURASIA AND GONDWANA

I

In 1985, Cristiano Grottanelli and I coauthored a short article, reprinted as chapter 1 of this volume, in which we observed that none of the most important theoretical work on religion has come from disciplines devoted to its study. Rather, this fell to outsiders—Marx, Weber, Durkheim, Malinowski, and a few others—who were not interested in religion per se, but who struggled to understand how it affects and is affected by other aspects of human experience. Thus, they paid particularly close attention to social dynamics and historic, also cultural context, using comparative methods to identify general categories and recurrent patterns. Once religious studies was constituted as an independent discipline, however, theologians, phenomenologists, and others concerned themselves little with context or dynamics, preferring to construe religion as a transcendent, atemporal essence. At the same time, the field clung to comparatism, even as such methods lost favor elsewhere. The situation struck us as troubling, but not without promise. "It is the historians of religion," we wrote, "whatever their other failings, who managed to keep comparatism alive, as in the works of such disparate figures as [Raffaele] Pettazzoni, Geo Widengren, Mircea Eliade, and Georges Dumézil."

Following that *apologia pro domo nostra*, we pressed the argument incautiously further. "One need not be a prophet to understand that a return to comparatism in all the human sciences lies in the very near future," we brashly proclaimed, "and that comparatism will be a central issue once more in the decades ahead. For whatever the errors of past comparatists—and they are legion, as is well known—it is only comparative research that can yield generalizations of a truly probative nature. The problem is not *whether* to compare, but *how*."

Thirty years later, I would stand by the principle, while acknowledging our prediction a fiasco, for comparatism, along with the grand theories and master narratives with which it existed in symbiosis, has been abandoned even by the discipline that clung to it longest and most faithfully. To be sure, we have seen recurrent pleas to revive a comparative spirit, along with suggestions on how this might be done,[1] but most professional students of religion, like scholars everywhere, now construct themselves as specialists who bring finely honed skills to bear on one text, one sect, one era, or—at most—one religious tradition. In large measure, it is the history of comparatism that is responsible for this, if "history" in the present context denotes the narrative we have cultivated, which places comparison in a predisciplinary Dreamtime of founding ancestors who were giants, tricksters, and sometimes both: figures like Bartolomé de las Casas, Giambattista Vico, and Friedrich Max Müller, who lived in an age when scope and daring were encouraged, appreciated, and often enough led to inspired folly. The story might be brought to a satisfying closure with a flawed hero like Claude Lévi-Strauss or a shallow pitchman like Joseph Campbell, depending on one's preference of genre. Tragedy, farce, horror story, and epic are among the available options.[2] In all forms, however, such narratives have a cautionary effect, and it has been a long while since anyone was rash enough to attempt comparatism on the grand scale.

Hence the 2012 appearance of a big, bold, and learned work based on systematic comparisons, global in scale, executed with self-conscious attention to issues of method, and written by a distinguished scholar who was an accomplished specialist before taking the comparative plunge occasions a mix of surprise, excitement, and anxiety.[3] Indeed, one might reasonably ask: Has Michael Witzel, Wales Professor of Sanskrit at Harvard, author of *The Origins of the World's Mythologies*, learned nothing from the sad history of comparison? Better, however, to ask in more measured fashion: Exactly what has Professor Witzel learned from that history? What (if anything) has he failed to learn, and how has this affected his work?

## II

According to Witzel, his book was forty years in the making and had its origin when, as a young Indologist, he noticed similarities between Indic and Japanese myths too suggestive for him to ignore. The impression grew stronger in 1990, when he, now a ranking expert on Vedic India, spent a year in Japan and immersed himself in aspects of Japanese culture.[4] Seeking a way to explain these resemblances, he read widely in the world's mythologies, while reflecting at length on the methods employed by his predecessors.[5] Starting from the premise that the task of comparative studies is to account for the "obvious similarities" even casual readers observe,[6] Witzel concludes that previous attempts were insufficiently systematic and did not take proper account of history.

The present approach is based on the mutual comparison of a sufficiently large number of mythologies of Eurasia, Polynesia, and Native America *over time*. In other words, the approach is both comparative and historical: it involves the axes of time and space; it works by collecting individual myths and analyzing their underlying structure, importantly including that of their arrangement in a myth collection.

Indeed, the main problem of the earlier types of explanations proposed so far is that they fail to address what I regard as the central but *unnoticed* problem briefly delineated earlier: the comparability of *whole systems of myths*. To use a linguistic simile, this entails something alike to the comparison of complete grammars of various languages, not just of particular words, forms, declensions, conjugations, or syntactical features. . . .

The structure common to these mythologies is a well-arranged and well-constructed narrative framework, a *story line* extending from the original creation of the world to its destruction. It underlies the original form of many mythologies of Asia, the Americas, and Europe.[7]

Although Witzel stresses the importance of history for his research, he uses that term to indicate his interest in the vast spans of *prehistoric* time during which myths developed and were transmitted across the earth's surface. History of a more conventional sort concerns him much less, as he pays little attention to the contexts and temporal processes relevant to individual narratives, texts, and traditions. Rather, his chief concern is to situate the origin of the world's myths (and the communities responsible for them) in the chronology of a very *longue durée*. The following passage gives some indication of what he has in mind.

The historical comparative approach is not one of old-fashioned Romanticism looking for and speculating on distant *ur*-situations, but it is the cladistic procedure also used by genetics, human anthropology, archaeology, linguistics, and philological manuscript research; all of them present pedigrees or stemmas of subsequent historical layers and their interrelations, filiations, or branchings.[8]

Essentially, Witzel proposes to extend the model Dumézil and others used for the reconstruction of Indo-European myth and religion, venturing beyond that temporal horizon (3000–4000 BCE?) to the extremely controversial notion of a "Nostratic" stratum (i.e., before Indo-European supposedly diverged from the Kartvelian, Finno-Ugrian, and Altaic language families, ca. 12,000–15,000 BCE?) and, more audacious still, to a previously unrecognized "Laurasian" entity (i.e., before migrations across the Bering Strait, ca. 20,000 BCE?) including most of Eurasia, the Americas, Polynesia, and North Africa.[9] The term is taken from theories of continental drift and describes the northern landmass that separated from its southern counterpart ("Gondwanaland") some 200 million years before the present.

Witzel believes systemic differences distinguish "Laurasian" mythologies from those of "Gondwana," which he takes to include sub-Saharan Africa, Australia, Melanesia, and parts of southern India. Most importantly, he takes Laurasians to have organized their myths into a story line moving from the world's creation to its destruction, while Gondwanalanders employ no encompassing narrative frame and show little interest in creation.[10] Rather, they recount episodes detailing the emergence and foundational acts of ancestral figures, as summarized in table 5.1.

The contrast drawn here and elsewhere is not just between *"our oldest complex story . . . a novel* of the creation, growth, and destruction of the world" and a collection of short stories, as Witzel sometimes puts it,[11] but between a rich plenum and relative scarcity, between integrating coherence

Table 5.1. Contrast of Laurasian and Gondwana mythologies

| LAURASIAN Mythology | GONDWANA Mythology |
| --- | --- |
| Creation from nothing, chaos, etc. | — |
| Father Heaven/Mother Earth created, separated | Earth, Heaven, sea preexist |
| Father Heaven engenders | High God in/toward heaven |
| Two generations ("Titans/Olympians") | Sends down his son, totems, etc. |
| Four (five) generations/ages | — |
| Heaven pushed up, sun released | — |
| Current gods defeat/kill predecessors | — |
| Killing the dragon/sacred drink | — |
| Humans: *somatic* descendants of Sun god | . . . to create humans: from tree/clay |
| They (or a god) show hubris | They show hubris |
| Are punished by a flood | Are punished by a flood |
| Trickster deities bring culture | Trickster deities bring culture |
| Humans spread, emergence of "nobles" | — |
| Local history begins | (Local tribes) |
| Final destruction of the world | — |
| New heaven and earth emerge | — |

*Source:* Following Witzel's Table 5.5 (*Origins of the World's Mythologies*, 352, emphasis in the original).

and its lack, between interest in The Big Picture and an absence thereof, also between peoples of the global north and those of the global south. It is a troubling picture that reproduces many stereotypes and binary oppositions of a sharply prejudicial sort. Were Witzel's method sound, his application of it rigorous and thorough, and his sources dependable, we should have to take these results seriously. Fortunately, that is not the case.

## III

With regard to method, I will venture four observations. First, it is a mistake to treat similarities as "obvious," since this obscures agency (and the possibility of error) by reversing the relations of subject and object, making it seem that resemblances reside in the data and force themselves on the reader. On the contrary, the impression that certain things are similar is an inference readers draw from their reading of things they *construe* as comparanda. In this, their judgment is inevitably inflected by preexisting desires, expectations, knowledge, disposition, and experience, all of which may be misleading. Second, to privilege similarity without giving serious consideration to difference leads one to aggregate large bodies of data in relatively uncritical fashion, based on shared features that may be superficial, accidental, insignificant, and/or illusory. Third, to construe the observed (or imagined) similarities first as the result of, and second, evidence for, a shared prehistory is to engage in circular reasoning based on examples recorded long after the presumed period of unity. And the more distant that hypothetical *Urzeit* might be, the more it provides a blank screen onto which even the most scrupulous scholars can project all manner of fantasies. Fourth, and perhaps most important, stark binary oppositions are always hierarchic and prejudicial. Organizing one's data in two master categories based on the presence or absence of a desirable feature (e.g., a coherent story line) implicitly elevates—and justifies elevating—one of these groups above the other.[12]

## IV

Although Witzel stresses the novelty of his method and conclusions, he frequently reproduces positions and problems associated with an important tradition in the history of comparison, the German *Kulturkreislehre*, which was influential from the end of the nineteenth to the middle of the twentieth century.[13] His account of myths that describe the separation of a primordially conjoined Heaven and Earth provides a good example and a useful point of departure.

"There are innumerable variations of this topic from Iceland to Tierra del

Fuego,"[14] Witzel states, although he quotes only the Maori myth of Rangi and Papa.[15] In this choice, he follows the lead of Andrew Lang (1844–1912), who compared it to Hesiod's story of Kronos already in 1884. Lang used the Maori variant to deprivilege Greek civilization and to support his argument that peoples throughout the globe react to the same stimuli by developing similar narrative explanations. "The mythmaker's fancy of Heaven and Earth as father and mother of all things naturally suggested the legend that they in old days abode together, but have since been torn asunder," Lang wrote, then appealed to E. B. Tylor (1832–1917) and others for similar stories from China, India, and elsewhere, on the strength of which he suggested "this view of Heaven and Earth is natural to early minds."[16] Such similarities he explained neither by diffusion nor—as Witzel would have it—as the result of a common inheritance.

> Of course it is not pretended that Chinese and Maoris borrowed from Indians and Greeks, or came originally of the same stock. Similar phenomena, presenting themselves to be explained by human minds in a similar stage of fancy and of ignorance, will account for the parallel myths.[17]

Such an argument was consistent with Lang's general view that "similar conditions of mind produce similar practices, apart from identity of race, or borrowing of ideas and manners."[18] For him, Greeks, Maori, and most all the world's peoples stand as equals on this ground. Others saw things differently.

Particularly noteworthy in this regard is Willibald Staudacher's monograph, *Die Trennung von Himmel und Erde* (1942), which took the ubiquity of such myths as its point of departure, but disputed Lang's conclusions about how this state of affairs arose and how it should be interpreted.

> In the following collection of HET [ = *Himmel-Erde-Trennung*, "Separation of Heaven and Earth"] myths, I hope to shed light on the wide distribution and meaning of a cosmogonic motif that Frobenius already judged a primordial possession of humanity. Unfortunately, however, all of us do not receive this myth in its pure form. For among the *Naturvölker*, whom it reached via radiation from the ancient *Hochkulturen* of the Mediterranean area, it was a "sunken cultural good," often combined with other sorts of ideas or fully distorted.[19]

Here, Staudacher (1914–57) defends the distinction *Kulturkreise* theorists regularly drew between high cultures and primitives (*Hochkulturen* and *Naturvölker*) against Lang, who threatened to destablize those categories by placing people like the Maori on the same plane as Greeks.[20] Staudacher went beyond Lang in one respect, however, adding a great many variants of the Heaven-Earth separation myth from Africa, as well as Siberia, East Asia, the Americas, and the Pacific.[21] But by mentioning Frobenius, he invoked the latter's view that this extremely ancient myth originated in western Asia, from which it diffused to the rest of the globe.[22] This is the position Staudacher develops at length, thereby reasserting the categorical divide in three ways: (1) Not all people have the same relation to this myth, since (2) it originated only among *Hochkulturen*, and (3) when diffused to *Naturvölker*, it assumes bastard form.

Racial issues enter the passage in veiled, but potent fashion, as in its association of *Hochkulturen* with purity (*in reiner Form*) and *Naturvölker* with *gesunkenes Kulturgut, andersartigen Vorstellungen* (not just other sorts of ideas, but the ideas of racial others), and the status of *Mischlingen*. Racism surfaces more blatantly, as one might expect in a volume whose foreword is signed "In the field, June 1942" by an author "in military service since spring 1939."[23] Accordingly, Staudacher argued that this myth originated in a high civilization of great antiquity, which he identified as "a pre-Aryan cultural *and racial* community encompassing the Mediterranean region and India."[24] From that primordial center, it spread to the various *Naturvölker* who tell such tales, along lines of diffusion he purports to trace.[25]

When considering the same question and much the same evidence treated by Lang and Staudacher, Witzel takes a position almost isomorphic to the latter, whom he has read and cites, although he modifies Staudacher's position in several ways.[26] First, he includes Polynesia and the Americas in the group for whom the Heaven-Earth myth is original and authentic. As a result, he no longer has to account for diffusion into and across the Pacific. Second, he assigns a date of 20,000 BCE to the originating group, while Staudacher leaves this unspecified. Third, he introduces a new terminology, "Laurasian" and "Gondwana," in place of *Hochkulturen* and *Naturvölker*.[27]

Given these modifications, the chief problem facing Witzel is how to account for the myth's presence in sub-Saharan Africa. To do so, he adopts the same explanation as did Staudacher, appealing to lines of diffusion they both took from Hermann Baumann's *Schöpfung und Urzeit des Menschen im Mythus der afrikanischen Völker* (1936), the same source from which Witzel and Staudacher took most of their African examples.[28] Staudacher adopts Baumann's arguments fully and enthusiastically, however, while Witzel shows more ambivalence and hesitation. Although his wording is cautious, even evasive at points, he seems to know that establishing his overall position depends on accepting this piece of diffusionist explanation, while resisting the larger claims of *Kulturkreislehre* diffusionism. It is a delicate balance that he does not always successfully maintain.[29]

V

Although Witzel typically—and problematically—relies on German ethnologists associated with the *Kulturkreislehre* for his information about the myths of non-literate peoples,[30] he leans on none of them so heavily as Baumann (1902–72), whom he cites no fewer than seventy-three times.[31] It is thus important to understand both the school and this individual for the way they influenced Witzel's vision and project.

Arising in a number of nascent disciplines (*Anthropogeographie, Anthropologie, Ethnologie, Volkskunde, Völkerkunde, Rassenkunde*) at the end of the nineteenth century, *Kulturkreise* theory took the world's populations to exist in a series of "culture areas," each with its own mode of production, technology, characteristic material objects, kinship system, and *Paideuma*, the term Frobenius coined to describe the intellectual and cultural style giving form and integrity to the ensemble.[32] *Kulturkreise* of this sort exist in specific geographic and ecological niches, but the theory also situated them in hierarchically differentiated positions in a sequence running from the lowest to the highest levels of material and spiritual (*geistlich*, also *seelisch*) development (i.e., bands of hunters and gatherers to powerful state societies). Given the way all aspects of a *Kulturkreis* were intimately interrelated and mutually reinforcing, it was understood that change normally comes, not as the result of an internal dynamic, but when superior technologies, goods, ideas, and/or beliefs are transmitted from more to less advanced areas. Diffusion of this sort began with the *Hochkulturen* of ancient Egypt, Mesopotamia, India, and the Mediterranean, and continues through history, culminating in modern Europe's relation to the rest of the globe.

As theorized by its founding figures—Friedrich Ratzel (1844–1904), Bernhard Ankermann (1859–1943), Leo Frobenius (1873–1938), and Fritz Graebner (1877–1934)—*Kulturkreislehre* helped legitimate the Second Reich's imperial ambitions, portraying colonial rule as the means for transmission of high culture to backward peoples and territories. Since most of Germany's new colonies were in Africa, as a result of the 1885 Berlin accords, it was thus important to cast the continent as always having needed and benefited from outside influence, which involved showing that all traits associated with higher cultures (states, kingship, organized military, sophisticated religion and philosophy, e.g.) were exogenous to Africa, having been introduced by "Hamitic" and other intrusive populations.[33] In the Weimar period, after Germany had lost its colonies, *Kulturkreise* theory shifted toward the orientation of Viennese scholars around Wilhelm Schmidt (1868–1954) and Wilhelm Koppers (1886–1961), priests and missionaries who understood "the white man's burden" more in terms of religious conversion than those of colonial administration.[34]

During these years, Baumann studied under leading *Kulturkreise* scholars at Freiburg (1920–21) and Berlin (1921–26),[35] conducted field research in Angola (1930–31), and worked closely with Bernhard Ankermann himself at both the Berliner Museum für Völkerkunde and the *Zeitschrift für Ethnologie* (1927–38). Politically, he gravitated toward the far right and in 1932 became active in Alfred Rosenberg's Kampfbund für deutsche Kultur, the same year he joined the Nazi Party and assumed responsibilities as chief (*Politischen Leiter und Amtswalter*) of the party's Charlottenburg section.[36]

In the late 1920s, Baumann began publishing articles relevant to the application of *Kulturkreise* theory to Africa, dealing with aspects of material culture,[37] subsistence activities,[38] kinship structure,[39] art,[40] and religion.[41] He made his mark, however, with an article of synthetic and schematic nature, in which he revised the work of Frobenius and others, dividing Africa into seven discrete culture areas, the lowest of which were properly African, while the more advanced ones showed an increasingly strong admixture of exogenous populations and features of high culture. His most important intervention, however, was to make race the basis of material and spiritual culture, replacing Frobenius's *Paideuma* as the central category of *Kulturkreislehre*.[42] The crucial passage reads as follows.

> Frobenius overshot the mark, however. He came to exaggerate the idea of an independent life of cultures, detached from the full-blooded substratum of race and the history of a *Volk*, which has its own laws. The way for future research is clear: It must lead away from the statistical formalism of the beginnings of *Kulturkreise* theory, also from all attempts that would let a mystical, autonomous *Volk*-soul be revived. Rather, it must always reckon with the substratum of the living human communities that are bearers of its culture. Therefore, attention to racial classification, patterns of migration, conquest, and other historical events is the absolute prerequisite for any study of cultures.[43]

This was published in 1934, the year after Hitler came to power, when all other discourses were being subordinated to that of race, and German colonial ambitions were stirring once more. Witzel mentions this article in passing, but seems to have misunderstood its significance, for he cites it as evidence that Baumann rejected the *Kulturkreislehre*, whereas in actuality he updated it to meet the demands of the National Socialist era.[44]

The schema Baumann developed in this article provided the template that undergirds—and claims verification in—his first major book, *Schöpfung und Urzeit* (1936).[45] Here he presented, then skillfully manipulated massive documentation (roughly 2,500 myths and folktales, drawn from a wide variety of sources), purporting to show how the creation myths of those groups indigenous to Africa correlated with their racial identity and low cultural level, in contrast to those groups who possessed more sophisticated myths, which they received via diffusion from and intermingling with higher races ("Hamites" and others).[46] That template is summarized in table 5.2.

This is the book that made Baumann's reputation, establishing him as Germany's foremost Africanist (alongside Diedrich Westermann [1875–1956], his teacher) and the foremost *Kulturkreise* theorist of his generation (alongside Wilhelm Mühlmann [1904–88], his sometime rival). The book was not just a catalogue or dispassionate study of African mythology, but was meant to show the continent's long-term dependence on superior civilizations for progress and spiritual guidance. Two years after *Schöpfung und Urzeit* appeared, in the immediate aftermath of the Anschluss, Baumann was given the chair in *Völkerkunde* at the University of Vienna, which the Nazis stripped from Wilhelm Koppers, who had opposed their racial theories.[47] In subsequent years, Baumann reorganized the Vienna institute to support German colonial efforts[48] and coauthored the highly influential volume that put race at the center of African studies.[49]

It is in this context that Baumann developed the argument Stadaucher and subsequently Witzel adopted, whereby the myth of Heaven's forcible separation from Earth was not developed by any of Africa's indigenous *Naturvölker* (categories 1–3 in table 5.2), but reached only the racially mixed peoples of Africa (categories 4–7), to whom they diffused from Mediterranean and Asian *Hochkulturen*. Stadaucher understood why Baumann advanced this argument, appreciated its place in a larger set of issues, and shared Baumann's views, also his values, on virtually all points. The same cannot be said of Witzel, who distanced himself from Baumann's broadest ideas regarding diffusion,[50] as well as his attempt to connect myth "too closely" to modes of production.[51] Conceivably, Witzel had only a limited grasp of Baumann's project, one specific piece of which he naively accepted, since it helped solve a problem that otherwise threatened the theories he sought to develop.

Things are not so simple, however, for Witzel took other ideas from Baumann, including his crucial argument that Gondwanalanders have no interest in stories of creation.

## VI

At one time, it was not uncommon for scholars—and not just Germans—to assume that *Naturvölker* were intellectually incapable of the speculative thought that finds expression in creation mythology. Witness, for instance, a 1908 rant Edwin Stanley Hartland (1848–1927) directed against Andrew

Table 5.2. Baumann's African *Kulturkreise*

| Culture level (lowest to highest) | Name | Geographic locus | Mode of production | Relation to other peoples | Race | Religion and mythology |
|---|---|---|---|---|---|---|
| 1. | Pygmies | Primordial forest of the Congo and Kalahari | Hunting with bow and arrow | Connection only to immediate neighbors in forest areas | Original | Ethical High God; primitive sacrifices |
| 2. | Bushmen | Northeast Africa and Sudan | Higher forms of hunting, using masks, poison, spears, etc. | Connections to a few isolated groups | Originally light skinned; now small and negroid due to intermixture with Pygmies and black Africans | Preanimistic; Uranian myths dealing with stars; animal mythology involving half-human forms; totemism |
| 3. | Ancient black Africa (*Altnigritisch*) | Sudan and East Africa, spreading into South Africa | Intensive hoe agriculture | Some relation to splinter groups in the Sudan and some in South Africa; uninfluenced by Hamites | Extremely crude, strongly Negroid (*besonders klobigen, stärkst negroiden*) | Chthonic; primitive mythology focuses on ancestral beings who emerge from the earth |

| | | | | | | |
|---|---|---|---|---|---|---|
| 4. | West African | Originally from Senegal, Guinea, and Congo to upper Zambezi; later spreading to area from Loango to Tanzania | Agriculture and exploitation of the forest | Invasions from the north | Strongly hybrid | Animist |
| 5. | East Hamitic | From Northeast Africa to South Africa | Herding of large livestock | Connections to Semites and the East Mediterranean | Hamitic | Rituals and religious ideas derived from Semites and East Mediterranean |
| 6. | Northern Hamites | From Senegal to southern Nigeria | Plow agriculture | Strong influences from the ancient Mediterranean, which this group diffuses through black Africa; later Islamic influence | Hamitic | Rituals and religious ideas derived from Semites and Mediterranean |
| 7. | Young Sudanic | Sudan and Ethiopia to Senegal south of the Sahara; also Southeast Africa | Very complex, with a feudal state | Origins in Sumer or India | | Divine kingship, ritual regicide; polytheism involving clan and occupational deities |

*Source:* Following Baumann, "Die afrikanischen Kulturkreise" and *Schöpfung und Urzeit.*

*Note:* In Baumann's view, categories 1–3 were indigenous to Africa, while categories 4–7 benefited from the introduction of exogenous populations and culture elements, which made them more advanced.

Lang's contention that a celestial creator can be found among the world's most primitive populations, such as aboriginal Australians.[52]

> When we are told that Baiame is the Kamilaroi creator, we must ask in what sense the word is used. Unfortunately, we have no details of the creative act. But we know that the idea of creation, as we use it, is completely foreign to savage ideas. The sublime conception of the creative fiat as set forth in the book of Genesis, and interpreted by Christian dogma, is the product of ages of civilisation; and to use the word *creation* is to import into the deeds of an imaginary being, who is presented, if not as "a deified blackfellow," at least as hardly more than a very exalted savage wizard, ideas which do not belong to them and therefore are utterly misleading to the reader.[53]

Going further, Hartland argued that in those instances where Baiame appears as creator, this is the result of missionary influence—another instance of diffusionist explanation.[54]

By the end of the Weimar period, such crudely disparaging views were becoming hard to sustain, especially in light of the theories of *Urmonotheismus* being developed by Fathers Schmidt and Koppers in Vienna. Drawing heavily on their work, Herbert Schlieper (1906–93?) devoted his dissertation to *die kosmogonischen Mythen der Urvölker* (1931), concluding that "with the exception of one group only—the Eskimo—all the *Völker* from the earliest levels of humanity known to us provide evidence of their concern with the question of the origins of the world and the earth."[55]

Schlieper's work was not so much influential as reflective of changing views. If the old attitudes were to be preserved, this would require more nuanced argumentation of the sort Baumann provided when he wrote that black Africans—that is, the original populations of Africa representing the three lower groups in his schema—cultivated myths describing the origin of people and their immediate environment, but showed no interest in the creation of the world as a whole.

> Regarding the origin of the human environment, to the extent that the inorganic is at issue, Africans devote little thought. At the center of ancient black African mythology stands man, i.e., the first man. Any thoughts that extend further point to cultures external to Africa.[56]

In this passage, Baumann advances two arguments that complement each other in perverse ways to establish a non-falsifiable, but utterly specious conclusion built on circular logic. The first asserts that there are no *real* creation myths in Africa, implicitly reasserting the notion that *Naturvölker* are incapable of such advanced thought. The second acknowledges that one does, in fact, find creation myths in Africa, then asserts these are not *really* African, but imports from elsewhere. In the subsequent discussion, he considers some of the (many) examples that threaten his first point and require the second, claiming—on no real evidentiary basis—that myths of creation from the primordial sea or a world egg must have come from the *Hochkultur* of the Nile Valley, earth-diver cosmogonies from Asia, astral myths and lunar ancestors from India, and creation myths where rain and rainmaking figure from Hamites or "Eurafrican hunters."[57]

On both points, Witzel adopts Baumann's strategies to defend the binary distinction central to his theory. Often, he is content to insist there are no creation myths in Gondwanaland.

> Myths about the beginning of the universe and the earth are the most prominent feature in Laurasian mythology. They constitute the very beginning of "mythic time." The Laurasian stress on cosmogony, however, is entirely absent in Gondwana mythologies.[58]

> As will be readily seen, the mythologies of these [Gondwana] areas differ so much from Laurasian ones that they cannot be included in the Laurasian scheme. Most notable is the highlighted absence of myths of primordial creation and final destruction. The question of how the universe and the world came into being is simply not asked.[59]

> In Gondwana myth, the earth already existed and was a hot, dry, and sometimes dark place. The only question that is of interest for Gondwana myth is how the earth can be shaped properly so as to make human life possible. . . . Laurasian myth, in contrast, is characterized by the myth of the original emergence (or "creation"), though how that took place is left unclear to some extent or shrouded in mystery.[60]

When this fails, arguments for diffusion become necessary.

> Some [Andaman Island] myths rather look like adaptations from Laurasian mythology: there is the typical separation of Heaven and Earth and an axis mundi.[61]

> If we did not take into account northern, Afro-Asiatic, and Nilotic influences, many of the features discussed in this section would align much of sub-Saharan African mythology with the Laurasian system.[62]

> In sum, these Laurasian motifs in Africa [(1) Primordial ocean; (2) Fishing up the floating earth and spreading it; (3) The world egg; (4) Creation of light; (5) Primordial waters are guarded by a monster; (6) Father Heaven/

Mother Earth] are isolated and can be explained as intrusions from areas that have Laurasian mythology.[63]

At one point, Witzel suggests that when "Laurasian" traits show up among a people he normally classifies as "Gondwana," these are likely to be mixed populations at the borders of Gondwana territory, open to Laurasian diffusion. One is thus justified to "subtract" the extraneous materials and seek the *real* Gondwana mythology among "backwoods" groups insulated against foreign influence. Underlying these extraordinary moves is Baumann's separation of Pygmies, Bushmen, and *Altnigritisch* Africans from Hamites, Sudanites, and *Mischlingen*, as Witzel acknowledges, while simultaneously (and rather comically) trying to suggest that he and Baumann reached their conclusions independently.

> Obviously, in the cases mentioned so far, the Laurasian traits have to be carefully "subtracted" from what we find in Gondwana myths. This can best be done by starting out from the mythology of isolated areas, such as the "backwoods," literally speaking, of Central Africa. We therefore begin with the central Bantu peoples of the Congo Basin, who were fairly isolated due to their habitat within the rain forest. Central African mythology is characterized as *not interested in creation myths*. This feature has been stated by scholars who could not yet know of the present theory. In the summary of his book, Baumann formulates in general and rather stark terms:

>> [These myths] are indeed much less colorful . . . They lack the speculation of nature philosophy of the Polynesians and some Amerindians, the close intertwining of human fate with the astral world as found with the Amerindians, and the grotesque fantasy of the Eskimos. The center of African myth is occupied by a creation principle that in most cases is identical with the High God, and the First Man, who has been begat, formed or brought forth by him. How this first man came to earth, how he lived and what he experienced is the topic of almost all African mythology. Next to this, the myths are almost insignificant of the emergence of heaven and earth, of the stars, and of supernatural beings that occupy a large portion of the mythology of other continents.[64]

With the parenthetical phrase "[These myths]" and an ellipsis, Witzel hides Baumann's original words and obscures the latter's meaning. In the original, Baumann specified it is only "black Africans" (*Neger*) whose myths are relatively colorless, unspeculative, and disinterested in creation,[65] a description he reserves for peoples of the lower African *Kulturkreise*. Hamites, in contrast, could engage in cosmogonic narrative and speculation without causing classificatory problems. The reason for this is obvious if one understands the logic of his system, which theorized the Africanity of "Hamites" as geographic only, *and not racial.* In the estimation of Baumann, his colleagues, and contemporaries, it is the latter that really mattered.

Normally, Witzel does not follow Baumann where the latter's racism is most obvious and offensive, but he rarely identifies it as such or rejects it outright. Rather, he modifies terminology, reworks the categories, softens the discourse, and rethinks the issues in non-racial terms, while salvaging whatever he finds persuasive and valuable, which amounts to quite a lot.[66] The result is a theory less novel than its author believes, for its master categories, many of its chief lines of argument, and its broad conclusions all modify and recode, but largely reflect and ultimately derive from, those of racist scholarship from the National Socialist era. Let me make clear that I do not think this is Witzel's intent, given the points where he took pains to distance himself from Baumann, but it is all the more regrettable—perhaps also more dangerous—for being unacknowledged and unconscious.

## VII

By way of general conclusions, we can recognize two ways that an inadequate model of and superficial engagement with the history of comparatism have influenced its practice. Thus, we began by noting how most contemporary scholars react to the litany of comparison's failures by renouncing such attempts altogether. The example of Michael Witzel provides an alternative, showing that this history can also be read as a challenge to do better. Toward that end, Witzel rummaged through prior attempts, discarding what he took to be bad, salvaging what he took to be good, then improving and expanding on the latter to produce a new comparative method that he hoped would yield dependable, even astounding results. His failure does not mean such efforts are always misguided, nor will it deter all brave souls in the future. But if such efforts are to succeed, they require a better understanding of what history is, also how one learns from and about it.

And here, I would make two points. First, history is not a classic narrative that has already been settled, but an ongoing process of inquiry. More precisely, it is an inquiry that seeks to improve our always-imperfect knowledge of the past, first by assembling as much evidence as survives (understanding that the past is more complex than we will ever know, large parts of it being irretrievably lost); and second, interrogating this evidence as thoroughly and as shrewdly as possible, with acute attention to (a) subtle and potentially revealing detail; (b) points of tension or contradiction internal to and between testimonies; (c) annoying lacunae, and (d) unexpected connections. To tell and retell a familiar story is not to practice history, even if one gives the narrative a revisionist twist or draws a new moral from it. If we are to learn from the history of comparatism, we need to reread the sources with fresh eyes, doing so in depth and detail, with close critical attention, and we need to look at a great many now-obscure works, as well as the old warhorses.

Second, history is a total, and not a compartmentalized inquiry. To study the "history of comparatism" as if this existed in isolation from the broader history of scholarship, and to study the history of scholarship as if this existed in isolation from political, social, and cultural history, yields results that are not just narrow and impoverished, but distorted and downright misleading. To understand any text—written or oral, monograph or myth—in historic fashion, one begins by placing its gestation, production, circulation, and reception in their proper temporal contexts, because this permits one to connect them with other texts and, more important still, with their contemporary social, cultural, and political currents. Only then can one understand the influences and pressures to which a text responded, the audience it sought and engaged, the reactions it provoked, the ambitions it harbored, the strategies with which it pursued them, the resistance it encountered, and the ripples it set in motion.

Failure to understand the extra-scholarly nature of Baumann and the *Kulturkreislehre* led Witzel into serious error, for the sources he took to be relatively unproblematic were, in fact, thoroughly entangled with the imperial ambitions of the Second Reich, the complexities of the Weimar period, the Third Reich's renewed desire for colonial *Lebensraum*, and the discourses of race that figured prominently in the scholarship and popular sentiments of all three eras. Similarly, a thorough discussion of Witzel's comparatism ought locate it in an era and a nation that likes to think itself anti-imperial (rather than neocolonial) and postracial (rather than racist). In such a context, grandiose scholarly discourses asserting the superiority of the collective self over the categorical other can no longer do so in open, straightforward fashion. Rather, they are obliged to code that message more deeply and obliquely, providing opportunities for denial, but also resulting in moments of confusion, illogic, and embarrassment, as well as bad faith and contradiction.

If the history of comparatism can help improve comparative practice, it might begin by providing us with a model of how to critically cross-examine the texts we study, how to place them in context, how to probe their subtexts, and how to better understand two (or more) pieces of evidence by paying close attention to their similarities, their differences, and the nature of their relation to the worlds of which they were simultaneously products and potentially transformative interventions.

# III
# A COMPARATIST'S LABORATORY: THE ANCIENT SCYTHIANS

# 6: REFLECTIONS ON THE HERODOTEAN MIRROR

## SCYTHIANS, GREEKS, OATHS, AND FIRE

I

Thirty-nine years after its publication, François Hartog's *Miroir d'Hérodote* remains a wonderfully provocative book: rich in insight, shrewd in argument, challenging in its insistence that book 4 of Herodotus does not describe the Scythian way of life *wie es eigentlich gewesen*, but undertakes quite a different task.[1] As Hartog saw it, the *Skythikos logos*, like the *Histories* in general, is a highly rhetorical work that elaborates and (re)circulates well-structured images, reinforcing its readers' sense of the ethnic other as an inversion or antithesis of the normalized Greek self. Thus, to take his two favorite examples, the text's representation of the Scythians as nomads construes them, above all, as people without a polis, the defining institution of civilized Greek existence,[2] while its description of sacrifice emphasizes the elements of Greek practice that the Scythians lack: temple, altar, sacrificial knife (*makhaira*), and axe (*pelekus*), concern to obtain the victim's (fictive) consent, accompanying libations, scattering of grain, blood poured out for the gods, and special portions of meat reserved for them.[3]

Renouncing positivistic attempts to mine Herodotus for evidence of Scythian realia, Hartog shifted focus to the assumptions, conventions, and distortions operative in the text itself. Attuned to emerging interest in discourse and perspective, also to the critique of orientalism Edward Said had just introduced,[4] Hartog's book met a strong and enthusiastic response, opening the path for a generation of classicists to engage a novel set of issues and methods.[5] Specialists in Scythian studies, however, have been less taken with his position, which marginalized (or even ignored) evidence they consider important.

Before Hartog, it was common for scholars in all disciplines to adduce Iranian comparanda (archaeological, textual, linguistic, and folkloric) as a means to construct a coherent picture of Scythian culture from Herodotus's account. Three major attempts were made along these lines. First was a classic article of Karl Meuli (1891–1968), connecting Herodotus's description of the Scythian sweat bath (4.73–75), the mystic travels of Aristeas (4.13–15) and Abaris (4.36), and the sexually ambiguous diviners known as Enarees (1.105, 4.67) to central Asian shamanism.[6] Second were the efforts Georges Dumézil (1898–1986) sustained over many decades, adducing counterparts to the Scythian creation account (4.5–7), deities (4.59 and 62), head-hunting practices (4.64), drinking rituals (4.66), and other details in Ossetic folklore, which he understood to have preserved ancient Scythian traditions and the trifunctional ideology he considered characteristic of Indo-European religions in general.[7] Finally, there was the suggestion of V. I. Abaev (1900–2001) that certain peoples mentioned in the Avesta were actually Scythians, who played an important part in the development of Zoroastrianism and displayed many of the same features described by Herodotus, including their dependence on their herds (4.2, 46, and 121), proximity to rivers and concern with hydrology (4.47–57), martial pursuits and cattle raiding (4.64–65), and festive consumption of meat (4.61) and intoxicating beverages (4.66 and 70).[8]

Others continue to work in this vein, sometimes engaging Hartog polemically and sometimes ignoring his work altogether. Along these lines, studies of Scythian creation mythology,[9] shamanism,[10] slavery,[11] androgyny,[12] funerary rituals,[13] gnomic discourse,[14] head-hunting,[15] lycanthropy,[16] and milking practices[17] have appeared in recent years. To be honest, some of these are relatively mechanical attempts to validate the Herodotean testimony by overreading the importance of one comparandum or another.[18] More sophisticated work tends to integrate Hartog's argument with an improved understanding of relations between Scythians and Greek colonists north of the Black Sea.[19] What emerges is a sense of the *Skythikos logos* as the product of complex interaction and multiple mediations: not a description of Scythians per se, but of those Scythians who were in closest proximity to Greek emporia, as they were perceived (and misperceived) by a few informants from the city of Olbia, whose reports were further inflected by Herodotus, as he reprocessed the material they gave him.[20]

Such an understanding makes clear the Herodotean text is no window transparent to the Scythian other, nor a mirror reflecting an inverted self. To pursue the optical metaphor, one might consider it a lens of limited scope, flawed in its manufacture and smudged with multiple fingerprints in the course of its use. As such, it provides neither a fully reliable picture nor one that is utterly useless. In the absence of better instruments, it continues to command our attention, notwithstanding its acknowledged defects.

## II

In broad terms, this is true not just of Herodotus, but of ethnography, scholarship, and human perception in general. All observers see what they are culturally prepared to see, and their vision is conditioned by their perspective and situation of interest. Accordingly, all reports are partial, in every sense of the word. It is not the case, however, that observers inevitably see and speak only about themselves while systematically misperceiving and misconstruing the other. If ethnographic reporting is never so objective or scrupulously disinterested as its practitioners once claimed, neither is the knowledge it purports to offer fully reducible to solipsism and the camouflaged workings of power.

Reading ethnography is thus a difficult operation. Unless one has independent sources of information (preferably originating from the people described) to serve as a control, it is easy for naive readers to accept an ethnographic report as reliable, but equally easy for skeptics to dismiss the same text as deluded and prejudicial. Reception that appropriately balances critical and appreciative moments thus depends on the use of evidence independent of the ethnographer. Had we ancient Scythians to interview or texts written by them, our task would be easier, but no such data being available, the best evidence consists of archaeological remains from Scythian territories, comparanda from their Achaemenid and Zoroastrian contemporaries, and folklore from their Ossetic descendants. Only when these are given serious consideration can one reach more reasonable—if still only approximate—judgments about the value of Herodotus's report, as well as the degree and nature of its distortion.

The limits of my own competence lead me to focus on comparanda from Old Persian and Avestan texts, which share a Pan-Iranian linguistic and cultural inheritance with the Scythians. This is evidenced by the thirty-six Scythian words for which Manfred Mayrhofer established cognates in other Iranian languages, including such culturally significant lexemes as the self-referential ethnonym "Aryan, Iranian" (*ariįa-; cf. Old Persian ariya-, Avestan ariia-)[21] and words denoting "religion, religiously informed way of life" (*daįna-; cf. Avestan daēnā-, Pahlavi dēn),[22] "sovereignty, glory" (*farnah-; cf. Old Persian farnah-, Avestan xᵛarənah-),[23] "herd, possessions" (*gaįθā-; cf. Old Persian gaįθā-, Avestan gaēθā-),[24] "true" (*haθįa-; cf. Old Persian hašiya-, Avestan haiθiia-),[25] "intoxicant" (*madu-; cf. Avestan maδu-),[26] and "ruler" (*xšaįa-; cf. Old Persian xšay-, "to rule"; xšāyaθiya-, "king"; Avestan xšayant-, "ruling").[27] Other continuities can be established through cognate resemblances of a nonlinguistic sort, e.g., the way special belts (Greek zōstrē, Avestan aiwyåŋhana, Pahlavi kustīg) are used as markers of male maturity,[28] or the priestly practice of pressing the sap from a symbolically significant plant (Scythian *askhu*; cf. Avestan and Old Persian *haoma*) and mixing it with milk to produce a drink that is theorized as combining the essence of plants and that of animals.[29]

## III

In the following pages, I propose to consider one such example: the Scythian practice of swearing oaths by the royal hearth in light of Avestan and Old Persian comparanda. Herodotus's account (4.68–69) reads as follows.

> When the Scythian king falls sick, he summons the three most highly reputed diviners, who practice divination. Usually they say that someone has foresworn an oath by the royal hearths (*tas basileias histias epiōrkēke*), naming one of the people.[30] For the custom of the Scythians is that when they wish to swear the greatest oath (*ton megiston horkon*), they swear by the royal hearths. Straightaway this person is seized and brought in, and they accuse him of having foresworn. The diviners say it is shown by their divination that he has foresworn an oath by the royal hearths, and for this reason the king is suffering. The accused man denies it, saying he has not foresworn, and he makes a great fuss. When he makes this denial, the king summons a second set of diviners, and if after looking into the divination they should convict him of having foresworn, straightaway they cut off his head and the first set of diviners divide up his possessions. But if the second group of diviners should acquit him, then other diviners arrive, and others still. And if the majority should acquit the man who was accused, it is customary for the first group of diviners themselves to be killed. They execute them in this fashion. After they put a cartload of firewood on a wagon and yoke oxen to it, having shackled the diviners, tied their hands behind them, and having gagged them, they shut them up in the middle of the firewood. Then they set fire to it and let the terrified oxen loose. Many oxen burn themselves up along with the diviners, and others escape with a scorch after the wagon-pole burns through. They also burn diviners (*mantias*) in this fashion for other reasons, calling them liar-diviners (*pseudomantias*). And when the king kills them, he does not let their children survive. Rather, he kills all the males, but does no injustice to the females.[31]

In his discussion of this remarkable text, Hartog focused on the hearth itself, which Herodotus elsewhere describes the Scythians as having personified and regarded as a goddess, whom he identified with the Greek Hestia.[32] From this starting point, Hartog ingeniously explicated the many ways the passage inverts Greek norms.[33] Thus, whereas Greek hearths were either those of a family or that of a city, the Scythian hearth is royal, recalling the deep past of Greek history, when there were kings, but no civic hearth, nor yet a polis.[34] Further, because the Greek hearth served as the center of a fixed dwelling space, Hestia was often paired contrastively with Hermes, the god in constant motion.[35] Given Scythian nomadism, one would expect Hermes to figure prominently, rather than Hestia, but he is unattested. Rather, the Scythian Hestia is to Greek eyes an oxymoronically *mobile* hearth, since the king had many hearths in different places, each of which served to center social, not geographic space.[36] Finally, there is almost no evidence of Greeks swearing oaths by Hestia, and when oaths were foresworn, the consequences were expected to fall on the perjurer, not on a king.[37]

These differences are real enough, but before embracing the idea that the description of these (putative) Scythian practices represents an inversion of Greek norms, we might entertain a simpler explanation. For in Greece, the hearth was divinized, while fires were not; in ancient Iran, the opposite situation obtained.[38] Further, ancient Iranian languages had no proper name for a hearth, speaking rather of "fire-places,"[39] while the Scythian name of the goddess in question seems to suggest fire, rather than containers for same: Tabiti, "She who heats."[40] Conceivably, "Hestia" was a misleading near equivalent, through which Herodotus (or his informants) described the Scythians' divinized fire, for which the Greek world had no more precise counterpart.[41]

If we focus on the way fire was understood among ancient Iranians, instead of the way Greeks regarded their hearths, other points emerge that have relevance for the Scythian oaths. One of the first things to note is that the most ancient surviving texts—those of the Older Avesta (ca. 1000 BCE)—consistently place fire in close association with truth, treating it as the instrument through which liars are identified, the righteous rewarded, and the order of the cosmos maintained.[42] To cite just a few examples:

Wise Lord, we want your fire, which is powerful with truth,
To be clear help for your supporter
And visible harm for the one who is hostile.[43]

I will think you strong and beneficent, O Wise One,
When with that hand you give two different
Compensations to the liar and to the truthful person
By the heat of your fire, whose power is truth.[44]

What do you give, Wise One, as protection for one like me
When a liar would constrain me to what is wrong?

Figure 6.1. Xerxes's tomb at Naqš-ī Rustam. Photograph: Courtesy of the Oriental Institute of the University of Chicago.

What other than your fire and mind,
By whose deeds you promote the truth, O Lord.[45]

Described as one "whose power is truth" (*ašā.aojah*), fire differentiates truthful people (*ašavan*) from liars (*drəgvant*), conferring this-worldly and otherworldly rewards on the former, with corresponding punishments for the latter. This is consistent with the givens of ancient Iranian religions, which construed truth (Old Persian *ṛta*, Avestan *aša*; cf. Vedic *ṛtá*, Mitanni *arta*) as the basis of the social, moral, and cosmic order: an order constantly threatened by the corrosive force of "the Lie" (Old Persian *drauga*, Avestan *drug*; cf. Vedic *drúh*).[46] In this perilous situation, kings were charged to preserve and protect the truth, and should a king's truthfulness be compromised in any fashion, catastrophe was expected to follow.

A highly significant representation of the Achaemenid king worshipping at a fire under the benevolent eye of the Wise Lord survives in a privileged site: the monumental relief sculptures carved in front of all the monarchs' tombs located at Naqš-ī Rustam (figure 6.1). Apparently these signaled the king's devotion to the truth incarnate in fire, as in the inscription Darius placed there: "Proclaims Darius the King: By the Wise Lord's will, I am the sort of person that I am a friend to Right. I am not a friend to Wrong. . . . The Right, that is my desire. I am not friend to a lying man."[47]

## IV

Two classic Iranian narratives highlight the king's responsibility for defending truth against falsehood, one a piece of Achaemenid history, the other of Zoroastrian myth. The first appears in Darius's Bisitun inscription of 521–520 BCE, which recounts that when King Cambyses stayed too long in Egypt, "the people became vulnerable to deception and the Lie became great."[48] In particular, "the Lie" (*Drauga*) asserted its power in and through an ambitious priest named Gaumāta.

> Then a man who was a Magus named Gaumāta . . . lied (*adurujiya*) to the people, [saying] thus: "I am Bardiya, the son of Cyrus, the brother of Cambyses." Then the people all became rebellious from Cambyses. It went over to him—Persia and Media and the other lands/peoples. He seized the kingship.[49]

From that initial act of deception, further catastrophes followed: the death of the legitimate king,[50] then a reign of terror,[51] then damage to plants, animals, and humans (i.e., life in all its forms).[52] All this is consistent with the Achaemenian view, expressed in a later inscription of Darius, that the Lie is the greatest of evils, opening the way to all others.[53] Rescuing the world from its troubles thus begins with the restoration of truth or, in the case at hand, with the Wise Lord's recognition of the man best suited for that job.

> Proclaims Darius the King: For this reason the Wise Lord bore me aid, he and the other gods that are: Because I was not vulnerable to deception, I was not a liar, I was not a deceit-doer, neither I nor my lineage. I conducted myself according to rectitude. I did deceit neither to the lowly nor to the powerful.[54]

In the struggle that followed, this (self-described) hero-of-truth killed and replaced the liar-king, with the Wise Lord's active support. His first act upon winning the throne holds particular interest.

> Proclaims Darius the King: The kingship that had been usurped from our lineage, I put it back on its proper footing. I set it back in place. Just as before, so I made the *āyadanas* that Gaumāta the Magus demolished.[55]

The word *āyadana-* occurs only in this passage, and its interpretation is contested. Some think it denotes temples or altars Gaumāta destroyed; others, rites he abolished.[56] Regardless of this, one thing is certain: its derivation from the verb *yad-*, "to sacrifice."[57] As his first act on the throne, Darius thus restored the practice of sacrifice, a key part of which was the fire in which oblations and libations were offered, which was itself construed as sacred and identified with the value of truth. With this, Darius began the process of restoring the moral, political, and cosmic order that had been gravely damaged by the perfidious Gaumāta.

Darius's story of his rise to kinghip is not identical to Herodotus's account of oaths by the Scythian royal hearth, but the two texts share details and themes drawn from their common Iranian inheritance. Thus, order and well-being were understood to depend on the quality of truth, which had the cultic fire as its material counterpart, it being the king's responsibility to maintain, defend, and restore, if necessary, truth and fire alike. Both stories derive their drama from much the same point: should falsehood enter at any point in this system, serious troubles follow and strenuous redressive action becomes necessary.

## VI

An important Zoroastrian myth involves much the same set of ideas. This is the story of Yima, last of the Pēšdādian ("primordial," lit. "created-before") line of kings who presided over the golden age.[58] Further, he was most possessed of the radiant glory (*x^varənah*) that is the material counterpart of royal legitimacy and excellence.[59] This came to an abrupt end, however, as the Avestan hymn to *x^varənah* recounts.

> We sacrifice to the mighty royal glory (*x^varənah*) created by the Wise Lord . . . that accompanied radiant Yima for the long time when he ruled over the earth. . . . Under his rule there was neither heat, nor cold, neither old age, nor death, nor demon-created envy, due to his non-lying until he took up lying, untruthful speech (*draoγəm vācim aŋhaiϑīm*). And when he was seen taking up this lying, untruthful speech, then the royal glory departed from him in the form of a bird.[60]

In the moment he told his first lie, Yima's kingship was over, as were the wonders of his golden age. He himself fled, was overtaken by enemies, killed, and dismembered.[61] Meanwhile, the *x^varənah* changed its form from the "royal" (*kauuaēm*) type enjoyed by legitimate kings to an "unappropriated" (*ax^varətəm*) variety that remains independent and disincarnate, holding unworthy candidates at bay until such time as someone qualified to be king appears.[62]

*X^varənah*'s flight opened a power vacuum, to which the rival forces of the cosmos responded. As the hymn continues, the Beneficent and Evil Spirits

(*Spənta* and *Aŋra Mainiiu*) both send teams in pursuit of the departed glory. These teams include spiritual entities: Truth (*Aša*) and Good Mind (*Vohu Manah*) on the one hand, Evil Mind (*Aka Manah*) and Wrath (*Aēšma*) on the other. The physical struggle, however, falls to their material members: Fire (*Ātar*) representing the side of the Good versus Aži Dahāka, a tricephalous monster hostile to all Iranians.[63] In this tense situation, Fire makes the first advance.

> Then Fire, son of the Wise Lord, sprang forward, thinking thus: "I will take hold of this glory, which is unappropriated." Then Aži [= "the Dragon"] with three gaping maws, whose religion is evil, rushed at him from behind, voicing a vicious threat: "Ha! Consider this, O Fire: If you take hold of this [glory], which is unappropriated, I will trample you—You will not flare up again on the earth, created by the Lord, to protect the world of truth." Then Fire pulled back its hands, concerned for preservation of its life when Aži was so fearful.[64]

In the next phase of conflict, the positions of the two rivals reverse, as Aži rushes to seize the *x<sup>v</sup>arənah*, only to be deterred by the violence of Fire's threats.

> Then Aži [the Dragon] with three gaping maws, whose religion is evil, rushed forward, thinking thus: "I will take hold of this glory, which is unappropriated." Then Fire, son of the Wise Lord, advanced at him from behind, speaking with these words: "Ho! Consider this, Aži of the three gaping maws: If you should take hold of this [glory], which is unappropriated, I will sprout up your ass and flare out your mouth. You will not scamper about again on the earth, created by the Lord, to destroy the world of truth." Then Aži pulled back its paws, concerned for preservation of its life when Fire was so fearful.[65]

The two passages parallel one another closely, inverting a few key points of diction. Most important is the nature of the threats the adversaries voice, each of which causes his rival to retreat. Thus, where the Dragon says he will trample the Fire so that it can no longer "*protect* the world of truth" (*θrāθrāi ašahe gaēθanąm*), Fire responds by saying he will scorch the Dragon so it can no longer "*destroy* the world of truth" (*mahrkāi ašahe gaēθanąm*).

The story of Yima's fall advances an ideology in which, once again, the world order depends on the king, kingship depends on the truth, and untruthful kings automatically lose their legitimacy, power, and lives. Episodes following Yima's death develop the ideology further, as Fire becomes the protector of truth in the absence of a rightful king. So long as Fire survives, the story asserts, truth will not be destroyed, although Fire alone cannot reconnect truth and kingship when the two have been sundered by a royal lie. For proper relations to be fully restored, it is necessary for a deserving candidate to acquire the "unappropriated" $x^v ar\partial nah$ and make it "royal" again. Between Yima and Kavi Haosravah, who accomplished that feat, an unspecified period of time elapsed, during which kingship— but neither truth nor $x^v ar\partial nah$—fell to foreigners and dangerous tyrants, including Aži Dahāka. The story is long and fascinating, but following its complications would take us far from the issues at hand.

## VII

When one considers Herodotus's description of Scythian oaths by the royal hearth alongside Darius's account of how he became king and the myth of what happened to Yima's $x^v ar\partial nah$, what emerges is not a precise correspondence, but a looser set of values, institutions, symbolic constructs, narratives, and practices that were all part of the Pan-Iranian culture that Scythians, Achaemenids, and Zoroastrians shared.

The Herodotean passage shows a structure in which the king, the value of truth, and a highly valorized fire were intimately interrelated and collectively responsible for the preservation of well-being. Further, this set of relations was subject to challenges and threats that could throw the king, the realm, and the world into disorder and crisis. In all these ways, the Herodotean testimony strikes me, *pace* Hartog, as mostly reliable and highly instructive, even if slightly distorted in certain predictable ways.

We have identified one place where culturally conditioned preconceptions led the father of history into error: his misidentification of the Scythian goddess Tabiti with Greek Hestia, which—as Hartog recognized—produced a certain confusion about relations between domestic and civic space, and the mobile or fixed nature of the polity. There is another point where the Herodotean lens was prejudicial, although in its own way revealing. This is his depiction of the Scythian court as a hotbed of political intrigue in which any ailment of the king produced a crisis; where accusations were quickly leveled and just as quickly contested; where priests stood to profit from transforming accusations into convictions, as they took possession of the malefactor's property upon his conviction; but where rival teams of diviners jockeyed for advantage in high-stake games of power politics, in which the king executed the losers—and their families!—in spectacularly violent fashion.

One could, perhaps, locate Iranian comparanda for all these details. Achaemenian kings, for instance, not only dispatched those they regarded as liars, but made public displays of their tortured bodies on occasion.[66]

That the Scythian kings dealt with those whose errors revealed them to be *pseudo-mantides*—i.e., lying priests, rather like Gaumāta—holds interest, as does the use of fire to produce their demise. Most striking, however, is a stark contradiction between the brutal competition for royal favor and the high ideals (truth, fidelity, knowledge) that all actors espoused (perhaps sincerely), but which provided the rhetorical instruments through which competition was waged. Such a contradiction was neither a projection nor a product of Greek ethnocentricism. Rather, it is one more example—as if one were needed—of the contradiction that is the essence of ideology: that between theory and practice, lofty ideals and grubby dealings.

Even the most ethnocentric ethnography does not invent such contradictions: indeed, it does not need to do so, for they are ubiquitous. What it does is identify contradictions *in the other*, then exaggerate their frequency and severity, so that the contradictions of one's own people appear relatively minor in (explicit or implicit) contrast. In his account of the Scythian royal hearth, Herodotus engages in exaggeration of just this sort, but not so much as to render the phenomena he describes so distorted as to be parodic or unrecognizable. As I hope to have shown, the picture he paints had its basis in real Scythian practices, Pan-Iranian ideology concerning the king's (idealized) relation to truth, and the inevitable contradictions this entailed.

# 7: GREEKS AND SCYTHIANS IN CONVERSATION

### I

In the Coen brothers' 2013 film *Inside Llewyn Davis*, the title character offers a definition of the music he loves and plays: "If it never was new and it never gets old, then it's folk." One could make similar claims regarding myth, another genre that admits no originals, no singular masterworks produced by a solitary genius, no authentic or definitive versions, just recirculation through countless anonymous iterations. Like folk songs, myths represent themselves as eternal wisdom and the very voice of a people.

Such views, which derive from Herder's theories of the *Volk* and German romanticism more broadly, remain as attractive as they are misleading. Most importantly, while mythic narrators may remain nameless, this does not make their products authorless, trans-temporal, or collective. Rather, it occludes the author's identity, agency, position within the social whole, and situation of interest, all of which makes it easy to misperceive a given variant as "the myth," to misperceive a given narrator as "the people," and to misrepresent the specific interests advanced through the way that narrator tells the tale to a given audience on a given occasion as "the people's abiding values."

Accordingly, critical scholarship on myth begins by declining the seductions of romanticism, insisting on the particularities of each variant, seeking to identify as best as possible the unnamed narrators, and attempting to understand the way the details of a given variant not only correlate with, but actively advance the interests of the narrator and that fraction of society s/he represents.

### II

Herodotus provides us with a convenient example of how such inquiry might proceed—and what it can offer—in his summary of the Scythian myth of creation, which he presents in two variants. One of these has received considerable scholarly attention over many decades,[1] while the other has more recently become an object of interest.[2] The important task, however, is to consider them in relation to each other, exploring their commonalities, differences, and the implications of the latter. The first text reads as follows.

> The Scythians say they are the youngest of all peoples and this is how it came to be so. A first man was born in this country, which was (previously) uninhabited. His name was Targitaos. The parents of this Targitaos, they say—saying things that aren't credible to me—were Zeus and the daughter of the river Borysthenes. This was the lineage from which Targitaos was born and of him were born three sons: Lipoxais, Arpoxais, and Kolaxais, the youngest. In the time of their reign, golden products fell from the sky: a plow and also a yoke, a battle-axe, and a *phialē* fell to Scythia. Seeing these first, the oldest went close, planning to take them, but as he approached, the gold burst into flame. When he had departed, the second son approached the gold, and it flared up again. And when the flaming gold had repelled them, the fire was extinguished at the approach of the third and youngest son, and he carried it off as his own. The older brothers then accepted that the whole kingship be handed over to the youngest. From Lipoxais was born the tribe of those Scythians who call themselves Auchatai, from Arpoxais, the middle brother, were born those who call themselves Katiaroi and Traspies, and from the youngest, who was king of them, those who call themselves Paralatai. The name of them all together is Skolotai, taken eponymously from the king. The Greeks call them Skythai.[3]

Although Herodotus recounts the story in Greek, most of its characters bear Scythian names with good Iranian etymologies. This includes the first man Targitaos (< Old Iranian *\*darga-tavah-*, "he whose strength is long lasting"),[4] the river deity Borysthenes (< Old Iranian *\*ṷaru-stānā-*, "wide standing"),[5] and the three brothers Lipoxais, Arpoxais, and Kolaxais, whose names all end in the element *-xais* (< Old Iranian *\*xšaịa*, "ruling").[6] Numerous etymologies have been suggested for the first element in these names but there is little agreement on the details, only a common desire to construe them as a coherent set (table 7.1). Finally, there is the name of the royal line (or tribe) founded by Kolaxais: Paralatai (< Old Iranian *\*para-dhāta*, "first established" or "set in front").[7]

The narrative itself unfolds in three episodes, each of which involves cosmological constructs well attested in Iranian cosmogonies. The first involves the sexual union of Zeus and a daughter of the Borysthenes, elsewhere given the Scythian name Api ("the watery").[8] Like the originary coupling of Ahura Mazdā (= sky) and Armaiti (= earth) in Zoroastrian myth,[9] this is a conjunction of opposite principles—above and below, male and female, warm and moist—that produced the first human. In the second act of the drama, the unity embodied in Targitaos is subjected to fragmentation along multiple lines, including kinship (his three sons), class (the fiery golden

Table 7.1. Etymologies suggested for the names of the three brothers who competed to be the first Scythian king

| | Lipo-xais | Arpo-xais | Kola-xais |
|---|---|---|---|
| Christensen, Le premier homme et le premier roi (1918) | | "King of the Ŗpa" | "King of the Skolotai" |
| Brandenstein, "Die Abstammungssagen der Skythen" (1953) | "He who leads the *seniores*" | "He who leads the middle-age class" | "He who leads the *juniores*" |
| Dumézil, *Romans de Scythie et d'alentour* (1978) | "Chief of the young men belonging to a *Männerbund*" | "Chief of (agricultural) work" | "Chief of the lineage" |
| Cornillot, "De Skythes à Kolaxais" (1981) | "He who bears the axe" | "He who bears the yoke" | "He who bears the crown (*skuδa*)" |
| Ivantchik, "Une légende sur l'origine des Scythes" (1999a) | "King of the (mythic) mountain" | "King of the (watery) abyss" | "Sun King" or "Heavenly King" |
| Loma, "Namenkund-liches zur skythischen Abstammungssage" (2011) | "Ruler of the peninsula" | "Small king" | "Ruler over all, i.e., Great King" |

objects, each associated with a different occupation and social stratum), ethnicity and territory (the four *genoi* that descend from his sons).[10] The story then reaches closure by establishing kingship as the solution to the problem of fragmentation, insofar as the king encompasses and reintegrates all elements of the primordial whole. Thus, Kolaxais gains possession of all four golden objects, which constitute "the whole kingship" (*tēn basilēiēn pasan*), his elder brothers having been proven less worthy by the ordeal of the fiery gold.[11] Accordingly, the *genoi* they established remain forever subordinate to all subsequent kings descended from Kolaxais, who maintained the four golden objects as the sign of their royal power, which they ritually renewed each year.[12]

The fact that the story of creation culminates in the establishment of kingship reveals the identity of those who were the narrative's prime beneficiaries and the likeliest agents responsible for its production, reproduction, and circulation, just as the cosmogonic account produced by the Achaemenian scribes climaxes in the Wise Lord's elevation of Darius (or one of his successors) to the Persian imperial throne.[13] Given this, Herodotus is incor-

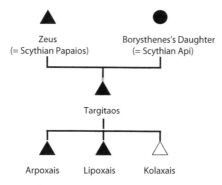

Figure 7.1. Mythic genealogy presented in the first version of the Scythian origin myth (Herodotus 4.5–6). The white triangle indicates the son who won the four heavenly objects constitutive of kingship.

rect to describe this as the story "the Scythians tell regarding themselves."[14] More precisely, it is the story Scythian kings and their apologists liked to tell to their countrymen, as it established the divine origins of kingship and the right of Kolaxais's descendants to rule. Presumably, the story was attractive to non-royal Scythians for the way it legitimized and stabilized their central political institution and an intriguing detail also contributed to its appeal. Thus, in thematizing the superiority of the youngest (*neōtaton*) brother, the myth imputed similar preeminence to the Scythians, who regarded themselves as "youngest of all peoples" (*neōtaton pantōn ethneōn*) and thus, by implication, superior to Greeks and others.[15]

This claim of preeminence was countered by a minor revision to the story effected, in all probability, by Greek colonists on the Black Sea, who had close relations with Scythians and served as Herodotus's informants.[16] This is the name given the god at the head of the mythic genealogy, whom the Scythians knew as Papaios ("Daddy"),[17] but who bears the name "Zeus" in the Herodotean text (figure 7.1). Although this might represent nothing more than the normal workings of *interpretatio graeca*, the revision invited Herodotus's readers to view the Scythians as patrilineal descendants of the Greek god and thus half-Greek in their origins.[18]

### III

The second version involves a much more thorough reworking of Scythian materials by the Olbian Greeks to better advance their interests.[19] Here, the union of Heaven and Earth disappears, as does the primordial unity represented by Targitaos. When the story begins, humanity has already come into existence, as have divisions of gender, geography, status, and ethnicity.

Driving the cattle of Geryon, Herakles arrived at this land, which was desolate, but which the Scythians now inhabit. . . . Having arrived there, he pulled the lion-skin over himself to fall fast asleep, for he was overtaken by winter and frost. At this time, his horses, which had been grazing under the chariot, disappeared by divine fortune. When Herakles awoke, he searched for the horses, roaming over all of the country. Finally, he arrived at the land called Hylaia and in a cave there, he found a certain half-maiden, a biform viper who was a woman above her buttocks and a serpent below. Seeing and marveling at her, he asked if she had seen his horses wandering about. She said that she had them herself and would not give them up to him until she had slept with him. Herakles slept with her for this reward. She delayed restitution of the horses, planning thus to be together with Herakles for a long time, since he would wish to depart once he obtained them.

At last, having given them back, she said: "These horses came here and I kept them for you, and you have furnished me with a reward, for I have three sons from you. Tell me what is right to do with them when they have grown big. Should I settle them here (for I myself hold power over this country) or should I send them to you?" They say he responded thus: "When you see the boys grown to men, if you do these things, you will not err. Whichever one of them you see stringing this bow and girding himself in this way with this belt (*zōstrē*), make that one the inhabitant of this land. Whoever of them leaves these things that I command undone, send him away from this land. Having done these things, you will make yourself happy and you will accomplish the things I ordered." Then, having drawn one of his bows (for until then Herakles carried two), he presented to her that bow and a belt that had a gold *phialē* at the top of its clasp, and having given them, he departed.

And when the sons born to her had grown to be men, she assigned names to them: Agathyrsos to the first of them, Gelonos to the next one, and Skythes to the youngest. And remembering Herakles's instructions, she did the things he had ordered. Two of her children, Agathyrsos and Gelonos, not having become capable of the task set before them, were cast out by their mother to dwell apart from their country. Having accomplished it, Skythes, the youngest of them, settled down in the country. This alone his mother contrived for Skythes. These things are told by the Greeks dwelling in Pontus.[20]

Set in Hylaia ("Woodland"),[21] the story begins with two people who have markedly different relations to that territory: Herakles, a Greek who enters from outside, and a woman identified as an autochthon by the serpentine lower members that connect her to the soil and her dwelling inside the earth.[22] An ambiguous creature (*mixoparthenon . . . ekhidnan diphuea*), simultaneously human and bestial, high ranking and base, monstrous and seductive, she is the model of the Scythian "native." Initially, her situation is characterized by isolation, deprivation, and lack. Although she rules over the land, her realm is empty (*gēn . . . herēmēn*), wintry, without other inhabitants, assets, or marks of civilization. The arrival of Herakles changes things, however. As a "stranger-king" of the sort described by Marshall Sahlins, he embodies the power of alterity and the radical alterity of power.[23] Union with him provides the means to transform the precivilized status of Scythia into something more like the world of the Greeks by introducing the potent, but morally ambiguous institution of kingship. To accomplish that end, the serpent-woman makes use of her thievish and feminine wiles, stealing Herakles's horses and refusing to return them until the hero shares her bed.

As a result, she bears three sons, and before the hero departs, she seeks to define her children's identity. "Tell me what is right to do with them when they have grown big," she says. "Should I settle them here or send them to you?"[24] Which is to say, Are they mine or yours? Scythian or Greek? By way of answer, Herakles gave her three novel instruments of culture—a bow, a belt, and a *phialē*—and told her to use them as a test. When the boys reached adulthood, he explained, the one able to string this bow and to gird himself with the belt should remain in place and assume royal power (4.9).[25] Note, however, that the Greek visitor claimed none of these youths as his own. The ablest—i.e., the one most Heraklean in his physical and cultural capacities—was to inherit Scythia. His less able brothers—i.e., those who received a lesser portion of their father's gifts—were to be sent, not to their father, but in the opposite direction. Thus, the first-born son, Agathyrsos, emigrated to the northwest and founded the people known as Agathyrsoi, whom Herodotus elsewhere describes as living a dissolute, unmanly existence.[26] Similarly, Gelonos moved to the northeast, where his people lead a sedentary, non-heroic and non-nomadic life, working the soil, tending gardens, eating bread, and speaking a language half Greek and half Scythian.[27]

Bringing Herakles into the story thus serves to construe the serpent-woman's offspring as Greek in their descent, but only partially so. That Skythes was more Greek than his brothers is suggested in four different ways. First, it was the physical excellence he inherited from his father that let him win the kingship. Second, he obtained implements of Greek culture (bow, belt, *phialē*) that his brothers were denied. Third, as an adult he dwelt closer to the Greeks, while his brothers were exiled far to the north. Finally, he established a more virile cultural style for his people than did his brothers, whose mores would strike a Greek audience as deriving from their Asian mother (figure 7.2).

Understanding Skythes as largely, but not fully Greek helps one recognize the cultural goods he received as an incomplete set. Thus, the bow,

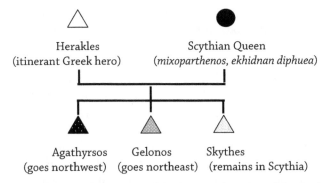

Herakles                          Scythian Queen
(itinerant Greek hero)    (*mixoparthenos, ekhidnan diphuea*)

Agathyrsos           Gelonos           Skythes
(goes northwest)  (goes northeast)  (remains in Scythia)

Figure 7.2. Mythic genealogy presented in the second version of the Scythian origin myth (Herodotus 4.8–10). White indicates Greek identity; black, Scythian; and shading depicts intermediate mixes of Greek and Scythian. The most Greek ( = least shaded) of the three sons wins the Scythian kingship.

belt, and horses Herakles introduced to Scythian terrain are construed as the Greek gifts that gave Scythian troops their powers of offense, defense, and mobility. Herakles's club, however, goes unmentioned, implicitly explaining why the Scythians, unlike the Greeks, preferred to avoid close combat. In contrast, the first version of the myth gave Scythians a battle-axe (*sagaris*) as their distinctive offensive weapon, an object derived not from the Greeks, but from Heaven itself.[28]

The Greek adaptation of the Scythian origin myth thus retains a plot in which the youngest of three brothers becomes first king of his people. At the same time, it drops the first version's cosmological concerns (divine origins, conjunction of opposites, fragmentation, reunification through kingship), erases most of the Iranian terminology, and reworks the genealogy to introduce an ethnogonic, rather than sociogonic line of analysis. Toward that end, it construes the Scythians as largely, but not entirely Greek in their origins and ethnic identity, while characterizing certain traits as defects peculiar to non-Greeks (e.g., the luxury and promiscuity of the Agathyrsoi, the agrarian passivity of the Gelonoi, Scythian avoidance of close combat and their thefts of livestock), all of which the barbarians in question inherit from their primordial, autochthonous mother.

IV

To propagate this version, presumably in competition with the other, the craftsmen of Olbia and other Greek outposts on the Black Sea produced splendid artistic renditions of the story for distribution as trade goods to their Scythian neighbors. Surviving examples include a representation of the serpent-woman from Tsymbalova Moguila (figure 7.3), the vase

Figure 7.3. Scythian horse frontlet in gold from Tsimbalka Kurgan near the Dnepr (4th century BCE), depicting the serpent-woman. Greek manufacture for Scythian trade. The State Hermitage Museum, St. Petersburg (Collection #Dn 1868, 1/8). Photograph © The State Hermitage Museum. Photography by Vladimir Terebenin, Leonard Kheifets, and Yuri Molodkovets.

Figure 7.4. Silver vessel from Tchastje Kurgan #3 (near Voronež, 4th century BCE), showing an older warrior bestowing a bow on an unbearded youth. The figures quite probably represent Herakles and Skythes. Greek manufacture for Scythian trade. The State Hermitage Museum, St. Petersburg (Collection #Do 1911). Photograph © The State Hermitage Museum. Photography by Vladimir Terebenin, Leonard Kheifets, and Yuri Molodkovets.

from Voronezh that seems to show Herakles bestowing his bow on Skythes (figure 7.4), or the one from Kul Oba, which, as D. S. Raevskiy first recognized, juxtaposes a scene of Skythes stringing that bow (figure 7.5) with pictures of his two brothers receiving medical attention for the kind of wounds typically suffered from the recoil of an unsuccessful attempt (figures 7.6 and 7.7).[29]

What we have been able to establish is that neither of the two variants Herodotus preserved is rightly regarded as a "Scythian" myth, if that term

Figure 7.5. Vase from Kul-Oba Kurgan in the Crimea (4th century BCE). Skythes stringing the bow. Greek manufacture in electrum for Scythian trade. The State Hermitage Museum, St. Petersburg (Collection #KO 11–3). Photograph © The State Hermitage Museum. Photography by Vladimir Terebenin, Leonard Kheifets, and Yuri Molodkovets.

designates a story of, by, and about the people as a whole. Rather, as we have seen, the first variant is not the Scythian people's account of their origins, but that of their kings, lightly adapted by the Greek colonists of Olbia, from whom Herodotus got the story. Prior to revision, it asserted the superiority of the royal line to all other Scythians and the superiority of Scythians to all other peoples. Revision rendered the latter half of this argument more problematic, by raising the question of whether the Scythians really were Greeks. The second variant represents a more thorough appropriation and transformation of the story that asserts (a) the superiority of Greeks to Scythians, (b) the dependence of Scythia on Greece for whatever civilizing arts it has come to possess, and (c) the superiority of the most hellenized Scythian to their more barbarous northern neighbors. Beyond the intrinsic interest of these materials lies a broader point of theory and method. Here, as elsewhere, rescuing a variant from its anonymity by identifying those who told the story *in precisely this way* and the audience they

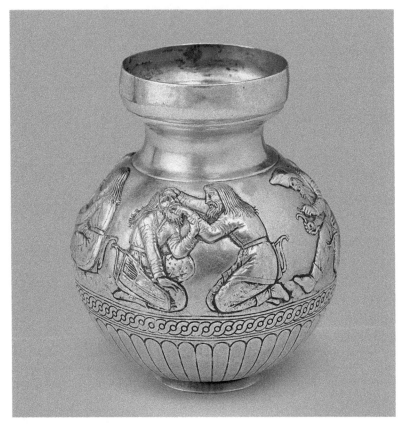

Figure 7.6. Agathyrsos (?) treated for a tooth broken by the bow's recoil. Greek manufacture in electrum for Scythian trade. The State Hermitage Museum, St. Petersburg (Collection #KO 11–2). Photograph © The State Hermitage Museum. Photography by Vladimir Terebenin, Leonard Kheifets, and Yuri Molodkovets.

hoped to influence thereby is the crucial step in discovering what it was all about. Here, as is so often true elsewhere, differences among the variants represent the instruments through which rival narrators and populations jockeyed for position, each one attempting to turn the story into a brief for the superiority of those groups they represented.

Figure 7.7. Gelonos (?) treated for a leg wound inflicted by the bow's recoil. Greek manufacture in electrum for Scythian trade. The State Hermitage Museum, St. Petersburg (Collection #KO 11–1). Photograph © The State Hermitage Museum. Photography by Vladimir Terebenin, Leonard Kheifets, and Yuri Molodkovets.

# 8: SCYTHIAN PRIESTS AND
# SIBERIAN SHAMANS

I

One of the earliest and boldest exercises in comparative ethnography already shows some of the genre's most dangerous traits, including

1. the way preconceived theoretical patterns and commitments dispose an author to construe as "evidence" those data—whether empirically observed, wholly imaginary, or imaginatively massaged into shape—that serve to confirm a theory;
2. the way the theory's elegance and systematicity seduce naive readers into accepting the author's tendentious selection of evidence and superficial, at times distorted presentation of examples;
3. the way ethnocentric prejudices are naturalized, normalized, and built into the theory's structure, then seemingly confirmed in the discussion of specific examples;
4. the way an unspoken group—that to which the author belongs—is the chief beneficiary of the comparison's results, even when it enters the discussion only in oblique, tacit, or subtextual fashion.

The text in question is the Hippocratic treatise *On Airs, Waters, and Places*, composed circa 430 BCE, which introduced a wide-ranging theory of ecological determinism.[1] While its first eleven chapters are presented as a guide for itinerant physicians needing to inform themselves about the cities they visit before treating their residents,[2] the second half of the text opens by announcing the author's intention "to show how much Europe and Asia differ from each other in every way, as the bodily forms of their peoples are quite distinct and resemble each other not at all."[3] Pursuing this agenda, it contrasts the rough terrain and varied climate of Europe to the richer soil, smoother landscape, and more uniform weather of Asia, while drawing inferences about the effect of these environs on human health and character, concluding most pointedly, à propos of Asia:

This place is most like spring in its nature, the most moderate of the seasons. Manliness, hardihood, willingness to labor, and greatness of spirit cannot come into being in this nature, neither among those races who are born there, nor those of other races who now live there. Rather, pleasure necessarily rules.[4]

Asians are thus defined as lacking a set of valorized qualities the text associates with the male gender: manliness (*andreion*), hardness (*talaipōron*), industriousness (*emponon*), and spirit (*thumoeides*), and this is said to result from the force of nature itself, as exercised through the environment. A bit later, the text suggests that cultural forces, particularly the institution of kingship, contribute to the "unmanliness" (*an-andreia*) of Asians, construing the importance of culture or custom (*nomos*) as a secondary amplification of effects chiefly caused by nature (*physis*), since topography and climate produce the soft bodies and weak spirits of Asia that kingship subsequently exploits and makes worse.

Regarding the lack of spirit and unmanliness of certain peoples, their dwelling places and seasons are the most important reasons that Asians are less warlike and more docile than Europeans, as these produce no great changes, tending neither to warmth, nor to cold, but a near-equal situation. For no disruptions of the mind, nor powerful changes of the body, come into being, which are more likely to make the temperament wild and to share its hot temper and harshness than is a situation that remains always the same. For changes of all things arouse people's minds and do not permit them to rest quiet. It seems to me that these are the reasons the Asian race is lacking strength, but their customs also contribute. For most of Asia is ruled by kings and where people are not autonomous and in control of themselves, but are ruled by despots, they may train for battle, but they do not have the character to be warlike.[5]

Having argued that the Asian landscape and climate suppress the qualities it judges "manly" (strength, industry, bellicosity, e.g.),[6] the text considers two examples—one from the extreme north of what was classified as Europe and one from the extreme south[7]—to demonstrate that it is not Asiatic mildness, but uniformity of terrain and weather wherever this might occur that weakens both body and spirit. These examples round out the text's constitutive architecture, permitting it to show why the North (Scythia), East (Asia), and South (Egypt and Libya) were all inferior to the West (Europe, with Greece at its center).[8]

Unfortunately, the chapters treating Egypt and Libya have not survived (a lacuna is apparent following chapter 12), but the Scythian *logos* (chs. 17–22) hammers at the central point, as when it describes the bodies of Scythian men as moist and flabby, lacking in muscle tone, and easily fatigued;[9] incapable of handling weapons without remedial surgery;[10] or suffering from sexual and reproductive inadequacies.[11] It describes Scythian men as "the least prolific in their offspring" (*hēkista polygonon*) as a result of their sustained exposure to cold plus moisture, a situation that produces their phlegmatic disinterest in and incapacity for sexual reproduction.[12]

> Such a nature as this is not conducive to prolific reproduction, as a desire for sex does not arise much in a man because of the moisture of his nature, the softness and coldness of his inner body. For these reasons such a man is least disposed to have sex.[13]

Certain Scythian habits are alleged to exacerbate this condition, especially wearing trousers and riding horses (the latter associated with the effete noble class).[14] As in the case of kingship, culture here works with and builds on the disposition nature has already implanted in Scythian bodies through the unchanging cold and moisture of their environment.

## II

The Hippocratic treatise is thus organized so that the Scythians play a dual role in a field of comparative relations. Associated with Asia by the constancy of their climate, they provide the extreme example of the feminizing effects of such an environment. For the same reason, they are contrasted with the virility produced by climatic and topographic change, as is supposedly normal in the rest of Europe.[15] As Edmond Lévy demonstrated,[16] this represents a change from the way Scythians were depicted in many older works, including Homer,[17] Hesiod,[18] Alcman,[19] Hecataeus,[20] and the traditions surrounding Aristeas,[21] where Scythians were invested with a reputation for peace, justice, wisdom, and other aspects of the "soft primitivism" described by Arthur Lovejoy and George Boas.[22]

Herodotus's attitude, as we shall see, is considerably more nuanced than either of these extremes. Unlike the earlier sources, he was not inclined to idealize the wisdom or the peacefulness of the Scythians, to whom he attributed a good many practices troubling in their ferocity (head-hunting, blood-drinking, and human sacrifice, e.g.).[23] At the same time, unlike the near-contemporary Hippocratic treatise, he held Scythian masculinity and martial prowess in high respect. Thus, of all the peoples who figure in the *Histories*, he reserves the adjective "unconquerable" (*amakhos*) for the Scythians alone,[24] describing how their nomadic habits gave them the means to repel the Persians, and whom he thus implicitly aligns with, rather than contrasts to, the Greeks. Differences in the way Herodotus and the Hippocratic treatise depict the Scythians are thus conditioned by the different ways they attempt to explain Greek victory in the Persian Wars, the latter attributing it to the natural superiority of the Greek body, the former acknowledging the importance of culturally conditioned temperament (specifically the love of freedom) and tactics (including the use of strategic withdrawal, following the Scythian model).[25]

## III

The structure of the Hippocratic text is quite elegant. Having construed the Scythians as the paradigmatic example of softness, weakness, and effeminacy, it accords a similar position to one particular set of Scythians, who are taken to exemplify the nature of the *ethnos* as a whole. These are the people it calls Anarieis, whom it describes at length in its twenty-second chapter.

> The majority of Scythians become eunuch-like. They perform female tasks, live like women, and converse in corresponding fashion: such types are called Anarieis. Truly, the people of this country attribute the cause of this to a god, and they revere these people and make obeisance before them, each one fearing for himself. It seems to me that these conditions are divine like all others are and none is more divine, nor more human than any other, but all are the same and all are divine. Each of them has its own nature, and none comes into being outside of nature. And I will explain how I think this condition comes into being. As a result of riding, *kedmata*[26] seize them, because they are constantly straddling their horses. Then they become lame, and their hips are lacerated, so they suffer badly. And they treat themselves in this way: whenever the illness begins, they cut the blood vessel behind each ear. When the blood flows, weakness and fatigue come over them, and they lie down to sleep. Then they wake up, some being healthy and others not. Truly, it seems to me that the power of procreation is destroyed by this remedy, for there are blood vessels beside the ears, and when someone cuts them, those who have them cut become incapable of producing progeny. It seems to me that these are the blood vessels they cut. After that, when they approach a woman, and they do not suffer to have sex with her, at first they do not take this to heart, but they are calm and peaceful. But when they have tried twice, thrice, and more, and things did not turn out any differently, they blame a god, whom they believe they have wronged, and they put on women's clothes, convicting themselves of unmanliness. They act like women and work alongside women in their manner. The rich Scythians suffer this, not those who are lowest, but the best-born and those

who have acquired most strength. It comes through their horse-riding, and ordinary laborers have it less, because they do not ride. . . . And this illness comes into being among the Scythians for such a reason as I have said. It is the same among other people of similar type, for wherever they ride a great deal and very frequently, a majority are plagued by *kedmata*, hip ailments, and gouty feet, and they are the worst at sexual relations.[27]

In contrast to the indigenous interpretation and the Greek sources from which he gained his information, the Hippocratic author provides a thoroughly rational materialist explanation of the Anarieis's ailments, suggesting that divinity manifests itself in the workings of nature, not in the putative marvels naive observers theorize as "supernatural."[28] His aetiological argument then unfolds in four steps. First, as already established, the nature of the environment makes all Scythians soft, cold, and indisposed to sexuality, i.e., of an unmanly nature (*an-andreiē*).[29] Second, the equestrian activity of the upper class further damages lower parts of their bodies, making them the most sexually inept of all people (*lagneuein kakistoi*).[30] Third they treat these injuries by bloodletting from the parotid vein, which—according to other Hippocratic treatises—also transmits semen to the testicles. Such treatment thus renders them incapable of reproduction (*a-gonoi*).[31] Finally, they mistake their sexual and reproductive disorders for the sign and result of divine displeasure. Accordingly, they decide to act like women (*gynaikizousi*), adopting female dress, language, labor, and identity.[32] As a result of this process, in which culture augments nature, and the two are further compounded by iatrogenic malpractice, the Anarieis become "eunuch-like" (*eunoukhiai*).[33] But because there are so many of them—they constitute the majority (*hoi pleistoi*) of the population, we are told[34]—the text reaches a broader conclusion, pronouncing the Scythians in general "the most eunuch-like" (*eunoukhoeidestatoi*) of all peoples.[35]

IV

Herodotus describes a similar group, although he calls them Enarees, rather than Anarieis. Here, as in other details, his account differs sufficiently from that of the Hippocratic treatise to suggest that the two texts drew on a common source—most likely Hecataeus—rather than one depending directly on the other.[36] Two separate Herodotean passages treat the Enarees. The first comes toward the end of the *Histories*' account of the Scythians' conquest of Asia and subsequent retreat.[37]

When they were withdrawing, they came to the city of Ascalon in Syria. Most of the Scythians slipped past without harm, but a few who had been left behind plundered the temple of Uranian Aphrodite. The deity cast a female sickness onto those among the Scythians who had plundered the temple in Ascalon and their descendants forever after. The Scythians say it afflicts them for this reason, and those who come to Scythian territory see how it affects those whom the Scythians call Enarees.[38]

Where the Hippocratic treatise provides an aetiological analysis integrating environmental, physiological, and psychological factors, Herodotus offers an origin myth featuring divine retribution: precisely the kind of story the Hippocratic text introduces only in order to dismiss it.[39] Herodotus's second passage describes the situation of the Enarees in Scythia, with only passing reference to the issues of sex and gender that dominated the Hippocratic discussion.

The Enareis, who are androgynes, say that Aphrodite gave them the power of divination, and they divine with the bark of lime-trees. Thus, having cut the bark into three pieces, they proclaim oracles while weaving and unweaving it in their fingers.[40]

Conceivably, Herodotus meant to be discreet, and his coy reference to the Aphrodite of Ascalon was meant to conjure images of the Syrian goddess later described by Lucian and, more pointedly, to the priests who castrated themselves in devotion to her.[41] Any number of modern scholars have taken this to be so, but nowhere does Herodotus show knowledge of such practices or narrative traditions.[42] This detail notwithstanding, one is struck by how little attention Herodotus devotes to the Enarees and their "female sickness" (*thēlean nouson*), compared to the Hippocratic author. This difference itself is telling, and it can be related to the place of these people in the structure of the two texts. Where the Hippocratic treatise construed the Anarieis as the group whose extremity revealed the underlying nature of the Scythian people, whom it construed as the extreme case of the disorders a constant climate produces, Herodotus treated the Enarees as a minor curiosity with little importance for his overall argument, which is wider ranging, less theory-driven, and less tendentious than that of *On Airs, Waters, and Places*.[43] As we have seen, he harbored no doubts regarding the masculinity of Scythians, whose military prowess he considered superior to that of all others.[44] As he saw it, the Enarees were an exceptional case, affecting only "a few" (*oligoi*).[45] More precisely, they were men who had showed cowardice, greed, and impiety by lingering behind the bulk of the army to plunder a deity's temple, conduct that could well be regarded as "unmanly," although this point is not developed or rendered explicit. In the *Histories*' vast scope, the Enarees are introduced as an anomaly that departs from the Scythian norm, while the Hippocratic author makes them a centerpiece of his argument: a datum that reveals the nature of Scythians and Asians alike.

V

The differences of these two sources notwithstanding, modern scholarship has compared them in relatively uncritical fashion, assuming they provide complementary perspectives on the same phenomenon. Yet it is clear that both texts construct imaginary objects that suit their individual preconceptions and purposes, based on the (conveniently) scant information available to them. The two resemble each other (to the extent they do) because they draw on the same source(s), which themselves engaged in the same kind of operation. Neither Herodotus nor the Hippocratic author was utterly ignorant about these Scythians of ambiguous or mutable gender, but neither one was terribly well informed or deeply understanding. The same can be said of Hecataeus and any others in the chain of transmission. Combining the "two perspectives" that survive can make for great sport, but will not yield an accurate—or even an improved—picture.

Almost without exception, scholars of the nineteenth, twentieth, and twenty-first centuries have engaged in comparison of this sort, and many have expanded the inquiry further, believing—as Karl Meuli famously put it—"Die Lösung des Rätsels bringt auch hier das ethnographische Vergleichsmaterial."[46] For their part, medical specialists continued to look for syndromes that resemble what the Greek texts described, with venereal disease, contracted from the sacred prostitutes at the temple of Ascalon, being the early favorite,[47] and haemochromatosis (an inability to metabolize iron) the most recent entry.[48] Others have favored anthropological comparanda[49] that led them to connect the Anarieis/Enarees with practices of ritual transvestitism,[50] eunuch priesthoods,[51] couvade,[52] or third-gender constructions like the Native American berdache.[53] Most widely accepted, however, is a suggestion first introduced by William Reginald Halliday in 1911[54] and given its classic form by Meuli, who compared the Scythian "androgynes" to central Asian shamans whose gender identity was restructured as part of their religious vocation and ritual practice.[55]

Briefly, the Enarees/Anarieis were one of three data Meuli construed as evidence for shamanistic practices among the Scythians, the others being the sweat-lodge practices described by Herodotus (4.75) and the ecstatic voyages of Aristeas and Abaris (4.13–15 and 4.36, respectively). For each of these, he adduced Siberian comparanda, but with regard to our example he cited one example only, taken from Waldemar Bogoras's 1907 ethnography of the Siberian Chukchi, which he summarized as follows.

Among the Chukchee there are, albeit seldom, female shamans who feel themselves to be like men and behave accordingly. Far more frequently there are male shamans who feel themselves to be like women. The "transformation" normally takes place at the command of a spirit at the beginning of puberty, when the first visions and inspirations also press themselves upon those who are becoming shamans. There can be very different degrees of this transformation; it can extend to a change of coiffure only or, as is often the case, only a change of clothing. One Chukchee shaman known to Bogoras was freed of a disease through his transformation when he was a young man, after which he pursued the shamanic calling in women's clothes. That did not keep him from marrying and begetting four children with his wife. Obviously, temporary disturbance of normal sexual feelings could occur here, either caused or followed by small bodily changes. But according to Bogoras, such changes do not occur, even in the highest degree of "transformation." There, the shaman completely gives up the dress, manner of speech, and pursuits of men and exchanges them for those of the female sex. He also experiences himself as fully female and can even enter into the normal forms of marriage, establishing a lasting union with a man and founding an otherwise perfectly normal household.[56]

What led Meuli to this comparison was his sense that Herodotus emphasized the religious aspect of the Enarees, while the Hippocratic treatise stressed the Anarieis's peculiar relation to sex and gender. Combining the two yielded an image of religious specialists whose gender identity was fluid and subject to revision. Looking for examples of this sort, he found one in Bogoras's description of those whom the Chukchi call "soft men" (*yirka ʾɤ-la´ul*) or men "similar to women" (*ñe´uʧiʧä*).[57] Everything in the passage quoted above comes from Bogoras's description of these individuals, but there are serious problems in Meuli's use of the ethnographic material.[58] Thus, Bogoras discussed these "soft men" in a seven-page section of his fifty-six-page chapter on shamanism, making clear that they are a small subset of the broader category, and however distinctive their ascribed gender might be, this is not what makes them shamans.[59] As Bogoras explained in the full course of his chapter, every shaman's career begins with a call, usually associated with illness and an initiatory crisis. There follows a long period of preparation and training, defined as "gathering inspiration" (*eñe´ñɪvɪlɪn*), in the course of which they cultivate the ability to manage long-term relations with spirits and to manifest these spirits in states of possession. Great skill at drumming, song, and trance induction are necessary parts of a shaman's practice, as are powers of healing, animal transformation, and other forms of magic.[60] Most important, perhaps, is the relation with spirits: so much so that Chukchi shamans are called *eñe´ɪlɪt*, literally "those with spirits."[61] This is no less true of the "soft men" than of any others, for it is their relation to the spirits—and not their gender fluidity—that makes them shamans. Thus, as Bogoras states in a passage not noted by Meuli, "each 'soft man' is supposed to have a special protector among the 'spirits,' who, for the most part, is said to play the part of a supernatural husband (*keʾle-uwaᵉqučʾ*) of the transformed one. This husband is supposed to be the real head of the family and to communicate his orders by means of his transformed wife."[62]

None of Bogoras's broader discussion entered Meuli's discussion, however, and this was surely no accident, for not a single one of the key traits constitutive of shamanism—call, training, drumming, song, ecstasy, trance, healing, or relation to spirits—is attested for the Herodotean Enarees or the Hippocratic Anarieis.

## VI

Like the author of the Hippocratic treatise, Meuli saw in the "eunuch-like" Scythians what he wanted to see, and his interpretation of them was conditioned by his broader understanding of relations between Europe and Asia. Ultimately, what he hoped to show was that in the sixth century, Greeks encountered a new style of myth, ritual, and visionary experience that transformed important aspects of their poetry, religion, and cultural imagination.[63] Some years earlier, his search for the sources behind the stories of fabulous journeys, battles with monsters, and descents to the underworld that figure in Jason's quest and Odysseus's wanderings led him to consider *Helfermärchen*, *Jenseitsfahrten*, and *Urfabeln* from the region of the Black Sea.[64] Later, he came to view these as themselves deriving from the songs in which shamans—who were simultaneously healer-diviners (*iatromanteis*) and poets (*aoidoi*)—described their ecstatic journeys.[65] The problem, then, was how to connect the shamanism of central Asia and the far north with the developments he thought he observed in Greece. His discovery—or invention—of Scythian shamanism provided the necessary geographic and cultural mediation.

Meuli's argument pursued lines introduced by Bachofen and Nietzsche, who insisted that non-rational, ecstatic, and erotic elements were a central part of Greek culture, alongside (really, in dialectic tension with) the rationalism and moderation that were infinitely more attractive to bourgeois intellectuals of the nineteenth century. In turn, his views were adopted and taken further still by E. R. Dodds, who saw the influence of Scythian shamanism behind the novel theories of the soul, its separability from the body, and the need for its care in this world and beyond that were developed by Pythagoras, Empedocles, and the Orphics.[66] Dodds's views have been enormously influential, for reasons that are not hard to understand, for they call attention to potent "irrational" elements in Greek culture, while maintaining the privilege and prestige of classical Greece by defining these elements as intrusive, exogenous, and barbarian.

## VII

In recent years, the image of transgender Scythian shamans has acquired still further cachet. Thus, to cite the most important scholarly example, it plays a crucial role in Carlo Ginzburg's sprawling attempt to trace stereotypes of the witches' Sabbath (and many other phenomena) to an archaic stratum of shamanistic popular religion that Scythian shamans helped disseminate from central Asia through most of Europe.[67] Meanwhile, our own primary instrument for disseminating popular culture, the internet, is replete with Scythian androgyne shamans, particularly the many sites where enthusiasm for new age religions and that for the restructuring of gender identities meld and overlap.[68] Here, as in the stodgier and slightly more sober sources we have considered, the descriptions put forward rework the little that is known to produce an image (in the new age sites, utopian; for the Hippocratics, derogatory) that is powerfully conditioned by and reinforcing of the beliefs and desires of individual authors, as well as those of the communities for and to whom they speak.

Just how little do we know? As I see it, one word only, but a word whose significance has been widely misunderstood. The word is Scythian *\*a-narya-*, the original form of the lexeme Herodotus rendered (in the plural) as *enarees* and the Hippocratic treatise as *anarieis*. Since the early nineteenth century, it has been recognized that the initial *a-* is privative, modifying an adjective in *-yo-* built on a root noun *nar-*.[69] This noun being cognate to Avestan *nar-*, Vedic *nr̥-*, Old Persian *nar-*, and Ossetic *nart* (all of which denote "man"), the Scythian term has been understood to mean "unmanly." As this title presumably bore some relation to the bodies and lives of the people it denoted, while also signaling the way they were regarded by others, Greek descriptions of them as "androgynes" or "eunuch-like" seem to reflect the Scythian terminology, ideology, and realia.

There is, however, more to be said.

First, we must recognize that the semantics of the nouns that have been compared to Scythian *\*a-narya-* and provide the basis for its interpretation are more complex than is generally realized. If we start with Vedic Sanskrit, the oldest of the surviving Indo-Iranian languages, the most complete reference dictionary, that of Hermann Grassmann, distinguishes three different levels of denotation for Vedic *nr̥-*, which are constructed through different contrasts and degrees of marking.[70] The results can be graphed as shown (figure 8.1).

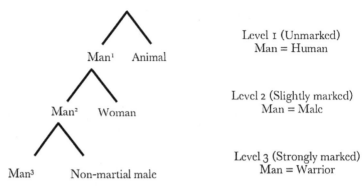

Figure 8.1. Semantics of Vedic ṇṛ- (following the analysis of Hermann Grassmann).

It is not clear that Grassmann carefully differentiated between the first two levels, but neither one is attested with great frequency. He lists thirty-one instances of the unmarked sense "human" and only three of the slightly marked sense "male." Included in the latter category, however, should be all those instances where the noun occurs in a context or with an adjective identifying the ṇṛ- in question as holding a ritual office reserved for males, a situation that adds another 107 occurrences. Best attested of all, however, is the strongly marked sense "warrior," i.e., a male particularly possessed of the qualities culturally understood as characteristic of the male gender: bodily strength, courage, and a capacity for both aggressive and defensive violence. Intriguingly, this meaning can be applied not only to humans, but also to deities, provided they are martial males. The term is used in this sense a full 243 times.

The situation in Avestan differs only slightly. Here, the strongly marked nar- = "warrior" is least common (twenty occurrences), followed by the unmarked form nar- = "human" (thirty-two), while the slightly marked nar- = "male" is most common of all (sixty-seven occurrences), as listed in Christian Bartholomae's standard reference dictionary.[71] There are, however, a large number of instances where Bartholomae felt the term was indeterminate, often translatable as "one" (German man). Close study of these might change the picture somewhat, but even without this, one can conclude that in Avestan these three semantic domains and levels of marking are differentiated from each other, and all three are reasonably well attested.[72]

If the semantic relations are clear in Vedic and Avestan, they are less so in Old Persian, where there is not enough information to let us fill in the whole picture. As it happens, nar- occurs only once in the entire corpus, not as an independent noun, but in a compound where it is modified by the prefix ū-, which adds the sense of "good." The compound thus denotes the qualities of a good nar-—but are these the virtues of a good human (man¹), a good male, as a husband perhaps (man²), or a good warrior (man³)? The word appears in the funerary inscription of Darius the Great in a passage that leaves no doubt about this question.

> I am fervent in counterattack with both hands and feet. As a horseman, I am a good horseman. As an archer, I am a good archer, both on foot and on horse. As a spearman, I am a good spearman, both on foot and on horse. Those skills [*ūnarā*, lit. "capacities of a good *nar-*"] that the Wise Lord bestowed on me, I was strong enough to bear them. By the Wise Lord's will, that which has been done by me, I did these things by the skills [*ūnaraibiš*] that the Wise Lord deposited in me.[73]

Having named three specialized types of combat—cavalry, archery, infantry—Darius claims to have mastered each skill, using the same prefix to advance his claim via formulae of this sort: "As a horseman (*asabāra*), I am a good horseman (*uv-asabāra*)."[74] He then uses that same prefix in combination with *nar-* to summarize what has just been said and raise it to a higher level of generalization. He has all the skills (*ū-narā*) of a warrior (*nar-* = man³), having mastered all branches of military service. Then, to make clear that he uses *nar-* in its strongly marked sense, he says these skills were of use to him only because he was "strong enough to bear them."[75]

Compared to the others, the case of Ossetic is more straightforward, for there *nart* denotes mythic heroes of giant stature and extraordinary strength, daring, and boldness: exemplary "men" in the strongly marked sense.[76] Two plausible etymologies have been proposed for the term: one deriving it from Iranian *\*nar-tama-*, "most manly,"[77] the other from *\*nr̥-θra-*, "actively exhibiting *nar*-force . . . that of vigorous or violent men (or gods conceived as men)."[78]

Based on these linguistic comparanda, I would suggest that translation of Scythian *\*a-narya-* as "unmanly" (in the marked sense) = "womanish," "androgynous," or "eunuch-like" is premature and possibly erroneous. Logically possible is translation as "unmanly" (in the unmarked sense) = "inhuman," "bestial," but this has little to recommend it. Best, I think is "unmanly" (in the most highly marked sense) = "unwarlike," "pacific," or "priestly," since within the Scythian social order, as among Indo-Iranians in general, priests are those males who are most pointedly contrasted with warriors, constituting an alternate model of human excellence.[79] This is clear from Herodotus's description of the one set of Scythian priests other than the Enarees that he treats at any length.

> No one does them any injustice, for they are said to be sacred, and they possess no weapons of war. They are the ones who resolve the quarrels

of those who dwell around them, and should a fugitive take refuge with them, no injustice would be done him by anyone. Their name is Argippaioi.[80]

Although these holy men "possess no weapons of war" (*oude ti arēion hoplon ekteatai*), there is no suggestion that they were disrespected or culturally defined as effeminate. Rather, the form of strength they had—spiritual, intellectual, and verbal—was contrasted with, and judged superior to, the physical strength of other males, as evidenced by the fact that the latter would not dare to harm the Argippaioi, to whom they submitted their disputes for adjudication.

As priests who specialized in divination, the Scythian *A-naryas would have been like the Argippaioi with regard to their status as sacred, inviolable, and categorically held apart from warfare and physical violence.[81] That some might misunderstand their name and their nature, taking them to be (pathological and somewhat pathetic) "non-males" rather than (highly valorized) "non-warriors," is an understandable error, but not an innocent one, given the way it aligns with the desire to demonstrate the natural superiority of (martial) Europe to (effeminate) Asia.

## VII

Returning to the theme of comparison, I would observe that the author of the Hippocratic treatise compared whole continents for their landscape and climate, then compared this to the bodies and characters of their people, to yield an understanding of how nature and health interrelate in the micro- and macrocosm. The result was one of the world's first theories of "scientific" racism, whose historic consequences have been catastrophic, long lasting and far reaching.

More modestly, Meuli compared the religious practices and sensibility of three peoples at select moments in time (Greeks and Scythians in the sixth and fifth centuries, Siberians in the nineteenth). His goal was not to produce general theory, but to explain a specific historic transformation as the result of cultural contact, influence, and diffusion. In order to forge the links in the chain of transmission he hypothesized, he misread some sources, overread others, and ignored others still, selectively recombining those elements that served his purpose. In the process, he produced an attractive fantasy that has become a countercultural icon of sorts, intriguing scholars and delighting countless others for eight decades and counting. His relation to empirical reality, however, was little better than that of his Hippocratic predecessor, whose correlated binary oppositions—Europe/Asia and male/female—Meuli effectively revalorized by associating his transgender Scythian shamans, not with phlegmatic effeminacy and weakness, but with ecstatic experience, spiritual adventure, and divine inspiration: positive qualities regrettably lacking in masculinized European rationality.

Strong comparative arguments, i.e., those that make sweeping claims, marshal large bodies of data, and are concerned to suggest general, even universal patterns, are always exciting and seductive. They are, however, consistently misguided, for the claims they make outrun the evidence they can muster, while their demands on authors and audience alike outrun the limits of their competence. Although such systems often generate initial excitement—one thinks of the vogue for Max Müller or Lévi-Strauss—their overreach makes collapse inevitable. This is sad, not only for the crash of lofty reputations and the waste of massive labors, but because it discredits comparison in general.

In the latter sections of this chapter, I have tried to provide a more modest and therefore more viable form of "weak" comparative method of the sort discussed in chapter 3. This involved initial comparison of two texts—the Hippocratic treatise and Herodotus—that offered accounts of the "same" (putative) phenomenon, and whose differences proved even more instructive than their similarities. Second, I compared the most influential prior study of these texts (Meuli) with the ethnography that let him introduce his novel interpretation (Bogoras), stressing the non-congruence of the two, which revealed the tendentious nature of Meuli's selectivity. Finally, I focused on the sole datum in any of these texts that is irreducibly and incontestably Scythian: the word *a-narya-*. Comparison to four cognate terms in other Indo-Iranian languages (Vedic, Avestan, Old Persian, Ossetic) permitted me to suggest reinterpretaton of that term's significance.

Ultimately, I would like to suggest that we have no alternatives to comparison, since no knowledge is possible without it. The issue is not whether to compare, but how to do so responsibly and productively. Weak comparison has the advantage of letting one remain within the limits of one's competence; it permits one to assemble the full range of relevant evidence, instead of cherry-picking examples that reinforce one's preconceptions; it gives one the chance to study all the data in depth and detail, with appropriate emphasis on nuanced differences, as well as the points of continuity or resemblance; finally, it lets one frame plausible hypotheses, instead of grandiose theories. There are still a great many ways one can go wrong, but the risks of comparison are better acknowledged honestly than boldly and rashly ignored.

# IV
# WEAK COMPARISONS

# 9: FURTHER ON ENVY AND GREED

I

In chapter 3, I noted an intriguing similarity between the Anglo-Saxon poem *Beowulf* and certain medieval Zoroastrian texts written in Pahlavi. Although the scope of these two literatures differs widely—*Beowulf* treats the life and exploits of a single hero, while the Zoroastrian texts sketch the history of the cosmos—both make their point of departure a malevolent creature who assails a physical manifestation of moral perfection. In *Beowulf*, this is King Hrothgar's mead-hall Heorot, most brilliant of the world's structures, which the monster Grendel ravages by night.[1] In the Zoroastrian texts, it is the Wise Lord Ohrmazd's original creations (sky, water, earth, plant, animal, human, and fire), which were pure and flawless until assaulted by Ahreman (the "Evil Spirit"). In both cases, the aggressor is described as motivated by envy, a complex emotion involving bitter resentment, destructive rage, and a self-pitying sense of deprivation. In both cases, this envy is of an extraordinary sort, being directed not just at those who possess things the monster lacks, but at God, his creation, and all that is beautiful, joyous, and good.

Rather than seeking a common source behind the two bodies of literature or imagining that one influenced the other, I interpreted both as having engaged similar (socioeconomic *cum* ethical) problems and having arrived at similar (narrative *cum* ideological) solutions. Both treat envy as rooted in the frustration of actors located at the bottom of a hierarchic order, who experience their situation as unjust and resent the position others enjoy. Discontent of this sort can prompt agitation for social change, threatening the privilege—also the security, and sometimes the lives—of the elite, who try to delegitimate these sentiments by stigmatizing them as "envy." The texts in question deploy a particularly aggressive form of this rhetoric, depicting envy not just as a destructive, shameful, or childish emotion, but a primordial sin, monstrous and demonic in nature.

Given this analysis, I was led to conclude that by making "envy" the source of all ills and treating it as an offense against God, the Anglo-Saxon poem and the Zoroastrian scriptures both intervened on behalf of elites in the social struggles of their era. Further reflection, however, with particular attention to the way greed is handled in these texts has led me to revise that conclusion. For if both literatures begin their story with envy, they end it with greed, a quality they depict as equally monstrous. In doing so, they claim to occupy a position of moral authority that transcends the two vices, from which they offer somewhat different solutions to the problem of economic inequality and social stratification.

## II

Thus, while *Beowulf* begins with Grendel, it ends with the Dragon, who deserves equal attention. Medieval literature knew many dragons and regularly depicted them jealously guarding piles of gold.[2] An Anglo-Saxon maxim summarizes this view: "Dragons are found in barrows, old and wise, glorying in treasures."[3] *Beowulf* concurs, repeatedly calling its dragon *hordweard* ("hoard-guardian"), *beorges hyrde* ("barrow guardian"), *goldweard* ("gold-guardian"), and *frætwa hyrde* ("guardian of treasure").[4] Although this dragon possesses vast riches, its claim to ownership is fortuitous, for it neither produced, conquered, inherited nor was given this wealth (the normal processes that yield ownership), but merely stumbled upon it. The origin of his hoard is as follows.

|  |  |
|---|---|
|  | In ancient times, |
| a thoughtful man | there hid |
| the great legacy | and precious treasures |
| of a noble lineage. | In former times, |
| death took all the others away | and there was still one |
| of the nobles of the race, | who survived longest. |
| Mourning his friends, this guard | expected the same fate: |
| that he would be allowed | little time to enjoy |
| the ancient treasures. | A new barrow |
| stood ready on a plain | by the headland |
| near the sea-waves, | secure and difficult of access. |
| There, inside, he deposited | all the noble line's treasures.[5] |

As this narrative makes clear, a hoard consists of wealth that has been withdrawn from circulation, losing its exchange-value, use-value, and sign-value in the process. It is the massive residue of profit—and honor—from many generations of successful enterprise, but once buried, it is "useless" (*unnyt*).[6] Hidden away and jealously guarded, it becomes a fetish, as much as a treasure.[7] It is this the dragon stumbles across and appropriates as his own.

| | |
|---|---|
| | An ancient dawn-predator |
| found that delightful hoard | standing open. |
| . . . | There, for countless years |
| he wards heathen gold, | but it is not any better for him. |
| Thus, for three hundred years | this immensely powerful |
| enemy of the people[8] | clung tight to a treasure-house |
| in the ground | until a man enraged him |
| deep in his heart.[9] | |

The dragon's rage was prompted by the loss of a single cup,[10] picked up by a desperate man who chanced upon the barrow.[11] The loss was minimal, but prompted the beast to ravage the countryside, burn Beowulf's palace, and terrorize the population, leading to the final combat and Beowulf's death. The excessive nature of the dragon's reaction highlights his miserly greed, any diminution of his goods being intolerable.[12]

### III

Such greed is particularly problematic in a gift economy, where actors use wealth to forge the (asymmetric) relations of reciprocity that constitute the social order. Consistent with Marcel Mauss's description of gift-exchange as a "total social fact," the system described in *Beowulf* was simultaneously a political, moral, and prestige economy, in which the value of wealth was multivalent.[13] As Ernst Leisi first observed, all the relevant Anglo-Saxon terminology associates riches with such qualities as divine favor, good fortune, well-being, fame, power, and nobility.[14] Overdetermined treasure-objects— the cup, weapons, or rings, for instance—brought honor to giver and receiver alike, especially when conferred in ceremonial contexts, where the donor's wealth and benevolence, like the recipient's worthiness and favor, were publicly displayed, or—to put it in terms of process, rather than those of preexisting state—ritually constructed. By giving liberally, the giver (most often and most prominently the king) showed he possessed so abundant a surplus that he could bestow value-bearing goods on people he found deserving. Those who accepted became his retainers, obliged to repay such largesse with subsequent service. In turn, they too could redistribute wealth to those lower on the social scale, with whom they established the same kind of patron-client reciprocity.

At the apex of the system was God himself, theorized as the ultimate source of wealth and divine model for giving.[15] *Beowulf* makes this clear in two important passages. The first describes Hrothgar's decision to build Heorot.

It came into Hrothgar's mind
that he wanted to command / the building of a hall,
a great mead-hall / for men to make
so that men and children / would ever hear of it.
And inside there, / to young and old
he would distribute all things, / *such as God gave him.*[16]

Second, there is Hrothgar's advice to Beowulf concerning what happens when a king grows irresponsible.

The things he has long possessed / now seem insufficient to him.
Disposed to anger, he covets; / dishonorably, he gives no
ornamented rings. / *Exulting in all God gave him in the past—*
*the portion of honor* / *Heaven's Ruler bestowed—*
he forgets and neglects / the world to come.
In the end, / it comes to pass
that as death approaches, / his perishable body
declines and falls. / Another man takes hold of
his ancient wealth, / one who has no anxieties
and distributes treasures / without reservation.[17]

*Beowulf* treats the king's largesse as a cardinal virtue, as seen in the common epithets of rulers, e.g., *bēag-gyfa* ("ring-giver"), *beaga bryttan* ("distributor of rings"), *gold-wine gumena* ("gold-friend to men"), *sinces brytta* ("distributor of treasure"), *sinc-gifa* ("treasure-giver"), and *wil-geofa* ("liberal giver").[18] Here, "royal generosity" was understood as a mix of kindness, wisdom, justice, and grace that set the moral/political economy in motion, constructing a social order through the (purportedly) meritocratic distribution of wealth and honor. As such, it represented the antithesis of envy on the one hand, greed on the other.

*Beowulf* thus sanctified a hierarchic order by claiming it descended from God to kings, then to nobles and others below: an order in which wealth and the capacity for generosity co-vary with status, and status covaries with merit. In practice, however, things differed from this ideal. Kings' prestations were hardly altruistic or uncalculating, but shrewd, self-interested, and highly profitable investments, through which they converted some of their economic assets into two kinds of social capital that were readily convertible back into wealth: (a) the prestige they gained as their gifts were seen, discussed, and remembered; (b) the long-term patron-client relations they established, which obliged their retainers to render ongoing highly valuable service.[19]

That this was a fully conscious strategy is clear in the advice offered to princes.

| So should a young man | work with goods and goodness |
| in splendid gifts of wealth, | even while in his father's lap, |
| so that later, in his old age | he will still have |
| good companions | and when war comes, |
| men will stand by him.[20] | |

Here and elsewhere the text articulates retainers' obligation to defend the kings who gave them gifts, as when Wiglaf helps Beowulf against the dragon precisely because "he remembered the honor gifts that man previously gave him."[21] Martial service was not always defensive, however, and retainers were also expected to win booty for the king that would more than compensate for the gifts they had received. This is something the text does not emphasize, preferring to veil the sources of the king's wealth, which he obtained in two fashions. First was extraction from outsiders (= booty + tribute), which the text normally ascribed to divine favor and the king's martial excellence, thereby minimizing his retainers' contributions. Second was extraction from the king's own people (= taxes + fines + tolls and other impositions), which go completely unmentioned. Between these two revenue streams, successful kings could build up a large surplus, only a fraction of which they redistributed.

*Beowulf* thus provides critique of both envy and greed, depicting the one as the failing of resentful have-nots, the other of stingy haves. Placing envy at the beginning of its narrative and greed at the end, it structures their opposition in such a way that a third term can emerge, one designed to transcend and overcome them both. This is the ideal of "royal generosity,"

Table 9.1. Royal generosity in relation to envy and greed

| | Possessions (in abundance) | Benevolence toward others |
|---|---|---|
| **Envy** | − | − |
| | | = resentment of nongivers |
| **(Royal) generosity** | + | + |
| | | = gifts and honor given liberally according to merit |
| **Greed** | + | − |
| | | = unwillingness to give |

the virtue that conjoins abundance and benevolence, creating the basis of moral and social order.[22] Or so the story would have it.

## IV

The medieval Zoroastrian texts also place greed at the end of their story in the form of a demon named Āz.[23] As an abstract noun, this name is sometimes translated simply as "greed," but its semantic range encompasses multiple forms of appetitive drive and acquisitive desire.[24] Thus, the *Selections of Zādspram*, which contains the fullest discussion of Āz, recognizes three different aspects: hunger, sexual desire, and material greed, each with two subcategories.[25]

> Āz ("Appetite"), being one in nature, was not able to corrupt the Wise Lord's creatures as long as they are scattered. So she divided her powers into three portions: that which is natural, that which is at the limits of nature, and that which is beyond nature. (1) The natural is that whose life-force is enslaved to eating. (2) At the limits of nature is the desire for excessive sexual intercourse, which itself is called Lust, when by seeing something, one's inner organs are aroused and the substance of the body is excited. (3) That beyond nature is the desire for whatever good things one sees or hears about. Each level has two components. Those of the natural are (1a) hunger and (1b) thirst. Those of nature at its limit are (2a) ejaculation and (2b) reception (of semen). Those beyond nature are (3a) greedy acquisition and (3b) miserly refusal to give.[26]

Greed is thus described as the extreme form ("beyond nature," *bērōn az cihr*) of a general phenomenon, whose most basic form ("natural," *cihrīg*) is hunger, and whose intermediate form ("at the limits of nature," *be cihrīg*) is sexual desire. Implicit is a scale of how necessary the correlated objects of desire are for life's preservation. Thus, deprivation of food and water produces death in a matter of weeks, while deprivation of sex leads to extinction after one generation, deprivation of wealth and material goods having less dire consequences. The ranking also reflects myths of how the human condition developed. Thus, in response to Ahreman's original assault and the introduction of mortality, the first humans committed a series of sins necessary for their survival: first taking milk from an animal and drinking it,[27] then killing an animal and eating its meat,[28] then enjoying sexual intercourse and bearing children.[29] Rudimentary material goods—firewood, clothing, metal tools, and wooden bowls—were acquired fortuitously along the way, as a much less important part of the story.[30]

V

Like all Zoroastrian demons, Āz was theorized as a spiritual force that acquires material substance—and with it the capacity for physical action— only by colonizing the body of someone whose cravings for food, sex, goods, and wealth then vary with (and testify to) the force of the demon's presence.[31] Every body thus becomes a battleground, in which Appetite seeks to expand and meets resistance from the person's better tendencies (self-sufficiency, self-discipline, will-power, e.g.). The human condition being marked by mortality, this struggle cannot be decisively won as long as people need to eat, drink, and reproduce in order to survive.[32] The best one can do in the present world-age is to keep Appetite at a minimum, while anticipating a more definitive victory on history's far horizon.[33]

In its eschatological account, *Zādspram* tells that Ahreman will name Appetite commander in chief of the demonic horde before the final battle.[34] At that time, the most urgent task facing the forces of good will be to find a remedy, antidote, or counterforce (Pahlavi *cār*) capable of overcoming Appetite.[35]

> Appetite is that which encompasses all evil. At the end, in order to establish a remedy for Appetite, truth will come to earth, together with Airyaman, and will show the creatures how sinful it is to kill animals and how little use there is to it. This too he will command: "You who are humans—cease to be animal-killers."[36]

The effects of following this command are both immediate and longer term. Thus, those who renounce their carnivorous ways not only reverse part of the first humans' fall;[37] they also cut off Appetite's meat supply, meat being understood as the most potent of foods, as well as the most sinful.[38] As a result, the power of Appetite—both in those she inhabits, and as an aggregate force—will diminish abruptly by a full one-quarter. The noxious effects of Appetite being reduced, the world will become less foul and less dark, while people become more spiritual and more intelligent.[39]

The first intervention is thus at the level of hunger, i.e., the "natural" aspect of Appetite, while lust and greed remain unaddressed and undiminished. The assault on hunger will continue, however, as the children of the meat-renouncers, having been born with less Appetite than their parents, go on to abjure dairy products, thereby reducing Appetite's power by another one-half.[40] These mathematically precise calculations suggest that the text considered hunger to account for the great bulk of Appetite's strength.[41] Once hunger has been disarmed, the less pressing problem of sexual desire (Appetite's second most powerful component) will find relatively easy resolution, as the milk-renouncers' children are destined to bear no children.[42] The implications of this are clear: having overcome the need for food, humans attain immortality and have no further need for sexual reproduction. Less clear is the question of libidinal appetite, on which *Zādspram* is silent, but other Zoroastrian sources addressed the issue with considerable ingenuity. Thus, they recognize a positive, Ohrmazdian aspect of sexuality, including pleasure, fulfillment, and satisfaction, that will persist when Appetite is overcome, while a negative, Ahremanian aspect—i.e., lustful craving for erotic pleasure, reflecting the absence of the latter—can be expected to disappear.[43]

The conquest of Appetite's two most basic levels (hunger and lust) sets the stage for a similar victory over greed, but that is never narrated. Rather, in the exquisitely ironic last act of the drama, *Zādspram* describes how a needy, malnourished Appetite seeks help from the Evil Spirit. No longer able to gain nourishment through parasitism on human bodies, as has been her wont, Appetite will find herself desperate for food. At this point, Ahreman lets her devour all the other demons, but when she finishes these, she will be ravenous still, consistent with her insatiable nature.[44] Accordingly, she will turn on Ahreman at a crucial moment, when the two of them face their mortal opponents. Together, we are told, Appetite and the Evil Spirit are a match for the forces of good, but their bickering makes it possible for Sraoša ("Obedience, Discipline," here personifying the virtues of self-control and adherence to religious doctrine) to vanquish Appetite, just as Ohrmazd overcomes Ahreman.[45] This definitive victory will bring history and its conflicts to an end, clearing the way for humans to recover—and retain—immortality, perfect self-sufficiency, and absolute contentment.[46]

Greed's role in the eschatological drama is thus ambiguous: simultaneously prominent (as part of Āz), but near-invisible, having been encompassed in the broader category of Appetite. Implicitly, it is suggested that if hunger and lust are conquered by divinely mandated acts of renunciation, greed automatically follows, with no need to address its specific defining features. Logically elegant, this solution is also politically convenient, obviating the need to consider the origins of greed in socioeconomic inequity, the persistent maldistribution of wealth, the systemic reproduction of privilege, and elites' tenacious defense of their assets.

## VI

All things considered, the discussion of chapter 3 thus needs correction in four ways. First, the similarity between *Beowulf* and the Zoroastrian texts goes further than I recognized. Not only do they both make cosmic envy the beginning of evil; they also treat greed as the final monster/demon to be overcome. Second, one cannot read condemnation of envy (the vice of lower strata) as a straightforward intervention on behalf of elites, since the texts condemn greed with equal force. Ultimately, what they promote is the status quo, which includes (of course!) the position and privileges of the elite. To that end, they acknowledge the serious problems of envy and greed, but suggest these could best be redressed if actors of all stations and classes would live up to the society's ideals.

Third, one needs to consider not only the vices the texts condemn, but the ideals they advocate. For *Beowulf*, this is economic circulation, such that goods and the honor they convey ought be in constant motion among those who deserve them. As the prime engine of this system, kings need to be generous, while the rest of society needs be correspondingly worthy of such generosity, also more loyal in return for it. In contrast, *Zādspram's* ideal is non-consumption, full realization of which is deferred to the eschatological future. People can pursue it here and now, however, by reducing their appetitive desires to the barest minimum required for survival. Where *Beowulf* implicitly counsels the poor to be grateful for what they receive, *Zādspram* urges them to make do with less, reaching much the same end—reduction of malcontent and stabilization of the status quo—by an alternate route.

Finally, while the two texts provide similar narrative resolutions for the same set of socioeconomic, political, and moral problems, they do so in generically different fashion. Thus, in its unrealistically idealized treatment of "royal generosity," *Beowulf* serves to mystify and legitimate the status quo, thereby helping to reproduce it. In contrast, *Zādspram* provides a fantastic alternative to the world as it is, allaying discontentment in the present with promises of a radically different future to be realized with God's help, when all needs will be overcome and all desires satisfied. To put it in Karl Mannheim's terms, *Beowulf* advances an ideology, while *Zādspram* entertains a utopia.[47]

# 10: KING AUN AND THE WITCHES

I

The story of King Aun was a favorite of Sir James George Frazer, for whose theories it seemingly offered powerful confirmation.[1] Thanks to Frazer's influence, this datum entered much early scholarship on sacrifice, and it still figures prominently in studies of human offerings among pre-Christian Germanic peoples.[2] Such literature regularly brings together three bodies of evidence: (a) the ethnographic testimony of foreigners from Tacitus through Adam of Bremen (often tendentious and ill informed); (b) some (suggestive, but ambiguous) archaeological remains, particularly from Danish moors and bogs; (c) episodes from Old Norse literature (written centuries after conversion). Each body of evidence has its problems, and the hope is that when all three are combined, their difficulties will cancel out, rather than compound and multiply. The literary accounts are thus introduced in the hope of confirming what is known—or thought to be known—from archaeology and ancient ethnography, and Aun's story is one of three or four privileged data regularly introduced toward that end.[3] While relatively few scholars think it records an actual historic episode, most take it to accurately reflect sacrificial ideology and practice of the pagan era.[4]

The fullest and best-known version is *Ynglingasaga* 25, a text composed some time between 1220 and 1235, most probably with Snorri Sturluson (1178–1241) as its chief compiler and redactor (rather than "author" in the modern sense).[5] The passage is worth citing in its entirety.

> Jörund's son was named Aun or Áni. He was King over Sweden following his father. He was a wise man and great sacrificer, but not a warrior. He stayed in his own lands. At that time Dan the Proud first ruled over Denmark. He was extremely old. Then ruled his son, Fróði the Proud or the Peaceful, then his sons Halfdan and Friðleif. They were great warriors. Halfdan was the oldest and superior in all things. He came to Sweden with his army against King Aun and they fought some battles. Halfdan

was always victorious and finally King Aun fled to West Gautland. At that time he had been king over Uppsala for twenty years. He was in Gautland another twenty years while King Halfdan was in Uppsala.

King Halfdan died a natural death at Uppsala and he was buried there. After that, King Aun came back to Uppsala and he was then sixty years old. He then performed a great sacrifice. He sacrificed that he should have a long life and he gave Óðinn his son, who was sacrificed to him. King Aun asked of Óðinn that he should live another sixty years.

Aun then was king at Uppsala for another twenty years. Then Áli the Valiant, son of Frilleif, came to Sweden with his army against King Aun and they fought some battles. Áli was always victorious and finally King Aun fled his realm again and went to West Gautland. Áli was king at Uppsala for twenty years, until Starkað the Old killed him.

After Áli's death, King Aun came back to Uppsala and then he ruled the realm another twenty years. Then he performed a great sacrifice and sacrificed another of his sons. Then Óðinn told him that he would always live, as long as he gave Óðinn one of his sons every ten years. Also, he should give a name to some district in his land after the number of his sons whom he had sacrificed to Óðinn.

But when he had sacrificed seven of his sons, he then lived for ten years in a state where he could not walk and was carried about in a chair. He then sacrificed his eighth son and he lived another ten years, lying in bed. Then he sacrificed his ninth son and lived another ten years, drinking from a horn like a baby.

Aun then had one more son and he wanted to sacrifice him and he wanted to give Uppsala and the surrounding districts to Óðinn and to have them called Tíundaland ["Ten-hound-land"]. The Swedes forbade him that and there was no sacrifice. Thereafter, King Aun died and he was buried at Uppsala. Thereafter, when a man dies painlessly of old age, it is called ánasótt [lit. "grandfathers' disease," but folk-etymologically "Áni's Disease"].[6]

Although most have limited their discussion to this richly detailed passage, it is useful to consider the five other surviving texts in which Aun appears. Most of these are genealogical lists that trace the royal Yngling line from mythic prehistory to the founding of the Norwegian state. Two of the variants are very short, but consistent with the others, they identify Aun as Jörund's son, Egil's father, and give him the epithet "Aun the Old" (Aun hinn gamle).[7] Two others provide a bit more information, detailing the old king's decrepitude. Historia Norwegiæ, written some decades before Ynglingasaga (perhaps as early as 1170 and no later than 1220), thus states the following.

Jörund begot Aun,[8] who, in the long decline of old age desisted from solid
food for nine years before his death and was lifted up to suck milk from
a horn like an infant.[9]

The "Genealogy of King Harald from Óðinn" (*Ættartala Haralldz fra Odni*),
written some decades later, tells much the same story, while adding the
alternate name "Áni" (a learned invention it borrowed from *Ynglingasaga*).[10]

Jörund was father of Áni the Old. We call him Aun. For nine years he
drank from a horn because of his old age before he died.[11]

Although these genealogies all trace the Yngling line to a prestigious
antiquity, they do so in different fashion. One begins the lineage with Noah
and Japheth, then incorporates Jupiter, Erechthonius, Priam, and other
heroes of classic antiquity.[12] Another starts with the primordial deities Buri,
Bur, and Óðinn.[13] Others make the younger gods Yngvi, Njörð, and Freyr
their point of departure.[14] Such differences show that these texts do not
descend from the same source, but are semi-independent variants operating
with a traditional set of methods, contents, and interests.[15] Regarding Aun,
however, all stress his old age and the majority (three out of five) develop
this theme by describing the pathos of his last years' infantile diet. The
sources also agree in what they do not tell, for none save *Ynglingasaga*
makes Aun sacrificer of his sons.

## II

There is, however, one last surviving variant to consider: the oldest, most
prestigious, and most significant of all. This is *Ynlingatal*, a ninth-century
poem written by the royal skald Thjóðólf of Hvin. As quoted by Snorri—
who elsewhere names this poem as his most important source[16]—*Ynglingatal*
15–16 recounts this story.

Finally, at Uppsala
Old-age sickness (*ánasótt*)
was able
to stop Aun.
Earlier,
his obstinate yearning for life
made him accept
an infant's food.
He turned
the narrower part

of a bull's horn
to himself.
Lying down,
the *áttunga rjóðr*
drank from
the point of an ox's horn.
The white-haired
King of the east
was just able
to hold up the horn.[17]

Once again, the text focuses on Aun's old age and the humiliating diet of his senescence. There is, however, one phrase that bears examination: the otherwise unattested kenning *áttunga rjóðr*, which I have initially left untranslated. Apparently Snorri took these words to identify Aun as "sacrificer of his sons," and his narrative was meant to unpack what he thought was compressed in that kenning. Although modern critics have generally followed his lead,[18] close philological analysis shows this to be mistaken.[19]

In the first place, *áttunga* does not mean "sons." Rather, the base-form *áttung-* is an extension of *átt* (alternate form: *ætt*), a culturally salient noun that denotes "family, kindred, lineage" or, more precisely, the descent group within which rights of inheritance and obligations for vengeance were shared.[20] Aun's sons would have been members of his *átt*, to be sure, but so would his father, grandfather, brothers, patrilineal uncles, granduncles, cousins, nephews, grandnephews, and great-grandnephews. The kenning tells us that some members of this relatively large group suffered something nasty at Aun's hands, but it doesn't specify who it was, nor just what happened.

The second element of the kenning sheds light on the latter question, for the agent noun *rjóðr* derives from the verb *rjóða*, "to redden."[21] Seventy-four occurrences of this verb are cited in the *Lexicon Poeticum Antiquæ Linguæ Septentrionalis* (the work that inventories all surviving eddic and skaldic verse, the oldest works of Old Norse literature). Eleven are listed under a relatively broad definition: "to color red, as when the color is produced by the sun."[22] Examples include a shield's rim gleaming as it is hardened in the fire,[23] a woman's cheek that flushes as she weeps,[24] roses,[25] banners,[26] and weapons tipped with gold.[27]

The remaining sixty-three occurrences are grouped under a second definition, summarizing usages that were more marked, more grim, and much more common: "to redden with blood."[28] The objects of such action include bedsheets stained with gore,[29] runic spells activated by their carvers' vital fluid,[30] soil and water discolored by mortal combat.[31] Most often it is martial equipment that is reddened with blood,[32] although the fangs and claws of wild animals also show sanguinary hues,[33] and parts of the human body can be similarly stained: a victim's foot,[34] a killer's mustache,[35] or the throat of a decapitated warrior.[36] In all these cases, moreover, the blood is human, and it does not flow by accident.

In the vast majority of poetic contexts (a full 85 percent of the total), the verb *rjóða* thus describes the polluting discoloration that follows on—and bears witness to—acts of violence performed (in decreasing order of frequency) by martial men, predatory beasts, and homicidal women. But in the entire corpus, there is only one poem where *rjóða* is used in an unambiguous context of sacrifice. If one wishes to interpret the kenning *áttunga rjóðr* as "sacrificer of kinsmen," the case stands or falls on that passage.

The text in question is *Hyndluljóð* 10, which is hard to date. Most experts would place its composition in the latter half of the twelfth century, i.e., decidedly post-conversion.[37] One might thus question the value of its testimony regarding fine points of pagan discourse about sacrifice, but for our purposes there is no need to do so. Better simply to consider the text itself, where a goddess says the following of the poem's hero.

| | |
|---|---|
| He built a sacrificial cairn for me | of piled up stones— |
| Now that stone | is becoming slick like glass— |
| He reddened it anew | with the blood of cattle; |
| Óttar always believed | in the goddesses.[38] |

Beyond this text, there are also several prose texts (all written well after the conversion) that employ *rjóða* in sacrificial contexts, using a diction so similar as to be formulaic.[39] In all instances (a) the sacrificer appears in the nominative case as subject of the action; (b) an altar or other material object is named in the accusative as direct object of the action; (c) blood, and the animal from which it came,[40] are named in oblique cases (dative and genitive, respectively) as the instruments with which the sacrificer carries out the action.

Considering all the relevant evidence, we may thus conclude that no Old Norse text of any sort or any date ever described a sacrificial victim as having been "reddened," for it is only inanimate objects—altars, cairns, and the like[41]—that are treated in this fashion. Moreover, in the context of sacrifice, "to redden" does not mean "to kill"; rather, it denotes the action of sanctifying an inanimate object by ritual application of the victim's blood. When *Ynglingatal* names King Aun "reddener of kinsmen," it thus cannot be accusing him of having offered up his relatives. Rather, it employs *rjóða* in the same way as do the vast majority of texts that use this verb, identifying him as one who has spilt other men's blood in a situation of warfare or homicide.

Of the six authors who discuss King Aun, Snorri is the only one to portray the aged monarch as sacrificer of his sons, and this reflects his creative misunderstanding of a phrase he found in his oldest, most trusted source. The elaborate story he wove thus tells us nothing reliable about the realities of pagan sacrifice, kingship, or family relations. It does, however, reveal much about Snorri's situation of interest and the perspective from which he engaged these topics.

### III

As we have seen, *Ynglingatal* charged Aun with violence against his kin, and most likely these were homicides he committed (or had committed) as he fought his way to the throne, rather like Shakespeare's Richard III.[42] *Ynglingasaga* expands the critique from considerations of family and politics to include those of religion. Written more than two centuries after conversion, the later text develops a Christian caricature of a wicked king who is not only a serial slayer-of-kin, but a heathen sacrificer, sorcerer, and devil worshipper.[43] Not just Richard III, but also Macbeth.

Snorri thus introduces Aun as "a wise man and great sacrificer" (*vitr maðr ok blótmaðr mikill*).[44] Hardly accidental, the correlation of these two qualities identifies the wisdom in question as a form of knowledge/power antithetical to Christian truth and associated with sinister deities of old, especially Óðinn, who dominates the first ten chapters of *Ynglingasaga*. There, Óðinn is described not only as founder of the Yngling line—and thus Aun's ultimate ancestor—but as a great sacrificer[45] and fearsome magician, skilled in necromancy,[46] shape-shifting,[47] clairvoyance and foresight,[48] spells,[49] incantations,[50] illusions,[51] mystic knowledge,[52] and the most sinister types of black magic.[53] The text concludes by connecting magic directly to sacrifice, and it makes Óðinn responsible for the continued practice of both.

> He taught most of his magic arts to the sacrificial priests [= Njörð, Freyr, and his other companions]. They were next to him in all knowledge and sorcery. Many others took much from him, and as a result sorcery was scattered wide and lasted long. But men sacrificed to Óðinn and the twelve priests and called him their god and believed (in him) for long thereafter. The name Auðun is taken from that of Óðinn, and men call their sons in that fashion.[54]

Consistent with his Christian identity and euhemerist views, Snorri here treats "Óðinn" not as a god, but as an extraordinarily wise, powerful, and sinister magician, who established sacrificial rites, installed himself as primordial king, and deluded his people so thoroughly that they mistook him for a deity. On death, this man was succeeded by others whom he had trained in the mystic arts. Above all, he taught them to perform sacrifice, which remained their primary ritual until the Yngling kings converted to Christianity and outlawed the practice. Of all his successors, moreover, none was more devoted to sacrifice than Aun, who alone is described as a "*great* sacrificer" (*blótmaðr mikill*),[55] and whose very name—an abbreviated form of *Auðun*[56]—Snorri construed as evidence of Óðinnic origins and nature.[57] Like Óðinn, Aun was a morally dubious sacrificer and magician who entered a diabolical bargain with the sinister deity for whom he was named whereby the old king butchered his sons in exchange for decades added to his increasingly miserable life.

## IV

Our understanding of (Snorri's version of) Aun's story has been enriched at many points by those who compared it to the Greek myth of Kronos[58] and Indian legends of King Yayāti.[59] Although the parallels are real enough, the explanations offered for them (direct influence in the first instance, common Indo-European ancestry in the second) strike me as unlikely. Alternatively, I would suggest that the points of narrative resemblance are better understood as reflecting similar points of tension in the social structure of the peoples among whom these stories circulated, which produced problems the stories sought to resolve by reshaping the consciousness of the audiences they reached and influenced.

From this perspective, it is hardly surprising that one finds similar stories far from medieval Scandinavia or, for that matter, from anything vaguely "Indo-European." Consider, for instance, certain reports that reached the desk of Captain R. M. Downes, a colonial officer of northern Nigeria in November 1929.[60] Although details varied somewhat, all of these concerned a group described as a secret society or coven of witches, known among Tiv-speakers as *Mbatsav*. Members were said to possess potent ritual instruments that could be used for good or ill and to renew the power of these objects—as well as their own life-force—by magically assassinating members of their families, whose bodies they later exhumed, dismembered, and distributed to other members of the group for secret cannibalistic consumption. Were that not enough, this gift was said to establish "flesh-debts," so that one day's recipients were obliged to reciprocate by later supplying meat of their own kin. Horrified at reports he found all too credible, Downes took steps to investigate and suppress the grisly rituals in question. The first ethnographies of the Tiv resulted from the inquiries he launched, with the cooperation of Major Roy C. Abraham, anthropological officer for northern Nigeria.[61] In their books, both men repeated and amplified the alarmist charges, while also admitting they had found no concrete evidence of magico-sacrificial homicide.[62]

Maj. Abraham concluded that the initial reports must have conveyed memory of practices from an earlier era.[63] Subsequent research, however, has shown that rather than being a secret society, *Mbatsav* was a discursive construct grounded in the indigenous ideology of "power" (*tsav*).[64] Traditionally, Tiv have a diffuse and informal leadership structure with no fixed offices, a segmentary lineage system of organization, and a relatively egalitarian ethos. Accordingly, power excites ambivalence and suspicion.[65] Recognizing that some people exert disproportionate influence, command respect, and can control the outcome of events more than others, they posit that such persons have more *tsav* than others. While it resembles such concepts as "power," "charisma," or *mana*, *tsav* is also theorized as having a material base. Most precisely, it is a tissue that grows around the heart in layers of the pericardium, and as such it is available for inspection by forensic autopsy.[66]

Normally, one's *tsav* is expected to grow over the course of a lifetime, which is why elders tend to accumulate power, and there are also variations in the rate of individuals' accumulation (which is why some people have more power than others). In addition to the natural growth and development of *tsav*, however, it is understood that one can accelerate and amplify the process by feasting on human flesh, especially that of one's closest kin.[67]

The panicked reactions of credulous administrators notwithstanding, these beliefs do not reflect (or inform) the practices of dangerous witches; rather, they voice a popular sense that the pursuit of power—and, to a certain extent, power itself—is something unnatural, immoral, monstrous, and violent that grows through predation on others. As such, they help check ambition, for anyone thought to have acquired too much *tsav* can quickly become the object of denunciation.

Such views were part of precolonial culture, but they gained new relevance as the British tried to establish a system of indirect rule and found it difficult to locate "chiefs" among the "acephalous" Tiv or to recruit for the role of officials and tax collectors. For the most part, it was younger men, especially those who "knew the way of the whites," who were willing to take such positions, reaping the opportunities they carried and accepting their risks.[68] Foremost of those risks was the perception that they had more *tsav* ("power") than could be acquired by ordinary means, with the corollary inference that they had elevated themselves beyond what was normal and decent by sacrificing and feasting on their kin, betraying the deepest and most binding of human connections.

Over the colonial period, Tiv society was convulsed by a series of "witchfinding" movements excited by such perceptions. In each instance, popular sentiments were mobilized against tribal officers of the colonial regime and others felt to have abandoned the more egalitarian indigenous ethos. Such persons were accused of being *Mbatsav*, a term the British authorities took to mean "witches," but which literally denotes "men of power." The earliest movement of this sort for which we have records is the precolonial Budeli movement of uncertain date, followed by the Ijôv of 1912–13, the Ivase, which followed in rapid succession, and the Nyambua of 1939. Most important, however, was the Haakaa (from *ha akaa*, the call for *Mbatsav* to "throw away" their ritual implements and ill-gotten powers) of 1929, an opening salvo of which were the complaints lodged with Maj. Downes.[69]

Downes and Abraham erred, not in taking these complaints too seriously, but by misconstruing their nature. These were not literal descriptions of actual events; rather, they constituted a vernacular critique of illicit power, couched in vivid metaphor to denounce those who sacrificed the interests of their people to those of the colonial state, discarding the moral obligations of kinship in pursuit of personal profit. All of this the British officers heard, but their understanding of it was distorted by their presumption of cultural and religious superiority.[70] Although the Tiv lodged a protest against the power of the powerful, Downes, Abraham, and their colleagues heard a lurid account of the horrors practiced by pagan savages. For them, the focal issues were not ambition, corruption, arrogance, and betrayal, but ignorance, superstition, and primitivity, as most emphatically marked by human sacrifice and cannibalism.

Although I would not want to exaggerate the points of resemblance, something similar seems present in the way Snorri transformed the narrative of King Aun from the form it took in *Ynglingatal*. The earlier text advanced a political and moral critique of Aun by his coreligionists, who charged the king with having bloodied his kinsmen and then having lingered overlong on his ill-gotten throne. Centuries later, Snorri recast this as an explicitly religious critique, grounded in the presumed superiority of Christians to non-Christians. Thus, in his version Aun was not just a bad—i.e., ruthlessly aggressive—king, but a bad *pagan* king: a sorcerer and great sacrificer, who offered the flesh of his sons to a treacherous deity. To put it in a different idiom, Snorri's Aun became a Scandinavian *Mbatsav*.

V

Snorri's story of King Aun and Tiv rumors about the *Mbatsav* permit one to make one last point. Although there are surely cases where human sacrifice was real enough, in most parts of the world and most periods of history, discourse about human sacrifice is more prevalent, more significant, and more revealing than its actual physical practice.

Similar conclusions were reached by our regretted colleague Cristiano Grottanelli in one of his last—and best—articles, where he considered the way Roman discourse relegated the practice of human offerings to other times, places, and social strata, thereby defining the collective Roman self as people *who no longer do such terrible things*. More precisely, he recognized an ideology consisting of four interrelated propositions.

1) In ancient times, Romans used to offer human sacrifices;
2) later, such practice was abandoned, and now Rome prohibits ritual homicides of any type.
3) But in special cases even Romans may be forced by difficult circumstances to practice such awful *sacra prodigiosa*;
4) while different kinds of barbarians and the enemies of the Roman order are given to such *sacra*.[71]

In place of "Romans," one could also say "Scandinavians," "Britons," and "Tiv," and the examples we have considered permit us to add one interesting nuance to Grottanelli's elegant schema. For in their critiques of King Aun and the *Mbatsav*, Snorri and the agitators of the Haakaa movement made clear that the "enemies of the Swedish (or Tiv) order" whose continued practice of human sacrifice was thought antithetical to the people's culture and morality might not be limited to criminals, deviants, lunatics, and witches, but might also include those at the very pinnacle of political power: kings and government officials. Indeed, it was possible to imagine they had reached that pinnacle precisely because they were willing to sacrifice their children and to betray their people, and it is this point that provided the basis for a critical denunciation, not just of specific malefactors, but of power in general.

# II: CONTRASTING STYLES OF APOCALYPTIC TIME

I

It is hardly uncommon for a religious community to orient itself toward a past it regards as foundational and to cultivate a strong sense of tradition. Reflecting this, much scholarship in history of religions has focused on the tendency of religious texts, traditions, institutions, and communities to privilege the time of sacred origins that Mircea Eliade famously termed *illud tempus*.[1] This concern with religious reverence for the primordial past also informed Eliade's tendency to contrast cyclical with linear time, and the way he aligned that binary opposition with others: myth and history, religion and secularity, the archaic and the modern.[2]

I would like to complicate that picture, first by noting a third construction of time that is well attested, profoundly religious, and neither linear nor cyclic, but apocalyptic. Second, I will insist that constructions of time have political implications, a point familiar to historians and anthropologists, if not to students of religion.[3] Third, I will suggest that the binary oppositions do not line up so neatly as is often assumed, but are rather fluid categories, open to human manipulation by actors and scholars alike.

Before taking up the relations of past, present, and future, as these are continually—if unacknowledgedly—reconfigured in discourse and practice, it seems appropriate to begin with a moment of autobiographical reflection: an origin story of sorts. This chapter thus starts with the flawed arguments I introduced in a paper titled "The Politics of Myth" (1980) that marked my first public departure from the theories developed by Eliade, my friend, *Doktorvater*, and mentor.[4]

The argument I advanced in that paper was twofold. First, beginning from Eliade's sense that *homines religiosi* find in myth not just an intellectually satisfying account of origins, but a sacred model on which to base their rituals, institutions, and lives, I suggested that such a construction implies—and effects—a fundamentally conservative program. Much like the valorization of "tradition" in general, it construes continuity, stability, and fidelity as cardinal virtues, while treating the reproduction of the past in the present as an ongoing imperative.

Second, I suggested that although this is, indeed, the way many myths operate, it is not true of myth in general, for some myths have a different temporal—and thus a different political—orientation. Where Eliade erred, I thought, was in privileging cosmogonic accounts, i.e., myths that invest the most primordial past with the greatest prestige and highest importance. Eschatologies, millenarian accounts, and apocalypses operate in different fashion, focusing on an imminent future, when cataclysmic change is expected to overwhelm a present that is depicted—and experienced—as intolerable.

## II

To demonstrate my argument, I cited a large number of examples, focusing prime attention on two pieces of rhetoric relevant to the Spanish Civil War, the most intense ideological battleground of the twentieth century. Here, forces from the most extreme left to the most extreme right made serious bids for power, deploying not just armed force, but skilled discourse to advance their cause. Although thoroughly engaged in the struggles at hand, political discourse frequently had a mythic dimension, gesturing well beyond its immediate moment. As an example of the cosmogonic mode, I cited a speech that José Antonio Primo de Rivera (1903–36), founder of the fascist Falange Española, delivered in Valladolid on March 4, 1934.[5] Building to his rhetorical climax, the young leader shifted from cataloguing the troubles plaguing the Spanish Republic (1931–39) to the glorious origins of the Spanish nation.

> We have no personal ambitions, except, perhaps, the ambition to be in the forefront of danger. All we want is to see Spain become once again herself, and to say with honor, social justice, youthfulness, and patriotic enthusiasm what this very city of Valladolid said in a letter to the emperor Charles V in 1516:
>
>> "Your Highness ought to come and take up in one hand that yoke bequeathed to you by the Catholic king, your grandfather [ = Ferdinand], with which so many men of courage and pride have been tamed, and in the other hand the arrows of that incomparable queen, your grandmother Doña Isabella, with which she removed the Moors so far away."
>
> Well, here in this selfsame city of Valladolid, which pleaded thus,

you have the yoke and the arrows: the yoke of toil and the arrows of authority. Thus we have come, beneath the emblem of the yoke and arrows, to say right here, in Valladolid: "Castilla, once again for Spain!"[6]

As in cosmogonies of a more traditional sort, José Antonio here invoked foundational moments of the past—a glorious time of heroic commitment, sovereign authority, and militant faith—that he construed as a transcendent model for actors and action in the present, while not so subtly suggesting that he and his movement best realized that ideal, for the yoke and the arrows were the Falange's emblem, after the model of Mussolini's fasces and Hitler's swastika.[7]

In contrast, I cited the apocalyptic response Buenaventura Durruti (1896–1936), foremost leader of the Spanish Anarchists, gave to a journalist who tried to provoke him by saying, "You will be sitting on top of a pile of ruins even if you are victorious."

"We have always lived in slums and holes in the wall," [Durruti] said quietly. "We will know how to accommodate ourselves for a time. For, you must not forget that we can also build these palaces and cities, here in Spain and in America and everywhere. We, the workers. We can build others to take their place. And better ones. We are not in the least afraid of ruins. We are going to inherit the earth. There is not the slightest doubt about that. The bourgeoisie might blast and ruin its own world before it leaves the stage of history. We carry a new world here, in our hearts," he said in a hoarse whisper. And he added: "That world is growing in this minute."[8]

In Durruti's rapturous language, one finds all that is typical of apocalyptic discourse: soteriological promise, redemptive potential, a sense of one's group as the righteous elect, absolute confidence in the world's imminent transformation, urgent anticipation of that sweeping change, and an inspiring vision of the world to come.[9] It is worth stressing that these words came from a committed revolutionary who had robbed banks, organized unions, led general strikes, battled police, served jail time, been condemned to death on multiple occasions, raised an anarchist militia without officers or conventional discipline, and battled fascist troops across Spain, before becoming a martyred hero a few months after this interview.[10] Particularly noteworthy is the absolute novelty of the future he anticipated: a world cleansed of its past and purged of all bosses. A world of equality, beauty, and justice realized through a leveling process precipitated by the violence of the ruling classes, but brought to a righteous conclusion by the efforts of the workers.

III

For some time, it has been fashionable to think that much, if not all apocalyptic discourse encodes revolutionary visions, desires, and purpose.[11] In my 1980 article, I gestured toward a half dozen comparanda supporting such a view, while treating none of these in detail. At the head of my list stood the Lakota (a.k.a. "Sioux") Ghost Dance (*wanaǧi wačipi*, lit. "spirit dance") of 1890, the last and most desperate form of resistance adopted by Plains Indians, culminating in the Wounded Knee Massacre.[12] Adapting prophecies that originated in Wyoming among the Paiute the previous year, Lakota leaders organized strenuous dances in which exhausted dancers were guided toward visionary encounters with ancestral spirits. These ecstatic experiences were construed as fulfillment and validation of prophecy, also as anticipations of the cataclysm the dance would soon produce: an earthquake, flood, or great wind that would bring back the Indian dead, restore the buffalo, remove whites, and cleanse the earth of evil.

Late in 1890, the Ghost Dance gained influence among the Lakota, a people who had been militarily worn down (but not conquered), confined to reservations, and subjected to betrayals, broken treaties, and countless humiliations. Others have chronicled this shameful history at length, and there is no need to rehearse its details.[13] I would, however, begin by citing a document that shows how things looked to white authorities around the advent of the Ghost Dance. To that end, consider the annual report by James T. McLaughlin, agent for the Standing Rock Reservation, home of Sitting Bull, for the fiscal year ending June 30, 1890 (the report is dated August 26 of that year).

> In conclusion I desire to state that the Indians of this agency, with a few exceptions, show steady progress and wholesome advancement in civilization. Increased interest and efforts to provide permanent habitations and more comfortable homes are manifest from year to year, also better care of stock, more intelligent cultivation of fields, and accumulation of property are very apparent, as are also an acceptance and increasing knowledge of the precepts of Christianity, with less opposition to placing their children in school and a gradual abandonment of Indian customs. Some of the older persons however, cling tenaciously to the old Indian ways, are jealous of seeing their former power pass from them, and can not be brought to accept the new and better order of things. But this retarding influence is gradually losing its weight, and as the old non-progressive Indians pass away, there will be none among the rising generation found to pose as "obstructionists," as some of the old men of the present day do.[14]

McLaughlin's views were typical of the reservation agents, who were charged with transforming Lakota culture in ways dictated by the U.S. government. This project, which they consistently defined as benevolent and civilizing, began with confinement to reservations (so that white settlers could take Indian lands), encouraged the adoption of agriculture (since hunting was no longer possible), promoted a shift from communal to private property (to facilitate sales of land, also to break the power of kin and tribal groupings), sought conversion to Christianity (to encourage individualism, traditional religious practice having been banned in 1883), and tried to enforce education in boarding schools (where children were separated from the influence of their elders, then deprived of their native dress, language, and traditions). Such measures were meant to consolidate the conquest of the Plains tribes and to transform the Lakota into a dominated, unthreatening, and assimilable population.[15] All this was defined as "progress," an unquestioned good that faced one obstacle only, at least in the agents' view: traditionalists like Sitting Bull, who would not get with the program.[16] McLaughlin's text provides a map of social segmentation circa 1890 as perceived by the government agents, who saw—and encouraged—a crucial line of cleavage dividing "non-progressive" Lakota elders from the younger, more malleable "progressives." Further, they felt confident that the former group was losing influence and would disappear, after which all Indians would be assimilated to white culture (figure 11.1).

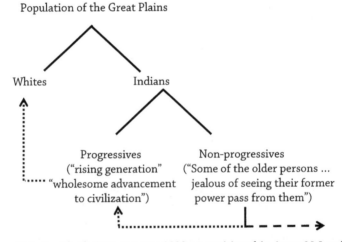

Figure 11.1. Social relations, summer 1890, as envisioned in Agent McLaughlin's report. Solid lines represent the pattern of segmentation then extant; dotted lines represent processes anticipated in the future, larger dashes standing for obsolescence and shorter dots for assimilation. The bifurcated line at the bottom of the diagram represents an alternative: those non-progressives who will not adapt to the policies advanced by the agents are fated to disappear.

From the Lakota viewpoint, however, conditions were tenuous at best, and rapidly deteriorating. Having surrendered much of their best land in a controversial treaty of 1889, they subsequently saw the federal government ignore most of its commitments. Drought and crop failure brought people near starvation, and government rations were slashed, just as word arrived concerning the prophecies of the Paiute holy man Wovoka.[17] Accordingly, at a great council held in fall 1889, the Lakota decided to send a delegation of seven men to Wyoming to consult with Wovoka and assess his teachings.[18] Upon their return the following spring, two of these men, Kicking Bear and Short Bull, took the lead in organizing Ghost Dances.[19] Initially, McLaughlin and the other agents were relatively unconcerned and viewed the dance as a fantasy of the old non-progressives, little more than a fleeting annoyance.[20]

This changed rather abruptly on October 9, 1890, when Kicking Bear arrived at McLaughlin's Standing Rock Reservation without the requisite government permission, having been invited by Sitting Bull himself. To the excited throng that assembled, Kicking Bear relayed these instructions of the Great Spirit (Wakan Tanka).

The Great Spirit spoke to us, saying: Take this message to my red children and tell it to them as I say it. I have neglected the Indians for many moons, but I will make them my people now if they obey me in this message. The earth is getting old, and I will make it new for my chosen people, the Indians, who are to inhabit it, and among them will be all those of their ancestors who have died, their fathers, mothers, brothers, cousins, and wives—all those who hear my voice and my words through the tongues of my children. I will cover the earth with new soil to a depth of five times the height of a man, and [1] under this new soil will be buried the whites, and all the holes and the rotten places will be filled up. The new lands will be covered with sweet-grass and running water and trees, and herds of buffalo and ponies will stray over it, that my red children may eat and drink, hunt and rejoice. And the sea to the west I will fill up so that no ships may pass over it, and the other seas will I make impassable. And while I am making the new earth [2] the Indians who have heard this message and who dance and pray and believe will be taken up in the air and suspended there, while the wave of new earth is passing; then set down among the spirits of their ancestors, relatives and friends. [3] Those of my children who doubt will be left in undesirable places, where they will be lost and wander around until they believe and learn the songs and the dance of the spirits.[21]

Like other leading advocates of the Ghost Dance, Kicking Bear here differentiated three groups, foreseeing a different fate for each.[22] Thus, the

Population of the Great Plains

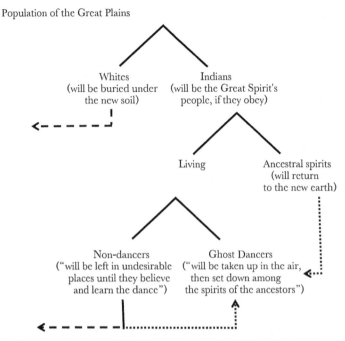

Figure 11.2. Social relations, fall 1890, as envisioned in Kicking Bear's speech. Solid lines represent current pattern of segmentation; dotted lines represent processes anticipated in the future, larger dashes standing for obsolescence and shorter dots for reunion. The bifurcated line at the bottom of the diagram represents an alternative: those Indians who will not learn and practice the Ghost Dance are fated to disappear.

whites now resident in North America were to be buried under the new earth, serving as landfill for the world's most rotten places. Oceans would then be made impassable, so the whites of Europe could never return. Indians who participated in the dance would be lifted into the air during the earth's renewal, then set gently on its surface, where they could rejoin their ancestors and the buffalo, brought back from the world beyond.[23] Non-participants, however, would be "left in undesirable places" until such time as they began to sing and dance. Intriguingly, Kicking Bear's speech describes a pattern of segmentation quite similar to that of McLaughlin's report, but with very different evaluations of the relevant groups and a different expected outcome (figure 11.2).

It is important to note that Kicking Bear did not incite violence against whites; rather, he prophesied that divine vengeance would fall upon them, such that they would be excluded from the glories of the world to come.[24] Alarmed by the level of interest Kicking Bear aroused, McLaughlin sent a squad of his Indian police to remove him from the reservation. Although these were choice "progressives," whom McLaughlin cultivated, rewarded, and used to advance the government's policies, they "returned without executing the order, both officers being in a dazed condition and fearing the powers of Kicking Bear's medicine."[25] Nearly a week went by before Kicking Bear was finally persuaded to head home (October 15), by which time a great many at Standing Rock were enthusiastically dancing.[26]

This setback made McLaughlin reevaluate the situation. Previously, he associated the dance exclusively with non-progressives and viewed it as one more piece of superstition that was sure to pass. The possibility that his Indian police could be swayed was thus cause for concern.[27] His anxiety mounting, McLaughlin pressed his superiors in Washington for the arrest of Sitting Bull and other prominent "mischief-makers."[28]

In late October and November, other agents also began calling for action, as did white settlers and the press. Roughly a month after the incident at Standing Rock, President Harrison directed the military to take precautions against a Lakota uprising (November 13, 1890). Troops arrived at Pine Ridge on November 19, and less than a month later, Sitting Bull was killed by the Indian police McLaughlin sent to arrest him (December 15).[29] Two weeks later, nearly three hundred Lakota, more than half of them women and children, were slaughtered at Wounded Knee in the last military action of the Indian Wars (December 29).

I do not mean to suggest that McLaughlin's actions were causal, or that his shift of mid-October set in motion the events leading up to Wounded Knee. McLaughlin had long been locked in a struggle with Sitting Bull, and his general attitudes reflected U.S. policy, which championed cooperative and entrepreneurial young men (termed "friendlies," as well as "progressives"), while seeking to reduce the influence of former elites (called "traditionalists," "hostiles," "obstructionists," and worse, as well as "non-progressives").[30] Consistent with this, agents initially saw the line between dancers and non-dancers as identical to that between non-progressives and progressives. The idea that "progressives" might embrace the dance was thus a threat of the first order: in such a development McLaughlin saw not just the unraveling of his hard work, or the return of "old ways" and stubborn old men, but the reversal of progress itself, time turning back on itself to reanimate an earlier era.[31]

This mirrored the view of the dancers themselves, who saw such a reversal not as chaos, but salvation. The past whose return they sought to accomplish, even speed, was one of perfect purity, harmony, and abundance: a primordial paradise anterior to Columbus, when buffalo were ubiquitous and white men stayed in Europe.

## IV

Kicking Bear's expectations were no less apocalyptic than Durruti's, and his faith no less fervent, but he faced a different situation, occupied a different position within the field of conflict, and sought to accomplish different results. The temporal sensibilities of the two men also differed in ways that correspond to their social position and political goals.

Durruti represented workers who, having always been politically and economically dominated by others, fought to realize a future such as had never previously existed: a world of unprecedented equality, devoid of any elite. In contrast, Kicking Bear, Sitting Bull, and other Ghost Dance leaders represented an elite that had recently been displaced by foreign powers.[32] Accordingly, they sought to recover the situation of a not-too-distant past, when the position of men like themselves was neither subordinated to whites nor challenged by "progressives." Other similarities notwithstanding, Durruti's politics were utopian and revolutionary, while those of the Ghost Dance tended toward *ressentiment* and restoration.

One is thus led to recognize two different kinds of apocalyptic. That of Durruti—which one might designate *progressive* apocalypticism—admits two moments only: an oppressive present and its reversal in the near future, this being accomplished not through a gradual process of evolution and reform, but by a radical, violent, and/or supernatural leap (figure 11.3).

The apocalypticism of the Ghost Dance—which I would now style *recursive*—includes a third moment: a highly valorized past understood to have been catastrophically reversed in the present, but soon to be restored. Such a construction involves a narrative whose temporality is neither linear nor cyclical, for time and history effectively end when the primordial ideal is recovered.

The move from past to present (figure 11.4a) thus sets up a second move, which is not a continuation of the original process (figure 11.4b), but its reversal, given that the emergent future is modeled after and identified with the foundational past (figure 11.4c). The "past" in question, however, is not any past that actually *was*, but the idealized past of myth, accounts of which are strongly inflected by the interests and desires of those who speak in—but also *against*—the present.

This mirroring of past and future provides reassurance that however severe the woes of the current moment may be, they are only a temporary interruption of the world's authentic and proper order, which was divinely established in the beginning and will soon be divinely restored. The troubled present is thus construed as an accidental and inauthentic disruption of the way things were and ought to be, the product of fallible humans—foreigners and others alienated from the divine—whose removal

**-PRESENT**          **+FUTURE**

Figure 11.3. Progressive apocalypticism, which anticipates and seeks to accomplish an abrupt transition from a devalorized present to an idealized future.

**a)**

**+PAST**          **- PRESENT**

**b)**

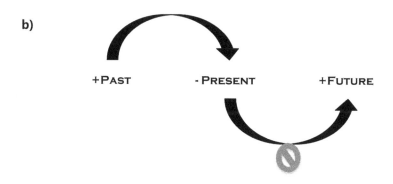

**+PAST**          **- PRESENT**          **+FUTURE**

**c)**

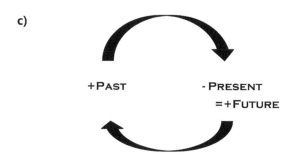

**+PAST**          **- PRESENT**
                        **=+FUTURE**

Figure 11.4. Recursive apocalypticism, the first moment of which involves the transition from an idealized past to a devalorized present (a). The move to an idealized future, however, is understood not as a continuation of historic process (b), but a reversal of same, such that time circles backward, restoring existence to its primordial state of perfection (c). With the recovery of this ideal, time, history, and change are expected to cease.

will help restore the world's original and future perfection. Put differently, the present is a sort of "enemy time" (on the analogy of "enemy territory"): an anomalous, but finite period when one's people have fallen under the control of illegitimate outsiders: a situation soon to be rectified and reversed, by divine intervention, if necessary.

V

Recursive apocalypticism characterizes many movements usually considered "religions of the oppressed."[33] On closer inspection, many of these prove to be like the Ghost Dance, i.e., led by old elites seeking to recover privileged positions from which they were recently displaced by foreigners and/or usurpers. In his classic work, *The King Is Dead*, S. K. Eddy understood this as the context for Persian, Egyptian, and Jewish apocalypticism in the Hellenistic era, all of which he interpreted as movements seeking to restore the indigenous kingships overthrown by the Macedonian empires, as in the case of the Maccabees.[34] Similar arguments have been made about Christian and Jewish apocalyptic vis-à-vis Rome,[35] and one can perceive the same dynamic elsewhere.

To cite but one dramatic example, consider the Xhosa cattle-killing movement of 1856–57.[36] As the British advanced in South Africa, eroding Xhosa autonomy,[37] a young girl named Nongqawuse conveyed a message from spirits, instructing her countrymen that all current ills—British encroachment on Xhosa territory, witchcraft accusations, and pneumonic plague among the herds—could be reversed and the world renewed, were the Xhosa to sacrifice all their cattle. In a sense, such an act marked the end of a world, since cattle were the basis of the Xhosa economy and social order. To sacrifice all the animals was thus to place one's self in God's hands and Nongqawuse promised that once this was done, "new herds" and "new people," purer and better than those of today, would miraculously appear.[38]

Like Wovoka, Nongqawuse herself was more catalyst than cause of subsequent events, and her prophecies gained traction only when embraced and disseminated by chiefs (Sarhili, Sandile, Maqoma, Mhala, et al.) who had seen their power diminish with the British advance. As the crisis developed, these traditional leaders found themselves challenged by their own sons and other young men who saw collaboration with the British as a means to improve their position.[39]

In the heat of events, a cleavage opened up rather like that between Lakota "progressives" and "non-progressives." On the one side were chiefs (and those loyal to them), who urged massive sacrifices to speed the events prophesied by Nongqawuse. On the other were young men, suspicious of the prophecy, increasingly uncomfortable under chiefly authority, and eager to preserve their wealth in cattle. J. B. Peires refers to the two factions as "believers" and "unbelievers," but the groups called themselves *amagogotya* and *amathamba*, literally "the hard" (i.e., the hard-headed young men who were sufficiently ambitious and insensitive to the moral demands of tradition and community that they refused to kill their cattle) versus "the soft" (i.e., the soft-hearted Xhosa, who responded to others' needs and the chiefs' requests by unselfishly sacrificing their herds). Alternatively, one could see them as the fading leaders of traditional culture and the constituents of a new proto-capitalist class with entrepreneurial ambitions.[40]

As in the Ghost Dance, an old elite was embattled on two fronts, facing superior foreign powers and opportunistic defectors among their own people. As their situation and that of their people rapidly deteriorated, these men embraced an apocalyptic prophecy and engaged in extraordinary rituals to speed the appearance of a new world. Once again, their apocalypticism was of the recursive sort, promising the reinvigoration of an old order and the disappearance of intrusive forces promoting unwelcome change. For all that Nongqawuse spoke of "new people," "new cattle," and a "new world," what Sarhili and the chiefs labored to realize was the restoration of a world in which they still ruled, their sons still submitted to their authority, and the British were nowhere to be found.

## VI

These examples prompt me to reconsider José Antonio Primo de Rivera, who also represented a recently displaced elite. Indeed, his father, Don Miguel Primo de Rivera y Orbaneja, 2nd Marquis of Estella, 22nd Count of Sobremonte, and Knight of Calatrava (1870–1930), was a landed aristocrat and a captain general of the Spanish army. After staging a coup d'état in support of the failing monarchy in 1923, he served as dictator and prime minister until 1930.[41] In the chaos that followed his fall from power, the monarchy collapsed, and the Spanish Republic was founded (April 1931).

Shortly thereafter, José Antonio (who himself bore an impressive string of titles)[42] founded the Falange (1933) to combat the newly founded Republic, which he understood as the spawn of foreign ideologies. As he saw it, Republican Spain came into existence under the influence of these alien forces, losing track of Spain's true, original, and eternal essence, which demanded unity above all.[43] In the moment, Spain was catastrophically dissolving in factional strife along the lines of partisan politics, regional separatism, and class conflict.[44] Accordingly, the task José Antonio claimed for his movement was to wage a ferocious struggle for the restoration of the true Spain against Rousseau, Marx, and those benighted Spaniards who had fallen victim to their seductions.[45] In practice, this would involve

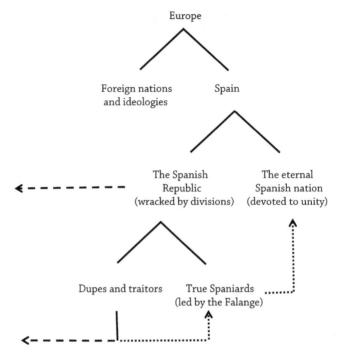

Figure 11.5. Social relations in Spain, 1934–36, as represented in the discourse of José Antonio Primo de Rivera. Solid lines represent the pattern of segmentation then extant; dotted lines represent processes anticipated in the future, larger dashes standing for obsolescence and shorter dots for assimilation. The bifurcated line at the bottom of the diagram represents an alternative: those republicans who will not return to the true Spain advocated by the Falange are fated to disappear.

the violent overthrow of the Republican state,[46] the suppression of labor unions, political parties, and movements for regional autonomy,[47] and the installation of a strong leader—someone like his father, and presumably himself—equipped with dictatorial powers (figure 11.5).[48] Although some of his appeals gestured toward the foundational past, most of his rhetoric stressed the woes of the present and the violent struggle that would soon restore Spain to its once and future authentic and glorious self. Contrary to my earlier suggestion, his style was not cosmogonic, but an apocalypticism of the recursive type, as when he declaimed: "All we want is to see Spain become *once again* herself."[49]

Surely there are important differences between the apocalyptic vision of a fascist group like the Falange and that of anticolonial movements like the Ghost Dance and the Xhosa cattle-killing movement. It is not just the former's bloody success under Franco that makes us recoil, nor the tragic end of the other two that demands sympathy and respect. In the ideals they cherished, the nature of the adversaries they confronted, the degree of violence and ruthlessness they were prepared to unleash, these movements differed sharply. In their temporal orientation, however, they were quite similar, insofar as all sought to recover a situation of the recent past, which they identified with a primordial ideal. Perceiving the present as a catastrophic fall from that ideal, they sought to produce sweeping change of a contradictory sort: difficult to achieve, but imminent and inevitable; divinely ordained, but requiring strenuous human effort; an overthrow of foreigners, their ideas and institutions, but also directed against those of one's own people who collaborate with the outsiders. Equally contradictory was the world they expected to establish: radically new, but a restoration of the old; beneficial for all, but especially for the older, displaced elites, who would recover their former positions.

## VII

As a side note, one can observe that recursive apocalypticism has become common in the contemporary United States among those who fetishize an originary past of "Founding Fathers" and "traditional values," see this as having been subverted by alien ideologies and actors ("liberalism," "progressivism," "judicial activism," "creeping socialism," "tenured radicals," e.g.), and expect salvation on the near horizon, whether this takes the form of "the Rapture" or "the End of History." What they long for in their call to "take back our country" or "make America great again" is the restoration of a world in which "real Americans" like themselves controlled policy, morals, and values. It is not just the present they decry, but the contentious processes, demographic shifts, cultural diversity, and political change that have deprivileged them (somewhat), but that also constitute history over the *longue durée*. To find history distressing is understandable, and to struggle against it can have a certain tragic grandeur, as in the case of Sandile, Sarhili, Sitting Bull, or Kicking Bear. It is, however, usually a losing battle.

Returning to the question of "the politics of myth," the materials I have considered suggest that although the temporal orientation of a myth may influence the politics it encodes, it does not do so in mechanical fashion. Thus, apocalypticism typically voices strong discontent with the present and is a convenient instrument for mobilizing the disaffected. Even so, a wide range of actors—anticolonialists, anarchists, fascists, and the Tea Party—have all found it relatively easy to develop a form of apocalyptic that speaks their particular discontents with the powers that be, while advancing their idiosyncratic ideals and desires. Ultimately, it is not the temporal orientation of a myth that determines its politics, but the specific interests, identities, ambitions, and values that bring narrators and audience together in relation to a story they embrace as absolute truth: a story that portrays their most desperate hopes as soon to be realized. Collectively, audience and narrators reshape the story's details over countless retellings, so that it makes the demands of their shared situation ever more clear and pressing. One sees this, for instance, as the Ghost Dance leaders reworked what they heard from Wovoka to better suit the situation of the Lakota, then further refined their message in the summer and fall of 1890 as conditions worsened and their following grew,[50] or in the way Nongqawuse, the chiefs, and other prophets modified their discourse to keep abreast of events, shifts in mood, and the fluctuating balance of acceptance versus skepticism.[51] Nor is it just the story that is reshaped through these repeated cycles of narration, reception, and revision. Through the same process, the group drawn to the story takes shape and transforms itself into a movement, party, or bloc committed to the often—but not always—futile project of realizing the change the narrative announces, which they imagine as history's end.

# 12: SLY GROOMS, SHADY MAGPIES, AND THE MYTHIC FOUNDATIONS OF HIERARCHY

I

In this and the following chapter, I want to consider two narratives that have numerous features in common. One is Herodotus's account of a critical turning point in world history, the other an equally critical moment in the newly republished "Origin Myth of Acoma Pueblo." As we will see, the two are similar—but not identical—in their general structure, and both center on an episode in which human actors seek resolution of an otherwise unsolvable problem by seeking a sign from the gods, with results whose consequences resonate over many centuries.

These materials provide a convenient example for the advantages of "weak comparison," i.e., a comparison that treats a small number of examples, is attentive to their differences as well as their points of resemblance, and takes their similarities to reflect the attempts of different groups to grapple with similar issues, not as evidence for common origin, direct influence, archetypes, or universals. When considered in this fashion, the two narratives are seen to take up a host of broad issues, including the human capacity to reimagine and radically restructure political institutions and social relations; the way such operations are affected by the way people manage (and manipulate) their relations with powers they see as more than human; the dangers and doubts that attend such operations; the way societies reflect on the very real limits to the viability and legitimacy of their social order in the stories they tell; and the ways individual narrators explore and exploit the possibilities present in those stories. More specifically, the two narratives—and others to which they are connected, as we will see—engage this central problem: once it becomes clear that egalitarian relations among people cannot be sustained, is there any way to establish a hierarchic order that will be legitimate, beneficial, and stable?

## II

Neither on his own account nor on Herodotus's treatment of the same events was it easy for Darius to become Great King of the Persian empire in 522 BCE.[1] Both versions tell how he recognized his predecessor on the throne to be a Magus and an imposter; how he conspired with six other nobles to overthrow him; and how he slew the false king with his own hands. The version Darius had inscribed on the rock face at Bisitun ends there, save for his formulaic—but ideologically crucial—summation of how and why these events came to pass: "By the Wise Lord's will I became king. The Wise Lord bestowed the kingship/kingdom on me."[2]

In contrast to the brevity of Darius's account, Herodotus continued the story at some length and with some different wrinkles. Thus, in the early episodes of his version, Darius did not organize the conspiracy of seven, but was last to join the group. And once they had overthrown the imposter, Herodotus describes the group as uncertain whether to restore the monarchy or to establish a political order of an entirely different type. Accordingly, Otanes—who had first recognized the Magian imposter and organized the conspiracy—made the case for a democratic system, arguing that "the rule of the multitude has the fairest name of all: equality (isonomiē)."[3] He was followed by Megabyzus, who spoke in favor of oligarchy, both for principled and self-serving reasons. "Having picked a small group of the best men," he counseled his colleagues, "let us confer power on them, for we will surely sit among them."[4] Speaking last, Darius argued that monarchy on the traditional Persian model remained the best system, since oligarchy inevitably produces internal struggles, while democracy devolves into chaos.[5]

Classicists refer to this scene as the "Constitutional Debate," and consider it a rhetorical tour de force that Herodotus patterned after models developed by Athenian sophists and others.[6] He sets the episode, moreover, in an extraordinary moment of anarchic equity, when all things are possible, and no mortal holds power over any other, the world's greatest state having been deconstructed by its own ineptitude (Herodotus describes the last legitimate Persian king as having gone mad, then having died by his own hand, leaving no son or other successor), by the machinations of others (the scheming of the Magus who usurped the throne), and by the righteous violence of the conspirators. The debate and its outcome are also particularly well-constructed; Herodotus gives voice to all the logical options, all of which figure in the way the question is resolved, as (a) a small elite group of an oligarchic sort (b) uses the democratic methods of debate, followed by vote (c) to decide in favor of monarchy. More precisely, by a vote of 5–1–1 (with Otanes and Megabyzus as holdouts), the former conspirators decided on a pyramidal order in which power would be vested in a single ruler, backed by a small group of uniquely privileged nobles, and exercised over the rest of the population.[7]

Otanes alone refused this decision. Although his inability to accept the results of the vote might seem hypocritical or ironic, it is actually consistent with his position and prompts a better understanding of it, for Otanes's model of democracy centers on the principle of *equality*, not majority rule. That being the case, he informed the others: "I will not compete with you, for I am willing neither to rule nor to be ruled. I renounce ruling power, and in exchange, neither I nor my descendants to come will be ruled by any of you."[8]

Otanes having opted out, the others considered how to select the next king from the remaining six candidates, all of whom had the same claim to the throne, being of noble birth and having cooperated equally in deposing the Magian imposter. After further deliberation, they decided that the "most just" (*dikaiotata*) method would be a contest in which all six would assemble on horseback at the city limits just before dawn. As the sun rose, that man whose horse whinnied first would become king.[9]

Regarding what happened next, Herodotus records two variant traditions that circulated among the Persians.[10] In both, the leading role fell to Darius's wily groom, a certain Oibares.[11]

> Some say this Oibares touched the genitals of a mare with his hand, then kept it hidden in his trousers until sunrise. When the others were about to let loose their horses, he brought his hand close to the nostrils of Darius's horse, which snorted and whinnied upon smelling that.[12]

This contest, by which a king was chosen to rule all Asia,[13] should be understood not as a random lottery on the order of drawing straws or tossing coins, but as a form of divination in which the sun—a potent deity in the Persian pantheon[14]—would act on the horses (aristocratic animals, each closely associated with its owner) to produce a sign identifying that man who was divinely chosen to rule.[15] Oibares's trick compromised the process, however, with the result that Darius gained power through a fraud perpetrated by a low-status trickster, not by God's will. Clearly, this variant was designed to undermine the legitimacy of Darius's kingship, contradicting the narrative of divine election he propagated in his Bisitun inscription.

The second variant constitutes a riposte to the first, whose anti-Darius story it modified so as to reassert the king's legitimating claim of divine election.

> When the group of contestants dispersed, Darius said to his groom, who was a shrewd man: "Oibares, it seemed good to us to award the kingship

in this fashion: the man whose horse whinnies first at sunrise after all have mounted, he should win the kingship. Now truly, if you have any cunning, contrive something so that we get this prize and no one else." Oibares answered: "My lord, do not fear and be of good heart. No one other than you will be king. I have the means to do this." Darius said: "If you have such a trick, set to work and don't delay, for when day arrives, the contest is upon us." Having heard these things, Oibares did this. When night came, he led one of the mares whom Darius's horse loved best, to the city limits. He tethered her there and brought in Darius's horse, which he led around and around, close to the mare. Finally, he let the horse mount her. At daybreak, as agreed, the six arrived on their horses. Riding toward the city limit, they came to the place where the mare had been tethered the preceding night, whereupon Darius's horse ran up and whinnied. And as his horse was doing this, thunder and lightning came from the sky. These things having happened subsequently to Darius, it confirmed him, as if it happened by some agreement. The other contestants jumped down from their horses and prostrated themselves before Darius.[16]

Up to its conclusion, this variant differs from the other only in the erotic details of Oibares's trickery and the elaborate vocabulary with which it emphasizes his guile (*sophos, sophiē, mēkhanō, pharmakon, sophisma*), details that build on the argument and judgment of the other version. Having initially accepted this scenario, however, the longer variant adds two details that reverse the other's conclusion. These are (a) the thunderbolt, which provides a non-manipulated and unimpeachable celestial portent to replace the one compromised by Oibares's guile, and (b) the nobles' prostration, which signals human acceptance of the gods' choice and submission to the new king.[17] Where the shorter version suggests Darius won the contest only because his underling cheated, making the new ruler a false king (like his deposed predecessor), this one acknowledges the cheating, but dismisses it as irrelevant, since it benefited the uniquely gifted man whom the gods chose, independent of any horseplay. The relation of the two rival variants is summarized in table 12.1.

Tracing the sources for the episodes in Herodotus's account of Darius's accession permits us to see it as a work of bricolage (table 12.2). Scholarly discussions of the Oibares episode have generally sought its origins in trickster tales[18] and folklore,[19] precedents established in Mesopotamian royal inscriptions,[20] or Indo-Iranian and Indo-European sacrificial rituals associated with kingship.[21] Although the arguments in each case may be plausible, none is compelling or has gained general acceptance. A different sort of approach is called for, employing a different sort of comparison

Table 12.1. Rival accounts of the contest in which Darius was chosen as king

|  | Variant A (Herodotus 3.87.1) | Variant B (Herodotus 3.85-86) |
| --- | --- | --- |
| **Premise** | Divine election of next king, signaled by solar omen | Divine election of next king, signaled by solar omen |
| **Premise negated** | Contest subverted by Oibares | Contest subverted by Oibares |
| **(Initial) conclusion** | Darius = illegitimate king | Darius = illegitimate king |
| **Premise reasserted and negation negated (I)** |  | Results of the contest ratified by thunderbolt omen |
| **Premise reasserted and negation negated (II)** |  | Results of the contest ratified by others' prostration before the man divinely chosen |
| **(Revised) Conclusion** |  | Darius = legitimate king |

and raising deeper, more wide-ranging, and more important questions than those of origins and influence.

III

No plausible case can be made that a relation of influence, diffusion, common origin, or archetypal unity connects the story of Darius and Oibares to the Acoma Pueblo origin myth, the longest recorded version of which describes how two sisters, Iatiku and Nautsiti, made their way to the earth's surface and thus were "born" at the same moment.[22] Although there was little difference between the sisters at the moment of their emergence, over time they developed distinguishing features. First were the names they acquired, reflecting their relation to the content of the basket each one received from the Creator, for Iatiku means "Bringing to Life" and Nautsiti, "More of Everything in the Basket."[23] Next, they established and affiliated with the first two clans of Acoma society, Nautsiti founding the Sun clan and Iatiku the Corn.[24] As a result of her closer connection to the sun, Nautsiti was more comfortable with its bright light, exposure to which turned her skin whiter and made her mind quicker than her sister's.[25] Conversely,

Table 12.2. Sources for Herodotus's account of Darius's accession to kingship

| | Episode | Herodotus | Source |
|---|---|---|---|
| 1 | A Magus usurps the Persian throne | 3.61–67 | Darius's Bisitun inscription §§10–12 plus additional material of unknown origin |
| 2 | Seven noble Persians conspire to overthrow him | 3.68–79 | Darius's Bisitun inscription §13 and §68 plus additional material of unknown origin |
| 3 | Constitutional debate | 3.80–82 | Greek sophists and rhetoricians |
| 4 | Divination by sun and horses, Variant A | 3.87 | Persian oral traditions critical of Darius |
| 5 | Divination by sun and horses, Variant B | 3.84.3–86 | Persian oral traditions defending Darius against the criticism of Variant A |

Iatiku was more scrupulous in taking care of the corn, while Nautsiti was "a litle lazy."[26] Nautsiti also became a bit selfish, hoarding the seeds and images in her basket, while Iatiku was eager to activate hers and watch them grow.[27] Their emergent differences notwithstanding, the two sisters got along well and cooperated in giving life to all manner of plants and animals, until they carelessly let come into being "a serpent . . . with power of its own . . . a strange snake . . . the snake that was to tempt Nautsiti."[28]

Up to this point, there had been no conflict between the two girls, nor signs of jealousy between them. Immediately after the appearance of this ominous reptile (conceivably modeled on the serpent of Genesis 3), the question arose: Which sister was born first and thus outranked the other? A difficult problem, given the peculiar circumstances of their birth and compounded by the fact that Acoma kinship terminology distinguishes siblings by sex, but not differences in age and birth order.[29]

Nautsiti spoke to Iatiku, who had used more of the seeds and images from her basket. She wanted the chance to give life to more of her images. Iatiku replied, "I'm the older, you're younger than I." But Nautsiti said, "We should both give equally because we were created equally. Is it true that you are the older? Let's try each other! Tomorrow, when the sun rises, let us see who is going to have the sun rise for her first." But Iatiku was afraid that her sister was going to get the better of her in some way. She knew a white bird that was named Magpie. She went to it and asked it to go on ahead to the east, where the sun was to rise, without resting or eating. There it was to shade the sun with its wings from Nautsiti. The bird went as instructed, for it was strong and skillful. . . . Finally, after a long time, the bird reached the east where the sun was ready to rise and it spread its wings on the left side of the sun, making a shade in the direction of Nautsiti. So the sun struck Iatiku first and she straightaway claimed to be the older. And Nautsiti was very angry for she had hoped to win.[30]

With her claim of seniority ("I'm the older"), Iatiku attempts to introduce hierarchy into the sisters' relations. Initially, Nautsiti defends the balanced relations they have enjoyed to this point ("We should both give equally because we were created equally") and questions her sister's assertion ("Is it true that you are the older?"). Quickly, however, she perceives the threat in Iatiku's claim of privilege and proposes a contest to settle the question of primacy. In that moment, however, she abandons her defense of an egalitarian ethic and order ("Let's try each other! Tomorrow, when the sun rises, let us see who is going to have the sun rise for her first"), while proposing a contest in which she has an advantage by virtue of her membership in the Sun clan.[31]

Even the most casual observer will recognize how closely this episode in Acoma myth resembles Herodotus's account of the competition for Persian kingship. Serious inquiry begins, however, not by noting the features these narratives share, but by identifying the fundamental issues, the deep and difficult problems, they address and the positions they develop via their characters, plot, and details. This is the work of weak comparison, which we can begin by observing that both stories center on a contest in which the sun will select the winner. At issue is the attempt to secure divine resolution of human competition, given that Acoma residents, like the Persians, construe the sun as a great deity, sacred source of all life and energy.[32]

The competition, moreover, is of no ordinary sort. Rather, it is exceedingly difficult to resolve, because (a) the stakes are extremely high, and (b) the competitors enter the contest from positions of structural equality. Indeed, the competition is designed to end a period of egalitarianism that existed from the creation at Acoma and came into existence in Persia when the imposter-king was deposed. Although some characters valued and enjoyed that situation of equity (Otanes, Nautsiti), it proved problematic to others, who successfully pressed for its termination. That being accomplished, none of the characters—who were still structural equals—had any compelling way to claim or dependable means to win primacy for him- or herself. As a result, those who in this moment became rivals, as well as equals, agreed to seek divine intervention so that one could be set legitimately and incontrovertibly above the others. (As a side note, one should observe the implicit gender hierarchy present even in the egalitarian imaginary, all the competitors being men among the patriarchal Persians and women at matrilineal Acoma.)[33]

Notwithstanding the attempt to let a deity resolve the question of rank, the Acoma myth—like both variants of the Persian story Herodotus collected—tells that one competitor was sufficiently ambitious and unscrupulous to subvert the contest with the help of a shrewd and lowly outsider. And just as Darius, the man who made the case for monarchy, was the one who sought help from his cheating groom, so Iatiku, the sister who first claimed to be elder, was the one who did the same with Magpie. One can interpret this point in terms of individual psychology and ethics, observing that the characters who introduce hierarchy show a certain ruthlessness in their desire to benefit from it, which they justify by imputing the same quality to their rivals ("Iatiku was afraid that her sister was going to get the better of her"). At a deeper level, the narratives suggest that the injustice inherent in hierarchy elicits aggression and unscrupulousness in those who enter a system where the most ruthless actors are most likely to rise to the top.

Two points of difference can be recognized in the narratives, however. Whereas the Persian story shows Darius's rivals as having accepted his kingship without resentment or further contestation, the Acoma describe Nautsiti as "very angry because she had hoped to win."[34] As the story continues, her attitude and behavior were far from the gracious submission shown by the Persian nobles.

> Now the sisters were thinking selfish thoughts. Nautsiti schemed to get the better of her sister. She often wandered off, making plans to outdo Iatiku, but Iatiku watched her and noticed everything.[35]

The second difference concerns the fate of the trickster whose guile produced the victory. Thus, Darius is described as having gratefully acknowledged Oibares's assistance in an inscription that read "Darius, son of Hystaspes, with the help of his horse's excellence and that of his groom Oibares, acquired kingship of the Persians."[36] In contrast, Iatiku ordered Magpie to keep her role secret and punished the bird, who had interrupted her sunward flight to eat the flesh of a dead deer. This momentary dereliction of duty resulted in a lasting physical-*cum*-moral stain, whereby she—and not Iatiku—bore the guilt for having reduced Nautsiti from a position of equity to one of subordination.

> Iatiku, who did not want her sister to know about the trick she had used, whispered to the bird when it returned from the east, telling it not to say anything, and she also punished the bird for disobeying her. So she said

Table 12.3. Relations between the stories of Darius's accession and Iatiku's seniority

| | Herodotus 3.84.3–87.1 | Acoma Origin Myth (Stirling, 11–12) |
|---|---|---|
| **Initial situation of unstable equality** | Seven conspirators overthrow an imposter and agree to reestablish the monarchy, but have no basis to decide who will be king | Two sisters emerge from the earth together and are uncertain who is the elder |
| **Solar divination as the means to establish rank** | The conspirators agree that when the sun's rays first cause one horse to whinny, its owner will be king | The sisters agree that when the sun's rays first touch one of them, she will be recognized as elder |
| **Subversion of the method** | Darius gets his groom to sexually arouse his horse, causing him to whinny first | Iatiku gets Magipe to block the sun's northern rays, which otherwise would have fallen first on Nautsiti |
| **Results for the competitors** | Darius becomes king; in one variant, he is recognized by the heavens and the other contestants | Iatiku is recognized as senior; Nautsiti becomes angry and seeks to outdo her sister in some other way |
| **Results for the trickster** | Oibares is honored in a royal inscription | Magpie is ordered to stay silent; colors change from white to spotted, bloody, and dirty; turns from hunter to despicable carrion scavenger |

to it, "For stopping and eating you will not know from now on how to kill your own meat. You will not be a hunter, you will eat what others have killed and left, and most of the time you will eat what is spoiled. Your color also will be spotted from now on, you will not be as white as you were at first."[37]

The common and divergent features of the two narratives can be represented as in table 12.3.

## IV

The point of departure for the two narratives is the recognition that since perfect equality is hard to sustain, the introduction of hierarchy comes to be seen as desirable. For hierarchy to be accepted as legitimate, however, it is best that it enter the human from above and beyond, so that the distinctions of rank that will henceforward set one person above others are understood to have been introduced by divine powers. In this moment, the asymmetric relation of gods to humans provides both the template and the justification for hierarchy.[38]

Accordingly, those who desire to establish hierarchies regularly seek divine support for their initiative and may even do so in good faith. But the divine being available only in mediated fashion, what they actually seek is *signs* of divine election or favor, all of which are open to subversion by the unprincipled, ingenious, and ambitious. That being the case, whatever results may be obtained in this fashion are likely to be less conclusive than anticipated, since those dissatisfied with the results can always find grounds for suspicion and disputation.

In Herodotus's account, most of Darius's rivals accepted his accession without complaint, although one of the six voiced principled objections before the fact and one staged a misguided protest on a later occasion. Thus, as we have seen, Otanes negotiated an arrangement whereby he opted out of competition for the kingship on condition that he and his family would never have to submit to the king, only to Persian law.[39] All the other conspirators accepted Darius's election happily enough, rose to prominent positions, and were granted unique privileges.[40] Attempting to exercise these, however, one of their number challenged the king in ways that revealed lingering envy and resentment.

The privilege in question granted the six nobles direct access to the king at all times, except when he was in bed with a woman. When Intaphernes sought to exercise this right, however, royal gatekeepers asked him to wait until the king finished his lovemaking. Certain they were lying—the worst offense any Persian could commit and the gravest charge any Persian could level, here implicitly aimed at the king[41]—he assaulted the guards, inflicted disfiguring wounds on them, then boasted of what he had done.[42] When the king learned of this, he judged Intaphernes' violence to be rebellious and suspected all six nobles of plotting against him. Under questioning, the others assured Darius of their loyalty, at which point he had Intaphernes executed, along with most of his family.[43]

The scorecard is thus decidedly mixed, as shown in table 12.4.[44] Two-thirds of the group accepted the new hierarchy and their position in it without apparent problem. One individual rejected the system on principle, but negotiated terms that made it acceptable in practice. The last noble Persian, however—whom other sources treat as the group's foremost member[45]—reacted to the asymmetry of his relation to the king with such violence that he brought suspicion on the whole group and provoked a crisis that was resolved only with his elimination from Persian society.

Table 12.4. Darius's relations with his coconspirators after becoming king

| Herodotus's Six Noble Persians | Old Persian Names (Bisitun §68) | Attitude toward Darius's Preeminence, as Reported by Herodotus | Fate, as Reported by Herodotus | Fate, as Attested in Darius's Inscriptions |
|---|---|---|---|---|
| **Otanes** | Utāna | Rejects kingship, refuses to compete for the throne (3.83.2) | Retains freedom and insures that of descendants (3.83.2–3) | Descendants will be cared for (Bisitun §69) |
| **Gobryas** | Gaubaruva | Prostrates himself before Darius, accepting him as king (3.86.2) | Becomes adviser to Darius and commander in his army (4.132.2–135.1) | Commander in army (Bisitun inscription §71); Darius's spear-bearer (Naqš-i Rustam); descendants cared for (Bisitun §69) |
| **Aspathines** | Ardimaniš or Aspacanah[1] | Prostrates himself before Darius, accepting him as king (3.86.2) | Son becomes admiral in Xerxes's navy (7.97) | (a) Descendants cared for (Bisitun §69) (b) Darius's bow-bearer (Naqš-i Rustam) |
| **Megabyzus** | Bagabuxša | Prostrates himself before Darius, accepting him as king (3.86.2) | Son recaptures Babylon, earning Darius's gratitude (3.153.1–160.2) | Descendants cared for (Bisitun §69) |

(continued)

Table 12.4. (*continued*)

| Herodotus's Six Noble Persians | Old Persian Names (Bisitun §68) | Attitude toward Darius's Preeminence, as Reported by Herodotus | Fate, as Reported by Herodotus | Fate, as Attested in Darius's Inscriptions |
|---|---|---|---|---|
| Hydarnes | Vidr̥na | Prostrates himself before Darius, accepting him as king (3.86.2) | Son becomes commander in Darius's army (7.66.1) | Commander in army (Bisitun §25); descendants cared for (Bisitun §69) |
| Intaphernes | Vindafarnah | Prostrates himself before Darius, accepting him as king (3.86.2); mistakenly disputes an abridgment of his privileges (3.118.1–2); charges Darius's guards with falsehood, assaults, and disfigures them (3.118.2) | Darius suspects him of rebellion, has him and his sons executed (3.119.1–7) | Commander in army (Bisitun §50); descendants cared for (Bisitun §69) |

1 This is the sole point where Herodotus's list of conspirators differs from that which Darius provides at Bisitun §68. There, Ardumaniš stands in the place of Herodotus's Aspathines, whose name matches that of Aspacanah, whom Darius mentions at Naqš-i Rustam.

## V

The story of Intaphernes reveals the tension and potentially explosive resentment that are part of any hierarchic system, alongside the relative contentment, good relations, and good order represented by the other noble Persians. Having a much smaller set of characters, the Acoma emergence myth focuses exclusively on the destabilizing aspects of hierarchy, while developing a more poignant, if less violent narrative arc.

After Iatiku's victory, we are told that relations between the sisters worsened. Both became selfish. Nautsiti turned resentful and sought to avoid her sister, a development Iatiku watched with regret and apprehension.[46] Lonely, unhappy, and seeking to outdo her sister in some unanticipated fashion, Nautsiti took advice from the serpent and conceived twin sons by the rainbow, notwithstanding the Creator's instruction that the sisters postpone engaging in sexual relations. Angered at this transgression, the deity withdrew from contact with humans.[47] After a brief period of relative calm, there followed a second disjuncture.

> Nautsiti said to Iatiku, "We are not happy together. Let us share what we have in our baskets and separate. I still have many things. These animals in my basket, these sheep and cattle I will share with you, but it is understood that these animals will demand much care." Iatiku answered that it would be too hard a task to care for them and that she did not want her children to have them. Nautsiti also pointed out some seeds and told Iatiku to take some of them. They were seeds of wheat and vegetables. Nautsiti knew also that these were going to be hard to raise, but she wanted to share them with Iatiku. But Iatiku again did not want them for her children. In Nautsiti's basket, too, there were many metals. She offered to share these, but Iatiku did not take any. When Nautsiti had looked this far into her basket she found something written. Nautsiti also offered this, but Iatiku did not want it. Nautsiti said, "There are still many things that are very good for foods in my basket but I know that all of these things will require much care. Why is it, sister, that you are not thankful, why do you not take some of the things I have offered? I am going to leave you. We both understand that we are to increase our kind, and in a long time to come we shall meet again and then you will be wearing clothes. We shall still be sisters, for we have the same father, but I shall have the better of you again. I am going away into the East."[48]

With that, Nautsiti disappears from the story, leaving behind Tiamuni, the son she did not like, whom Iatiku raised, then took as her mate.[49] Each child born of that union founds a new Acoma clan, and Iatiku goes on to

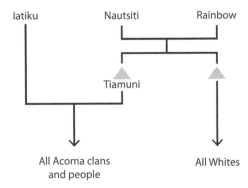

Figure 12.1. Descent of Acoma and whites from Iatiku and Nautsiti.

establish all the core institutions that define Acoma religion and culture thereafter.[50]

The competition of Iatiku and Nautsiti thus produces a schism whereby one small, intimate, family group suffers lasting estrangement, morphing into two radically different peoples who live at opposite ends of a vast continent, further separated by culture, religion, and ethnicity. Over many generations, the differences between the two groups only increase, as Nautsiti's distinctive qualities—restlessness, ambition, innovation, curiosity, adventurousness, quickness of thought, and sexual immodesty—lead her descendants to become much more numerous, wealthy, and powerful than those of her more faithful, cautious, and hardworking sister. This divergence notwithstanding, the primordial unity of the sisters remains latent in Iatiku's offspring, who descend from both their mother and their aunt, the latter via Tiamuni, Nautsiti's discarded son (figure 12.1).[51] Nautsiti's descendants by her second son, in contrast, preserve that unity neither in their bodies nor in their memories, having lost all connection with Iatiku, lacking the good qualities associated with her, and never having received the components of Acoma ceremonial life that Iatiku established after her sister's departure (table 12.5).

## VI

Pueblo Indians needed no help in understanding the import of their primordial ancestors' separation, nor of the promise-*cum*-threat Nautsiti spoke on that occasion: "In a long time to come we shall meet again and then you will be wearing clothes. We shall still be sisters, for we have the same father, *but I shall have the better of you again.*"[52] By 1928, when this myth was recorded, Nautsiti's descendants had not only returned to the West, they had done so in sufficient numbers and with sufficient economic, material,

Table 12.5. Differences between the two sisters Iatiku and Nautsiti (and their descendants)

|  | Iatiku | Nautsiti |
|---|---|---|
| **Distinctive physical traits** | Weaker eyes<br>Darker skin<br>Right-handed | Stronger eyes<br>Lighter skin |
| **Distinctive mental qualities** | Slower mind | Faster mind |
| **Distinctive material possessions** | Corn | Sheep<br>Cattle<br>Wheat<br>Vegetables<br>Metals<br>"Something written" |
| **Distinctive moral qualities** | Industriousness<br>Care in handling corn<br>Hesitation to satisfy her appetites<br>Desire to see things grow<br>Fear of her sister's competitiveness<br>and scheming ambition<br>Communal responsibility<br>and surveillance<br>Modesty<br>Obedience<br>Sexual reserve<br>Disinterest in accepting | A little laziness<br>Roughness in handling corn<br>Eagerness to satisfy her appetites<br>Selfishness<br>Competitiveness<br>Scheming ambition<br>Independence<br>Individualism<br>Vulnerability to temptation<br>Disobedience<br>Sexual adventurousness<br>Willingness to give |
| **Distinctive ceremonial items, institutions, and practices** | Prayers to spirits of the four quarters<br>Katsinas<br>Pueblo with central plaza<br>Altars<br>Prayer sticks<br>Masks<br>Kivas<br>Hunters' societies and fetishes<br>War chief<br>Country chief<br>Sand paintings<br>Medicine societies<br>Medicine and medicine bowls<br>Drum and rattle<br>Corn fetish<br>Koshari ritual clowns<br>Rules and etiquette for all ceremonies<br>Songs<br>Initiation rituals<br>Public dances | |

and military advantages to overwhelm the cousins whom they no longer recognized as such.

Hierarchy entered the world with Iatiku's dubious claim of seniority and her dishonest victory in the competition for a solar omen. With it came few benefits. In the short run, it brought resentment, envy, spoiled relations, and schism. In the long run, things became even worse, as her people suffered political domination, territorial expropriation, and a condescending paternalism from people whom they regarded as younger siblings who had become their material and numerical superiors, while remaining their moral and religious inferiors.[53]

It is here that the Acoma myth and the Persian story differ most sharply. Nowhere is there a suggestion that the hierarchic order established with Darius's kingship backfired on him or the other Persians (save the unfortunate Intaphernes). Nowhere do the victors or their descendants show remorse or regret, suffer ill effects, or seek to reverse what was done. The point is significant, and we will pursue it in the next chapter. For now, however, it is useful to summarize what the two narratives have in common.

To begin, both explore the nature of hierarchy, describing how it emerged from an earlier egalitarian situation with which some actors, but not all, came to be dissatisfied. Once again, a psychological reading of their dissatisfaction is possible, but inadequate. Rather than stressing Darius's ambition or Iatiku's insecurity as motivating factors, the narratives use these particularities to make a deeper, more interesting point. However equitable the distribution of wealth, power, status, and other conditions may be in a given social order, if the people who participate in that order are not equally satisfied, this imbalance of contentment constitutes a contradiction within egalitarianism—an inequity inside of and reacting to equity—that makes it unstable and ultimately nonviable.

That being the case, a transition to hierarchy must follow, and the two narratives pursue the questions that inevitably arise. Most important of these is not "What precise kind of hierarchy?" for which each story supplies its own specifics (kingship supported by nobles in Persia; seniority among kin at Acoma). Much more significant is the question on which the stories agree: "How can a hierarchic order (of whatever sort) be introduced and established?" As we have seen, both suggest this is best done through divine intervention, while making clear that actual practice falls far from that ideal. Rather than obtaining actual divine guidance, the proponents of hierarchy in both stories find ways—in fact, the same way—to produce a sign legible as an expression of the divine will, but open to manipulation, so that they can be sure to benefit from the system they introduce. Notwithstanding the claims, perhaps also the beliefs of its champions, both stories show hierarchy to be founded on deception and guile, a state of affairs that leaves it ever open to doubt, suspicion, and contestation. Internally contradictory, for it is not what it represents itself to be, hierarchy is therefore as unstable and nonviable as the egalitarianism it displaced.

This leads to one last point. Although myths regularly serve to naturalize, sacralize, and/or legitimate the institutions whose origins they narrate, the two narratives we have considered do the reverse. Quite openly—also quite brilliantly—they stress the artificiality of the institutions they treat, and that in the most literal sense, for they reveal the artifices through which interested and deeply flawed human actors conspired to bring such hierarchic systems as kingship, seniority among siblings, and ethnic division into existence through corrupt and deceitful means.

# 13: IN HIERARCHY'S WAKE

I

For all their similarities, the narratives considered in the last chapter differ sharply in the long-term consequences of their solar contests. Thus, Darius profited handsomely from his cheating, and his progeny ruled Asia for another two centuries, while Iatiku's backfired terribly, as her people came to be dominated, exploited, and held in contempt by Nautsiti's descendants. In a passage we have yet to consider, the text makes clear that Iatiku anticipated at least some of the troubles to come and suffered sharp and immediate regret at the loss of her sister.

To appreciate the importance of this passage, one needs to recognize that the text we have been considering is not "the" Acoma origin myth, but one variant, and an atypical one at that. The version available to those outside the Acoma community, from which I quoted, was collected under extraordinary circumstances (of which more later), and has been published in three different editions (1930, 1942, and 2015). Those texts provide a convenient starting point for an inquiry that leads further.

The three published versions of the Acoma text give much the same information about how it was obtained, each in succession revealing more. Thus, in his article of 1930, Daryll Forde (1902–73) briefly identified his sources.

> The following creation story was obtained from a party of Indians from the Pueblo of Acoma visiting the Bureau of American Ethnology, Washington, D.C., in August 1928. The myth was told in Keresan by the old man of the party and translated by one of his sons.[1]

Forde published only the myth's first sections, including the solar episode, and it took another twelve years before Matthew W. Stirling (1896–1975) brought out a monograph with the full text, having received additional help on the project from Elsie Clews Parsons (1875–1941) and Leslie A. White (1900–75).[2] In his preface to the volume that resulted from this collaboration, Stirling expanded on—and at two points contradicted—the information Forde had given.

> The following information was obtained in *September and October* of 1928 from a group of Pueblo Indians from Acoma *and Santa Ana* visiting Washington. The Acoma origin and migration myth is presented as it was learned by the chief informant during his initiation in youth into the Koshari, the group of sacred clowns to whom theoretically all religious secrets are divulged.[3]

In 2015, Peter Nabokov's painstaking research let him resolve the dissonance between the earlier accounts, establishing that the group presented themselves at the Smithsonian in late August 1928, then worked with Forde, Stirling, and others through October.[4] The group included four family members from Acoma—Edward Proctor Hunt (whose Keresan name was Gaire, "Daybreak"), his wife, Marie ("Morning Star") Valle Hunt, their sons Henry Wayne ("Wolf Robe") Hunt and Wilbert Edward ("Blue Sky Eagle") Hunt—and the Hunts' adoptive son Philip ("Silvertongue") Sanchez, who was originally from Santa Ana Pueblo.

Nabokov confirmed that Edward Hunt (1861–1948) was the chief narrator and had been initiated into the Koshari society, although he backs away from Hunt's sweeping claim that this gave him access to "all religious secrets."[5] Although Hunt sought to establish that his knowledge of esoteric lore was full and authoritative, his relation to Acoma tradition was much more troubled and complex than Stirling and his colleagues realized. Far from being a traditionalist, at the age of nineteen Hunt made the virtually unprecedented choice to leave his pueblo for education at the Duranes Indian School, a thoroughly paternalistic institution designed to "civilize" young Indians and facilitate their assimilation to white culture.[6] Over the course of three years (1880–83), the school worked on his body and his consciousness with considerable success, providing him with new clothes, skills, habits, values, and orientations, also the name he found inscribed in a secondhand Bible and thereafter took as his own.[7] The synthetic, interstitial, and conflicted nature of his religious and cultural identity are evident in a dream he related to Leslie White.

> A man of about 50 told me the following: He "did not believe in" the kachinas or the medicine men; he thought he believed in Cristo. One night he had a dream. He dreamed he had died and had gone to heaven. He found himself before God. He could not remember exactly how God looked, but he seemed to resemble in appearance and dress a successful American business man. He was in an office, seated behind a desk "just

like in a bank." The Indian stood before God at his desk. God asked him, "Where's your license?" (meaning, "Where is the sign that you have the right to enter heaven?"). The Indian had a Bible and showed it to God. God said, "No, that's not your license. This is your license," and he showed the Indian a prayer stick. God told him that the Bible was the white man's license. Then the Indian looked around and he saw different kinds of Indians there; some were Apaches, some Pueblos. God told him that the prayer stick was the Indian's license. I tried to learn what the Indian thought and felt about his dream, but it was very difficult. He said he didn't know, but that he guessed the dream was right; he seemed to feel that the white man's things were for the white man and the Indian had his own things.[8]

Upon returning to his pueblo, Hunt established himself as one of its leading progressives and as such, a controversial figure. Ultimately, his unwillingness to shoulder ritual responsibilities or have his children initiated led to his expulsion from Acoma (1918). After residing at Santa Ana Pueblo for some years, he and his family were expelled once again for the same reasons (1924), after which they lived in Albuquerque (1925–26) and toured with the Miller Brothers' Wild West show (1927–28), before presenting themselves at the Smithsonian.[9] To describe Hunt as being "from Acoma" without further explanation, as Forde and Stirling did, is technically correct, but veils the tortuous nature of his relation to the pueblo and its traditions.

Nabokov's research not only let him delineate these complexities; it also let him restore eleven of the seventy songs Philip Sanchez chanted to accompany Edward Hunt's narration. Although Stirling made mention of these songs, all of which were recorded on wax cylinders and stored in the Smithsonian's archives,[10] neither he nor Forde included them in their publications, despite the fact that the characters in Hunt's narrative are repeatedly described as singing songs that Sanchez would have supplied. The descriptions make clear, moreover, that consistent with pueblo traditions, the power present in the rhythms, melodies, and vibrations of these songs was understood to have activated creation in the first instance and sustained it with each repetition.[11] According to Nabokov, Hunt regarded these songs as "integral accompaniments to his story . . . whose function was to rekindle, in words and incantations, the same magical forces that brought to life each element in the world's creation before the dawn of time."[12]

As Hunt recounted, initially the sisters chanted these songs together, beginning with "the creation song" taught them by Tsichtinako, their divine instructor,[13] then the songs through which they animated the sun, moon, rainbow, and stars; corn and plants; small animals and game.[14] The first solo, however, represents a dramatic break with all the creative activity that came before. This is the song Iatiku performed "as a plea to her sister"[15] when Nautsiti announced her intention of departing.

Nautsiti, why are you crying?
No one [over there] wants to be related to you.
No one [over there] wants you to help in offerings.
Do not cry anymore.
Come back soon.
Iatiku wants to be your relative.
Iatiku needs you to help in offerings.
Do not cry anymore.[16]

Although Iatiku begins by imagining that her sister will find herself isolated and miserable in the far-off East, this is a reflection (and projection) of the loneliness and sorrow she herself feels. In her plaintive cry—"Come back soon. Iatiku wants to be your relative. Iatiku needs you to help in offerings"—we hear the remorse of a victor belatedly recognizing that her victory means the loss not only of her sister, but of the mutual support, affection, and respect the two of them previously enjoyed.

Just as Nautsiti tried to share the objects that gave her material advantage (cattle, wheat, metals, books, et al.), here Iatiku does the same with the sacred ceremonies that constitute her spiritual edge. Were both sisters able to accept their sibling's offer, they would become whole and equal. Such reconciliation was not possible, however, as neither could acknowledge the value and generosity of what the other one offered. And when Nautsiti contemplated the future, it was not equality she imagined, but a reversal of their newly established hierarchic relations.

In a long time to come we shall meet again and then you will be wearing clothes. We shall still be sisters, for we have the same father, *but I shall have the better of you again.*[17]

An artificial and offensive inequity, its establishment through guile, loser's resentment, victor's regret, and an inability to make amends result in a great distance that opens between the sisters, simultaneously spatial, emotional, cultural, and hierarchic. Together, these constitute the problem that haunts all subsequent generations. It is, moreover, the problem Edward Hunt sought to address (and redress) when he presented himself at the Smithsonian.

II

Although Hunt had never attempted something of this sort, he had a good deal of experience serving as an informant to anthropologists, government officials, and interested others, which let him formulate his plan to visit the Smithsonian with the expectation he would be well received and his gift would be appreciated.[18] In this, he was not mistaken. Subsequent to its publication by Forde and Stirling, the myth he narrated has been excerpted, paraphrased, studied, and hailed as a classic in various anthologies, novels, and scholarly volumes.[19] It has not met with the same reception at home, however, where Hunt was regarded with considerable suspicion. Feelings run strong to this day, as evidenced by the reaction of Fred S. Vallo Sr., governor of Acoma Pueblo, to Nabokov's republication of Hunt's text.

> Hunt never had the permission of the pueblo to impart any Acoma sacred information to anyone, much less to the Bureau of Ethnology for publication. The pueblo has always considered this publication by the Bureau of Ethnology to be a fundamental breach of trust by the United States. . . . *The Origin Myth of the Pueblo of Acoma* is the intellectual property of the pueblo, not the property of the United States, and surely not the property of Hunt or Nabokov to reproduce. The pueblo today has grave uncertainty as to Hunt's actual knowledge about Acoma beliefs, as he left the pueblo at an early age to attend school, and chose not to participate in the activities where traditional knowledge is passed on to the younger generations. This concern is strengthened by the many inaccuracies in the book.[20]

Vallo raises two objections: first, neither Hunt nor anyone else has the right to disclose the pueblo's sacred traditions without its consent; second, Hunt was not sufficiently knowledgeable to present this material accurately. The first is a point of principle not open to factual dispute, save on the question of whether Hunt sought or received the pueblo's authorization. Having been expelled from Acoma ten years earlier, this was surely not the case. The second point is difficult for an outsider to judge. If non-Acoma seek to identify the "many inaccuracies" to which Gov. Vallo alludes, the sole method available is to compare Hunt's text to other published versions of Acoma origins, of which there are only a few, none authorized by the pueblo and all much shorter than Hunt's. Most important is the one Leslie A. White, foremost ethnographer of the Keresan pueblos,[21] took to be normative.

Strikingly, neither in White's text nor in any of the published variants—save those traceable to Hunt—does one find any mention of Nautsiti, a quarrel between primordial sisters, a rigged contest to determine seniority, hurt feelings, departures, schisms, or lasting estrangement between descendants of the old rivals. Rather, in these variants, no ancestor appears alongside Iatiku, and no people other than those of the pueblo.

> They came out of the earth, from Iatiku, the mother. They crawled out like grasshoppers; their bodies were naked and soft. It was all dark; the sun had not yet risen. All of the little people had their eyes closed; they hadn't opened them yet. Iatiku lined them all up in a row, facing east. Then she had the sun come up. When it came up and shone on the babies' eyes they opened. They crawled around. In eight days they were bigger and stronger. They walk around now. There was a lake at Shipap. There was an island in the center of the lake, and there was a building on the island. Iatiku left her people when they got big enough to take care of themselves and went to live in this building. Before she went she told the people how to get food to eat. She also told them about the katsina who lived out west at Wenimats. She told them that the katsina would come to dance for them. She told the people that they must respect these spirits, for they were very powerful. Iatiku told her children to multiply and to teach their children to live as Iatiku wished. She said that she would always be near them to help them and to take care of them.[22]

White collected this text in 1926, during his pioneer fieldwork at Acoma. During this same period, he spoke frequently with Edward Hunt,[23] who was then residing at Albuquerque. When Hunt told him a shorter version of his Nautsiti story, it deviated so sharply from the accounts White obtained from his other Acoma informants, he was led to conclude, "I feel this particular version is largely the product of some individual fancy, perhaps the informant's."[24] An individual product, no doubt, but hardly fanciful or idiosyncratic. Rather, Hunt's variant skillfully reworked the mythic traditions of other pueblos, as well as those of Acoma, in ways that reflected, spoke to, and took advantage of his own interstitial situation.

### III

This is the variant Leslie White obtained from Hunt in Albuquerque, two years before the Hunts made their way to the Smithsonian.

> One night Uchtsiti [the Creator] gave the two sisters all kinds of fruits, vegetables, game, sheep, etc. It was all in a basket. There was a book in the basket. When the sisters woke up in the morning they found the basket. Nautsiti said, "Oh, look; this is our present from Uchtsiti. We will divide all the things." Nautsiti told Iatiku to pick out the things she wanted. So Iatiku picked out the wild game and the wild plants, things that grew by

themselves. The animals and plants that had to be planted and tended in order to grow she left to Nautsiti. Then Nautsiti offered the book to Iatiku, but Iatiku didn't want the book; she thought it would be too much trouble to read it. Then they called all the people together and told them to choose between the two sisters. Most of the people went with Iatiku; only a few went with Nautsiti. But Nautsiti told Iatiku that she was making a mistake. "You don't want to work," she told Iatiku, "but some day you may want what I have. I will get the best of you yet," she said. Then Nautsiti went to the east. She became the mother of the white people (who later came back to the land of the Indians). Iatiku was the mother of the Indians.[25]

Although the general argument of this variant is consistent with the version Hunt offered at the Smithsonian, it differs from the latter on the following points.

- There is only one basket, not two.
- Each sister chooses what she wants from the basket, and no goods are held in common,
- Particular emphasis is placed on possession of "the book."
- There is no contestation over seniority and no use of the sun to resolve this dispute.
- Magpie does not appear, and there is no question of trickery.
- There is no account of how subsequent humans came to be born; rather, a population already exists at the time of emergence, whose members will choose between the sisters.
- Iatiku does not claim to be elder, nor is she is recognized as such; rather, her superiority comes when she acquires more followers.
- Iatiku is mother of all Indians, not just the Acoma or Pueblo.
- Nautsiti charges Iatiku with laziness, which will let Nautsiti surpass her.
- Iatiku does not sing, nor does she show any sign of regret.

Apparently, the 1926 text constitutes an early draft of the version Hunt delivered to the Smithsonian, in which Nautsiti figures so prominently. It is impossible to say where, when, and how he got the idea to introduce this character into the Acoma traditions from which she was previously absent. As we will see, Nautsiti appears in the emergence myth told at other Keresan pueblos, to which Hunt was exposed on at least one occasion and probably numerous others. Thus, Nabokov records the following incident during Hunt's residence at Santa Ana (ca. 1922).

He was called on the carpet by Santa Ana's newly appointed conservative governor, who held progressives like the Hunts in low regard. "They stood me in the center of the Santa Ana Pueblo meeting house," Hunt remembered, where he was surrounded by community elders. What were his religious beliefs back at Acoma? they wanted to know. "I did all the old initiations and rituals," he replied. Then why not perform them here as well? they asked. . . . When another Santa Anan was more sympathetic, reminding everyone of a painting in their Catholic church that sympathetically portrayed Nautsiti, one of their mythic spirits, as the "mother of whites," he was told to be quiet. The mood forbade any accommodation between Indian and Anglo lifeways.[26]

There is much one could say about this meeting, which wrestled with the problem of whether Hunt was or could be a proper part of Santa Ana, setting in motion the processes that led to his expulsion from the pueblo.[27] The chief point of interest at present, however, is a minor detail. In a moment when the alterity of Indian and white was being construed as near-absolute, a sympathetic member of the pueblo compared Hunt favorably to Nautsiti, whom he—but apparently not all others—considered worthy of tolerance and respect as a figure who mediated the great divide.

## IV

If the more traditional variants of Acoma emergence mythology focus exclusively on Iatiku, this is not so at Santa Ana and several other Keresan pueblos. There, as indicated in table 13.1, the story regularly takes one of two forms. In one—current at Acoma, Santo Domingo, and San Felipe—there is one ancestor only, who emerges from underground and establishes the norms for her people. In all cases, she bears the name Iatik(u). In the other, which is found at Laguna, Cochiti, Santa Ana, and Sia, the creator appears, named Tsi(yo)stinako, along with two primordial sisters, one of whom becomes ancestor of the pueblos (or of Native Americans more broadly), while the other becomes ancestor of a rival people: most often whites, but sometimes the Navajo or "other nations" in general. The names of these two sisters are consistent everywhere (although reversed at Laguna),[28] and their common ending underscores the close relation between Ure-tsiti and Nao-tsiti, Utc-tsityi and Nau-tsityi, etc.

Strikingly, the names Edward Hunt gave his characters not only differ from the Acoma norm, but from what one finds in all other Keresan pueblos. Apparently, he adopted the two-sister pattern, but modified it by inserting the name Iatiku (elsewhere found only in the one ancestress pattern) in place of Utctsiti. The latter name he displaced to the Creator, whose usual name (Tsitsinako) he gave to the sisters' instructress (a role attested nowhere else, although Santa Ana has a mediating figure (named Iatik) with

Table 13.1. Characters in the emergence myths of the Keresan-speaking pueblos

| | Creator | Instructress | Indian Ancestor | Other Ancestor |
|---|---|---|---|---|
| **Acoma**[1] | | | Iatiku | |
| **Laguna**[2] | Tsitsinako | | Nautsiti | Itctsityi |
| **Cochiti**[3] | | | Uretsiti | Naotsiti |
| **S. Domingo**[4] | | | Iatik | |
| **San Felipe**[5] | | | Iatiku | |
| **Santa Ana**[6] | Tsiyostinako | (Iatik) | Utctsityi | Nautsityi |
| **Sia**[7] | Tsiyostinako | | Utctsiti | Naotsiti |
| **E. Hunt**[8] | Uchtsiti | Tshitinako | Iatiku | Nautsiti |

1 As recorded by White, "The Acoma Indians," 142–47.

2 As recorded by Boas, "Keresan Texts," 5–7 and 224–26; cf. Parsons, "Notes on Ceremonialism at Laguna," 95–97 and 114–15.

3 As recorded by Benedict, "Tales of the Cochiti Indians," 1–2; cf. Dumarest, "Notes on Cochiti, New Mexico," 212–15

4 As recorded by White, "The Pueblo of Santo Domingo, New Mexico," 29.

5 As recorded by White, "The Pueblo of San Felipe," 43.

6 As recorded by White, "The Pueblo of Santa Ana, New Mexico," 87.

7 As recorded by White, "The Pueblo of Sia, New Mexico," 113 and 115–21; cf. Stevenson, "The Sia," 26–34.

8 As recorded by Forde, "A Creation Myth"; Stirling, *Origin Myth;* and Hunt, *Origin Myth.*

some similarities). The text Hunt produced was thus neither strictly traditional nor radically innovative, but a bricolage that creatively reworked preexisting elements and a preexisting structure.

V

Within the two-sister pattern, further variations distinguish the way the story is told at Santa Ana from the variants collected at Laguna, Cochiti, and Sia pueblos. It is the latter that Hunt's version most closely resembles, although at some points he departs significantly from the model they provided (table 13.2). In all versions, the story begins with a situation of rough equality, in which one sister has a quantitative advantage (she is taller in Laguna A and B, Cochiti A and B, and Sia A; elder in Cochiti A and Sia A) offset by her sister's qualitative superiority (more generous in Laguna B; free of jealousy in Cochiti A; free of boasting in Cochiti B; better mind and heart in Sia A). Sia B makes this point in a way that differs from all others,

Table 13.2. Keresan pueblo myths of rivalry and schism between two primordial sisters

| | Initial Situation of Unstable Equality | Challenge | Victor | Cheating | Results |
|---|---|---|---|---|---|
| **Laguna Variant A[1]** | Primacy uncertain; Father of Whites (Itctsityi) taller | Father of Whites claims to be first | (a) Sun shines on Father of Whites<br>(b) Number of people inconclusive<br>(c) In stick game, rains kill white children, revived by Mother of Indians (Nautsiti) | | Mother of Indians recognized as more powerful, goes to Laguna; Father of Whites goes east; prediction that all will prosper |
| **Laguna Variant B[2]** | Relative power uncertain; Father of Whites (Itctsityi) taller | Father of Whites claims to have more power | (a) Sun shines on Mother of Indians (Nautsiti)<br>(b) Mother of Indians wins test of weapons<br>(c) In footrace, rains kill white children, revived by Mother of Indians | | Mother of Indians recognized as more powerful; Father of Whites and his children go east, predicting reversal of their status |

(continued)

Table 13.2. (*continued*)

| | Initial Situation of Unstable Equality | Challenge | Victor | Cheating | Results |
|---|---|---|---|---|---|
| **Cochiti Variant A**[3] | Mother of Whites (Naotsete) elder and bigger, but jealous of younger sister | Mother of Whites challenges right to inhabit the south | (a) Mother of Indians (Uretsete) wins guessing contest<br>(b) Sun shines on Mother of Indians | Spider (Creator) sends Magpie to shade sun's rays | Mother of Indians kills Mother of Whites and tears out her heart; squirrel and dove come from her body; Mother of Indians withdraws, counsels against disputes |
| **Cochiti Variant B**[4] | Mother of Navajo (Naotsiti) taller; Mother of Pueblos (Uretsiti) elder | Mother of Navajo challenges who is greater and whose children have value | Sun shines on Mother of Pueblos | | Mother of Pueblos changes Mother of Navajo into wood rat; pueblos safe, win fights with Navajo |
| **Sia Variant A**[5] | Mother of Other Nations (Nowutset) elder and bigger; Mother of Indians (Utset) better in mind and heart | Mother of Other Nations challenges Mother of Indians (Utset) to a guessing contest | (a) Mother of Indians wins guessing contest<br>(b) Sun shines on Mother of Indians | Mother of Indians sends bird to shade sun's rays | Indians conquer rivals; Mother of Indians kills Mother of Other Nations, cuts her heart out and turns pieces into rats |

| | | | | |
|---|---|---|---|---|
| **Sia Variant B**[6] | Things created by Mother of Whites (Naotsiti) more wonderful (e.g., paper that talks) | The sisters decide on competition to determine whose power is greater | (a) Mother of Indians (Utctsiti) wins guessing contest<br>(b) Mother of Indians wins test of weapons<br>(c) Sun shines on Mother of Indians | Magpie shades sun's rays | Mother of Whites flees, turns herself into wood rat |
| **Edward Hunt**[7] | Birth order uncertain; Mother of Indians (Iatiku) darker skin, slower thought | Mother of Indians claims to be elder | Sun shines on Mother of Indians | Mother of Indians sends Magpie to shade sun's rays | Mother of Indians recognized as elder; Mother of Whites (Nautsiti) goes east, predicting reversal of their status |

1 As narrated by Gyimi in 1919 and recorded by Boas, *Keresan Texts*, 5–7.

2 As narrated by Pedro Martín in 1919 and recorded by Boas, *Keresan Texts*, 224–26.

3 As collected by Father Noël Dumarest between 1894 and 1900 and published in his posthumous "Notes on Cochiti, New Mexico," 212–15.

4 As narrated by Ruth Benedict's "Informant 1" in 1926 and published in Benedict, "Tales of the Cochiti Indians," 1–2.

5 As recorded by Stevenson, "The Sia," 26–34.

6 As recorded by White, "The Pueblo of Sia," 120–21.

7 As narrated by Edward Proctor Hunt at the Smithsonian in 1928 and published by Stirling, *Origin Myth of Acoma*, 1–12; Hunt, *Origin Myth*, 3–30.

save Edward Hunt, contrasting the material advantage of paper with the spiritual advantage of constant contact with the Creator.

> Naotsityi invented things more wonderful than those that Utctsiti had created. Naotsityi created paper and it could talk to her and to her people. Utctsiti could not talk to paper and it would not talk to her. She felt bad about it and began to cry. But Tsiyostinako was always with Utctsiti. She told Utctsiti what the paper was saying.[29]

The situation of equality ends when the Ancestor of Non-Indians claims superior status.[30] And when her sister disputes this, the more aggressive, more ambitious sibling challenges her to some form of competition that will settle the issue, continued equality being excluded. As both sisters understand, the stakes are high, and the consequences will be enduring. Cochiti B states this most bluntly.

> Naotsiti challenged Uretsiti to a contest. She said, "Whoever the sun shines on first shall be the greater," for she was taller than her elder sister. Uretsiti and Naotsiti stood up before dawn and waited for the first rays of the sun. Naotsiti said, "Whoever the sun strikes first, her children shall be valuable; whoever the sun strikes last, her children shall be worthless." She was boasting.[31]

Here, as in Edward Hunt's variant, the question is resolved by a single act of solar divination. All other variants include the solar trial, but make it either the first or last in a series that includes guessing games, a test of weapons, and/or physical contests. Thus, at Laguna, the series starts with the sun and ends when the children of the rivals run a race around the world. Although the lead sways back and forth, the issue is settled when the Mother of Indians uses her magic power to produce rains that kill the white contestants. With this, the ancestor of whites concedes, crying out, "Enough, it is enough. Yourself, indeed, you are the first. . . . Please, make my people alive for me, for you have much magical power."[32] Gracious in victory, she grants the request and revivifies his dead children, but in the process their faces are disfigured by weeds or vomit.[33] As a result, white men have beards: a phenotypic trait this story transforms into a lasting reminder of their defeat, humiliation, and subordinate status.

At Cochiti and Sia pueblos, the dénouement is more discriminatory still and much more shocking. In Sia A, for example, after the Mother of Indians has won the last contest (sun), her people kill the majority of her sister's followers. Then comes the sisters' turn.

They fought like women—not with arrows—but wrestled. The men formed a circle around them and the two women fought hard and long. Some of the men said, "Let us go and part the women"; others said, "No; let them alone." The younger woman [= Utset, Mother of Indians] grew very tired in her arms, and cried to her people, "I am very tired." They threw the elder sister [= Nowutset, Mother of Other Nations] upon the ground and tied her hands; the younger woman then commanded her people to leave her, and she struck her sister with her fists about the head and face as she lay upon the ground, and in a little while killed her. She then cut the breast with a stone knife and took out the heart, her people being still in a circle, but the circle was so large that they were some distance off. She held the heart in her hand and cried: "Listen men and youths! This woman was my sister, but she compelled us to fight; it was she who taught you to fight. The few of her people who escaped are in the mountains and they are the people of the rats"; and she cut the heart into pieces and threw it upon the ground, saying, "Her heart will become rats, for it was very bad," and immediately rats could be seen running in all directions. She found the center of the heart full of cactus, and she said: "The rats for evermore will live with the cacti"; and to this day the rats live thus.[34]

Far from regretting her sister's death and the reduction of her people to rodentine status, Utset glories in her triumph, justifying her violent acts as the rightful and inevitable result of a conflict Nowutset initiated. Indeed, the story provides confirmation of the latter's bad character (envy, ambition, etc.) in the material nature of her heart, which is thorny and verminous at its core. "This woman was my sister," the victorious Utset acknowledges, before affixing blame, "but she compelled us to fight."

All other variants make the same point in gentler fashion, as it is always the non-Indian ancestor who terminates the egalitarian era by claiming primacy, issuing a challenge, and asking for competition. To this rule, Edward Hunt is a striking exception, for he—and he alone—shifted responsibility to the Mother of Indians. In his variant it is Iatiku, and not Nautsiti, who set the conflict in motion with her self-elevating pronouncement: "I am the older, you are younger than I."[35]

There are other ways in which Hunt's variant is unique. Thus, most versions have the Indian ancestor triumph by her superior strength, skill, intelligence, or magic power, while others have the sun's rays accurately identify the sister who enjoys divine favor. Three variants complicate the story, however, by introducing the episode of Magpie, whose trickery changes the outcome of the solar contest (Cochiti A, Sia A and B). These texts do not completely invalidate the results, however, for in all three, the Indian ancestor wins other forms of competition (guessing game, test of weapons) in perfectly honest fashion. Her victory is thus imperfect and somewhat tainted, but not entirely undeserved or unjust. Each of the three variants treats Magpie's intervention differently, but all are at pains to guard against the implications of cheating. Thus, Cochiti A has the Creator send the bird, with the result that the solar test reveals the divine will *through* (and not *in spite of*) Magpie's action.[36] Sia B has the bird act on its own volition, so Utctsiti bears no responsibility for the means of her victory.[37] And although Sia A has Utset enlist Magpie's help, it carefully frames this as a demonstration of the way superior intelligence bests physical advantage.[38] Only in Edward Hunt's version is there any implication that Iatiku and Magpie have done something wrong and have cause for regret. In no other variant does the victor—or narrator—express the slightest doubt about the rightness of what happened.

It thus becomes clear that Hunt departed sharply not only from Acoma traditions, but from the Keresan pueblo norm. He, and he alone, organizes events in the following sequence (the places where his version finds no parallel are marked in italics).

1. *Iatiku (Mother of Indians) claims primacy, saying she is older.*
2. *Nautsiti (Mother of Whites) defends equality.*
3. Nautsiti suggests they resolve their dispute by a solar contest.
4. Iatiku is frightened her sister will win.
5. Iatiku instructs Magpie to cheat on her behalf.[39]
6. *Since no other contests are staged, Magpie's cheating entirely determines the outcome.*
7. *Iatiku experiences remorse and regret, which she expresses most poignantly in the song she sings to her sister.*

## VI

Read in a vacuum, Edward Hunt's story of Iatiku and Nautsiti might seem like a Malinowskian "social charter," explaining how the asymmetric power relations of the present result from a trivial episode in the mythic past that granted Acoma Pueblo—and Native Americans more broadly—seniority over the whites, while producing the technological, economic, and demographic supremacy of the latter.[40] When one establishes the context and pragmatics of the Hunt text, however, a more subtle, dynamic, and complicated picture emerges. Asking the crucial questions "Whom did he seek to persuade? Of what? Toward what end?" permits one to see that Hunt's goal was not to explain, justify, or reproduce the extant sociopolitical order. Rather, he addressed Nautsiti's descendants, speaking on behalf of the pueblos (and perhaps all Indians), using the mystical powers of song to reanimate Iatiku's profound regret for the events that produced the hierarchic differentiation and subsequent estrangement of peoples, and suggesting that things might—and ought—be different. Toward that end, he called on his interlocutors (at the Smithsonian and beyond) to help him change their unequal relations of alterity into the full "mutuality of being" constitutive of kinship, as theorized by Marshall Sahlins: "Kin are persons who belong to one another, who are parts of one another, who are co-present in each other, whose lives are joined and interdependent."[41]

Just as Hunt reworked the Magpie episode to establish the nature of the problem, i.e., the artificial and regrettable nature of hierarchy and schism, he also attempted to implement its solution when he introduced Iatiku's song. For with the powers of song, he meant not just to recall past events with a whiff of nostalgia, but to reactivate the ideal situation of equality, intimacy, and interdependence and to reawaken in Nautsiti's descendants the sentiments and bonds of kinship that were not lost, however much they were damaged, even forgotten when their ancestor departed.

Come back soon.
Iatiku wants to be your relative.
Iatiku needs you to help in offerings.
Do not cry anymore.[42]

## VII

Recognizing that Hunt saw the Smithsonian as a conduit through which he, as emissary and mediator, might speak to white society helped us understand his text, not as a faithful repetition of traditional knowledge, but as his attempt to reshape old materials so they might help him repair troubled human relations of the present. Asking whom Herodotus addressed and what he hoped to accomplish by reworking the "Persian" story of Darius's accession is similarly productive. The answer to the first question is easy: he wrote for Greeks, especially Athenians in the 430s or early 420s, on the eve of the Peloponnesian War, when Persia remained a great power, but the threat of invasion was long past, and Athens itself was becoming an imperial power. The master narrative he developed tells how a long chain of events led Darius (in 490), then Xerxes (480–79), to attack Greece with vastly superior forces, but the quantitative advantages enjoyed by the Persians—demographic, territorial, military, and economic—could not overcome the Greeks' qualitative advantages, particularly their love of freedom (*eleutheriē*).[43]

The Keresan pueblo myth of two ancestors similarly juxtaposed "our"

Table 13.3. Discursive relations and projects of persuasion in three comparable texts

|  | Keresan Pueblos | Edward Hunt | Herodotus |
|---|---|---|---|
| **Narrator represents** | Vanquished | Vanquished | Victors |
| **Narrator addresses** | Vanquished | Victors | Victors |
| **Desired effect** | Console; maintain pride in spite of defeat | Reverse effects of defeat; restore lost equity | Preserve core virtues; warn against reversal of fortune and the hubris that comes with victory |

qualitative advantages to "their" material superiority, but did so in different circumstances. When that myth spoke of a spiritual superiority still perceptible in the pueblo, it offered consolation and helped maintain the pride of people politically dominated by and dependent on wealthier, more powerful others whom they regarded as their moral inferiors. Hunt modified this narrative to tell the victors that the vanquished remain worthy and should be treated as equals. Herodotus undertook yet a third project of persuasion, explaining the non-material bases of their strength to the victors, now tempted by the material benefits that come with victory, and warning them lest they lose their real source of strength and become rich, vain, and overconfident in the manner of their old enemy (table 13.3).

Herodotus makes his point most emphatically in the final paragraph of the *Histories* by placing it in the mouth of Cyrus the Great, founder of the Persian empire, in his moment of triumph. Having established their lordship over Asia, Cyrus's men wanted to leave the rough, impoverished soil of Persia for the lushest available terrain, arguing that seizing rich territory and booty is only right, since Zeus granted them supremacy (*hēgemoniē*).[44]

> Having heard this, Cyrus did not marvel at what was said. He ordered them to go ahead and do these things, but advised them to prepare themselves to rule no longer and to have others rule them, for the love of soft places gives birth to soft people, since splendid fruit and good, battleworthy men do not grow from the same soil. At this, the Persians withdrew in agreement. Yielding to the considered opinion of Cyrus, they chose to rule and dwell on miserable land, rather than to be slaves sowing the beautiful fields of others.[45]

With these closing words, Herodotus lets Cyrus himself warn against the destructive dynamic whereby power leads to wealth, which leads to luxury and self-indulgence, which leads to decadence and a reversal of fortune, whereby erstwhile rulers become new slaves. Three clear subtexts attend this passage. The first suggests that Persians could have been more like Greeks, had they heeded Cyrus's advice and not succumbed to the dangers of arrogance, ambition, and greed. The second inverts this point, suggesting that Greeks—more precisely, Athenians—are in danger of becoming (more) like Persians as a result of the same temptations and dynamic. The third combines these points and generalizes, suggesting that the difference between Persians and Greeks, self and other, victors and vanquished, is neither innate nor inevitable. Rather, human groups can move closer together or further apart as the result of their choices, events, and the shifting relations of power.[46]

Herodotus used the episode of Darius's ascension to make many of the same points he attributed to Cyrus, while shifting his emphasis from the dangers of wealth to those of kingship (*basileiē, mounarkhiē,* sometimes also *hēgemoniē*).[47] Once again, he placed his critique in the mouth of a Persian.

How can kingship be a proper thing, when the king is permitted to do whatever he likes with impunity? If this were so for the best of all men, even he would stray from his normal thoughts, for hubris arises in him as a result of all the good things he has available, while envy grows in people from the very beginning. The king thus possesses both these qualities and consequently possesses every vice. Being glutted in his appetites, he does many impious things, some out of hubris and some out of envy. Now, a king ought to be a man without envy, since he possesses all good things, but by nature he is the very opposite of this toward his countrymen, for he envies the best of them and takes pleasure at the worst of his subjects and he is quickest to believe false accusations. He is the hardest of all men to please, for if you marvel at him in moderate ways, he is angry not to be excessively flattered and if one flatters him greatly, he is as angry as if you do so inadequately. And I have even more serious things to say: he meddles with the ancestral laws, takes women by force, and kills people who have been condemned of nothing. In contrast, the rule of the multitude has the fairest name of all: equality. Further, it does none of the bad things a king does. It exercises its powers by vote, it holds power accountable, and it refers all decisions to the public. I put forth my considered opinion that we discard the kingship in order to exalt the multitude, for what is in the many is in all.[48]

Acknowledging that some Greeks might not believe a Persian could issue so scathing a denunciation of kingship or voice preference for democratic equality (*isonomiē, plēthos arkhon*), Herodotus insists it was so.[49] Nor were these the idle ruminations of some Persian misfit. On the contrary, this was the opening salvo in the "Constitutional Debate," as spoken by Otanes, a man "equal to the foremost Persians in birth and in wealth."[50] The same Otanes who first recognized the Magian imposter[51] and recruited the Persian nobles he most trusted to help overthrow the usurper.[52]

Darius, it should be noted, was not initially part of this group. Rather, he joined the conspiracy late, without anyone vouching for his character.[53] Rashly, he urged immediate action, warning that any delay would be their undoing.[54] Going further, he issued a blunt threat: "Either we act today or I myself will denounce you."[55]

At that, Otanes posed a practical question: How did Darius expect to get past the palace guards without making plans or preparations? Given Persian reverence for the cardinal virtue of truth, Darius's answer was truly shocking.[56] "If a lie needs to be told, tell it," he said, arguing that there is no difference between truth-tellers and liars, since both do what they must to accomplish their goals.[57] Astonishingly, he persuaded the others with this cynically unprincipled argument,[58] foreshadowing later episodes when he would persuade them to restore the kingship, then cheat to make it his own.[59]

In his Bisitun inscription, Darius represented himself as a paragon of truth[60] and took prime responsibility for killing the imposter, acknowledging he had help from a few supporters, but contrasting his courage, confidence, and certainty of divine favor to others' fear and hesitation.

Proclaims Darius the King: *There was not a man—not a Persian, nor a Mede, nor anyone of our lineage*—who could have deprived that Gaumāta the Magus of the kingship. The people feared him mightily. . . . *No one dared* to proclaim anything about Gaumāta the Magus *until I arose.* Then I prayed to the Wise Lord for assistance. The Wise Lord bore me aid. Ten days of the month Bāgayādi had passed (29 September 522) when I, *with a few men*, slew that Gaumāta the Magus and the men that were his foremost followers.[61]

In retelling this story, Herodotus shifts focus and makes quite a different point. Although Darius remains its protagonist and most vigorous actor, in the Herodotean variant, Otanes becomes its (tragic) hero, who engaged in three interrelated struggles. One of these was to save Persia from the usurper, a struggle he initiated and won, with the very significant help of six others. The second was to maintain control of his group, and this he lost to Darius, who proved more energetic and unscrupulous than he. The third, and most important struggle, in Herodotus's view, was his attempt to save

Persia from the institution of kingship, and here—regrettably—he lost to Darius once more.

In Herodotus's hands, the story of Otanes, Darius, and Oibares thus becomes an object lesson and an exercise in counterfactual history. Had Otanes won the "Constitutional Debate," the story suggests, the Persians would have abandoned kingship, embraced the values of freedom and equality, and become (more) like Greeks. Under such circumstances, Greeks and Persians might never have come into conflict, and it still might have been so, were it not for Oibares's ruse, since a man less ambitious, aggressive, and unprincipled than Darius would then have gained the throne. Here, as with the closing speech he attributed to Cyrus, Herodotus brings self and other together, subtextually juxtaposing the non-hubristic, non-imperial nation Persia could have been (had Otanes prevailed), and the hubristic, imperial state Athens threatened to become, should its liars, cheats, and bold men of action succeed in gaining control.

This is not the same message Edward Hunt brought to the Smithsonian in 1928, yet there are similarities between them, just as there are strong resemblances in their narrative structure and details. These narrative similarities reflect and result from the fact that both narrators, and both of the cultures they represent, were wrestling with similar issues that our practice of weak comparison is designed to elucidate. Most broadly, the problematic these narratives engage begins with their recognition of egalitarianism as a primordial state and utopian ideal that proves impossible to sustain. That which replaces equality, however—i.e., hierarchy of whatever sort—is understood to be artificial, dishonest, and discriminatory. As such, it leads to estrangement and conflict between peoples, with terrible suffering for some and real dangers for all. The issue that arises, for victors and vanquished alike, is whether there is some way to move back from a perilous, unjust, and ultimately nonviable hierarchic order and restore—or at least approximate—the lost egalitarian ideal. In the face of that problem, Edward Hunt and Herodotus reflected on the deep past and told a story where one character shrewdly manipulates the sun's rays to create the semblance of divine favor, thereby gaining supremacy over his or her rivals. Others had told that story before, but by the innovative way they reworked its details, both narrators sought to modify the consciousness and self-understanding of the audiences they engaged, as well as their attitudes toward and relations with people they regarded as other. In both cases, that intervention failed, such audacious projects not being easily accomplished, but their failure ought make their attempt no less admirable or fascinating.

# NOTES

## CHAPTER ONE

1. Here, one should note that "apples" and "oranges" relate to other entities (Macintoshes, Cortlands, Winesaps; Valencias, Navels, Mandarins) in much the same way, reducing those to the status of subcategories whose distinctive particularities risk being consigned to irrelevance within the encompassing category.

2. Jonathan Z. Smith, "The Glory, Jest, and Riddle: James George Frazer and *The Golden Bough*" (PhD diss., Yale University, 1969). Although Smith's dissertation was never published and remains difficult to access, one gets some idea of the content from an article published a few years later: Smith, "When the Bough Breaks," *History of Religions* 12 (1973): 342–71. Smith describes his struggle with Eliade in a more recent essay of similar title, "When the Chips Are Down," in *Relating Religion: Essays in the Study of Religion* (Chicago: University of Chicago Press, 2004), 1–60.

3. Wikander declined to publish his lectures, which acquired a somewhat legendary status. They were ultimately published long after his death by Mihaela Timus, "Les 'Haskell Lectures' de Stig Wikander, University of Chicago, 1967," *Archaeus* 8 (2004): 265–322. In contrast, Dumézil published his Haskell Lectures as *Mythe et epopée*, vol. 2, *Types épiques indo-européens: Un héros, un sorcier, un roi* (Paris: Gallimard, 1971), one of the culminating works of his much-acclaimed career. Translations into three separate English volumes followed: *The Destiny of the Warrior*, trans. Alf Hiltebeitel (Chicago: University of Chicago Press, 1970); *The Destiny of a King*, trans. Alf Hiltebeitel (Chicago: University of Chicago Press, 1973); and *The Plight of a Sorcerer*, ed. Jaan Puhvel and David Weeks (Berkeley: University of California Press, 1986).

4. J. A. Simpson and E. S. C. Weiner, *The Oxford English Dictionary*, 2nd ed. (Oxford: Clarendon Press, 1989), available online at http://www.oed.com.proxy .uchicago.edu/view/Entry/75072?rskey = ZtZh1l&result = 1&isAdvanced = false #eid, based on Henry Bradley, *A New English Dictionary on Historical Principles*, vol. 4, *F-G*, ed. James A. H. Murray (Oxford: Clarendon Press, 1901), 574–75.

5. Ibid. Several other definitions are given, but identified as rare, obsolete, or technical and late of origin. These include (a) a fruit-tree; also a foodplant (obsolete and rare); (b) a course of fruit; the dessert (obsolete, first attested 1577); (c) the seed of a plant or tree, regarded as the means of reproduction, together with its envelope

(technical, first attested 1794); (d) offspring, progeny (now rare, except in biblical phraseology); (e) a male homosexual (slang, first attested 1895).

6. *Cursor Mundi* (Galba), line 28833: Þe pouer man es like þe felde, Þat mekill fruit es wont to yelde.

7. *Cleanness*, line 1044: Þe fayrest fryt þat may in folde growe, As orenge & oþer fryt.

8. *Jacob's Well*, line 202: Þe fruyte & þe profyȝte of þat lande & of beeste in þi tyme.

9. *Pilgrim's Sowle* v.xiv.80: Alle the wyde world is fulfylled with the fryte of theyr good labour.

10. *Hali Meidenhad: An Alliterative Homily* 7: Þus hauen godes freond al þe fruit of þis world þat ha forsaken habbeð.

11. Charlton T. Lewis and Charles Short, *A Latin Dictionary* (Oxford: Clarendon Press, 1879), 784.

12. Cicero, *Oration on the Agrarian Law* 2.2.5: hoc tam singulare vestrum beneficium ad animi mei fructum atque laetitiam duco esse permagnum.

13. Livy 21.7.3: in tantas brevi creverant opes, seu maritimis seu terrestribus fructibus.

14. Cicero, *Oration on Behalf of Sulla* 1.1: Maxime vellem, iudices, ut P. Sulla . . . modestiae fructum aliquem percipere potuisset.

15. Lewis and Short, *A Latin Dictionary*, 785.

16. Ibid., 1939.

17. Alfred Ernout and Antoine Meillet, *Dictionnaire étymologique de la langue latine* (Paris: C. Klincksieck, 1951), 455–56. Cf. Alois Walde and J. B. Hofmann, *Lateinisches etymologisches Wörterbuch* (Heidelberg: Carl Winter, 1965), 1: 552–53. Comparison of the Latin terms to their cognates in Germanic makes clear that the general semantics of enjoyment preceded any botanical referent, since the latter is entirely lacking in all the relevant terminology, which includes Gothic *brūks* ("useful"), *unbrūks* ("useless"), and *brūkjan* ("to make use of"); Old High German *brūchan,* Old Frisian *brūka,* Old English *brūcan,* and Anglo-Saxon *brūkan* ("to make use of, enjoy; eat; spend"), and Anglo-Saxon *brýce* ("use, service; the occupation or exercise of a thing; profit, advantage"), as well as Dutch *gebruiken* and German *brauchen.* See further Sigmund Feist, *Vergleichendes Wörterbuch der gotischen Sprache* (Leiden: E.J. Brill, 1939), 107; Joseph Bosworth and T. Northcote Toller, *An Anglo-Saxon Dictionary* (Oxford: Oxford University Press, 1898), 128 and 129; and Julius Pokorny, *Indogermanisches etymologisches Wörterbuch* (Bern: Francke Verlag, 1959), 173.

18. Thus, *Priests, Warriors and Cattle: A Study in the Ecology of Religions* (Berkeley: University of California Press, 1981) combined an attempt to reconstruct Indo-Iranian religion with a comparison to the religious systems of Nilotic East Africa, based on similarities of ecology and economy; *Emerging from the Chrysalis: Studies in Rituals of Women's Initiation* (Cambridge, MA: Harvard University Press, 1981) considered five different examples scattered across the globe; *Myth, Cosmos, and Society: Indo-European Themes of Creation and Destruction* (Cambridge, MA: Harvard University Press, 1986) remained fully within the Indo-European paradigm; and *Death, War, and Sacrifice: Studies in Ideology and Practice* (Chicago: University of Chicago Press,

1991) voiced my growing dissatisfaction with it. Most interesting, diverse, and experimental, however, is *Discourse and the Construction of Society: Comparative Studies of Myth, Ritual, and Classification* (New York: Oxford University Press, 1989; 2nd ed., 2014), in which I was groping for alternatives.

19. Potent critiques of Eliade on other grounds had already been published, above all Edmund Leach, "Sermons by a Man on a Ladder," *New York Review of Books*, October 20, 1966, 28–31, but his involvement with Romanian fascism emerged as a major concern in debates that began with the publication of a Romanian dossier in an obscure publication: Th. Lavi, "Dosarul Mircea Eliade," *Toladot: Buletinul Institutului Dr. J. Niemirower* 1 (1972): 21–26. There followed Alfonso di Nola, "Mircea Eliade e l'antisemitismo," *La Rassegna Mensile di Israel* 43 (Jan.–March 1977): 12–15; Vittorio Lanternari, "Ripensando a Mircea Eliade," *La Critica Sociologica* 79 (1986): 67–82; Ivan Strenski, *Four Theories of Myth in Twentieth-Century History: Cassirer, Eliade, Lévi-Strauss, and Malinowski* (Iowa City: University of Iowa Press, 1987); Mac Linscott Ricketts, *Mircea Eliade: The Romanian Roots, 1907–1945* (Boulder, CO: East European Monographs, 1988); Claudio Mutti, *Mircea Eliade e la Guardia di Ferro* (Parma: Edizioni all' Insegna del Veltro, 1989); Adriana Berger, "Fascism and Religion in Romania," *Annals of Scholarship* 6 (1989): 455–65; Berger, "Mircea Eliade, Romanian Fascism, and the History of Religions in the United States," in Nancy Harrowitz, ed., *Tainted Greatness: Antisemitism and Cultural Heroes* (Philadelphia: Temple University Press, 1994), 51–74; Daniel Dubuisson, *Mythologies du XXe siècle: Dumézil, Lévi-Strauss, Eliade* (Lille: Presses Universitaires de Lille, 1993; English trans., 2006; 2nd ed. 2008); Dubuisson, *Impostures et pseudo-science: L'oeuvre de Mircea Eliade* (Villeneuve d'Asq: Presses universitaires du Septentrion, 2005); and a great many others.

20. Like Eliade, Dumézil had been criticized on other grounds, but the discussion shifted in the 1980s to the way his political commitments informed, inflected, and found expression in his scholarly writings. Significant contributions to this discussion include Arnaldo Momigliano, "Premesse per una discussione su Georges Dumézil," *Opus* 2 (1983): 329–41; English trans. in G. W. Bowersock and T. J. Cornell, eds., *A. D. Momigliano: Studies on Modern Scholarship* (Berkeley: University of California Press, 1994), 286–301; Carlo Ginzburg, "Mitologia germanica e Nazismo: Su un vecchio libro di Georges Dumézil," *Quaderni Storici* 19 (1984): 857–82; English trans. in *Clues, Myths, and the Historical Method*, 114–31; Georges Dumézil, "Une idylle de vingt ans," in *L'oubli de l'homme et l'honneur des dieux: Esquisses de mythologie* (Paris: Gallimard, 1985), 299–318; Dumézil, "Science et politique: Réponse à Carlo Ginzburg," *Annales ESC* 40 (1985): 985–89; Bruce Lincoln, "Shaping the Past and the Future," *Times Literary Supplement*, October 3, 1986, 1107–8, Didier Eribon, *Faut-il brûler Dumézil?* (Paris: Flammarion, 1992); and Cristiano Grottanelli, *Ideologie, miti, massacri: Indoeuropei di Georges Dumézil* (Palermo: Sellerio editore, 1993).

21. *Il nuovo dizionaria italiano Garzanti* (Rome: Garzanti Editori, 1984), 829: "sfruttare, v. tr. 1. ottenere il massimo rendimento possibile da un terreno; esaurirne il vigore; (fig.) trarre illecito profitto dal lavoro altrui; non remunerare adeguatamente chi lavora."

22. *Vocabolario degli Accademici della Crusca*, vol. 4, *Q–S* (Venice: Francesco Pitteri, 1741), 341: "Parlandosi di terreni, vale Renderli infruttuosi, sterili, e meno atti

al frutto, Indebolirli. . . . Trattandosi d'altre cose, vale Cercar di trarne più frutto, che si può, senza aver riguardo al mantenimento."

23. Ibid., vol. 2, p. 372: "Il parto degli alberi, e d' alcune erbe."

24. Ibid.: "Per Entrata, Rendita, Profitto annuale," with citation of Boccaccio, Introduzione, 25: "Non d' aiutare i futuri frutti delle bestie, e delle terre, e delle lor passate fatiche, ma di consumare quelli (Not to augment the future products [*frutti*] of animals, of the earth, and of their own past labors, but to consume them)."

25. Simpson and Weiner, *Oxford English Dictionary*, ad loc.

26. Anonymous [signed μ], "Revelations of a 'Clairvoyant'," *New Monthly Magazine and Humorist* 53 (1838): 301–9.

27. A neologism coined from Greek οὐδὲν, οὐδέις, "nothing." The word first appeared in another anonymous article titled "Nothing of a Leader," *London Medical and Surgical Journal* 7 (July 25, 1835): 825. Presumably, the same author was responsible for both of these texts.

28. "Revelations of a 'Clairvoyant'," 304.

29. Ibid., 305.

30. Ibid.

31. Ibid., 306 (emphasis in the original).


CHAPTER TWO

1. Clifford Geertz, *The Interpretation of Cultures* (New York: Basic Books, 1973), 87.

2. The most important of Marx's writings on religion have been conveniently collected in a volume entitled *Marx and Engels on Religion* (New York: Schocken Books, 1964). See, in particular, "Theses on Feuerback" (69–72, written in 1845) and "Contribution to the Critique of Hegel's Philosophy of Right" (41–58, written in 1844).

3. See, in particular, *The German Ideology* (1845–46). Part 1, dealing with Feuerbach, represents Marx's most fully developed ideas on the theme of religion.

4. Friedrich Engels, *The Peasant War in Germany*, trans. M. J. Olgin (New York: International Publishers, 1966; German original, 1850).

5. Max Weber, *Sociology of Religion*, trans. Ephraim Fischoff (Boston: Beacon Press, 1964; German original, 1922).

6. Max Weber, *The Protestant Ethic and the Spirit of Capitalism*, trans. Anthony Giddens (New York: Scribner's, 1976; German original, 1922–23).

7. Émile Durkheim, *Elementary Forms of the Religious Life*, trans. Joseph Swain (New York: Free Press, 1965; French original, 1912).

8. Along these lines, see Émile Durkheim and Marcel Mauss, *Primitive Classification*, trans. Rodney Needham (Chicago: University of Chicago Press, 1963; French original, 1901–2); Marcel Granet, *Religion of the Chinese People*, trans. Maurice Freedman (New York: Harper & Row, 1977; French original, 1922); Robert Hertz, *Death and the Right Hand*, trans. Rodney Needham (Glencoe, IL: Free Press, 1960); Henri Hubert and Marcel Mauss, *Sacrifice: Its Nature and Function*, trans. W. D. Halls (Chicago: University of Chicago Press, 1964; French original, 1902).

9. Bronislaw Malinowski, *Magic, Science, and Religion, and Other Essays* (Garden City, NY: Doubleday, 1954).

10. Claude Lévi-Strauss, *The Savage Mind* (Chicago: University of Chicago Press, 1966; French original, 1962), 3.

11. To give an idea of how recently this discipline took shape, one might note that at the University of Uppsala, one of the most active and influential centers for research in history of religions (along with the universities of Rome, Paris, Chicago, and several German institutions), it was only in 1938 that a Chair of History and Psychology of Religion was established (in the Faculty of Divinity; a second chair was added in the Faculty of Arts in 1948), research in this general area previously having been carried out by occupants of a Chair of Theological Propaedeutics and Theological Encyclopaedia. Significantly, the two twentieth-century occupants of this latter chair (Nathan Söderblom [1866–1931] and Tor Andrae [1885–1947]) both became archbishops of the Swedish National Church. In contrast, Andrae's successor, Geo Widengren (1907–96), as first occupant of the renamed chair, maintained a staunchly secular position and succeeded Raffaele Pettazzoni as president of the IAHR.

12. See, for instance, Pettazzoni's essay "History and Phenomenology in the Science of Religion," in his *Essays in the History of Religions*, trans. H. J. Rose (Leiden: E. J. Brill, 1967), 215–19. This piece originally appeared as the introductory article to the first issue of *Numen* (1954), the official publication of the IAHR.

13. Regrettably, only a small portion of Pettazzoni's writings are available in English. In addition to the essays included in the volume cited above, there is only *The All-Knowing God: Researches into Early Religion and Culture*, trans. H. J. Rose (London: Methuen, 1956; Italian original, 1957). A number of articles dealing with his life and work, together with a bibliography of his writings appear in a special issue of *Studi e Materiali di Storia delle Religioni* issued on the centenary of his birth (1983).

14. See, for instance, such widely read (and at one time acclaimed) works as Rudolf Otto, *The Idea of the Holy: An Inquiry into the Non-rational Factor in the Idea of the Divine and Its Relation to the Rational*, trans. John Harvey (London: Oxford University Press, 1958; German original, 1917); Nathan Söderblom, *The Living God: Basal Forms of Personal Religion*, trans. Yngve Brilloth (London: Oxford University Press, 1933; Swedish original, 1932); Wilhelm Schmidt, *Primitive Revelation*, trans. Joseph Bayerl (St. Louis and London: Herder, 1939; German original, 1910); Friedrich Heiler, "The History of Religions as a Preparation for the Cooperation of Religions," in Mircea Eliade and Joseph Kitagawa, eds., *The History of Religions: Essays in Methodology* (Chicago: University of Chicago Press, 1959), 132–60; Gerardus van der Leeuw, *Religion in Essence and Manifestation: A Study in Phenomenology*, trans J. E. Turner (New York: Harper and Row, 1963; German original, 1933); Joachim Wach, *The Comparative Study of Religions* (New York: Columbia University Press, 1958). This list could easily be multiplied many times over.

15. This trend was recognized and denounced (but ineffectively) by Pettazzoni's successor in the Chair of History of Religions at Rome, Angelo Brelich, in his account of the first meetings of the IAHR held after the death of Pettazzoni (Marburg, 1960). See Angelo Brelich, *Storia delle religioni: Perchè?* (Naples: Liguori Editore, 1979), 131–36.

16. Thus, e.g., Geertz, *Interpretation of Culture*; Lévi-Strauss, *The Savage Mind*; Lévi-Strauss, *The Raw and the Cooked*, trans. John and Doreen Weightman, (New

York: Harper and Row, 1969; French original, 1964), *From Honey to Ashes*, trans. John Weightman and Doreen Weightman, (New York: Harper and Row, 1973; French original, 1966); Lévi-Strauss, *The Origin of Table Manners*, trans. John Weightman and Doreen Weightman (New York: Harper and Row, 1978; French original, 1968); Lévi-Strauss, *The Naked Man*, trans. John Weightman and Doreen Weightman (New York: Harper and Row, 1981; French original, 1971); Victor Turner, *The Ritual Process: Structure and Anti-structure* (Chicago: Aldine, 1969); and Mary Douglas, *Purity and Danger: An Analysis of Concepts of Pollution and Taboo* (London: Routledge & Kegan Paul), 1966.

17. Inter alia, Max Gluckman, *Custom and Conflict in Africa* (London: Basil Blackwell, 1966); Vittorio Lanternari, *The Religions of the Oppressed: A Study of Modern Messianic Cults*, trans. Lisa Sergio (New York: Mentor, 1960; Italian original, 1960); Maurice Godelier, *Perspectives in Marxist Anthropology*, trans. Robert Brain (Cambridge: Cambridge University Press, 1977; French original, 1973); and Stephen Feuchtwang, "Interpreting Religion," in Maurice Bloch, ed., *Marxist Analyses and Social Anthropology* (London: Tavistock, 1984), 61–82.

18. Jacques Le Goff, *Time, Work, and Culture in the Middle Ages*, trans. Arthur Goldhammer (Chicago: University of Chicago Press, 1980; French original, 1977); Eric Hobsbawm, *Primitive Rebels: Studies in Archaic Forms of Social Movement in the 19th and 20th Centuries* (Manchester: University of Manchester Press, 1959); Christopher Hill, *The World Turned Upside Down: Radical Ideas during the English Revolution* (New York: Viking, 1972); Natalie Zemon Davis, *Society and Culture in Early Modern France: Eight Essays* (Stanford, CA: Stanford University Press, 1975); and Carlo Ginzburg, *The Cheese and the Worms: The World-View of a 15th-Century Miller*, trans. John Tedeschi and Anne Tedeschi (Baltimore: Johns Hopkins University Press, 1980; Italian original, 1970).

19. T. H. Aston, "*Past and Present*, Numbers 1–50," *Past and Present* 50 (1971): 3.

20. Jean-Pierre Vernant, *Myth and Society in Ancient Greece*, trans. Janet Lloyd (Sussex: Harvester Press, 1980; French original, 1974) or orientalists like Marshall Hodgson, *The Venture of Islam: Conscience and History in a World Civilization*, 3 vols. (Chicago: University of Chicago Press, 1974–77); and Joseph Needham, *Science and Civilization in China*, 5 vols. (Cambridge: Cambridge University Press, 1954–82).

21. Inter alia, Raffaele Pettazzoni, *La confessione dei peccati* (Bologna: N. Zanichelli, 1929); Geo Widengren, *King and Saviour*, 5 vols. (Uppsala: Uppsala Universitet Arsskrift, 1945–55); Mircea Eliade, *Shamanism: Archaic Techniques of Ecstasy*, trans. Willard Trask (Princeton, NJ: Princeton University Press, 1964; French original,s 1951); Georges Dumézil, *L'idéologie tripartie des indo-européens* (Brussels: Collection Latomus, 1958).

## CHAPTER THREE

1. On the general nature and importance of the *Bundahišn*, see Carlo Ceretti, *La letteratura Pahlavi: Introduzione ai testi con riferimenti alla storia degli studi e alla tradizione manoscritta* (Milan: Mimesis, 2001), 87–105. The standard edition is now Fazlollah Pakzad, *Bundahišn: Zoroastrische Kosmogonie und Kosmologie*, vol. 1,

*Kritische Edition* (Tehran: Centre for the Great Islamic Encyclopaedia, 2005). All translations that follow are original.

2. This is spelled out in *Greater Bundahišn* 1.1–11.

3. *Greater Bundahišn* 1.12: "In his omniscience, the Wise Lord knows that the Foul Spirit exists, because he [i.e., Ahreman] draws up plans in envious desire, as he mixes things up from beginning to end in countless ways. Spiritually, [the Wise Lord] created the creation that is necessary for his power." (Ohrmazd pad harwisp-āgāhīh dānist kū Gannāg-Mēnōg ast čē +handāzēd{ud kunēd} pad arešk-kāmagīh ciyōn / andar\ gūmēzēd <az> fragān /ta\ frazām abāg cand abzārān. u-š mēnōgīhā ān dām ī pad ān abzār andar abāyēd frāz brēhēnīd.)

4. *Greater Bundahišn* 1.14–15: Gannāg-Mēnōg pas-dānišnīh rāy az (h)astīh ī Ohrmazd an-āgāh būd. pas az ān zōfāyīg +axēzīd ō wimand ī didār ī rōšnān mad. ka-š dīd Ohrmazd ud ān rōšnīh ī a-griftār frāz +payrūd zadār-kāmagīh ud arešk-gōhrīh rāy pad murnjēnīdan tag abar kard. *Greater Bundahišn* 4.10 describes Ahreman's primordial assault, once again tracing the violent acts he committed to his preexisting sense of envy: "Then the Foul Spirit rose up against the lights, together with his demons and powers. He saw the sky. In envious desire, he launched an attack." (pas āxist Gannāg-Mēnōg abāg hāmist dēwān abzārān ō padīrag ī rōšnān. u-š ān asmān dīd {ī-šān mēnōgīhā nimūd ka nē astōmand dād estēd} arešk-kāmagīhā tag abar kard.)

5. Much recent scholarship has been concerned to show the association of Ahreman with non-being. See especially Shaul Shaked, "Some Notes on Ahreman, the Evil Spirit, and His Creation," in E. E. Urbach et al., eds., *Studies in Mysticism and Religion presented to Gershom G. Scholem* (Jerusalem: Magnes Press, 1967), 227–34; Jes P. Asumssen, "Some Remarks on Sasanian Demonology," in *Commémoration Cyrus: Actes du Congrès de Shiraz* (Leiden: E.J. Brill, 1974), 236–41; Hanns-Peter Schmidt, "The Non-Existence of Ahreman and the Mixture (*gumēzišn*) of Good and Evil," in *K.R. Cama Oriental Institute, Second International Congress Proceedings* (Bombay: K.R. Cama Oriental Institute, 1996), 79–95; Antonio Panaino, "A Few Remarks on the Zoroastrian Conception of the Status of Angra Mainyu and of the Daēvas," *Res Orientales* 13 (2001): 99–107; and Bruce Lincoln, "The Cosmo-logic of Persian Demonology," in *Gods and Demons, Priests and Scholars: Critical Explorations in the History of Religions* (Chicago: University of Chicago Press, 2012), 31–42.

6. *Dādēstān ī Dēnīg* 36.4–8: ōh-iz dādār ī dahišn dād ān ī mēnōg dām abēzag anahōgēnēd ud ān-iz ī gētīgīg dām amarg a-zarmān ud suyišn ud abandišn abēš ud adard. . . . u-š pad arešk ī purr-kēnwarīh ī spurr-druxtārīh nīxwarēd ō griftan wišuftan ud wanēnidan abēsīhēnidan ī im hukard dām ī yazdan. Text from Mahmoud Jaafari-Dehaghi, ed., *Dādestān ī Dēnīg*, part 1, *Transcription, Translation, and Commentary* (Paris: Association pour l'avancement des études iraniennes, 1998).

7. *Dēnkart* 5.24.4 makes complex emotions of this sort responsible for Ahreman's assault, listing envy alongside others, but not granting it primacy. On this last point, it differs from the analysis of the *Bundahišn*.

The reason for his waging combat to mix up existence is his improper vindictiveness, greed, lust, enviousness (*areškanīh*), shame, thievishness, quarrelsomeness, arrogance, perversity, ignorance, his lie about being able to destroy the basis of the light-substance, his malevolence, injustice, foolhardy combativeness, and all his functions correlated with these.

ud kōxšišn ī pad andar gumēxtan wihān ān-ēwēn kēnwarīh ud āzwarīh ud waranīgīh ud areškanīh ud nangwarīh ud apparag-xēmīh ud stēzgārīh ud abarmenišnīh ud tar-menišnīh ud a-frazānagīh ud mituxtīh ī pad abesīhēnidan šāyistan ī buništ <ī> rōšn gōhr ud anāk-kāmīh ud a-dādig-cihragīh ud halak-kōšāgīh ud hāmist imīn ham rāyēnišn.

Text from Jaleh Amouzgar and Ahmad Tafazzoli, eds., *Le cinquième livre du Dēnkard* (Paris: Association pour l'avancement des etudes iraniennes, 2000).

8. Any of the standard secondary sources contain summary discussions of these issues. See, for example, Herman Lommel, *Die Religion Zarathustras nach dem Awesta dargestellt* (Tübingen: J.C.B. Mohr, 1930), 93–129, 205–46; Jacques Duchesne-Guillemin, *La religion de l'Iran ancien* (Paris: Presses Universitaires de France, 1962), 308–54; Marijan Molé, *Culte, mythe et cosmologie dans l'Iran ancien* (Paris: Presses Universitaires de France, 1963), 389–422; Mary Boyce, *A History of Zoroastrianism*, vol. 1, *The Early Period* (Leiden: E.J. Brill, 1975), 192–246.

9. Dating of the text remains controversial. For a variety of positions, see Colin Chase, ed., *The Dating of "Beowulf"* (Toronto: University of Toronto Press, 1997). Citations are taken from Fr. Klaeber, ed., *Beowulf and the Fight at Finnsburg*, 3rd ed. (Lexington, MA: D.C. Heath, 1950). All translations are original.

10. *Beowulf* 104–14:

|  |  |
|---|---|
|  | fifelcynnes eard |
| wonsǣli wer | weardode hwile, |
| siþðan him Scyppend | forscrifen hæfde |
| in Cāines cynne— | þone cwealm gewræc |
| ēce Drihten, | þæs þe hē Ābel slōg; |
| ne gefeah hē þǣre fæhðe, | ac hē hine feor forwræc, |
| Metod for þȳ māne | manacynne fram. |
| Þanon untȳdras | ealle onwōcon, |
| eotenas ond ylfe | ond orcnēas, |
| swylce gigantas, | þā wið Gode wunnon |
| lange þrāge. |  |

11. The story of Cain appears at Genesis 4.1–16, and verses 3–5 establish his envy of Abel's privileged relation to God as motive for the murder. The theme of Cain's monstrous descendants entered Old English traditions via the pseudepigraphical Book of Enoch. See further David Williams, *Cain and Beowulf: A Study in Secular Allegory* (Toronto: University of Toronto Press, 1982); Ruth Mellinkoff, "Cain's Monstrous Progeny in *Beowulf*: Part I, Noachic Tradition," *Anglo-Saxon England* 8 (1979): 143–97; Mellinkoff, "Cain's Monstrous Progeny in *Beowulf*: Part II, Post-diluvian Survival," *Anglo-Saxon England* 9 (1981): 183–97; Stephen C. Bandy, "Cain, Grendel, and the Giants of *Beowulf*," *Papers on Language and Literature* 9 (1973): 235–49; R. E. Kaske, "Beowulf and the Book of Enoch," *Speculum* 46 (1971): 421–31.

12. The classic discussion of envy, including envy at the creation, as prompting Grendel's assault remains Oliver Farrar Emerson, "Grendel's Motive in Attacking Heorot," *Modern Language Review* 16 (1921): 113–19.

13. *Beowulf* 86–103:

| | |
|---|---|
| Ðā se ellengǣst | earfoðlīce |
| Þrāge geþolode, | sē þe in þȳstrum bād, |
| Þæt hē dōgora gehwām | drēam gehȳrde |
| hlūdne in healle; | þær wæs hearpan swēg, |
| swutol sang scopes. | Sægde sē þe cūþe |
| frumsceaft fīra | feorran reccan, |
| cwæð þæt se Ælmihtiga | eorðan worh(te), |
| wlitebeorhtne wang, | swā wæter bebūgeð |
| gesette sigehrēþig | sunnan ond mōnan |
| lēoman tō lēohte | landbūendum, |
| ond gefrætwade | foldan scēatas |
| leomum ond lēafum, | līf ēac gesceōp |
| cynna gehwylcum | þāra ðe cwice hwyrfaþ.— |
| Swā ðā drihtguman | drēamum lifdon, |
| ēadiglīce, | oð ðæt ān ongan |
| fyrene fre(m)man | fēond on helle; |
| wæs se grimma gǣst | Grendel hāten, |
| mǣre mearcstapa, | sē þe mōras hēold, |
| fen ond fæsten; | |

14. On Heorot as mirroring the creation and the text's polysemic blurring of microcosm and macrocosm, see Alvin A. Lee, *Gold-Hall and Earth-Dragon: "Beowulf" as Metaphor* (Toronto: University of Toronto Press, 1998), 152–76; Willem Helder, "The Song of Creation in *Beowulf* and the Interpretation of Heorot," *English Studies in Canada* 13 (1987): 243–55; Paul Beekman Taylor, "Heorot, Earth, and Asgard: Christian Poetry and Pagan Myth," *Tennessee Studies in Literature* 11 (1966): 119–30.

15. *Beowulf* 64–81:

| | |
|---|---|
| Þā wæs Hrōðgāere | here-spēd gyfen, |
| wīges weorð-mynd, | þæt him his wine-māgas |
| georne hȳrdon, | oðð þæt sēo geogoð gewēox |
| magodriht micel. | Him on mōd bearn, |
| þæt healreced | hātan wolde, |
| medoærn micel | men gewyrcean |
| þon[n]e yldo bearn | æfre gefrūnon |
| ond þær on innan | eall gedælan |
| geongum ond ealdum, | swylc him God sealde |
| būton folcscare | ond feorum gumena. |
| Ðā ic wīde gefrægn | weorc gebannan |
| manigre mægþe | geond þisne middangeard, |
| folcstede frætwan. | Him on fyrste gelomp, |

| ǣdre mid yldum, | þæt hit wearð ealgearo, |
|---|---|
| healærna mǣst . . . | |
| Hē bēot ne āleh, | bēagas dǣlde, |
| sinc æt symle. | |

16. On the hall and its significance, see Hugh Magennis, *Images of Community in Old English Poetry* (Cambridge: Cambridge University Press, 1996).

17. For the letters exchanged during the first year of our correspondence, see Bruce Lincoln, "Beginnings of a Friendship," *Mythos* 9 (2014): 13–33.

## CHAPTER FOUR

1. The trial transcript was first published by Hermann von Bruiningk, "Der Werwolf in Livland und das letzte im Wendenschen Landgericht und Dörpischen Hofgericht i. J. 1692 deshalb stattgehabte Strafverfahren," *Mitteilungen aus der livländischen Geschichte* 22 (1924–28): 203–20. The text is in Middle German, with occasional Latin phrases inserted, and at points it clearly represents a paraphrase, not a verbatim record of what was said. Whether Thiess and other witnesses testified in German or in the vernacular is unclear. The text is divided into seventy-nine numbered sections, plus a preamble introducing the court and the judges, and a transcript of the verdict. I am grateful to Kenneth Northcott, Ken Pennington, and Louise Lincoln for help with the translation. The incident of the witness's smile is described in paragraph 1.

2. I am grateful to Professor Jurgis Skilters, director of the Center for Cognitive Sciences and Semantics at the University of Latvia, Dr. Kristine Ante, and Dr. Marins Mintaurs for help in identifying the Latvian names now used for the locales the transcript gives in German.

3. Thiess trial, paragraph 1: R: "Es wüste ja jederman, dasz er mit dem teuffell umbginge und ein wahrwolff wehre; wie er den schwehren köndte, weil er solches selber nicht leugnen würde und von langen jahren solches getrieben."

4. Thiess trial, paragraph 2.

5. Ibid., paragraph 3.

6. The most important accounts of Livonian lycanthropy in learned literature of the early modern period are Olaus Magnus, *Historia de Gentibus Septentrionalibus* 18.45–46 (1555); Philip Melanchthon, *Publicas Lectiones* 131 (1558); Kaspar Peucer, *Commentarius de præcipuis generibus divinationum*, p. 141r (1560); Paul Einhorn, *Wiederlegunge der Abgötteren*, Chapter VI (1627); and Christian Kortholt, writing under the pseudonym Theophilius Sincerus, *Nord-Schwedische Hexerey, oder Simia Dei, Gottes Affe*, pp. 31–32 (1677).

7. Thiess used this image at paragraphs 19, 44, and 62.

8. No translation adequately captures all the nuances of this term (= modern German *Segen*), which figures prominently in Thiess's account. Most literally, it is a blessing that purports to secure prosperity, and in some passages it has that meaning only (paragraphs 64, 65, 68. 69, 71, and 72). In most occurrences, however (paragraphs 13, 15, 19, 30, 32, and 62), it denotes the blessing of prosperity, fertility,

abundance, and a good harvest, as well as the divine favor or grace that makes these possible and of which they are the material consequence and expression.

9. Thiess trial, paragraphs 11, 12, 15, 19, 24, 30, 35, 44, 62, and 63.

10. Ibid., paragraph 20, von Bruiningk, 207–8: "Q: Ob das nicht böse gethan sey, dasz er seinem nechsten sein vieh nicht nur eigener bekentnis nach raube, sondern vornemblich auch das ebenbild Gottes, worzu er als ein mensch erschaffen, seiner einbildung nach in einen wolff verstelle."

11. Ibid., paragraph 32, von Bruiningk, 210: "Wie solches möglich seyn könne . . . dasz es nur eine falsche einbildung und teüffelischer betrug und verblendung sey?" See also paragraphs 27, 31, and 63. Ever since Saint Augustine, orthodox theology maintained that metamorphosis from human to animal state was impossible, since this would nullify God's will as expressed in his creation of the human body after his own image. The putative experience of lycanthropic transformation was thus theorized as an illusion created by the Devil, which affected both what was seen by those who reported werewolf attacks and the consciousness of those who in sleep, dream, or hallucination believed they had passed into a wolf's body. This remained the standard explanation thereafter, although a small number of theologians, most notably Jean Bodin, entertained the possibility of real physical transformation. Paul Einhorn, *Wiederlegunge der Abgötteren* (Riga: Gerhard Schröder, 1627), Chapter VI provides a view of contemporary opinion in Livonia, where some thought the werewolf's soul entered a wolf's body, while others held that his body transformed into that of a wolf. Speaking on behalf of religious and legal authorities, however, Einhorn (who was both a Lutheran pastor and superintendent of the Kurland district) insisted that werewolfery "is nothing other than the Devil's work and doing, through which he deludes wretched people" (Ist aber nicht mehr als bey Teuffels Werck und Getrieb, damit er daß elende Volk bethöre). On these theories, see Nicole Jacques-Lefèvre, "Such an Impure, Cruel, and Savage Beast: Images of the Werewolf in Demonological Works," in Kathryn A. Edwards, ed., *Werewolves, Witches, and Wandering Spirits: Traditional Belief and Folklore in Early Modern Europe* (Kirksville, MO: Truman State University Press, 2002), 181–97; on their influence in early modern Livonia, Tiina Vähi, "The Image of Werewolf in Folk Religion and Its Theological and Demonological Interpretations," in Manfried L. G. Dietrich and Tarmo Kulmar, eds., *The Significance of Base Texts for the Religious Identity / Die Bedeutung von Grundtesten für die religiöse Identität* (Münster: Ugarit Verlag, 2006), 213–37.

12. *Seegensprecher* (Modern German *Segensprecher*) literally denotes one who pronounces blessings (*Segen*), but it usually has a pejorative connotation, indicating a conjuror and charlatan. The pastor entered the proceedings just after Thiess had been describing the magic formulae he recited as part of his healing practice, so it is likely that he meant to play on the term's ambiguity, describing Thiess as one who portrayed himself as a speaker-of-blessings, but whom religious authorities rightly regarded as a misguided poser.

13. Thiess trial, paragraph 60, von Bruiningk, 214: "Weil nun der Hr. Pastor hujus loci Magister Bucholtz mit anhero erbeten ward, dem actui beyzuwohnen, ward er ersuchet, diesen selbst geständigen seegensprecher und in des teüffels stricken gefangenen sünder auch zuzusprechen, ihme seine grobe sünde, wozu er sich verführen

laszen, und darinnen bishero so lange und viele jahre verharret, zu gemühte zu führen und das gewiszen zu rühren, ob er zu bekehren undt zur busze, auch einer recht-schaffenen reüe und zur ablassung von dergleichen teüffelischen wesen zu bewegen undt zu bringen stehen möchte."

14. Ibid., paragraph 61; cf. paragraph 75.

15. Ibid., paragraph 63, von Bruiningk, 215: "er verstünde es beszer als der Hr. Pastor, der noch jung wehre, und ärgerte sich über des Hrn Pastoris zurehden."

16. Ibid., paragraph 62, von Bruiningk, 215: "Ille erwiese sich hierauff gahr ver-stockt und blieb beständig dabey, dasz solches alles, was er begangen, keine sünde wieder Gott wehre, sondern Gott vielmehr dadurch ein dienst geleistet und deszen willen erfüllet würde, den sie nähmen dem teuffell den seegen, so die zauberer ihm zutrügen, wieder weg und thäten dem ganzen lande dadurch gutes."

17. Ibid., paragraph 78, von Bruiningk, 218: "Ob man auch zwahr folgig bey der session zu Wenden die acta vornahm, kondte und wolte man sich dennoch über einen so schwehren und miszlichen casum zu keinem definitiven auszspruch entschlieszen, sondern ward erhehblich erachtet, solches nochmahlsz bisz zu supplirung des collegii durch die ehist gewärtige ankunfft des neuen Hrn. Landrichters von Palmbergs." See also paragraphs 75, 77, and 79.

18. In the final sentence of his verdict, Herman Georg von Trautvetter, judge of the Royal High Court, makes reference to the process of *leuteratio*, which has placed the case in his hands. Regarding the details of this procedure, see Johann Ernest Olympius, *Promptuarium Juris Canonici, Reudalis, Civilis, et Criminalis* (Vienna: Georg Lehmann, 1720), 47–48. I am grateful to Ken Pennington for help with this issue.

19. Thiess trial, "Judgment," von Bruiningk, 219: "Demnach ausz inquisiti selbst eigener auszuge erhellet, dasz er von langen jahren hehr alsz wahrwolff sich erwiesen und mit andern herumb gelauffen, auch in der hölle gewehsen, und in solche maasze einen und andern raub an vieh und mehrere dergleichen actus mit begehen helffen."

20. Ibid.: "noch des Jürgensburgschen Hrn. Pastoris bewehgliche zurehde sich davon ableiten laszen wollen, auch seiner dem Hrn. Pastori loci vorhin gethaner angelobung zu wieder nicht davon abgestanden, noch sich zum gehör Göttl. wohrts und gebrauch der hl. Sacramenten selbst gestandener maaszen eingefunden, son-dern auch, weiln er wieder höchsten Gottes und weltlicher obrigkeit ernstlichen verboht allerhand wahrsagung und seegen sprechereyen getrieben und dadurch sich schwehrlich versündiget und andere nehben sich zum aberglauben verführet." At two other points the court showed concern about the influence Thiess enjoyed among the peasants. Thus, early in the proceedings, Judge Ackerstaff stated that as a result of Thiess's having escaped the Nitau court without punishment, "he was idolized by the peasants" (paragraph 3, von Bruiningk, 204: von den bauren gleich einem abgotte gehalten worden). Second, in pronouncing his verdict, Judge von Trautvetter specified that Thiess's flogging be public "to demonstrate the offense of this male-factor to the bystanders to warn others against the same vexatious and punishable conduct and to warn them to let superstitions flow away from themselves" (Verdict, von Bruiningk, 220: und ihnen dabenehben dieses maleficiantis hartes verbrechen vorzustellen, auch andere von dergleichen ärgerlichen und sträftlichen wandell auch aberglauben abzumahnen selbst gefliszen seyn wird).

21. Ibid., 220: "billig nach schärffe des rechten anzusehen und zu bestraffen, wie er den solches seines gahr ärgerlichen und schwehren verbrechens halber, ihme zur wollverdienten straffe und andern zum merklichen abscheu hiemit zum öffentlichen staupenschlage." As Tālivaldis Zemzaris, "Vilkaču prāvas Vidzemē ("Werewolf Trials in Vidzeme"), in Margers Steprmanis, ed., *Latviesu vesturnieku veltijums Profesoram Dr. hist. Roberta Viperam* (Riga: Gulbis, 1939), 115–41, first observed, the penalty was extremely light, perhaps because of complexities in Thiess's case, but more likely because of larger shifts in judicial practice and general opinion. A generation earlier convicted werewolves were still being burned at the stake, as in a 1647 case that Zemzaris used as a point of comparison.

22. In several interviews, Ginzburg has discussed the timing, circumstances, and consequences of his first reading the transcript of Thiess's trial. The fullest account I have found appeared in "De près, de loin: Des rapports de force en histoire; Entretien avec Carlo Ginzburg," *Vacarme* 18 (January 2, 2002), available at http://www.vacarme.org/article235.html. He also provides an extremely useful discussion of the way his studies developed in "Witches and Shamans," in Carlo Ginzburg, *Threads and Traces: True, False, Fictive*, trans. Anne C. Tedeschi and John Tedeschi (Baltimore: Johns Hopkins University Press, 2012), 215–27.

23. Carlo Ginzburg, *I Benandanti: Stregoneria e culti agrari tra cinquecento e seicento* (Turin: Giulio Einaudi, 1966); English trans. by John Tedeschi and Anne Tedeschi, *The Night Battles: Witchcraft and Agrarian Cults in the Sixteenth & Seventeenth Centuries* (Baltimore: Johns Hopkins University Press, 1983).

24. One can see the way the Thiess trial modified Ginzburg's view of the Benandanti from the passage in which he introduced it, reflecting an abrupt and somewhat awkward revision from the language of his dissertation.

> The trial of Gasparutto and Moduco was the first in a long series involving the benandanti (both men and women) who declared that they fought at night with witches and sorcerers to secure the fertility of the fields and the abundance of the harvests. This belief (we have hinted at its presumably ritual origins) does not appear to the best of our knowledge, in any of the countless trials for witchcraft or superstitious practices held outside the Friuli. *The sole and extraordinary exception is furnished by the trial of a Livonian werewolf which took place at Jürgensburg in 1692—more than a century after the trial of Gasparutto and Moduco, and at the other extremity of Europe.* (*The Night Battles*, 28–29; my italics, reflecting additions to the text of Ginzburg's 1964 dissertation and the published version of *I Benandanti* in 1966)

25. Ginzburg, *The Night Battles*, xx–xxi and 28–32.

26. Carlo Ginzburg, *Storia notturna: Una decifrazione del sabba* (Turin: Giulio Einaudi, 1989); English trans. by Raymond Rosenthal, *Ecstasies: Deciphering the Witches' Sabbath* (New York: Pantheon, 1991).

27. For the most part, Ginzburg uses the term "shamanism" in conventional fashion, much as it is described in such classic literature as M. A. Czaplicka, *Aboriginal Siberia: A Study in Social Anthropology* (Oxford: Clarendon Press, 1914); Geor-

gii Nioradze, *Der Schamanismus bei den sibirischen Völkern* (Stuttgart: Strecker und Schröder, 1925); Mircea Eliade, *Le chamanisme et les techniques archaiques de l'extase* (Paris: Payot, 1951); English trans. by Willard Trask, *Shamanism: Archaic Techniques of Ecstasy* (New York: Bollingen Foundation, 1964); Louise Bäckman and Åke Hultkrantz, *Studies in Lapp Shamanism* (Stockholm: Almqvist & Wiksell, 1978); Vilmos Diószegi, *Shamanism in Siberia* (Budapest: Akadémiai Kiadó, 1996). Ginzburg is well aware of the complicated genealogy of this term and category, which he discussed in an essay titled "The Europeans Discover (or Rediscover) the Shamans," in *Threads and Traces*, 83–95. Further along these lines, see Gloria Flaherty, *Shamanism and the Eighteenth Century* (Princeton, NJ: Princeton University Press, 1992); Andrei A. Znamenski, *The Beauty of the Primitive: Shamanism and Western Imagination* (New York: Oxford University Press, 2007); and Jeroen W. Boekhoven, *Genealogies of Shamanism: Struggles for Power, Charisma, and Authority* (Groningen: Barkhuis, 2011).

28. Carlo Ginzburg, *Il formaggio e i vermi: Il cosmo di un mugnaio del '500* (Turin: Giulio Einaudi, 1976); English trans. by John Tedeschi and Anne Tedeschi, *The Cheese and the Worms: The Cosmos of a 15th-Century Miller* (Baltimore: Johns Hopkins University Press, 1980).

29. On the reception of *I Benandanti*, see Yme Kuiper, "Witchcraft, Fertility Cults, and Shamanism: Carlo Ginzburg's *I Benandanti* in Retrospect," in Brigitte Luchesi and Kocku von Stuckrad, eds., *Religion im kulturellen Diskurs / Religion in Cultural Discourse: Festschrift für Hans G. Kippenberg* (Berlin: Walter de Gruyter, 2014), 33–59. Important early support came from E. William Monter, *European Witchcraft* (New York: Wiley, 1969); Monter, "The Historiography of European Witchcraft: Progress and Prospects," *Journal of Interdisciplinary History* 2 (1972): 435–51; Mircea Eliade, "Some Observations on European Witchcraft," *History of Religions* 14 (1975): 149–72, reprinted in *Occultism, Witchcraft, and Cultural Fashions: Essays in Comparative Religion* (Chicago: University of Chicago Press, 1976), 69–92; Anne Jacobson Schutte, "Carlo Ginzburg," *Journal of Modern History* 48 (1976): 296–315; and Peter Burke, "Good Witches," *New York Review of Books*, February 28, 1985, 32–34.

30. Among those who reacted to *Storia notturna* most enthusiastically were the Middle European folklorists who had previously studied the Hungarian *táltos*, Slavic *kresniki*, and others Ginzburg incorporated in his theory. Inter alia, see Gábor Klaniczay, *The Uses of Supernatural Power: The Transformation of Popular Religion in Medieval and Early-Modern Europe*, trans. Susan Singerman (Princeton, NJ: Princeton University Press, 1990), 129–50; Klaniczay, "Shamanism and Witchcraft," *Magic, Ritual, and Witchcraft* 1 (2006): 214–21; Éva Pócs, "Hungarian *Táltos* and His European Parallels," in Mihály Hoppál and Juha Pentikäinen, eds., *Uralic Mythology and Folklore* (Budapest: Ethnographic Institute of the Hungarian Academy of Sciences, 1989), 251–74; Pócs, "Le sabbat et les mythologies indo-européennes," in Nicole Jacques-Chaquin and Maxime Préaud, eds., *Le sabbat des sorciers VXe-XVIIIe siècles* (Grenoble: J. Million, 1993), 23–31; Pócs, "Nature and Culture—'The Raw and the Cooked': Shape-Shifting and Double Beings in Central and Eastern European Folklore," in Willem de Blécourt and Christa Agnes Tuczay, eds., *Tierverwandlungen: Codierungen und Diskurse* (Tübingen: Francke, 2011), 99–134. Also of interest is the "Round-Table Discussion with Carlo Ginzburg, Gustav Henningsen, Éva Pócs, Giovanni Pizza, and Gábor Klaniczay," in

Éva Pócs and Gábor Klaniczay, eds., *Witchcraft Mythologies and Persecutions* (Budapest: Central European University Press, 2008), 35–49. Serious critiques include Giovanni Filoramo, "Una storia infinita: La *Storia notturna* di Carlo Ginzburg," *Rivista di Storia e Letteratura Religiosa* 27 (1991): 283–96; Klaus Graf, "Carlo Ginzburgs 'Hexensabbat': Herausforderung an die Methodendiskussion der Geschichtswissenschaft," *Kea* 5 (1993): 1–16; Willem de Blécourt, "The Return of the Sabbat: Mental Archaeologies, Conjectural Histories, or Political Mythologies," in Jonathan Barry and Owen Davies, eds., *Palgrave Advances in Witchcraft Historiography* (Houndmills: Palgrave Macmillan, 2007), 125–45; and de Blécourt, "A Journey to Hell: Reconsidering the Livonian 'Werewolf,'" *Magic, Ritual, and Witchcraft* 2 (2007): 49–67.

31. Thiess trial, paragraph 23, von Bruiningk, 208: "weil ja kundbahrer weise er ein bettler und ganz unvermögend sey."

32. The sole exception is Marienburg (today's Alūksne), located more than 100 km west of the others. Since Thiess blamed a "scoundrel from Marienburg" for having first made him a werewolf, it may be that he was deflecting unwelcome questions by describing his powers as having a distant origin.

33. There is one exception, which is slight, but revealing. The court identified Gricke Jahnen as a "fellow" (*kerl*, cognate to English *churl*), and not a peasant, presumably because he had been adopted by "the blessed Herr Pastor" (perhaps following his mother's marriage to the latter).

34. Regarding the werewolf trials, see Maia Madar, "Estonia I: Werewolves and Poisoners," in Bengt Ankarloo and Gustav Henningsen, eds., *Early Modern European Witchcraft: Centres and Peripheries* (Oxford: Clarendon Press, 1990), 257–72; and Merili Metsvahi, "Werwolfprozesse in Estland und Livland im 17. Jahrhundert: Zusammenstöße zwischen der Realität von Richtern und von Bauern," in Jürgen Beyer and Reet Hiiemäe, eds., *Folklore als Tatsachenbericht* (Tartu: Sektion für Folkloristik des Estnischen Literaturmuseums, 2001), 175–84. Specialized studies of the Livonian werewolf tradition more broadly include not only von Bruiningk, but Karlis Straubergs, "Om Varulvarna i Baltikum," in Sigurd Erixon, ed., *Liv och folkkultur* (Stockholm: Samfundet för Svensk Folklivsforskning, 1955), 107–29; Andrejs Plakans, "Witches and Werewolves in Early Modern Livonia: An Unfinished Project," in Lars M. Andersson, Anna Jansdotter, Badil E. B. Persson, and Charlotte Tornbjer, eds., *Rätten: En Festskrift till Bengt Ankerll* (Lund: Nordic Academic Press, 2000), 255–71; Vähi, "The Image of Werewolf in Folk Religion"; Vähi, "Werwölfe—Viehdiebe und Räuber im Wolfspelz? Elemente des archaischen Gewohnheitsrechts in estischen Werwolfvorstellungen," in de Blécourt and Tuczay, eds., *Tierverwandlungen*, 135–56; Willem de Blécourt, "A Journey to Hell: Reconsidering the Livonian 'Werewolf'"; Stefan Donecker, "The Werewolves of Livonia: Lycanthropy and Shape-Changing in Scholarly Texts, 1550–1720," *Preternature: Critical and Historical Studies on the Preternatural* 2 (2012): 289–322; Donecker, "Livland und seine Werwölfe: Ethnizität und Monstrosität an der europäischen Peripherie, 1550–1700," *Jahrbuch des baltischen Deutschtums* 56 (2009): 83–98; and Donecker, "Werewolves on the Baltic Seashore: Monstrous Frontier of Early Modern Europe, 1550–1700," in Niall Scott, *The Role of the Monster: Myths & Metaphors of Enduring Evil* (Oxford: Inter-Disciplinary Press, 2009), 63–75.

35. Stefan Donecker, "The Medieval Frontier and Its Aftermath: Historical Discourses in Early Modern Livonia," in Imbi Sooman and Stefan Donecker, eds., *The "Baltic Frontier" Revisited: Power Structures and Cross-Cutural Interactions in the Baltic Sea Region* (Vienna: n.p., 2009), 41–62; Donecker, "Konfessionalisierung und religiöse Begegnung im Ostseeraum," in Andrea Komlosy and Hans-Heinrich Nolte, and Imbi Sooman, eds., *Ostsee 700–2000: Gsesellschaft, Wirtschaft, Kultur* (Vienna: Promedia, 2008), 91–109; Donecker, "Livland und seine Werwölfe"; and Donecker, "Werewolves on the Baltic Seashore." See further Vilho Niitemaa, *Die undeutsche Frage in der Politik der livländischen Städte im Mittelalter* (Helsinki: Annales Academiae Scientiarum Fennicae, 1949); Paul Johansen, "Nationale Vorurteile und Minderwertigkeitsgefühle als sozialer Faktor im mittelalterlichen Livland," in *Alteuropa und die Moderne Gesellschaft: Festschrift für Otto Brünner* (Göttingen: Vandenhoeck & Ruprecht, 1963), 88–115; Paul Johansen and Heinz von zur Mühlen, *Deutsch und Undeutsch im mittelalterlichen und frühneuzeitlichen Reval* (Cologne and Vienna: Böhlau, 1973); Juhan Kahk, "Heidnische Glaubensvorstellungen, Zauberei und religiöse Eifer in Estland um 1700," *Zeitschrift fûur Ostforschung* 34 (1985): 522–35; and Wilhelm Lenz, "*Undeutsch*: Bemerkungen zu einem besonderen Begriff der baltischen Geschichte," in Bernhart Jähnig and Klaus Militzer, eds., *Aus der Geschichte Alt-Livlands: Festschrift für Heinz von zur Mühlen* (Münster: Lit Verlag, 2004), 169–84.

36. Donecker, "The Medieval Frontier and Its Aftermath," 48.

37. Thiess's was one of the last trials for werewolfery. Most of the earlier trials ended with a confession extracted by torture, often to avoid conviction on the more serious charge of witchcraft. See Metsvahi, "Werwolfprozesse in Estland und Livland," 176–77; and Vähi, "Hexenprozesse und der Werwolfglaube in Estland," 226–27 and 230.

38. Thiess repeatedly cited the Nitau court's indulgent treatment of him as something like a precedent that ought lead the Wenden court to recognize not only his innocence, but that of werewolves in general. See paragraphs 2, 3, 63, 64, and 72.

39. Ibid., paragraph 20, von Bruiningk, 208: "und das gelübde, so er seinem erlöser Christo in der hl. Tauffe gethan, da er dem teüffel und allem seinem wesen und wercken entsaget, Gotts vergeszener weise breche und dergleichen höchst verbotene sünde andern zum abscheü und ärgernis so beharlich treibe und nicht zu Gottes hause, wo er sonst durch die predigt und christliche lehrer zu Gottes erkäntnis und dienste gelangen könte, sich begäbe, sondern lieber der höllen zulauffe."

40. Ibid., paragraph 33, von Bruiningk, 210: "Q: Ob er dann nicht des vorsatzes sey, vor seinem tode sich zu Gott zu bekehren, von seinem willen und wesen sich unterrichten zu laszen, von solchem teüffelischen unwesen abzustehen, seine sünde zu bereüen und seine seele von der ewigen verdamnis und höllen pein dadurch zu erretten? R: Hierauff wolte er nicht recht antworten, sagete, wer wüste, wo seine seele bleiben würde; er wäre nun schon alt, was könte er solche dinge mehr begreiffen."

41. Ibid., paragraph 18, von Bruiningk, 207:

Q: Where do the werewolves go after death?

A: They are buried like other people and their souls come to heaven, but the Devil takes the sorcerers' souls for himself.

Q: Is the witness diligent toward the Church, does he listen faithfully to the word of God, does he pray diligently and does he take the Lord's Supper?
A: No, he does neither the one nor the other.

Q: Wo die wahrwölffe nach dem tode hinkähmen? R: Sie würden begraben wie andere leüte und ihre seelen kähmen in den himmel; der zäüberer seelen aber nähme teüffel zu sich.—Q: Ob referent sich fleiszig zur kirchen halte Gottes wort mit andacht anhöre, fleiszig bäte und sich zum hl. Nachtmahl halte? Negat, er thue weder eines noch das andere.

Cf. paragraph 62.

42. Ibid., paragraph 5, von Bruiningk, 204: "Q: Wie dan referent nach der höllen gekommen und wo dieselbe gelehgen sey? R: Die wahrwölffe gingen zu fusz dahin in wölffe gestalt, der ohrt wehre an dem ende von der see, Puer Esser genand, im morast unter Lemburg, etwa 1/2 meyle von des substituirten Hr. Praesidis hoffe Klingenberg, alda wehren herliche gemächer und bestellete thürhüter, welche diejehnige, so etwas von der von den zauberern dahin gebrachter korn-blüte und dem korn selber wieder ausztragen wolten, dichte abschlügen. Die blüte würde in einem sonderlichen kleht verwahret und das korn auch in einem andern." Cf. paragraphs 11, 12, 13, 15, 19, 30, 44, and 62.

43. A fairly deep relation connected the judge and the defendant, as indicated by the trial transcript, paragraph 3, von Bruiningk, 204:

In addition to the others present who knew Thiess well, the substitute Herr Judge of District Court Bengt Johan Ackerstaff, who had known him well in previous times when Thiess worked for him for several years, declared that he understood his health never to have failed him, also that he never lied about such things, and that in his opinion, nothing happened in the earlier case with the aforementioned judges, so that he was set free and he was idolized by the peasants.

Wohrauff nehben dehnen andern anwehsenden, so den Thiessen woll kandten, der substituirter Hr. Landrichter Bengt Johan Ackerstaff, alsz unter wessen gute er in vorigen zeiten auch einige jahre gelehbett und gedienet, declarirte dasz es ihme an gesundem verstande nimmer gefehlet, er auch solches sein wehsen nimmer verleügnet und, nachdehme ihme vor diesem von den damaligen richtern desfalsz nichts geschehen, desto freyer solches getrieben und von den bauren gleich einem abgotte gehalten worden.

44. On Latvian constructions of the otherworld as close at hand, located in lakes, swamps, and burial grounds, also a realm where the seasons are the reverse of ours, such that fertility resides there in the winter when absent from the earth's surface, see Karlis Straubergs, "Zur Jenseitstopographie," *Arv* 13 (1957); 56–110, esp. 85–90.

45. Thiess trial, paragraph 16, von Bruiningk, 206–7.

46. The sorcerers' feasts with the Devil in Hell are mentioned at paragraphs 6, 11, and 24.

47. Thiess describes the sorcerers' thefts at paragraphs 5, 12, 13, 15, 19, 44, and 62.

48. Thiess trial, paragraph 24, von Bruiningk, 208:

Q: Did they receive any sign from the Devil through which they could know him?
A: No, but he branded the sorcerers and was generous with them.

Q: Ob sie kein zeichen von dem teüffel bekähmen, woran er sie erkennen könne?
[R:] Negat. Die zauberer aber zeichnete er undt dieselbe tractirte.

49. Ibid., paragraph 44, von Bruiningk, 212:

Q: Had he then made so strong a pact with the Devil that he cannot desist from it?
A: The Devil has nothing to do with him.

Q: Ob er denn einen so festen bund mit dem teüffel gemachet, dasz er nicht davon ablaszen wolle? R: Der teüffel hätte nichts mit ihm zu thun.

50. The judges (or pastor) place the Devil in antithetical opposition to God at paragraphs 19, 20, 33, 61. They speak of the Devil's temptations, lies, and delusions at paragraphs 27, 31, 32, 56, 63, and 75, describing how he leads people into sin at paragraphs 27, 33, 43, 60, and 61 and to damnation at paragraphs 33, 43, and 61.

51. Thiess trial, paragraphs 33–36, von Bruiningk, 210:

Q: Wo er denn das wahrsagen gelernet, weil ja viele leute zu ihm giengen und ihn befrageten, was ihnen begegnen würde? R: Er könte nicht wahrsagen, sondern er wäre ein pferdeartzt, und wann andere sünder jemands pferden leyd angethan hätten, so hiebe er sie wieder auff, und nehme solches wieder von ihnen hinweg, wozu er einige und nur etwa 3 worte gebrauchte, und ihnen salz oder brodt eingebe, welches er mit den worten vorhin gesegnet hätte.
Q: Was vor sünder er verstehe, so den pferden leyd anthäten? R: Dieselben teüffels-macher oder hexen, welche nichts als böses thäten.
Q: Was es dann vor worte wären, die er dabey gebrauchte? R: Sonn undt mond gehe übers meer, hole die seele wieder, die der teüffel in die hölle gebracht und gib dem vieh das leben und die gesundheit wieder, so ihm entnommen,—und solches hülffe so woll anderm viehe als den pferden.

Cf. paragraph 52, where sorcerers are also said to cause disease.

52. Ibid., paragraphs 5, 12, 13, 15, 19, 44, 62.

53. Ibid., paragraphs 11, 16, and 24.

54. Ibid., paragraphs 18 and 19.

55. Ibid., paragraphs 5, 12, 13, 15, 19, 39, 44, 62.

56. Ibid., paragraph 15, von Bruiningk, 206: "Q: Wie referent sagen könne, dasz sie den diesjährigen seegen bereit verwichene Lucien nacht aus der hölle wieder

heraus bekommen, welchen die zauberer dahin gebracht, weil ja die saat undt blühte zeit nun erst bevorstehe und also noch nichts dahin gebracht seyn könne? R: Die zauberer hätten ihre sonderliche zeit und säete der teuffel schon lange voraus. Davon nehmen die zauberer alsdann etwas und brächten es in die hölle und solchen seegen trügen die wahrwölffe wieder aus der hölle, und darnach fiele alsdann der wachsthumb von unserer saat ausz, wie auch von obst bäumen, dergleichen auch bey der höllen viele wären, undt von fischerey; auf Weynachten wäre schon vollkommen grün korn allerhand arth und baum gewächs imgleichen bey der höllen." Cf. paragraphs 12, 30, 44, 62. Of particular interest is paragraph 19, von Bruiningk, 207, where the Devil himself is identified as a thief.

Q: How can the soul of someone who does not serve God, but the Devil, and who does not go to church, seldom to confession, and does not take the Lord's Supper, as the witness has admitted of himself, ever come to God?

A: The werewolves do not serve the Devil, for they take away from him that which the sorcerers brought him and for that reason the Devil is so hostile to them that he cannot bear them. . . . Everything the werewolves do profits people best, for if they didn't exist and the Devil made off with the prosperity, robbed or stole it, all the world's prosperity would depart.

Q: Wie denn deszen seele zu Gott kommen könne, der nicht Gott dienet, sondern dem teüffel, auch nicht zur kirchen kommet, weniger zur beichte und zum hl. Nachtmahl sich hält, wie referent von sich selber gestehe? R: Die wahrwölffe dieneten dem teüffel nicht, denn sie nehmen ihme das jenige weg, was die zäuberer ihme zubrächten und deswegen wäre der teüffel ihnen so feind, dasz er sie nicht leyden könnte . . . alles was sie, die wahrwölffe, thäten, gereichte dem menschen zum besten, denn wenn sie nicht wären und dem teüffel den seegen wieder wegstiehlen oder raubeten, so würde aller seegen in der welt weg seyn.

57. Friedrich von Toll, "Zur Geschichte der Hexenprocesse: Auszug aus dem Protocoll des Wier- und Jerweschen Manngerichts," *Das Inland* 4 (1839): 258: "worauf sich der böse Persönlich präsentiret, *in schwartzen Teutschen Kleidern*" (emphasis added). The significance of this testimony has been discussed by Donecker, "Livland und seine Werwölfe," 95; Donecker, "Werewolves on the Baltic Seashore," 67–68. Much the same kind of testimony recurs in a 1641 trial in Pärnu, where the accused testified that the devil appeared to him "as a German" (cited in Madar, "Estonia I: Werewolves and Poisoners," 271).

58. Ülo Valk, "Reflections of Folk Belief and Legends at the Witch Trials of Estonia," in Eszter Csonka-Takacs, Gabor Klaniczay, and Eva Pocs, eds., *Witchcraft Mythologies and Persecutions* (Budapest: Central European University Press, 2008), 269–82; the passage cited appears at p. 273. See further Valk, *The Black Gentleman: Manifestations of the Devil in Estonian Folk Religion*, trans. Ülle Männarti (Helsinki: Suomalainen Tiedeakatemia, 2001), esp. sections 1.3.1 and 1.3.2, "The Devil as a Landlord" and "The Demonisation of the German Noblemen in the 17th and 18th Centuries," 74–85 and 86–92, respectively.

59. Thiess discussed sorcerers in paragraphs 5, 12, 13, 15, 18, 19, 24, 44, 52, and 62. This notwithstanding, neither the judges nor the pastor showed much interest in the topic, mentioning sorcerers only once, when they tried to trip Thiess up in a contradiction (paragraph 15).

60. Thiess trial, paragraph 19, von Bruiningk, 207: "Everything the werewolves do profits people best, for if they didn't exist and the Devil made off with the prosperity, robbed or stole it, all the world's prosperity would depart and (the witness) confirmed this with an oath." (Alles was sie, die wahrwölffe, thäten, gereichete dem menschen zum besten, denn wenn sie nicht wären und dem teüffel den seegen wieder wegstiehlen oder raubeten, so würde aller seegen in der welt weg seyn, und solches bestätigte er mit einem eyde.)

61. See Vähi, "Viehdiebe und Räuber im Wolfspelz?"

62. The judges introduced theft of livestock nine times (paragraphs 8, 9, 10, 11, 20, 29, 31, 32, and the Verdict), compared to only two times they asked about grain (paragraphs 15 and 30). Thiess responded to such concerns five times (paragraphs 8, 9, 10, 20, and 32), and mentioned seizing animals on three other occasions (paragraphs 6, 7, 12). In contrast, he introduced the recovery of agricultural items from the underworld nine times, usually dwelling on it at length (paragraphs 2, 5, 11, 12, 13, 15, 19, 30, 62).

63. Thiess trial, paragraphs 9–10, von Bruiningk, 205:

Q: Weil sie in wölffe verwandelt wären, warumb sie dann nicht das fleisch rohe, wie wölffe, verzehreten? R: Das wäre die weise nicht, sondern sie äszen es als menschen gebraten.

Q: Wie sie es handtieren können, weil sie ja wolffes häupter und pfoten seiner auszage nach haben, womit sie kein meszer halten noch spiesze bereiten und andere darzu erforderte arbeit verrichten können? R: Meszer gebrauchten sie nicht darzu, sie zerriszen es mit den zähnen und steckten die stücker mit den pfoten auf stöcker, wie sie dieselbe nur finden, undt wenn sie es verzehreten, so wären sie schon wieder als menschen, gebrauchten aber kein brodt darbey; saltz nähmen sie von den gesindern mit sich, wenn sie ausgiengen.

64. Ibid., paragraph 17, von Bruiningk, 207: "Q: Ob nicht weiber undt mägde mit unter den wahrwölfen, auch Deutsche sich darunter befinden? R: Die weiber wären woll mit unter den wahrwölffen, die mägde aber würden dazu nicht genommen, sondern die würden zu fliegenden Puicken oder drachen gebrauchet und so verschicket und nehmen den segen von der milch und butter weg. Die Deutschen kähmen nicht in ihre gemeinschafft, sondern hätten eine sonderliche hölle."

65. Thiess's remarks about young women allude to the belief that the Devil could steal the spirit from milk and butter, leaving them insipid and tasteless. Butter that had suffered such a fate was called "Dragon-Butter" (*Drachen-Butter*). A discussion of this is found in Christian Kortholt, under the pseudonym Theophilius Sincerus, *Nord-Schwedische Hexerey, oder Simia Dei, Gottes Affe. Das ist: Ausführliche Beschreibung der schändlichen Verführungen des leidigen Satans* (1677), 14–15.

66. Thiess trial, paragraph 19, von Bruiningk, 207 (cf. paragraph 62):

In the preceding year, the Russian werewolves came earlier and had recovered the prosperity of their land. Therefore they had also had good growth in their land, while that of this land failed, for they had come too late on this side. But this year they had come before the Russians and thus it was a fruitful year and good for flax.

Die Ruszischen wahrwölffe wären im vergangenen jahre was früher gekommen und hätten ihres landes seegen davon gebracht. Darumb hätten sie in ihrem lande auch ein gut gewächs gehabt, woran es diesem lande gefehlet, weil sie von dieser seiten obberichteter maaszen zu späte gekommen. Dies jahr aber wären sie den Ruszen zuvor gekommen undt würde also ein fruchtbahr auch ein gut flachs jahr seyn.

See also paragraph 14 for the assertion that those from different villages belong to different bands (*es wären unterschiedliche rotten*). Here, Thiess specifies that Skeistan, who broke his nose, belonged to another band of werewolves, although Ginzburg and others regularly misidentify him as having been a sorcerer.

67. Thiess described werewolves' relation to Hell as hostile and fleeting, in contrast to that of sorcerers, who were recurrent visitors, welcomed and entertained by the Devil. The contrast is drawn most clearly in paragraph 11, von Bruiningk, 205:

The sorcerers eat with the Devil in Hell. The werewolves were not admitted there with them. Nevertheless, they sometimes quickly run in and snatch something, then run back with it as if fleeing.

die zauberer aber äszen mit dem teuffel in der hölle, die wahrwölffe würden nicht mit dazu gestattet, sie lieffen dennoch bisweilen eilig hinein undt erschnapten etwas und lieffen denn wieder damit als fliehend hinaus.

Cf. paragraphs 11, 12, 20, and 24. Paragraph 16, von Bruiningk, 206–7, is particularly significant for its implication that sorcerers "belong" in Hell, along with the Devil.

Q: Whenever you go to other feasts at that aforementioned place in Hell, do you find such buildings and do the same ones consistently stay there?
A: Yes.
Q: How is it that the other people who dwell nearby can't also see this?
A: It's not on top, but under the earth and the entrance is protected by a gate that no one can find, except someone who belongs inside.

Q: Ob allezeit, wenn sie zu andern mahlen sich an dem gemelten orth der höllen begeben, sie solche gebäude da fanden und dieselbe beständig allda verbleiben? Affirmat.—Q: Wie es denn andere da herumb wohnende leüte nicht auch sehen können? R: Es sey nicht über, sondern unter der erden, und der eingang mit einer pforten verwahret, welche niemand finden könne, alsz der dahin gehöre.

68. There is only one other datum from early modern Livonia in which were-wolves are construed in similar terms. This is a story reported as fact by Hermann Witekind (1522–1603), a student of Philip Melanchthon (1497–1560), who taught in Riga and maintained an epistolary relation with his teacher. Melanchthon relied on Witekind for his knowledge of events in Livonia, occasionally making mention of the latter's reports in his own publications and sharing them with his nephew, Kaspar Peucer (1525–1602), professor of mathematics and sometime rector at the University of Wittenburg. Witekind published this story under the pseudonym Augustin Lercheimer von Steinfelden, in a volume titled *Christlich bedencken und erinnerung von zauberey* (1585). Peucer, however, had already published it in his *Commentarius de præcipuis generibus divinationum* (Wittenberg: I. Crato, 1560). Both authors take it as an actual occurrence and cite it as evidence that the reported occurrences of werewolfery, being physically impossible, ought be understood as illusions produced by the Devil. The item of most immediate interest to us, however, is that the accused describes werewolves as the enemies of witches in response to the charges against him, explaining that he did not mean to harm the horse he killed and dismembered, for he swung his weapon at a witch hiding behind the horse and accidentally struck the latter. Here, as in the case of Thiess, the werewolf-witch opposition emerges in a defensive gambit, whereby the accused sought to clear himself by inverting stereotyped images.

69. Ginzburg returned to methodological questions repeatedly as he struggled to justify the move from morphology to history, e.g., *Ecstasies*, 15–16, 133–36, 170, 186, 195–97, 212–17, 240–43, 257–58, and 266–67. The most revealing such discussion is at p. 213, where he states: "Given cultural convergences of the amplitude that we have described, the theoretically possible explanations are three: (a) diffusion; (b) derivation from a common source; (c) derivation from structural characteristics of the human mind." As he associates the third option with ahistoric archetypes or structures (Jung, Eliade, Lévi-Strauss) and the second with a geneticism that easily gives way to a fascist triumphalism, either with or without racism (Höfler in the first instance, Dumézil in the second), he rejects both of these in favor of a more complex model, in which diffusion and genetic descent both have their part.

70. Ginzburg, *Ecstasies*, 16.

71. Von Bruiningk. A prefatory note states that a shorter version of the article was presented "in der Sitzung der Gesellschaft für Geschichte und Altertumskunde in Riga den 9. April 1924" (p. 163). Volume 22 of the *Mitteilungen aus der livländischen Geschichte* is dated 1924–28, while volume 21 dates from 1911.

72. Particularly noteworthy in the interwar period are Kārlis Straubergs, "Vilkaču ideoloğia Latvijā (Werewolf ideology in Latvia)," in Margers Steparmanis and Arveds Švabe, eds., *Latviesu vesturnieku veltijums Profesoram Robertam Viperam* (Riga: A. Gulbis 1939), 98–114; and Tālivaldis Zemzaris, "Vilkaču prāvas Vidzemē (Werewolf Trials in Vidzeme)," ibid., 115–41. On the nationalist motives and subtexts of these and other scholars active in this period, see Plakans, "Witches and Werewolves in Early Modern Livonia: An Unfinished Project," 255–59. The post-Soviet literature is listed above, in note 33.

73. Otto Höfler, *Kultische Geheimbünde der Germanen* (Frankfurt am Main: Moritz

Diesterweg, 1934). Höfler credits the Uppsala philologist Olof von Feilitzen (1908–76) with having called his attention to von Bruiningk's article, which suggests it had already excited some interest in Sweden. Karl Meuli also made mention of it in *Die deutschen Masken* (Berlin: de Gruyter, 1933), §35 "Kriegsmaske," reprinted in his *Gesammelte Schriften* (Basel: Schwabe, 1975), 1: 160.

74. Höfler built on a number of earlier works that were much admired in Germanic-speaking countries, but remain relatively little known to anglophone scholars. These include Heinrich Schurtz, *Altersklassen und Männerbund: Eine Darstellung der Grundformen der Gesellschaft* (Berlin: G. Reimer, 1902); Hans Blüher, *Die Rolle der Erotik in der männlichen Gesellschaft: Eine Theorie der Menschlichen Staatsbildung nach Wesen und Wert* (Jena: Eugen Diederich, 1921); Jakob Wilhelm Hauer, *Die Religionen: Ihr Werden, ihr Sinn, ihre Wahrheit* (Berlin: W. Kohlhammer, 1923); Lily Weiser, *Altgermanische Jünglingsweihen und Männerbünde: Ein Beitrag zur deutschen und nordischen Altertums- und Volkskunde* (Baden: Konkordia A.G., 1927); and Alfred Baeumler, *Männerbund und Wissenschaft* (Berlin: Junker & Dünnhaupt, 1934). On the politics and importance of the Männerbund theme, see Claudia Bruns, *Politik des Eros: Der Männerbund in Wissenschaft, Politik und Jugendkultur (1880–1934)* (Vienna: Bohlau, 2008); Ulrike Brunotte, "Mannerbund zwischen Jugend- und Totenkult: Ritual und Communitas am Beginn der Moderne," in Luchesi and von Stuckrad, eds., *Religion im kulturellen Diskurs*, 401–22; and the essays in Gisela Völger and Karin von Welck, eds., *Männerbande, Männerbünde: Zur Rolle des Mannes im Kulturvergleich*, 2 vols. (Cologne: Ethnologica, 1990): esp. Jürgen Reulecke, "Das Jahr 1902 und die Ursprünge der Männerbund-Ideologie in Deutschland," 1: 3–10; Klaus von See, "Politische Männerbund-Ideologie von der wilhelminischen Zeit bis zum Nationalsozialismus," 1: 93–102; and Stefanie von Schnurbein, "Geheime kultische Männerbünde bei den Germanen—Eine Theorie im Spannungsfeld zwischen Wissenschaft und Ideologie," 2: 97–102.

75. Höfler, *Kultische Geheimbünde der Germanen*, esp. 28–33 and 188–205.

76. On Höfler, see Olaf Bockhorn, "The Battle for the *Ostmark*: Nazi Folklore in Austria," in James Dow and Hannjost Lixfeld, eds., *The Nazification of an Academic Discipline: Folklore in the Third Reich* (Bloomington: Indiana University Press, 1993), 135–55; Harm-Peer Zimmermann, "Männerbund und Totenkult: Methodologische und ideologische Grundlinien der Volks und Altertumskunde Otto Höflers 1933–1945," *Kieler Blätter zur Volkskunde* 26 (1994): 5–28; and Esther Gajek, "Germanenkunde und Nationalsozialismus: Zur Verflechtung von Wissenschaft und Politik am Beispiel Otto Höfler," in Richard Faber, ed., *Politische Religion, religiöse Politik* (Würzburg: Königshausen & Neumann, 1997), 173–204. Gerd Simon has also compiled a very thorough chronology of Höfler's activities, which is available at http://homepages.uni-tuebingen.de/gerd.simon/nordistikchr.pdf. Höfler reasserted the aggressive argument of *Kultische Gehembünde der Germanen*, not only throughout the National Socialist period, but for the duration of his life. Cf. the following works by Höfler: "Der germanische Totenkult und die Sagen vom Wilden Heer," *Oberdeutsche Zeitschrift für Volkskünde* 1 (1936): 33–49; "Über germanische Verwandlungskulte," *Zeitschrift für deutsches Altertum* 73 (1936): 109–15; "Die politische Leistung der Völkerwanderungszeit," *Kiele Blätter: Veröffentlichung der Wissenschaftlichen Akademie des*

*NSD-Dozentenbundes der Christian Albrechts Universität* 4 (1938): 282–97; *Germanische Sakralkönigtum* (Tübingen: Max Niemeyer, 1952); *Verwandlungskulte, Volkssagen und Mythen* (Vienna: Verlag der österreichischen Akademie der Wissenschaften, 1973); "Zwei Grundkräfte im Wodankult," in Manfred Mayrhofer et al. eds., *Antiquitates Indogermanicae: Gedenkschrift für Herman Güntert* (Innsbruck: Innsbrucker Beiträge zur Sprachwissenschaft, 1974), 133–44; "Staatsheiligkeit und Staatsvergottung," in Adolf Fink, ed., *Rechtsgeschichte als Kulturgeschichte: Festschrift für Adalbert Erler* (Aalen: Scientia Verlag, 1976), 109–33.

77. Höfler, *Kultische Geheimbünde der Germanen*, 345–57. The dissertation was approved in 1931, which means that Höfler read von Bruiningk's article some time between 1931 and 1933, as Hitler was moving toward power.

78. Ginzburg, *The Night Battles*, 186; see also Ginzburg's remarks in various interviews, including "De près, de loin: Des rapports de force en histoire"; "Carlo Ginzburg, 'L'historien et l'avocat du diable': Suite de l'entretien avec Charles Illouz et Laurent Vidal," *Genèses* 54 (2004), available at http://www.cairn.info/revue-geneses-2004-1-page-112.htm; and "On the Dark Side of History: Carlo Ginzburg Talks to Trygve Riiser Gundersen," *Samtiden* (2003), available at http://www.eurozine.com/articles/2003-07-11-ginzburg-en.html.

79. Carlo Ginzburg, "Mitologia germanica e Nazismo: Su un vecchio libro di Georges Dumézil," *Quaderni Storici* 57 (1984): 857–82; English trans. in *Clues, Myths, and the Historical Method*, 114–31. The passage cited (870–71 in the original, retranslated to better reflect the original Italian; cf. *Clues, Myths, and the Historical Method*, 125) occurs in the course of a long and highly critical discussion of Höfler, which spans 867–73 in the original, 122–27 in the translation.

80. Höfler, *Kultische Geheimbünde der Germanen*, 286–97: "Fruchtbarkeitsmythen und Fruchtbarkeitszauber."

81. Ibid., p. 355: "Das Kriegerische scheint bei diesem lettischen Verband (in Gegensatz zu dem germanischen!) ganz zu fehlen."

82. Ginzburg, *Storia notturna*, 92, retranslated to better reflect the original Italian (cf. *Ecstasies*, 115).

83. Ironically—or perhaps not—by emphasizing ecstasy as part of Thiess's experience (something for which there is little evidence) and that of other Livonian werewolves (for which there is much more), Ginzburg recuperated an argument leveled against Höfler by critics within the Nazi Party in the mid-1930s, when paramilitary organizations had fallen from favor after Hitler's purge of the SA in the "Night of the Long Knives" (June 30–July 2, 1934). Particularly interesting is Harald Spehr, "Waren die Germanen 'Ekstatiker'?" *Rasse: Monatszeitschrift der nordischen Bewegung* 3 (1936): 394–400, who argued that ecstasy was not a Nordic or Aryan trait, but something wild, uncivilized, and Asiatic. Along similar lines, see also Bernhard Kummer, "Männerbundgefahren," *Nordische Stimmen: Zeitschrift für nordisches Wesen und Gewissen* 5 (1935): 225–33.

84. Carlo Ginzburg, *Il giudice e le storico* (Turin: Giulio Einaudi, 1991), trans. by Antony Shugaar, *The Judge and the Historian: Marginal Notes on a Late Twentieth-Century Miscarriage of Justice* (London and New York: Verso, 1999).

85. Walter Benjamin, Thesis VI in his essay "On the Concept of History," in How-

ard Eiland and Michael W. Jennings, eds., *Walter Benjamin, Selected Writings,* vol. 4, *1938–1940* (Cambridge, MA: Belknap Press of Harvard University Press, 2003), trans. by Edmund Jephcott, 291 (emphasis in the original).

86. Regarding Benjamin's influence on Ginzburg, see Tony Molho, "Carlo Ginzburg: Reflections on the Intellectual Cosmos of a 20th-Century Historian," *History of European Ideas* 30 (2004): 121–48, esp. 144–48.

87. Ginzburg, *Ecstasies,* 24.

88. This summary follows the brief biography of Leone Ginzburg published by the Associazione Nazionale, Partigiani d'Italia available at http://www.anpi.it/donne-e -uomini/leone-ginzburg. For fuller detail, see the moving memoir by Natalia Ginzburg, *Lessico famigliare* (Turin: Einaudi, 1963) or more recent biographies by Florence Mauro, *Vita di Leone Ginzburg: Intransigenza e passione civile* (Rome: Donzelli, 2013) or Nicola Tranfaglia, ed., *L'itinerario di Leone Ginzburg* (Turin: Boringhieri, 1996).

## CHAPTER FIVE

1. Inter alia, Jonathan Z. Smith, *Imagining Religion: From Babylon to Jonestown* (Chicago: University of Chicago Press, 1982): François Bœspflug and Françoise Dunand, eds., *Le comparatisme en histoire des religions* (Paris: Cerf, 1997): Marcel Detienne, *Comparer l'incomparable* (Paris: Éditions du Seuil, 2000); Hugh Urban, "Making a Place to Take a Stand: Jonathan Z. Smith and the Politics and Poetics of Comparison," *Method and Theory in the Study of Religion* 12 (2000): 339–78; Kimberley Patton and Benjamin Ray, eds., *A Magic Still Dwells: Comparative Religion in the Postmodern Age* (Berkeley: University of California Press, 2000); Peter Antes, Armin Geertz, and R. R. Warne, eds., *New Approaches to the Study of Religion,* vol. 2, *Textual, Comparative, Sociological, and Cognitive Approaches* (Berlin: W. de Gruyter, 2004); Arvind Sharma, *Religious Studies and Comparative Methodology: The Case for Reciprocal Illumination* (Albany: State University of New York Press, 2005); Thomas Idinopulos, Brian Wilson, and James Hanges, eds., *Comparing Religions: Possibilities and Perils?* (Leiden: E.J. Brill, 2006); Pietro Clemente and Cristiano Grottanelli, eds., *Comparativa/mente* (Florence: SEID Editori, 2009); Claude Calame and Bruce Lincoln, eds., *Comparer en histoire des religions antiques: Controverses et propositions* (Liège: Presses Universitaires de Liège, 2012); Rita Felshi and Susan Stanford Friedman, eds., *Comparison: Theories, Approaches, Uses* (Baltimore: Johns Hopkins University Press, 2013).

2. For different attempts, cf. Hans Kippenberg, *Discovering Religious History in the Modern Age* (Princeton, NJ: Princeton University Press, 2006); Laura Ammon, *Work Useful to Religion and the Humanities: A History of the Comparative Method in the Study of Religion from Las Casas to Tylor* (Eugene, OR: Pickwick, 2012); and David Chidester, *Empire of Religion: Imperialism and Comparative Religion* (Chicago: University of Chicago Press, 2014).

3. E. J. Michael Witzel, *The Origins of the World's Mythologies* (Oxford and New York: Oxford University Press, 2012).

4. Witzel, *Origins of the World's Mythologies,* vii–xi.

5. Ibid., 1–104, including sections titled "What Is Myth, and How Do We Study

and Compare It?" (1–6), "Definition of Myth and Its Study in the Past" (6–8), "Comparative Mythology" (8–15), "Earlier Explanations of Myth" (20–26), and "Comparison and Theory" (37–104). In the course of these pages he discusses or at least gestures knowingly toward numerous comparatists and theorists of comparison, including Giambattista Vico (1668–1774), Montesquieu (1689–1755), G. W. F. Hegel (1770–1831), Rasmus Rask (1787–1832), Franz Bopp (1791–1867), Max Müller (1823–1900), E. B. Tylor (1832–1917), W. Robertson Smith (1846–94), Hermann Oldenberg (1854–1920), Sir James George Frazer (1854–1941), Sigmund Freud (1856–1939), Ferdinand de Saussure (1857–1913), Lucien Lévy-Bruhl (1857–1939), Émile Durkheim (1858–1917), Sylvain Lévi (1863–1935), Wilhelm Schmidt (1868–1954), Leo Frobenius (1873–1938), Ernst Cassirer (1874–1945), C. G. Jung (1875–1961), A. L. Kroeber (1876–1970), Marcel Granet (1884–1940), Bronislaw Malinowski (1884–1942), Lord Raglan (1885–1964), Stith Thompson (1885–1976), Vladimir Propp (1895–1970), Károly Kerényi (1897–1973), Georges Dumézil (1898–1986), Stanislaw Schayer (1899–1941), Hermann Baumann (1902–72), Joseph Campbell (1904–87), Mircea Eliade (1907–86), F. B. J. Kuiper (1907–2003), Claude Lévi-Strauss (1908–2009), Edmund Leach (1910–89), Max Gluckman (1911–75), Robert Bellah (1927–2013), Fredrik Barth (1928–), Noam Chomsky (1928–), Walter Burkert (1931–2015), Jaan Puhvel (1932–), Alan Dundes (1934–2005), Jonathan Z. Smith (1938–2018), Carlo Ginzburg (1939–), Wendy Doniger (1940–), Gregory Nagy (1942–), Merritt Ruhlen (1944–), Yuri Berezkin (1946–), Robert Segal (1948–), Charles Ragin (1950–), Ina Wunn (1954–), and myself (1948–). As some of these are only mentioned in passing, it is hard to judge how thoroughly Witzel studied their work, but there is no doubt he tried to engage the history of comparative studies in reasonably comprehensive fashion.

6. Witzel, *Origins of the World's Mythologies*, 2, 18, 50, 53, 75, and passim.

7. Ibid., 16 (emphasis in the original); cf. 28, 47, 50, 74–75, and 101–2. Regarding the approaches Witzel rejects (diffusion and universal structures), see 1–2, 8–15, and 45–46.

8. Ibid., 46.

9. Ibid., 59–65, 80–82, 188–202, 414–17.

10. Witzel repeatedly and emphatically restates his view that the existence of a story line leading from cosmic creation to destruction is the most important feature distinguishing Laurasian from Gondwana myth, as in the following passage.

> The main feature, the story line approach, cannot and must not be abandoned; it is central to the theory. . . . Even a certain accumulation of circumstantial counterevidence does not suffice to bring down the theory: for example, if someone were to show that certain individual items (diver, flood myth) are in fact also found in sub-Saharan Africa or in Papua/Australia, I would not concede: the main pillar of the Laurasian theory, the story line arrangement, and myths of primordial creation and impending destruction, would still stand. (Witzel, *Origins of the World's Mythologies*, 283; cf. 54, 101, 281, 321, 329, and passim)

11. Witzel, *Origins of the World's Mythologies*, 54 (emphasis in the original); cf. 80 ("the earliest, quasi-historical 'novel' that we have"). Consistent with this characteri-

zation, he titles chapter 3 "Creation Myths: The Laurasian Story Line, Our First Novel" (105–85). Use of the first-person plural here, as elsewhere, signals his assumption that readers will identify with Laurasia, and not Gondwana.

12. I have discussed these points à propos of attempts to reconstruct Proto-Indo-European myth, religion, and culture on several occasions, most extensively in *Theorizing Myth: Narrative, Ideology, and Scholarship* (Chicago: University of Chicago Press, 1999); *Death, War, and Sacrifice: Studies in Ideology and Practice* (Chicago: University of Chicago Press, 1991), xv–xix, 119–27, 231–68; and *Discourse and the Construction of Society: Comparative Studies of Myth, Ritual, and Classification* (New York: Oxford University Press, 1989), 131–41. Witzel identifies my position as a potential objection to his thesis and attempts to show why it fails, but he is more concerned to set up a straw man than to engage the substance of the argument; Witzel, *Origins of the World's Mythologies*, 27–28, 95–96.

13. For a recent overview of the school, see Hélène Ivanoff, Jean-Louis Georget, and Richard Kuba, eds., *Kulturkreise—Leo Frobenius und seine Zeitgenossen* (Berlin: Dietrich Reimer, 2015). More critical studies include Manfred Gothsch, *Die deutsche Völkerkunde und ihr Verhältnis zum Kolonialismus* (Baden-Baden: Nomos, 1983); Hans Fischer, *Völkerkunde im Nationalsozialismus: Aspekte der Anpassung, Affinität und Behauptung einer wissenschaftlichen Disziplin* (Berlin: Dietrich Reimer, 1990); Fischer, *Randfiguren der Ethnologie: Gelehrte und Amateure, Schwindler und Phantasten* (Berlin: Dietrich Reimer, 2003); Wolfgang Jacobeit et al., *Völkische Wissenschaft: Gestalten und Tendenzen der deutschen und österreichischen Volkskunde in der ersten Hälfte des 20. Jahrhunderts* (Vienna: Böhlau, 1994); Thomas Hauschild, ed., *Lebenslust und Fremdenfurcht: Ethnologie im Dritten Reich* (Frankfurt: Suhrkamp, 1995); Bernhard Streck, ed., *Ethnologie und Nationalsozialismus* (Gehren: Escher, 2000); Andrew Evans, *Anthropology at War: World War I and the Science of Race in Germany* (Chicago: University of Chicago Press, 2010); and Arno Sonderegger, "Africa in Austrian and German African Studies," in Wulf D. Huld, Christian Koller, and Moshe Zimmermann, eds., *Racisms Made in Germany* (Vienna: Lit Verlag, 2011), 123–44.

14. Witzel, *Origins of the World's Mythologies*, 128.

15. Ibid., 129.

16. Andrew Lang, *Custom and Myth* (London: Longmans Green, 1884), 45–51, passages cited at 51.

17. Ibid., 51.

18. Ibid., 22.

19. Willibald Staudacher, *Die Trennung von Himmel und Erde: Ein vorgriechischer Schöpfungsmythus bei Hesiod und den Orphikern* (Tübingen: Bölzle, 1942; reprint, 1968), 3: "Die im folgenden gegebene Sammlung von HETMythen soll die weite Verbreitung und die Bedeutung eines kosmogonischen Motives, welches bereits Frobenius zu dem mythischen Urbesitz der Menschheit gerechnet hat, vor Augen führen. Leider ist uns dieser Mythus nicht überall in reiner Form erhalten. Denn bei den Naturvölkern, zu denen er durch Ausstrahlung der antiken Hochkulturen des Mittelmeergebietes gelangte, wurde er als „gesunkenes Kulturgut" oft mit andersartigen Vorstellungen verbunden oder völlig entstellt."

20. Staudacher discusses Lang in the opening paragraphs of his text, *Die Trennung von Himmel und Erde*, p. 1.

21. Staudacher, *Die Trennung von Himmel und Erde*, 4–43. The discussion begins with "African tribes" (*Afrikanische Stämme*, 4–8), among whom Staudacher cited twenty-two variants of the myth from virtually all parts of the continent (Ekoi [Ejagham], Yoruba, Mossi, Lobi, Songye, Herero, Ndorobo, Nandi, Nuer, et al.).

22. In the passage cited above, Staudacher left unidentified the passage from Frobenius to which he was referring, but he quotes it a few pages later (*Die Trennung von Himmel und Erde*, 9n1): "One can trace this motif (sc. the world parents) back to its primitive appearance in the earliest times attested to by West Asian archeology." (Leo Frobenius, *Kulturgeschichte Afrikas* [Zurich: Phaidon Verlag, 1933], 154: "Dieses Motiv (sc. des Wel.elternpaares) läßt sich in seiner primitiven Darstellung bis in die ersten Zeiten westasiatisch-archäologischer Kulturbezeugung zurückverfolgen."

23. Staudacher, *Die Trennung von Himmel und Erde*, vii.

24. Ibid., 58 (emphasis added): "dieser vorarischen, das Mittelmeergebiet und Indien umfassenden Kultur und Rassengemeinschaft." Cf. 50 ("eine kulturelle und rassische Gemeinschaft"), 56 ("eine rassische und kulturelle Einheit"), and 57 ("rassenmäßig mit der mittelmeerländischen Rasse in Europa in Zusammenhang"). On p. 56, Staudacher also assures the reader that his results are supported by die Ergebnisse der Ethnologie und Rassenkunde.

25. For the lines of diffusion, see Staudacher, *Die Trennung von Himmel und Erde*, 50–51 (to Africa), 52–53 (to the Americas), 54–58 (the Pacific).

26. Witzel, *Origins of the World's Mythologies*, 484n228.

27. Witzel's fullest discussion of this myth is found at *Origins of the World's Mythologies*, 128–37, but he returns to it repeatedly, including 2–3, 54, 77–79, 131, 160, 311–12, 314–20, 324, 344, 345, 347, 444n46, 483n215, and 548n269.

28. Cf. Staudacher, *Die Trennung von Himmel und Erde*, 50–52, and Witzel, *Origins of the World's Mythologies*, 128–31, both of which cite and depend on Hermann Baumann, *Schöpfung und Urzeit des Menschen im Mythus der Afrikanischen Völker* (Berlin: Dietrich Reimer, 1936; reprint, 1964), 174–77. Baumann's discussion includes a citation from one of his sources, showing a racism of which he approves, but which drops out of Witzel's account.

The already recounted myths of the shaping of things through *the mating of the couple Heaven and Earth*, who are also frequently designated as the primordial couple, presupposes a number of highly developed individual mythic ideas, above all the consistent personification of Mother Earth, which can hardly be achieved at an early stage of civilization. Ehrenreich, *Die allgemeine Mythologie und ihre ethnologischen Grundlagen* (Leipzig: J. C. Hinrichs, 1910), p. 158, is of the opinion that Mother Earth "already presumes a high degree of abstraction and therefore is chiefly found among the spiritually advanced *Völker*." He numbers among them the Indo-Aryan *Volk* and the Indians of North America, who possess a surprisingly high spiritual culture with an accomplished mythology, seldom achieved by black Africans.

Jene schon erwähnten Mythen von der Erschaffung der Dinge durch die *Begattung des Paares Himmel-Erde*, das auch oft als Welturpaar bezeichnet wird, setzen eine Summe hochentwickelter mythischer Einzelvorstellungen voraus, vor allem aber die konsequente Personifikation der Mutter Erde, die ursprünglich kaum erreicht wurde. Ehrenreich, Allgem. Mythologie, S. 158, meint von der Mutter Erde, daß sie "schon einen hohen Grad von Abstraktion voraussetzt, und sich daher vorwiegend bei geistig fortgeschrittenen Völkern findet." Er zählt hierzu neben den indo-arischen Völkern auch die Indianer Nordamerikas, die ja eine überraschend hohe geistige Kultur mit vollendeter Mythologie besitzen und die von Negern selten erreicht wird. (Baumann, *Schöpfung und Urzeit*, p. 174, emphasis in the original)

29. Thus, Witzel shows considerable respect for Baumann and accepts his views at *Origins of the World's Mythologies*, 10, 171, 289, 292 315, 316, 343–46, 445n56, 483n15, 483n16, 551n339, 551n342, and 552n352, while distancing himself—sometimes only subtly and slightly—from him at 10, 15–16, 63, 317, 407, 444n46, 549n305, 549n309, and 551n338. At other points he implicitly follows Baumann, without citing him by name.

30. In addition to Frobenius, Baumann, and Staudacher, Witzel cites a large number of scholars who worked in the *Kulturkreise* paradigm, including Adolf Bastian (1826–1905), Wilhelm Schmidt (1868–1954), Otto Dempwolf (1871–1938), Roberto Lehmann-Nitsche (1872–1938), Carl Leonhard Schultze-Jena (1872–1955), Walter Lehmann (1878–1939), Martin Gusinde (1886–1969), Paul Schebesta (1887–1967), Josef Dominik Wölfel (1888–1963), Paul Wirz (1892–1955), Erich Brauer (1895–1942), Adolf Jensen (1899–1965), Johannes Maringer (1902–81), Hans Nevermann (1902–82), Hans Findeisen (1903–68), Alois Pache (1903–69), Hans Schärer (1904–47), Ernst Dammann (1904–2003), Fritz Bornemann (1905–93), Karl Jettmar (1918–2002), August Schmitz (1920–66), Heinz Reschke (1922–90), Hermann Hochegger (1931–2009), and Beatrix Heintze (1939–). In contrast, he only rarely consults the more recent (and less tainted) work of a very few British, French, and American anthropologists.

31. Baumann appears to be cited more than any other author, with the possible exception of Joseph Campbell. Very few scholars are listed in Witzel's index, but Baumann figures prominently, receiving more page references than any of the others who appear (Frobenius, Jung, and Lévi-Strauss tie for second place). When introducing Baumann, Witzel also makes the unique gesture of citing an encomium that describes him as "a typical German thinker of forceful philosophical ambitions, striving for 'ultimate explanations' and the will for systematic integration" (*Origins of the World's Mythologies*, 445n56). Written by Klaus E. Müller, one of Baumann's most loyal students, it appeared in Müller's laudatory preface to Baumann's *Das doppelte Geschlecht: Ethnologische Studien zur Bisexualität in Ritus und Mythos* (Berlin: Dietrich Reimer, 1955; reprint, 1986), vii, and was meant to help rehabilitate Baumann's reputation after his formal de-Nazification in 1949.

32. For recent discussions of the *Kulturkreislehre*, see the literature cited above in note 16. Most extensively on *Paideuma*, see Leo Frobenius, *Paideuma: Umrisse einer Kultur- und Seelenlehre* (Munich: C.H. Beck, 1921).

33. On the colonial utility of such discourse, see especially Gothsch, *Die deutsche Völkerkunde und ihr Verhältnis zum Kolonialismus*. On the role played by theories of "Hamitic" migrations and influence, see Edith Sanders, "The Hamitic Hypothesis: Its Origin and Functions in Time Perspective," *Journal of African History* 10 (1969):

521–32; Birgitta Farelius, "Where Does the Hamite Belong?," *Nomadic Peoples* 32 (1993): 107–18; Peter Rohrbacher, *Die Geschichte des Hamiten-Mythos* (Vienna: Afro-Pub, 2002); and Robin Law, "The 'Hamitic Hypothesis' in Indigenous West African Historical Thought," *History in Africa* 36 (2009): 293–314.

34. On the difference between German and Austrian interests and approaches, see Wolfgang Jacobeit et al., *Völkische Wissenschaft*; and Sonderegger, "Africa in Austrian and German African Studies." On the Vienna school, see Ernest Brandewie, *When Giants Walked the Earth: The Life and Times of Wilhelm Schmidt, SVD* (Fribourg: University Press, 1990); and Wolfgang Müller-Limberg, *Pater Wilhelm Schmidt und die Entwicklung der Wiener Schule der Ethnologie* (Cologne: Philosophische Fakultät der Universität zu Köln, 1991).

35. For details, see Jürgen Braun, *Eine deutsche Karriere: Die Biographie des Ethnologen Hermann Baumann (1902–1972)* (Munich: Akademischer Verlag, 1995), 31–37. Baumann's teachers included Eugen Fischer (1874–1967), a leading racial theorist; Ernst Grosse (1862–1967), who pioneered the study of non-Western art in the discipline of *Völkerkunde*; Diedrich Westermann (1875–1956), Germany's foremost expert on African languages; Felix von Luschan (1854–1924), a medical anthropologist who contributed physiological arguments for the Hamitic hypothesis; Alfred Vierkandt (1867–1953), who devoted his first book to the social psychology of *Naturvölker und Kulturvölker*; and Karl Theodor Preuß (1869–1938), Germany's foremost expert on the indigenous peoples of the Americas and author of *Die geistige Kultur der Naturvölker*, who organized a seminar on *Religionswissenschaft* along with Diedrich Westermann.

36. Braun, *Eine deutsche Karriere*, 41–46. Baumann joined the party on August 1, 1932, the day after it polled strongly in national elections. His membership in the Kampfbund came earlier that year.

37. Hermann Baumann, "Die materielle Kultur der Mangbetu und Azande," *Baessler Archiv* 11 (1927): 3–129; Baumann, "Negerbauten," in *Wasmuth's Lexikon der Baukunst* (Berlin: E. Wasmuth, 1931), 3: 671–73.

38. Hermann Baumann, "The Division of Work according to Sex in African Hoe-Culture," *Africa* 1 (1928): 289–319; Baumann, *Vom Grabstock zum Pflug: Frühformen des Bodenbaues* (Berlin: Museum für Völkerkunde, 1934).

39. Hermann Baumann, "Vaterrecht und Mutterrecht in Afrika," *Zeitschrift für Ethnologie* 58 (1927): 62–161; Baumann, "Ein Volk des Mutterrechts," *Woche* 15 (1931): 103–5.

40. Hermann Baumann, "Die Kunst der afrikanischen Naturvölker," *Übersee- und Kolonialzeitung* 40 (1927): 378–79; Baumann, "Die Kunst der Primitiven," in Hermann Gunkel and Leopold Zscharnack, eds., *Die Religion in Geschichte und Gegenwart* (Tübingen: J.C.B. Mohr, 1929), 1383–85; Baumann, "Afrikanisches Kunstgewerbe," in H. T. Bossert, ed., *Geschichte des Kunstgewerbes aller Zeiten und Völker* (Berlin: Wasmuth, 1929), 2: 51–148; Baumann, "Bénin," *Cahiers d'Art* 7 (1932): 1–7.

41. Hermann Baumann, "Likundu: Die Sektion der Zauberkraft," *Zeitschrift für Völkerkunde* 60 (1928): 75–85; Baumann, "Die Mannbarkeitsfeiern bei den Tsokwe," *Baessler Archiv* 15 (1932): 1–54; Baumann, "Junglingsweihe: Missionare beschneiden ihre Zöglinge," *Die Umschau* 36 (1932): 426–29.

42. Hermann Baumann, "Die afrikanischen Kulturkreise," *Africa* 7 (1934): 129–39. Baumann had been working to revise Frobenius's model for some years. For a 1927 attempt that makes no reference to race, see Baumann, "Die materielle Kultur der Mangbetu und Azande," 11–14.

43. Baumann, "Die afrikanischen Kulturkreise," 133–34: "Aber Frobenius schoss über das Ziel hinaus. Er kam folgerichtig zu einer Überspitzung der Idee vom selbständigen Leben der Kulturen, das losgelöst vom blutvollen Substrat der Rasse und der Völkergeschichte, seine eigenen Gesetze besitzt. Der Weg zur Weiterforschung erscheint klar: Er muss gleich weitab führen vom statistischen Formalismus der kulturkreistheoretischen Anfänge, als auch von allen Bestrebungen, die jene mystische, eigenkräftige Volksseele aufleben lassen wollen. Er muss immer mit dem Substrat der lebendigen menschlichen Gemeinschaften als den Kulturträgern rechnen. Deshalb ist die Beachtung der rassischen Gliederung, der Wanderungen, Eroberungen und anderer historischer Ereignisse unbedingte Voraussetzung jeder Kulturenkunde."

44. Witzel, *Origins of the World's Mythologies*, 445n52: "Frobenius was the originator of the idea of the *Kulturkreis* ('civilization circle' or region), which he first published in *Petermann's Mitteilungen* 43–44 (1897–98); it was eventually opposed by Baumann (in *Africa* 7 [1934])." This note appears in the section of Witzel's text where he introduces diffusionist theories (8–12).

45. Baumann, *Schöpfung und Urzeit*.

46. Regardung Baumann's use of the Hamite category, see Rohrbacher, *Die Geschichte des Hamiten-Mythos*, 211–25.

47. Most offensive in this regard was Koppers's role in organizing a special issue of the *Wiener Beiträge zur Kulturgeschichte und Linguistik* 4 (1936) devoted to "Die Indogermanen- und Germanenfrage," in which he and others argued strenuously against placement of the Aryan homeland in German territory.

48. On Baumann's reorganization of Koppers's Institute für Völkerkunde, see Braun, *Eine deutsche Karriere*, 62–76; and Peter Linimayr, *Wiener Völkerkunde im Nationalsozialismus: Ansätze zu einer NS-Wissenschaft* (Frankfurt: Peter Lang, 1994), 54–57 and 143–54. This period of his activity is defined by the volumes he edited or coedited: "Koloniale Völkerkunde: In Zusammenarbeit mit der Kolonialwissenschaftlichen Abteilung des Reichsforschungsrates in der deutschen Forschungsgemeinschaft," *Wiener Beiträge zur Kulturgeschichte und Linguistik* 6 (1941–44) and *Koloniale Völkerkunde, koloniale Sprachforschung, koloniale Rassenforschung: Berichte über die Arbeitstagung im Januar 1943 in Leipzig* (Berlin: Dietrich Reimer, 1943).

49. Hermann Baumann, Richard Thurnwald, and Diedrich Westermann, *Völkerkunde von Afrika: Mit besonderer Berücksichtigung der kolonialen Aufgabe* (Essen: Essener Verlangsanstalt, 1940), which is framed by Baumann's programmatic statement (p. 4).

Historic research on African cultures today takes greater account of the race of their representatives and their geographic environment, new sources of knowledge and powerful forces in the formation of culture, which previously received regrettably little attention.

Die historische Erforschung der afrikanischen Kulturen schafft sich heute mit der stärkeren Berücksichtigung der Rasse ihrer Träger und der geographischen Umwelt, den beiden früher leider wenig geachteten, aber mächtigen triebkräften der Kulturenformung, neue Erkenntnisquellen.

50. Witzel, *Origins of the World's Mythologies*, 8–12, 15, 63, 407.

51. Ibid., 551n338: "I prefer not to follow such writers as Frobenius and Baumann who wanted to link mythologies too closely with economic development, for example, in linking '*hoe-type*' mythologies with patriarchal or matriarchal societies." Elsewhere, however, Witzel seems to endorse the idea that myths correlate with a historic sequence of *Kulturkreise*, attributing this idea (rather curiously and perhaps disingenuously?) to Montesquieu and Durkheim, rather than Ankermann, Graebner, Frobenius, and Baumann.

The present book follows a comparative *and* historical approach that pays close attention to the historical situation in which the respective myths emerged. This approach is particularly appropriate in adjusting our interpretations of early myth and religion to the then prevailing type of society and its way of life, consecutively hunter-gatherer, horticulturalist, agriculturist, nomadic, early state society, and so on. These types of society were already proposed by Montesquieu and elaborated by Durkheim. (*Origins of the World's Mythologies*, 28, emphasis in the original)

52. Andrew Lang, *The Making of Religion* (London: Longmans Green, 1898).

53. Edwin Sidney Hartland, "The High Gods of Australia," *Folk-Lore* 9 (1908): 301.

54. Ibid., 302–3: "It seems reasonable on the whole to infer that, whatever may be the origin of [Baiame's] name and his earlier position in native thought, the points of his story most resembling the Christian conception of Creator have been unconsciously evolved, first by white explorers, then by missionaries, and lastly by the natives themselves under European influence."

55. Herbert Schlieper, *Die kosmogonischen Mythen der Urvölker* (Bonn: Universitäts-Buchdruckerei, 1931), 63: "Mit Ausnahme einer einzigen Gruppe—der Eskimos—weisen alle behandelten Völker dieser frühesten der uns bekannten Menschheits-stufen Zeugnisse über eine Beschäftigung mit den Fragen der Entstehung von Welt und Erde auf."

56. Baumann, *Schöpfung und Urzeit*, 202.

57. Ibid.

58. Witzel, *Origins of the World's Mythologies*, 105.

59. Ibid., 289. Here, Witzel attributed the idea that Africans have no interest in cosmogony to Hermann Hochegger, *Mythes d'origine: Variantes zairoises de 1905 à 1994* (Bandundu, Zaire: Ceeba Publications, 1994), adding that "Hochegger's view is echoed by several other scholars dealing with all of African mythology, such as Bauman [*sic*] and Bastide." Although Hochegger did voice this opinion, it is hardly his, as he adopted it from Baumann, cited prominently on the very first page of Hochegger's anthology. The article on Africa that Roger Bastide contributed to a coffee-table book (Pierre Grimal, ed., *Mythologies de la Méditerranée au Gange* [Paris: Larousse, 1963])

also adopts this position following Baumann, as does Louis-Vincent Thomas, René Luneau, and J. L. Doneux, *Les religions d'Afrique Noire: Texts et traditions sacrés* (Paris: Fayard, 1969), whom Witzel cites at 550n311 in support of "Hochegger's view." Rather than providing independent confirmation of African disinterest, these works demonstrate the extent of Baumann's influence. Witzel uses them, however, to deflect attention from their common source, on which he is also dependent.

60. Witzel, *Origins of the World's Mythologies*, 361. Cf. 5, 15, 80, 103–4, 124, 128, 183–84, 283, 290, 291, 295, 305, 307, 310, 313, 316, 317, 324, 325, 329, 358, and 410.

61. Ibid., 311.

62. Ibid., 321.

63. Ibid., 346; cf. 283, 285–86, 292–93, 295, 297, 306–7, 309, 311, 312, 315, 316, 318–19, 319–20, 322, 324, 340–41, 343–46.

64. Ibid., 316, citing Baumann, *Schöpfung und Urzeit*, 1.

65. The sentence Witzel mutilated reads as follows in the original: "The relatively weak aptitude of black Africans, who represent the chief component of the African population, for myth-making has perhaps resulted in the fact that the existing body of African myths has stimulated so little research." (Die verhältnismäßig schwache Begabung des Negers, der nun einmal das Hauptelement der Afrikaner darstellt, zur Mythenbildung hat es vielleicht mit sich gebracht, daß die vorhandenen Mythen der Afrikaner so wenig zur Untersuchung anreizten.)

66. Thus, for instance, Witzel maintains the thoroughly discredited "Hamitic hypothesis," although he recodes it as an "Afro-Asiatic (formerly, 'Hamitic') cultural area" (*Origins of the World's Mythologies*, 319; cf. 19, 191, 321, and 343) or "Highways" of diffusion into Africa, without mentioning considerations of race (292–93, 316, 318–21). A more complicated attempt at salvage occurs at 317.

Baumann sums up the culture of this region that he calls, in line with then prominent *Kulturkreis* theory, the "Old African" or "Old Sudan" culture, as one with hoe agriculture, patriarchal society, and a "manistic" (ancestor-centered) religion. Leaving this theory apart, his description of its mythology still holds: the primordial ancestor is at the center of the world, and all life grows from it. Heaven and stars are not very important. Instead of "creation" we find "emanation" or "calling forth" of the mundane beings, animals, and humans.

## CHAPTER SIX

1. François Hartog, *Le miroir d'Hérodote: Essai sur la représentation de l'autre* (Paris: Gallimard, 1980); English trans. by Janet Lloyd, *The Mirror of Herodotus: The Representation of the Other in the Writing of History* (Berkeley: University of California Press, 1988). In the year preceding publication of his book, Hartog published those pieces of it treating these issues of nomadism and sacrifice: "Les Scythes imaginaires: Espace et nomadisme," *Annales ESC* 34 (1979): 1137–74; "La question du nomadisme: Les Scythes d' Hérodote," *Acta Antiqua Academiae Scientiarum Hungaricae* 27 (1979): 135–48; and "Le boeuf autocuiseur et les boissons d'Ares," in Marcel Detienne and

Jean-Pierre Vernant, eds., *La cuisine du sacrifice en pays grec* (Paris: Gallimard, 1979), 251–69.

2. Hartog, *Mirror of Herodotus*, 55–57, 193–205, 318–19.

3. Ibid., 8–9, 173, 176–88.

4. Edward W. Said, *Orientalism* (New York: Pantheon, 1978). A French translation by Catherine Malamoud appeared in the same year as Hartog's book: Edward Said, *L'Orientalisme: L'orient créé par l'occident*, with a preface by Tzvetan Todorov (Paris: Éditions du Seuil, 1980). It is not clear if Hartog had read Said, whom he never cited, but he was well aware of emergent poststructuralist and postmodern theory, as indicated by his references to Michel Foucault, Michel de Certeau, Gérard Genette, Pierre Clastres, and Hans Jauss.

5. A succession of works in this vein rapidly followed, including Jacques Jouanna, "Les causes de la défaite des Barbares chez Eschyle, Hérodote et Hippocrate," *Ktema* 6 (1981): 3–15; Anna Beltrammetti, *Erodoto, una storia governata dal discorso: Il racconto morale come una forma di memoria* (Florence: La Nuova Italia, 1986); Claude Calame, "Environnement et nature humaine: Le racisme bien tempéré d'Hippocrate," in *Sciences et racisme* (Lausanne: Payot, 1986), 75–99; Martin Bernal, *Black Athena: The Afroasiatic Roots of Classical Civilization,* vol. 1 (New Brunswick, NJ: Rutgers University Press, 1987); Catherine Darbo-Peschanski, "Les barbares à l'épreuve du temps (Hérodote, Thucydide, Xénophon)," *Metis* 4 (1989): 233–50; Edith Hall, *Inventing the Barbarian: Greek Self-Definition through Tragedy* (Oxford: Clarendon Press, 1989); Paul Cartledge, "Herodotus and 'the Other': A Meditation on Empire," *Échos du Monde Classique* 34 (1990): 27–40; Walter Burkert et al., *Hérodote et les peuples non-grecs* (Geneva: Fondation Hardt, 1990); G. Ceausescu, "Un topos de la littérature antique: L'éternelle guerre entre l'Europe et l'Asie," *Latomus* 50 (1991): 327–41; Pericles Georges, *Barbarian Asia and the Greek Experience* (Baltimore: Johns Hopkins University Press, 1994).

6. Karl Meuli, "Scythica," *Hermes* 70 (1935): 121–76, reprinted in his *Gesammelte Schriften* (Basel: Schwabe, 1975), 2: 817–79.

7. The culminating work along these lines was Georges Dumézil, *Romans de Scythie et d'alentour* (Paris: Payot, 1978), building on earlier publications that included *Légendes sur les Nartes, suivies de cinq notes mythologiques* (Paris: Institut d'études slaves, 1930); "Les légendes de 'Fils d'aveugles' au Caucase et autour du Caucase," *Revue de l'Histoire des Religions* 117 (1938): 50–74; "Les 'énarées' des Scythes et la grossesse de Narte Hamyc," *Latomus* 5 (1946): 249–55; "Les trois 'Trésors des ancêtres' dans l'épopée Narte," *Revue de l'Histoire des Religions* 157 (1960): 141–54; "À propos de quelques représentations folkloriques des Ossètes," *Paideuma* 7 (1960): 216–24; "La société scythique avait-elle des classes fonctionnelles?," *Indo-Iranian Journal* 5 (1962): 187–202; and *Mythes et epopées,* vols. 1–2 (Paris: Gallimard, 1968–69; 2nd ed., 1973).

8. V. I. Abaev, "Skifskiy byt' i reforma Zoroastra," *Archiv Orientalnì* 24 (1956): 23–56; Abaev, "Zoroastr i Skify," in *Monumentum H. S. Nyberg* (Leiden: E.J. Brill, 1975), 3: 1–12. Beyond the major works of Meuli, Dumézil, and Abaev, one should also note Hans-Joachim Diesner, "Skythische Religion und Geschichte bei Herodot," *Rheinisches Museum* 104 (1961): 202–12; and W. D. Blawatsky and G. A. Kochélenko,

"Quelques traits de la religion des scythes," in *Hommages à M. J. Vermaseren* (Leiden: E.J. Brill, 1978), 1: 60–66.

9. François Cornillot, "De Skythes à Kolaxais," *Studia Iranica* 10 (1981): 7–52; Dmitriy Raevskiy, *Scythian Mythology* (Sofia: Secor Publishers, 1993), 24–57; Askold Ivantchik, "Une légende sur l'origine des Scythes (Hdt. IV 5–7)," *Revue des Études Grecques* 112 (1999): 141–92; idem, "La légende 'grecque' sur l'origine des Scythes (Hérodote 4.8–10)", in Valérie Fromentin and Sophie Gotteland, eds., *Origines Gentium* (Paris: de Boccard, 2001), 207–20; Monica Visintin, "Echidna, Skythes e l'arco di Herakles: Figure della marginalità nella versione greca delle origini degli Sciti, Herodot 4.8–10," *Materiali e Discussioni per l'Analisi dei Testi Classici* 45 (2000): 43–81; Aleksander Loma, "Namenkundliches zur skythischen Abstammungssage," *Studia Etymologica Cracoviensia* 16 (2011): 75–92; and Sébastien Barbara, "Encore sur le mythe de royauté des scythes d'après le *logos skythikos* d'Hérodote (IV, 5–7) et le problème des sources du *scythicos logos* d'Hérodote," in Sébastien Barbara, Michel Mazoyer, and Jain Meurant, *Figures royales des mondes anciens* (Paris: Harmattan, 2011), 31–57.

10. Donat Margreth, "Skythische Schamanen? Die Nachrichten über Enarees-Anarieis bei Herodot und Hippokrates" (PhD diss., Universität Zurich, 1993); Andrea Piras, "Le tre lance del giusto Wirāz e la freccia di Abaris: Ordalia e volo estatico tra iranismo e ellenismo," *Studi Orientali e Linguistici* 7 (2000): 95–109; George Hinge, "Sjælevandring Skythien tur-retur," in Pia Guldager Bilde and Jakob Munk Højte, eds., *Mannesker og guder ved Sortehavets Kyster* (Aarhus: Aarhus Universitetsforlag, 2004), 11–27.

11. Fridrik Thordarson, "Herodotus and the Iranians: ὄψις, ἀκοή, ψεῦδος," *Symboloe Osloenses* 71 (1996): 42–58; David Braund, "Royal Scythians and the Slave-Trade in Herodotus' Scythia," *Antichthon* 42 (2008): 1–19.

12. Margreth, *Skythische Schamanen?*; Alain Ballabriga, "Les eunuques scythes et leurs femmes: Stérilité des femmes et impuissance des hommes en Scythie selon le traité hippocratique *des airs*," *Métis* 1 (1986): 121–39; and Charles Chiasson, "Scythian Androgyny and Environmental Determinism in Herodotus and the Hippocratic πέρι ἀέρων ὑδάτων τόπων," *Syllecta Classica* 12 (2001): 33–73. See also the earlier work of Albert Esser, "Ueber ein skythisches Männerleiden," *Gymnasium* 64 (1957): 347–53.

13. Bruce Lincoln, "On the Scythian Royal Burials," in Susan Skomal and Edgar Polomé, eds., *Proto-Indo-European: The Archeology of a Linguistic Problem; Festschrift for Marija Gimbutas* (Washington, DC: Journal of Indo-European Studies Monograph Series, 1987), 267–85; Fridrik Thordarson, "The Scythian Funeral Customs: Some Notes on Herodotus IV, 71–75," in *A Green Leaf: Papers in Honour of Professor Jes P. Asmussen* (Leiden: E.J. Brill, 1988), 539–47; A. I. Kubysev, "Der Bratoljybovka-Kurgan: Die Grabanlage eines skythischen Nomarchen?," *Beiträge zur Archäologie* 18 (1991): 131–40; A. Yu. Alekseyev, "Scythian Kings and 'Royal' Burial-Mounds of the Fifth and Fourth Centuries BC," in David Braund, ed., *Scythians and Greeks: Cultural Interactions in Scythia, Athens, and the Early Roman Empire* (Exeter: University of Exeter Press, 2005), 39–55; Igor Lisovy and České Budějovice, "Wenn der skythische König starb . . . (Die Kulte der Skythen im nördlichen Schwarzmeergebiet)," *Wiener humanistische Blätter* 48 (2006): 5–46.

14. Stephanie West, "The Scythian Ultimatum," *Journal of Hellenic Studies* 108 (1988): 207–11.

15. Peter Riedlberger, "Skalpieren bei den Skythen: Zu Herodot IV 64," *Klio* 78 (1996): 53–60; Elfriede R. Knauer, "Observations on the Barbarian Custom of Suspending the Heads of Vanquished Enemies from the Neck of Horses," *Archäologische Mitteilungen aus Iran und Turan* 33 (2001): 283–332; Eileen Murphy, Ilia Gokhman, Yuri Chistov, and Ludmila Barkova, "Prehistoric Old World Scalping: New Cases from the Cemetery of Aymyrlyg, South Siberia," *American Journal of Archaeology* 106 (2002): 1–10.

16. Askold Ivančik, "Les guerriers-chiens: Loups-garous et invasions scythes en Asie Mineure," *Revue de l'Histoire des Religions* 210 (1993): 305–29; Yulia Ustinova, "Lycanthropy in Sarmatian Warrior Society: The Kobyskovsko torque," *Ancient West and East* 1 (2002): 102–23.

17. Stephanie West, "Introducing the Scythians: Herodotus on Koumiss (4.2)," *Museum Helveticum* 56 (1999): 76–86.

18. Archaeologists seem particularly prone to this kind of positivism. See, for instance, E. M. Murphy and J. P. Mallory, "Herodotus and the Cannibals," *Antiquity* 74 (2000): 388–94; Eileen M. Murphy, "Herodotus and the Amazons Meet the Cyclops: Philology, Osteoarchaeology, and the Eurasian Iron Age," in Eberhard W. Sauer, ed., *Archaeology and Ancient History: Breaking Down the Boundaries* (New York: Routledge, 2004), 169–84.

19. The classic works on the topic are E. H. Minns, *Scythians and Greeks* (Cambridge: Cambridge University Press, 1913); Mikhail Rostovtzeff, *Iranians and Greeks in South Russia* (Oxford: Clarendon Press, 1922); Rostovtzeff, *Skythien und der Bosporus*, vol. 2, *Wiederentdeckte Kapitel und Verwandtes*, ed. Heinz Heinen (Berlin: H. Schoetz, 1993). More recently, see the essays brought together in Braund, ed., *Scythians and Greeks*; and David Braund and S. D. Kryzhitskiy, eds., *Classical Olbia and the Scythian World: From the Sixth Century BC to the Second Century AD* (Oxford: Oxford University Press, 2007).

20. Debate continues about whether Herodotus visited the Black Sea, as he claims, but most who find this credible acknowledge it is unlikely he got far beyond Olbia, although a trip to Exampaios is mentioned at 4.52 and 81. The most skeptical view remains O. Kimball Armayor, "Did Herodotus Ever Go to the Black Sea?," *Harvard Studies in Classical Philology* 82 (1978): 45–62. More sympathetic and nuanced is the discussion of Stephanie West, "Herodotus and Scythia," in Vassos Karageorghis and Ioannis Taifacos, eds., *The World of Herodotus* (Nicosia: Foundation Anastasios G. Leventis, 2004), 73–89; West, "Herodotus in the North? Reflections on a Colossal Cauldron (4.81)," *Scripta Classica Israelica* 19 (2000): 15–34; West, "Herodotus and Olbia," in Braund and Kryzhitskiy, eds., *Classical Olbia and the Scythian World*, 79–92. On Greek-Scythian relations in the region, see the essays brought together in the last-named volume and in Braund, ed., *Scythians and Greeks*. The sole informant Herodotus cites by name is Tymnes, the deputy, steward, or viceroy (*epitropos*) of the Scythian king Ariapeithes (4.76; further on Ariapeithes, 4.78).

21. Manfred Mayrhofer, *Einiges zu den Skythen, ihrer Sprache, ihrem Nachleben* (Vienna: Verlag der Österreichischen Akademie der Wissenschaften, 2006), 10. Scyth-

ian attestations include the proper names Ariantas (< *Ariya-anta) and Ariapeithēs (< *Ariya-paēsah-, "Ornament of the Aryans"), as well as the ethnonym Alans (used of certain Scythian tribes of Europe) and Iron (one of the two Ossetic subgroups). For the other Indo-Iranian cognates and their much-debated etymology, see Manfred Mayrhofer, *Etymologisches Wörterbuch des Altindoarischen* (Heidelberg: Carl Winter, 1992–2001), 1: 174–75 and the literature there cited.

22. Mayrhofer, *Einiges zu den Skythen*, 20. The term occurs in an inscription at Tanais dated 188 CE, in the proper name of a Scythian Xo-dainos (< Iranian *hu̯adaina-*, "One who follows his own religion"; cf. Avestan *x*v*ādaēna-*, which occurs as an adjective at *Yašt* 10.2 and as a proper name at *Yašt* 13.104). On the meaning of Avestan *daēnā-*, see Marijan Molé, "Daēnā, le pont Činvat et l'initiation dans le mazdéisme," *Revue de l'Histoire des Religions* 157 (1960): 155–85.

23. Mayrhofer, *Einiges zu den Skythen*, 21. The Scythian attestation comes in the name Xo-pharnos, found in an inscription of the third century, reflecting Scythian *Hu-farnah-*, "Good in glory." See further Philippe Huyse, "Gab es eine Lautentwicklyng /k/ → /x/ im Skytho-Sarmatischen?," *Hyperboreus* 4 (1998): 169–70. Old Persian *farnah* appears in the proper name Vinda-farnah (= Greek *Intaphernes*), "Glory-finder," and fifty other names of high-ranking Persians, for which, see J. Tavernier, *Iranica in the Achaemenid Period (ca. 550–330 B.C.): Lexicon of Old Iranian Proper Names and Loanwords, attested in Non-Iranian Texts* (Louvain: Peeters, 2007), 586–87 and passim. The initial *f-* is inconsistent with Old Persian phonology and has usually been taken as an indication that the Achaemenids took this word over from their Median predecessors. For different reasons, this has been challenged by P. Oktor Skjærvø, "Farnah: Mot mede en vieux-perse?," *Bulletin de la Société Linguistique* 78 (1983): 241–59; Pierre Lecoq, "Le mot *farnah* et les Scythes," *Comptes Rendus de l'Académie des Inscriptions et Belles-Lettres* (1987): 671–81; and Alexander Lubotsky, "Scythian Elements in Old Iranian," in Nicholas Sims-Williams, ed, *Indo-Iranian Languages and Peoples* (Oxford: The British Academy, 2002), 191–95, the last two of whom suggest Scythian origin. Preferable, however, is the analysis of Josef Elfenbein, "Splendour and Fortune," in Maria Gabriela Schmidt and Walter Bisang, eds., *Philologica et Linguistica: Festschrift für Helmut Humbach* (Trier: Wissenschaftlicher Verlag, 2001), 485–96. Regarding Avestan *x*v*aranah*, see Gherardo Gnoli, "Farr(ah)," in *Encyclopaedia Iranica* (London: Routledge, 1983–), vol. 9, pp. 312–19 and the large literature cited therein. Numerous cognates are also found in Middle Iranian languages, including Pahlavi *xwarrah* and *farr*, Manichaean Middle Persian *frh*, Parthian *prh, prnhw*, Manichaean Parthian *frh*, Sogdian *frn*, Khotanese *phārra*, Bactrian φαρρο, and Ossetic *farn*. Finally, the fiery gold objects described in Herodotus 4.5 and 7 bear striking resemblance to the Avestan description of *x*v*aranah* in such texts as *Yasna* 9.1–5, *Yašt* 18, 19, and 10.127.

24. Mayrhofer, *Einiges zu den Skythen*, 12. The Scythian term appears in the name of the god whom Herodotus identifies with Poseidon (4.59): Goitosyros, "strong in his herds" (with comparison to Avestan *gaēθā-* + *sūra-*). Old Persian *gaiθa-* appears at DB §14 and as a loanword in Elamite *gaiθa-pati-*, "protector of the herd." Preferable, however, might be the interpretation of Helmut Humbach and Klaus Faiss, *Herodotus's Scythians and Ptolemy's Central Asia: Semasiological and Onomasiological*

*Studies* (Wiesbaden: Ludwig Reichert, 2012), 5–6, positing Scythian *\*gauyauti-sūra-*, "ruler of the grassland," with comparison to Avestan *\*sūra gəušca vāstraheca*, "rich in/ ruler of cattle and pasture" (*Yašt* 19.54), and *vouru.gaoyaoiti-*, "of wide grasslands," the most common epithet of the god Miθra.

25. Mayrhofer, *Einiges zu den Skythen*, 19. This is one of two Indo-Iranian terms denoting "truth," the other of which (*\*r̥ta,*) is discussed below at pp. 77–78. The term in question is built on the present participle of the copula (thus I-I *\*sat-ya-*, < *\*√as-*, "to be") and denotes "truth" as that which is actually extant. The Scythian reflex occurs in the name of King Ateas, mentioned by Plutarch and Strabo. Old Persian *hašiya* figures in the solemn oath sworn by Darius at DB §57, and Avestan *haiθiia* in numerous important passages of the Older and Younger Avesta (see esp. *Yasna* 30.5, 31.6, and 34.15). On the distinction between the two forms of truth, see Hjalmar Frisk, *"Wahrheit" und "Lüge" in den indogermanischen Sprachen: Einige morphologische Beobachtung* (Göteborg: Eilanders Bogtryckeri, 1936).

26. Mayrhofer, *Einiges zu den Skythen*, 13. The word appears in the name of the Scythian king called Madyēs by Herodotus (1.103) and Madus by Strabo. Avestan *mad-*, "to intoxicate, invigorate," and *mada-*, "intoxicant," are found in the Older Avesta (*Yasna* 54.1 and 48.10, respectively), *maδu-* only in the Younger Avesta (*Vidēvdāt* 5.52–54 and 14.17). See further Rüdiger Schmitt, "Die skythischen Personennamen bei Herodot," *Annali del Istituto Orientale di Napoli* 63 (2003): 12–13.

27. Mayrhofer, *Einiges zu den Skythen*, 10–11. This royal title appears in the compound names of the three primordial figures who competed for the Scythian kingship according to the myth recounted in Herodotus 4.5–6: Arpo-xais, Lipo-xais, and Kola-xais. *xšāyaθiya* is the standard royal title in the Achaemenid inscriptions, where the verb *xšay-* appears in the royal name Xšaya-aršan ("Ruler of heroes," Greek Xerxes), and with the preverbs *upari-* ot *pati-*, yielding the sense "to rule over." The numerous Avestan occurrences are listed in Christian Bartholomae, *Altiranisches Wörterbuch* (Berlin: Walter de Gruyter, 1904), 551–53.

28. Herodotus 4.9–10. Cf. *Yasna* 9.26; *Yašt* 1.17, 15.57; *Dādestān ī Dēnīg* 38; *Selections of Zādspram* 13; *Dēnkart* 5.24.16c; *Šāyest nē Šāyest* 4 and 10.13. See further J. J. Modi, *The Religious Ceremonies and Customs of the Parsees* (Bombay: British India Press, 1922), 178–96; Geo Widengren, "Le symbolisme du ceinture," *Iranica Antiqua* 8 (1968): 133–55.

29. Herodotus 4.23. Cf. the treatment of *haoma* in general, which is at the center of the *Yasna* sacrifice and is well attested in the Persepolis archives. The Achaemenid designation of some Scythians as *haumavarga* is also relevant (DNa §3; DSe §3; XPh §3); the term is rendered in Greek as *Amyrgioi Skythoi*, Herodotus 7.64). See further E. D. Phillips, "The *Argippaei* of Herodotus," *Artibus Asiae* 23 (1960): 124–28; Ronald Bowman, *Aramaic Ritual Texts from Persepolis* (Chicago: Oriental Institute, 1970); Hugo Mühlenstein, "Kirschmus und Kahlköpfe," in *O-o-pe-ro-si: Festschrift für Ernst Risch* (Berlin: Walter de Gruyter, 1986), 561–64; and Dastur Firoze M. Kotwal and James W. Boyd, *A Persian Offering: The Yasna; A Zoroastrian High Liturgy* (Paris: Association pour l'avancement des études iraniennes, 1991).

30. Following Aristotle, *Politics* 1278a and derivation of the term from *astu*, "city,"

Hartog, *Mirror of Herodotus*, 124 takes *astoi* to denote "citizens," a concept he considers incompatible with the a-political nature of the nomadic Scythians, but such an implication is not necessary. Herodotus's usage of the term is considerably looser, such that J. Enoch Powell, *A Lexicon to Herodotus* (Cambridge: Cambridge University Press, 1938; reprint, 2004), 50 gave the definitions "native, fellow-countryman" for the singular and "the people" (Greek or non-Greek) in the plural.

31. Herodotus 4.68–69: Ἐπεὰν δὲ βασιλεὺς ὁ Σκυθέων κάμῃ, μεταπέμπεται τῶν μαντίων ἄνδρας τρεῖς τοὺς εὐδοκιμέοντας μάλιστα, οἳ τρόπῳ τῷ εἰρημένῳ μαντεύονται· καὶ λέγουσι οὗτοι ὡς τὸ ἐπίπαν μάλιστα τάδε, ὡς τὰς βασιληίας ἱστίας ἐπιώρκηκε ὅς καὶ ὅς, λέγοντες τῶν ἀστῶν, τὸν ἂν δὴ λέγωσι. τὰς δὲ βασιληίας ἱστίας νόμος Σκύθῃσι τὰ μάλιστα ἐστὶ ὀμνύναι τότε, ἐπεὰν τὸν μέγιστον τῶν τὸ ὅρκον ἐθέλωσι ὀμνύναι. αὐτίκα δὲδιαλελαμμένος ἄγεται οὗτος, τὸν ἂν δὴ φῶσι ἐπιορκῆσαι· ἀπιγμένον δὲ ἐλέγχουσι οἱ μάντιες, ὡς ἐπιορκῆσαι φαίνεται ἐν τῇ μαντικῇ τὰς βασιληίας ἱστίας καὶ διὰ ταῦτα ἀλγέει ὁ βασιλεύς· ὁ δὲ ἀρνέεται, οὐ φάμενος ἐπιορκῆσαι, καὶ δεινολογέεται. ἀρνεομένου δὲ τούτου ὁ βασιλεὺς μεταπέμπεται ἄλλους διπλησίους μάντιας· καὶ ἢν μὲν καὶ οὗτοι ἐσορῶντες ἐς τὴν μαντικὴν καταδήσωσι ἐπιορκῆσαι, τοῦ δὲ ἰθέως τὴν κεφαλὴν ἀποτάμνουσι καὶ τὰ χρήματα αὐτοῦ διαλαγχάνουσι οἱ πρῶτοι τῶν μαντίων· ἢν δὲ οἱ ἐπελθόντες μάντιες ἀπολύσωσι, ἄλλοι πάρεισι μάντιες καὶ μάλα ἄλλοι· ἢν ὦν οἱ πλεῦνες τὸν ἄνθρωπον ἀπολύσωσι, δέδοκται τοῖσι πρώτοισι τῶν μαντίων αὐτοῖσι ἀπόλλυσθαι. ἀπολλῦσι δῆτα αὐτοὺς τρόπῳ τοιῷδε· ἐπεὰν ἄμαξαν καμάρης φρυγάνων πλήσωσι καὶ ὑποζεύξωσι βοῦς, ἐμποδίσαντες τοὺς μάντιας καὶ χεῖρας ὀπίσω δήσαντες καὶ στομώσαντες κατεργνῦσι ἐς μέσα τὰ φρύγανα, ὑποπρήσαντες δὲ αὐτὰ ἀπιεῖσι φοβήσαντες τοὺς βοῦς. πολλοὶ μὲν δὴ συγκατακαίονται τοῖσι μάντισι βόες, πολλοὶ δὲ περικεκαυμένοι ἀποφεύγουσι, ἐπεὰν αὐτῶν ὁ ῥυμὸς κατακαυθῇ. κατακαίουσι δὲ τρόπῳ τῷ εἰρημένῳ καὶ δι᾽ ἄλλας αἰτίας τοὺς μάντιας, ψευδομάντιας καλέοντες. τοὺς δὲ ἂν ἀποκτείνῃ βασιλεύς τούτων οὐδὲ τοὺς παῖδας λείπει, ἀλλὰ πάντα τὰ ἔρσενα κτείνει, τὰ δὲ θήλεα οὐκ ἀδικέει.

32. Herodotus 4.59 and 127.

33. Hartog, *Mirror of Herodotus*, 119–33, esp. 119–25.

34. Ibid., 122.

35. Jean-Pierre Vernant, "Hestia-Hermes," in *Myth and Thought among the Greeks* (London: Routledge & Kegan Paul, 1983), 127–76.

36. Hartog, *Mirror of Herodotus*, 120–22 and 125.

37. Ibid., 118–19 and 123.

38. The divinized fire is known as *Ātar* in the Avesta, which contains a hymn in its praise, the *Ātaš Nyāyišn* (*Yasna* 62.1–10). Old Persian *\*ātar* is preserved in *Āçiyādiya*, "Fire-worship month" (from *ātar* + *yad-*), on which see Roland Kent, *Old Persian* (New Haven, CT: American Oriental Society, 1953), 166; and Wilhelm Brandenstein and Manfred Mayrhofer, *Handbuch des Altpersischen* (Wiesbaden: Otto Harrassowitz, 1964), 100; or, for a slightly different interpretation, A. Meillet and E. Benveniste, *Grammaire du Vieux Perse* (Paris: Honoré Champion, 1931), 154.

39. Carl Darling Buck, *A Dictionary of Selected Synonyms in the Principal Indo-European Languages* (Chicago: University of Chicago Press, 1949), 474–75. The fullest discussion of the topic is Wilhelm Eilers, "Herd und Feuerstätte in Iran," in Manfred

Mayrhofer et al., eds., *Antiquitates Indogermanicae: Gedenkschrift für Hermann Güntert* (Innsbruck: Innsbrucker Beiträge zur Sprachwissenschaft, 1974), 307–38. Most common among the Middle Iranian terms for the hearth that have an Indo-Iranian etymology are those that call it "fire-place" (Persian *ātaš-gāh*, Kurdish *āwiryā* [< *ādur-gāh*], Sīvandi *ārd-gā*, Pašto *ōryalai* [< *āθr-yālai*]) or "fire-holder" (Persian *ātaš-dān*, Tajik *ōtaš-dōn*, Kurdish *āgir-dān*).

40. Mayrhofer, *Einiges zu den Skythen*, 17; Humbach and Faiss, *Herodotus's Scythians and Ptolemy's Central Asia*, 7. Formally, the name is a present participle in the singular nominative feminine, built on the verbal root *\*tap-*, "to warm up, heat," on which see Johnny Cheung, *Etymological Dictionary of the Iranian Verb* (Leiden: Brill, 2007), 378–80. In some Iranian languages, this verb also acquires a sense "to shine" (thus Pahlavi, Parthian, Manichaean Middle Persian, Buddhist Sogdian, and Farsi). Dumézil,*Romans de Scythie et alentours*, 125–45, connected the Scythian goddess with Sanskrit Tapatī and Ossetic Acyrūs, but the attempt fails for reasons identified by George Hinge, "Herodots skythiske nomader," in Tønnes Bekker-Nielsen and George Hinge, eds., *På ronden af det ukendte* (Aarhus: Aarhus Universitetsforlag, 2003), 23–25. Thus, Tabiti and Tapatī share an ethmology; Tapatī and Acyrūs, some similarities in their narrative; Tabati and Acyrūs, nothing at all. Further, Tapatī appears in the *Māhabhārata* only and seems to be an invention of the epic.

41. Cf. Plutarch's identification of the Persian Areimanios with Greek Hades (*Isis and Osiris* 369e-f).

42. In addition to the verses cited below, see also *Yasna* 31.3, 31.19, 43.9, 47.6, and 51.9. The intimate association of truth and fire present in these ancient texts, traditionally attributed to Zarathuštra himself, was given fuller elaboration in subsequent literature, like *Greater Bundahišn* 1.49, 3.18, 26.44–45; *Supplement to the Šāyest nē Šāyest* 15.5; *Selections of Zādspram* 35.17 and 35.39, which worked out the theory that the most important spiritual entities have material instantiations or counterparts (*daxšag*), truth and fire being a prime example of such relationships. See further Herman Lommel, "Die Elemente in Verhältnis zu den Aməša Spəntas," in Bernfried Schlerath, ed., *Zarathuštra* (Darmstadt: Wissenschaftliche Gesellschaft, 1970), 377–96; Johanna Narten, *Die Aməša Spəntas im Avesta* (Wiesbaden: Otto Harrassowitz, 1982), 106–7 and 121–23; Mary Boyce, "*Ātaš*," in *Encyclopaedia Iranica*, 3: 1–5; Antonio Panaino, "Il culto del fuoco nello Zoroastrismo," in *Il fuoco nell' Alto Medioevo* (Spoleto: Centro Italiano di Studi sull' Alto Medioevo, 2013), 65–93.

43. *Yasna* 34.4:

| | |
|---|---|
| at tōi ātrəm ahurā | aojōŋhuuantəm ašā usəmahī |
| asīštīm əmauuantəm | stōi rapantē ciθrā.auuaŋhəm |
| at mazdā daibišiiantē | zastāištāiš dərəštā.aēnaŋhəm. |

44. *Yasna* 43.4:

| | |
|---|---|
| at θβā məŋghāi, | taxməmcā spəntəm mazdā |
| hiiat tā zastā | yā tū hafšī auuå |
| yå då ašīš, | drəguuāitē ašāunaēca |
| θβahiiā garəmā | āθrō ašā.aojaŋhō. |

45. *Yasna* 46.7:

| | |
|---|---|
| kəmnā mazdā | mauuaitē pāiiūm dadå |
| hiiat mā drəguuå | dīdarəšatā aēnaŋhē |
| aniiəm θβahmāt | āθrascā manaŋhascā |
| yaiiå šiiaoθanāiš | ašəm θraoštā ahurā. |

46. For linguistic analysis of the relevant lexemes, see Mayrhofer, *Etymologisches Wörterbuch des Altindoarischen*, 1: 254–55 and 1: 760–61. More broadly on the issues, see Onorato Bucci, "L'impero achemenide come ordinamento giuridico sovrannazionale e *arta* come principio ispiratore di uno *jus commune Persarum (dātā)*," in *Modes de contacts et processus de transformation dans les sociétés anciennes* (Pisa: Scuola Normale Superiore, 1983), 89–122; Bernfried Schlerath and P. O. Skjærvø, "*Aša*," in *Encyclopaedia Iranica*, 2: 694–96; Jean Kellens, "*Druj-*," in *Encyclopaedia Iranica*, 7: 562–63; P. O. Skjærvø, "Truth and Deception in Ancient Iran," in Carlo G. Cereti and Farrokh Vajifdar, eds., *Ataš-e Dorun: The Fire Within; Jamshid Soroush Soroushian Commemorative Volume* (N.p.: Mehrborzin Soroushian, 2003), 383–434; and Bruce Lincoln, *"Happiness for Mankind": Achaemenian Religion and the Imperial Project* (Louvain: Peeters, 2012), 20–40 and passim. Cf. Herodotus 1.136 and 138. Old Persian *r̥ta* and the related adjective *r̥ta-van* appear only in the famous "daiva inscription" of Xerxes at Persepolis (XPh §4b and 4d). It is present, however, in the royal name Artaxerxes (*R̥ta-xšaça*, "He whose kingship is truth") and scores of names attested at Persepolis and elsewhere, on which see Tavernier, *Iranica in the Achaemenid Period*, 542–43; and Manfred Mayrhofer, *Onomastica Persepolitana: Das altiranische Namengut der Persepolis-täfelchen* (Vienna: Österreichischen Akademie der Wissenschaften, 1973), as summarized in the index, 330–31. Translation of this complex term as "truth" generally follows from the analysis of Heinrich Lüders, *Varuṇa: II, Varuṇa und das R̥ta* (Göttingen: Vandenhoeck & Ruprecht, 1959).

47. Darius, inscription at Naqš-ī Rustam (DNb §§2a–2b): θāti Dārayavauš xšāyaθiya: vašnā Auramazdāhā avākaram ami, taya rāstam dauštā ami, miθa nai̯ dauštā ami . . . taya rāstam, ava mām kāma; martiyam drau̯janam nai̯ dauštā ami.

48. Darius's inscription at Bisitun (DB §10): yaθā Kambujiya Mudrāyam ašiyava, pasāva kāra arīka abava utā drauga dahyau̯vā vasai̯ abava. Regarding the significance of the phrases "vulnerable to deception" (*arīka*) and "became great" (*vasai̯ abava*), see Lincoln, *"Happiness for Mankind,"* 25–29 and 213–17.

49. DB §11: pasāva 1 martiya maguš āha, Gau̯māta nāma . . . hau̯ kārahyā avaθā adurujiya: "adam Br̥diya ami, haya Kurau̯š puça, Kambujiyahyā brātā." pasāva kāra haruva hamiçiya abava hacā Kambujiyā. abi avam ašiyava, utā Pārsa utā Māda utā aniyā dahyāva. xšaçam hau̯ agr̥bāyatā. The charge that Gau̯māta lied is repeated in the minor inscription that serves as a caption to his sculptural representation, DBb.

50. The phrase describing Cambyses's death has been much discussed. Immediately following its account of Gau̯māta's usurpation, the inscription states (DB §11): "Then Cambyses died his own death" (pasāva Kambujiya uvamr̥šiyuš amariyatā). There is now general agreement that the phrase "his own death" (*uvamr̥šiyuš*) was meant to establish this was not a case of homicide. It does not, however, define it as a natural death in anything like our sense. Rather, the phrase suggests that Cam-

byses was the victim of processes he himself had unleashed by his failures of royal responsibility: processes in which the motive force was not "nature," but "the Lie."

51. DB §13:

Proclaims Darius the King: There was not a man—not a Persian, nor a Mede, nor anyone of our lineage—who could have deprived that Gaumāta the Magus of the kingship. The people feared him mightily. He would kill greatly among the people those who knew Bardiya in the past. For that reason, he would kill among the people, (thinking): "Lest they might recognize me and know I am not Bardiya, the son of Cyrus." No one dared to proclaim anything about Gaumāta the Magus.

θāti Dārayavauš xšāyaθiya: naị āha martiya naị Pārsa naị Māda naị amāxam taụmāyā kašci, haya avam Gaụmātam tayam magum xšaçam dītam caxriyā. kārašim hacā dṛšam atṛsa. kāram vasaị avājaniyā, haya paruvam Bṛdiyam adānā. avahyarādī kāram avājaniyā; "mātaya mām xšnāsāti, taya adam naị Bṛdiya ami, haya Kuraụš puça," kašci naị adṛšnaụš cišci θanstanaị pari Gaụmātam tayam magum.

52. This follows from Darius's description of the works of restoration he had to accomplish, after replacing Gaumāta on the throne.

I restored the pastures and livestock and servants and houses of the people, of which Gaumāta the Magus had deprived them. I set the people back in place, in Persia and Media and in the other lands/peoples.

adam niyaçārayam kārahyā ābicarīš gaịθāmcā māniyamcā viθbišcā, tayādiš Gaụmāta haya maguš adinā. adam kāram gāθavā avāstāyam Pārsamcā Mādamcā utā aniyā dahyāva.

53. DPd §3, on which see Lincoln, "Happiness for Mankind," 406–19.

54. DB §§63–64: θāti Dārayavauš xšāyaθiya: avahyarādīmaị Auramazdā upastām abara utā aniyāha bagāha, tayaị hanti, yaθā naị arīka āham, naị draụjana āham, naị zūrakara āham, naị adam naịmaị taụmā, upari ṛštām upariyāyam; naị škaụθim naị tunuvantam zūra akunavam.

55. DB §14: θāti Dārayavauš xšāyaθiya: xšaçam, taya hacā amāxam taụmāyā parābṛtam āha, ava adam patipadam akunavam. adamšim gāθavā avāstāyam. yaθā paruvamci, avaθā adam akunavam āyadanā, tayā Gaụmāta haya maguš viyaka.

56. On the translation of Old Persian āyadana-, see Pierre Lecoq, "Un aspect de la politique religieuse de Gaumāta le mage," in Rika Gyselened, Au carrefour des religions: Mélanges offerts à Philippe Gignoux (Bures-sur-Yvette: Groupe pour l'étude de la civilisation du Moyen-Orient, 1995), 183–86. Lecoq's argument centers on the fact that in place of Old Persian āyadana, the Elamite version of the Bisitun inscription has ᵈzí-ia-an ("rite, doctrine, custom, usage") and not si-ia-an ("temple"), which typically lacks the dingir-determinative. Based on this, plus Herodotus's assertion that the Persians had no temples or altars (1.131), Lecoq thinks āyadana- best translated as "cult." The Akkadian, however, has Émeš ("temples"), and the destructive acts attributed to Gaumāta, denoted by the verb vi-kan- (lit. "to dig apart"; more broadly, "to demolish, destroy")

seem better suited to a building or an altar than to a set of ritual practices. Given that the term occurs in this passage only, it is hard to be certain just what *āyadana-* denotes.

57. On the verb *yad-*, "to sacrifice; to worship, venerate," cognate with Avestan *yaz-*, Vedic *yáj-*, Pahlavi *yaštan*, see Cheung, *Etymological Dictionary of the Iranian Verb*, 219–20; Émile Benveniste, *Le vocabulaire des institutions indo-européennes* (Paris: Éditions de Minuit, 1969), 2: 223; Benveniste, "Sur la terminologie iranienne du sacrifice," *Journal Asiatique* 252 (1964): 45–58; Mayrhofer, *Etymologisches Wörterbuch des Altindoarischen*, 2: 392–93.

58. Passages describing the perfection of Yima's reign include *Yasna* 9.4–5; *Vīdēvdāt* 2.4–5; *Yašt* 9.9–10, 15.16, 17.29–30, 19.31–33; *Greater Bundahišn* 32.10; *Dēnkart* 3.229, 7.1.23; *Dādestān ī Dēnīg* 38.19; and *Mēnōg ī Xrad* 27.24–26. The classic discussion remains Arthur Christensen, *Le premier homme et le premier roi dans l'histoire légendaire des Iraniens*, vol. 2, *Jim* (Uppsala: Appelberg, 1934). More recently, see Prods Oktor Skjærvø, "Jamšid: i. Myth of Jamšid," in *Encyclopaedia Iranica* 14: 501–22; and Audrey Tzatourian, *Yima: Structure de la pensée religieuse en Iran ancien* (Paris: L'Harmattan, 2012), both with abundant bibliography.

59. Yima is named "most glorious," lit. "most possessed of *xᵛarənah*" (Avestan *xᵛarənaŋuhastəma-*, Pahlavi *farraxtom*) at *Yasna* 9.4, *Yašt* 15.16, and *Dādestān ī Dēnīg* 38.19. Descriptions of him as possessing *xᵛarənah* in great abundance occur at *Yašt* 19.30–31, *Dādestān ī Dēnīg* 36.26, *Pahlavi Rivāyat accompanying the Dādestān ī Dēnīg* 46.21, *Greater Bundahišn* 26.4, and *Dēnkart* 3.129. On the *xᵛarənah* itself, see the literature cited above in note 23.

60. *Yašt* 19.30–34: uγrəm kauuaēm xᵛarənō mazdaδātəm yazamaide . . . yat upaŋhacat yim yiməm xšaētəm huuąθβəm darəyəmcit aipi zruuānəm yat xšaiiata paiti būmīm haptaiθiiąm . . . yeŋhe xšaθrāδa nōit aotəm åŋha nōit garəməm nōit zauruua åŋha nōit mərəiθiiuš nōit araskō daēuuō.dātō ⁺parō anādruxtōit para ahmāt yat hīm aēm draoγəm vācim aŋhaiθīm āat yat hīm aēm draoγəm vācim aŋhaiθīm cinmāne paiti.barata vaēnəmnəm ahmat haca xᵛarənō mərəyahe kəhrpa frašusat. I follow Helmut Humbach and Pallan R. Ichaporia, *Zamyād Yasht: Text, Translation, Commentary* (Wiesbaden: Harrassowitz, 1998), 109, in emending the incomprehensibly contradictory phrase *para anādruxtōit* of *Yašt* 19.33e to the semantically appropriate ⁺*parō anādruxtōit*. For other attempts to solve the problem, see Eric Pirart, *Kayān Yasn (Yasht 19.9–96): L'origine avestique des dynasties mythiques d'Iran* (Barcelona: Aula Orientalis, 1992), 46; Almut Hintze, *Der Zamyād-Yašt: Edition, Übersetzung, Kommentar* (Wiesbaden: Ludwig Reichert, 1994), 186–88.

61. *Yašt* 19.45; *Selections of Zādspram* 35.46; *Pahlavi Rivāyat accompanying the Dādestān ī Dēnīg* 31c6, 47.8, and 48.66; *Greater Bundahišn* 18.6, 33.1, and 35.5.

62. On the relation between the two kinds of *xᵛarənah*, see the discussion of Humbach and Ichaporia, *Zamyād Yasht*, 15–18. That which I am calling "royal" is more properly "Kavian," named after the dynasty of kings that came to possess the *xᵛarənah* after its flight from Yima.

63. *Yašt* 19.45–46:

We sacrifice to the mighty unappropriated glory created by the Wise Lord . . . for which the Beneficent and the Evil Spirit struggled. For this, which is unappropriated, each one sent his swiftest messengers. The Beneficent Spirit sent his messengers: Good Mind, Best Truth, and Fire, the Wise Lord's son. The Evil Spirit sent his messengers: Evil Mind, Wrath of the Bloody Club, Aži Dahāka, and Spityura, who cut Yima in pieces.

uɣrəm ax<sup>v</sup>arətəm x<sup>v</sup>arənō mazdaδātəm yazamaide . . . yahmi paiti parəx<sup>v</sup>āiθe spəntasca maniiuš aŋrasca. aētahmi paiti at ax<sup>v</sup>arəte aδāt ašte fraŋharəcaiiat āsište katarascit. Spəntō maniiuš aštəm fraŋharəcaiiat vohuca manō ašəmca vahištəm ātrəmca ahurahe mazdå puθrəm. Aŋrō maniiuš aštəmca fraŋharəcaiiat akəmca manō aēšməmca xruui.drum ažimca dahākəm spitiiurəmca yimō.kərəntəm.

On Aži Dahāka, see P. O. Skjærvø, "*Aždahā*: i. In Old and Middle Iranian," in *Encyclopaedia Iranica*, 3: 191–99.

64. *Yašt* 19.47–48: aδat fraša hạm.rāzaiiata ātarš mazdå ahurahe uiti auuaθa maŋhānō: "aētat x<sup>v</sup>arənō hangərəfšāne yat ax<sup>v</sup>arətəm." āat hē paskāt fraduuarat ažiš θrizafå duždaēnō uiti zaxšaθrəm daomnō: "inja auuat handaēsaiiaŋ<sup>u</sup>ha ātarš mazdå ahurahe yezi aētat niiāsåŋhe yat ax<sup>v</sup>arətəm frā θβạm paiti apāθa nōit apaiia uzraocaiiāi zạm paiti ahuraδātạm θrāθrāi ašahe gaēθanạm." aδa ātarš zasta paiti apa.gəuruuaiiat fraxšni uštānō.cinahiia yaθa ažiš biβiuuåŋha.

65. *Yašt* 19.49–50: aδat fraša hạm.duuarat ažiš θrizafå duždaēnō uiti auuaθa maŋhānō: "aētat x<sup>v</sup>arənō hangərəfšāne yat ax<sup>v</sup>arətəm." āat hē paskāt hạm.rāzaiiata ātarš mazdå ahurahe uiti vacəbiš aojanō: "tinja auuat handaēsaiiaŋ<sup>u</sup>ha aže θrizafəm dahāka yezi aētat niiāsåŋhe yat ax<sup>v</sup>arətəm frā θβạm zadaŋha paiti uzuxšāne zafarə paiti uzraocaiieni nōit apaiia afrapatāi zạm paiti ahuraδātạm mahrkāi ašahe gaēθanạm." aδa ažiš gauua paiti apa.gəuruuaiiat fraxšni uštānō.cinahiia yaθa ātarš biβiuuåŋha.

66. Note, for instance, Darius's treatment of the rebels Fravarti and Tritantaxma (DB §§32 and 33).

## CHAPTER SEVEN

1. Important discussions include Arthur Christensen, *Le premier homme et le premier roi dans l'histoire légendaire des Iraniens* (Uppsala: Appelberg, 1918–34), 1: 137–43; Emile Benveniste, "Traditions indo-iraniennes sur les classes sociales," *Journal Asiatique* 230 (1938): 530–37; W. Brandenstein, "Die Abstammungssagen der Skythen," *Wiener Zeitschrift für die Kunde des Morgenlands* 52 (1953–55): 183–211; Georges Dumézil, "La société scythique avait-elle des classes fonctionnelles?," *Indo-Iranian Journal* 5 (1962): 187–202; Dumézil, *Romans de Scythie et alentours* (Paris: Payot, 1978), 169–203; François Cornillot, "De Skythes à Kolaxais," *Studia Iranica* 10 (1981): 7–52; Askold Ivantchik, "Une légende sur l'origine des Scythes (Hdt. IV 5–7)," *Revue des Études Grecques* 112 (1999): 141–92; Aleksander Loma, "Namenkundliches zur skythischen Abstammungssage," *Studia Etymologica Cracoviensia* 16 (2011): 75–92; and Sébastien Barbara, "Encore sur le mythe de royauté des scythes d'après le *logos skythikos* d'Hérodote (IV, 5–7) et le problème des sources du *scythicos logos* d'Hérodote," in Sébastien Barbara, Michel Mazoyer, and Jain Meurant, *Figures royales des mondes anciens* (Paris: Harmattan, 2011), 31–57.

2. Askold Ivantchik, "La légende 'grecque' sur l'origine des Scythes (Hérodote 4.8–10)," in Valérie Fromentin and Sophie Gotteland, eds., *Origines Gentium* (Paris: de Boccard, 2001), 207–20; Monica Visintin, "Di Echidna, e di altre femmine anguiformi," *Métis* 12 (1997): 205–21; Visintin, "Echidna, Skythes e l'arco di Herakles: Figure della marginalità nella versione greca delle origini degli Sciti, Herodot 4.8–10," *Materiali e Discussioni per l'Analisi dei Testi Classici* 45 (2000): 43–81; Yulia Ustinova, "Snake-Limbed and Tendril-Limbed Goddesses in the Art and Mythology of the Mediterranean and Black Sea," in David Braund, ed., *Scythians and Greeks: Cultural Interactions in Scythia, Athens, and the Early Roman Empire* (Exeter: University of Exeter Press, 2005), 64–79. Other variants of the myth are found in Valerius Flaccus 6.48–59, Diodorus Siculus 2.43, and the Tabula Albana (*IG* XIV 1293 A 93–96).

3. Herodotus 4.5–6: 5. Ὡς δὲ Σκύθαι λέγουσι νεώτατον πάντων ἐθνέων εἶναι τὸ σφέτερον, τοῦτο δὲ γενέσθαι ὧδε. ἄνδρα γενέσθαι πρῶτον ἐν τῇ γῇ ταύτῃ ἐούσῃ ἐρήμῳ τῷ οὔνομα εἶναι Ταργιτάον· τοῦ δὲ Ταργιτάου τούτου τοὺς τοκέας λέγουσι εἶναι, ἐμοὶ μὲν οὐ πιστὰ λέγοντες, λέγουσι δ᾽ ὦν, Δία τε καὶ Βορυσθένεος τοῦ ποταμοῦ θυγατέρα. γένεος μὲν τοιούτου δή τινος γενέσθαι τὸν Ταργιτάον, τούτου δὲ γενέσθαι παῖδας τρεῖς, Λιπόξαΐν καὶ Ἀρπόξαΐν καὶ νεώτατον Κολάξαϊν. ἐπὶ τούτων ἀρχόντων ἐκ τοῦ οὐρανοῦ φερόμενα χρύσεα ποιήματα, ἄροτρόν τε καὶ ζυγὸν καὶ σάγαριν καὶ φιάλην, πεσεῖν ἐς τὴν Σκυθικήν· καὶ τῶν ἰδόντα πρῶτον τὸν πρεσβύτατον ἆσσον ἰέναι βουλόμενον αὐτὰ λαβεῖν, τὸν δὲ χρυσὸν ἐπιόντος καίεσθαι· ἀπαλλαχθέντος δὲ τούτου προσιέναι τὸν δεύτερον καὶ τὸν αὐτις ταὐτὰ ποιέειν. Τοὺς μὲν δὴ καιόμενον τὸν χρυσὸν ἀπώσασται, τρίτῳ δὲ τῷ νεωτάτῳ ἐπελθόντι κατασβῆναι, καὶ μιν ἐκεῖνον κομίσαι ἐς ἑωυτοῦ· καὶ τοὺς πρεσβυτέρους ἀδελφεοὺς πρὸς ταῦτα συγγνόντας τὴν βασιληίην πᾶσαν παραδοῦναι τῷ νεωτάτῳ. Ἀπὸ μὲν δὴ Λιποξάιος γεγονέναι τούτους τῶν Σκυθέων οἳ Αὐχάται γένος καλέονται, ἀπὸ δὲ τοῦ μέσου Ἀρποξάιος οἳ Κατίαροί τε καὶ Τράσπιες καλέονται, ἀπὸ δὲ τοῦ νεωτάτου αὐτῶν τοῦ βασιλέος οἳ καλέονται Παραλάται· σύμπασι δὲ εἶναι οὔνομα Σκολότους, τοῦ βασιλέος ἐπωνυμίην. Σκύθας δὲ Ἕλληνες ὠνόμασαν.

4. Mayrhofer, *Einiges zu den Skythen*, 17, following Rüdiger Schmitt, "Die skythischen Personennamen bei Herodot," *Annali del Istituto Orientale di Napoli* 63 (2003): 24 and n. 91. See also Helmut Humbach and Klaus Faiss, *Herodotus's Scythians and Ptolemy's Central Asia: Semasiological and Onomasiological Studies* (Wiesbaden: Ludwig Reichert, 2012), 1–2.

5. Mayrhofer, *Einiges zu den Skythen*, 11, following Fridrik Thordarson, in *Studia grammatica Iranica: Festschrift für Helmut Humbach* (Munich: R. Kitzinger, 1986), 502. *Pace* their reconstruction, the original gender of the name would have been feminine, as recognized by Humbach and Faiss, *Herodotus's Scythia and Ptolemy's Central Asia*, 2. Greek authors treated it as masculine, however, associating the second element of the compound with Greek *sthenos*, "bodily strength," as in familiar names like *Demo-sthenēs*.

6. Mayrhofer, *Einiges zu den Skythen*, 10–11; Schmitt, "Die skythischen Personennamen bei Herodot," 2; Humbach and Faiss, *Herodotus's Scythia and Ptolemy's Central Asia*, 2. Cf. Old Persian *xšāyaθiya*, "king," Avestan *xšayant-*, "ruling" (singular nominative *xšayąs*).

7. Mayrhofer, *Einiges zu den Skythen*, 15; Humbach and Faiss, *Herodotus's Scythia and Ptolemy's Central Asia*, 3. Cf. Younger Avestan *Para-δāta*, the standard epithet of the primordial king Haošyaŋha, also attested in the Elamite of the Persepolis Fortification Tablets as *Pa-ra-da-da* and *Par-da-ad-da*.

8. Herodotus 4.59. On the name (cognate to Avestan *āp-*, "water"), see Mayrhofer, *Einiges zu den Skythen*, 9; Humbach and Faiss, *Herodotus's Scythians and Ptolemy's Central Asia*, 9.

9. Regarding the Zoroastrian comparandum, see Prods Oktor Skjærvø, "Ahura Mazda and Armaiti, Heaven and Earth, in the Old Avesta," *Journal of the American Oriental Society* 122 (2002): 399–410. Although Armaiti was identified with earth, this also included the terrestrial waters. Scythian Api seems to have the same associations, as evidenced by the fact that Herodotus identified her with Gē (4.59).

10. See further Bruce Lincoln, "The One and the Many in Iranian Creation Myths: Rethinking 'Nostalgia for Paradise'," *Archiv für Religionsgeschiche* 13 (2012): 15–30. Marijan Molé, "Le partage du monde dans la tradition iranienne," *Journal Asiatique* 240 (1952): 455–63 is also relevant.

11. Ordeals by fire are attested in the earliest Avestan texts, as is the association of fire with the cardinal virtue of truth, as at *Yasna* 31.19, 32.7, and 51.9. The heavenly gold of the Scythian myth is also comparable to Avestan *xᵛarənah* (a term with Old Persian, Median, and Scythian cognates), the radiant nimbus that identifies and bestows good fortune on legitimate kings, on which see Gherardo Gnoli, "*Farr(ah)*," in *Encyclopaedia Iranica*, 9: 312–19.

12. Kolaxais's possession of "the whole kingship" is specified at Herodotus 4.5, his founding of the royal lineage at 4.6, and the kings continued possession of the gold at 4.7: τὸν δὲ χρυσὸν τοῦτον τὸν ἱρὸν φυλάσσουσι οἱ βασιλέες ἐς τὰ μάλιστα, καὶ θυσίῃσι μεγάλῃσι ἱλασκόμενοι μετέρχονται ἀνὰ πᾶν ἔτος.

13. Most extensively on the Achaemenian cosmogony, see Clarisse Herrenschmidt, "Les créations d'Ahuramazda," *Studia Iranica* 6 (1977): 17–58; and Bruce Lincoln, *"Happiness for Mankind": Achaemenian Religion and the Imperial Project* (Louvain: Peeters, 2012).

14. Herodotus 4.8: Σκύθαι μὲν ὧδε ὕπερ σφέων τε αὐτῶν . . . λέγουσι.

15. Ibid. 4.5: Ὡς δὲ Σκύθαι λέγουσι νεώτατον πάντων ἐθνέων εἶναι τὸ σφέτερον.

16. See note 20 in chapter 6.

17. Herodotus 4.59: Ζεὺς δὲ ὀρθότατα κατὰ γνώμην γε τὴν ἐμὴν καλεόμενος Παπαῖος. For the etymology of this *Lallwort*, see Mayrhofer, *Einiges zu den Skythen*, 15; Humbach and Faiss, *Herodotus's Scythians and Ptolemy's Central Asia*, 6. Note that Ahura Mazdā is also designated the divine father in Zoroastrian mythology, as at *Yasna* 31.8, 44.3, 45.4, and 47.2.

18. The point is emphatically restated in a speech put in the mouth of the Scythian king. Responding proudly to Darius's call that he submit, Idanthyrsos is reported to have said, "I acknowledge only Zeus, *my ancestor*, and Hestia, Queen of the Scythians, as my masters." (Herodotus 4.127, emphasis added: δεσπότας δὲ ἐμοὺς ἐγὼ Δία τε νομίζω τὸν ἐμὸν πρόγονον καὶ Ἱστίην τὴν Σκυθέων βασίλειαν μούνους εἶναι.)

19. Herodotus begins and ends his presentation of the second variant by attributing it to "the Greeks dwelling on the Black Sea" (4.10: *tauta de Hellēnōn hoi ton Ponton oikeontes legousi*; cf. 4.8).

20. Herodotus 4.8–10: Ἡρακλέα ἐλαύνοντα τὰς Γηρυόνεω βοῦς ἀπικέσθαι ἐς γῆν ταύτην ἐοῦσαν ἐρήμην, ἥντινα νῦν Σκύθαι νέμονται. . . . ἐνθεῦτεν τόν Ἡρακλέα ἀπικέσθαι ἐς τὴν νῦν Σκυθίην χώρην καλεομένην, καὶ καταλαβεῖν γὰρ αὐτὸν χειμῶνα τε καὶ κρυμόν, ἐπειρυσάμενον τὴν λεοντέην κατυπνῶσαι, τὰς δὲ οἱ ἵππους τὰς ὑπὸ τοῦ ἅρματος νεμομένας ἐν τούτῳ τῷ χρόνῳ ἀφανισθῆναι θείῃ τύχῃ. ὥς δ᾽ ἐγερθῆναι τὸν Ἡρακλέα, δίζησθαι, πάντα δὲ τῆς χώρης ἐπεξελθόντα τέλος ἀπικέσθαι ἐς τὴν Ὑλαίην καλεομένην γῆν· ἐνθαῦτα δὲ αὐτὸν εὑρεῖν ἐν ἄντρῳ μιξοπάρθενον τινά, ἔχιδναν διφυέα, τῆς τὰ μὲν ἄνω ἀπὸ τῶν γλουτῶν εἶναι γυναικός, τὰ δὲ ἔνερθε ὄφιος. ἰδόντα δὲ καὶ θωμάσαντα ἐπειρέσθαι μιν εἴ κου ἴδοι ἵππους πλανωμένας· τὴν δὲ φάναι ἑωυτήν ἔχειν καὶ οὐκ ἀποδώσιν ἐκείνῳ πρὶν ἢ οἱ μιχθῇ· τό δὲ Ἡρακλέα μιχθῆναι ἐπὶ τῷ μισθῷ τούτῳ. κείνην τε δὴ ὑπερβάλλεσθαι τὴν ἀπόδοσιν τῶν ἵππων, βουλομένην ὡς πλεῖστον χρόνον συνεῖναι τῷ Ἡρακλεῖ, καὶ τὸν κομισάμενον ἐθέλειν ἀπαλλάσσεσθαι· τέλος δὲ ἀποδιδοῦσαν αὐτὴν εἰπεῖν Ἵππους μὲν δὴ ταύτας ἀπικομένας ἐνθάδε ἔσωσα τοὶ ἐγώ, σῶστρά τε σὺ παρέσχες· ἐγὼ γὰρ ἐκ σεῦ τρεῖς παῖδας ἔχω. τούτους, ἐπεὰν γένωνται τρόφιες, ὅ τι χρὴ ποιέειν, ἐξηγέο σύ, εἴτε αὐτοῦ κατοικίζω (χώρης γὰρ τῆσδε ἔχω τὸ κράτος αὕτη) εἴτε ἀποπέμπω παρὰ σέ. τὴν ἐν δὴ ταῦτα ἐπειρωτᾶν, τὸν δὲ λέγουσι πρὸς ταῦτα εἰπεῖν "ἐπεὰν ἀνδρωθέντας ἴδῃ τοὺς παῖδας, τάδε ποιεῦσα οὐκ ἄν ἁμαρτάνοις· τὸν μὲν ἄν ὁρᾷς αὐτῶν τόδε τὸ τόξον ὧδε διατεινόμενον καὶ τῷ ζωστῆρι τῷδε κατὰ τάδε ζωννύμενον, τοῦτον μὲν τῆσδε τῆς χώρης οἰήτορα ποιεῦ· ὅς δ᾽ ἄν τούτων τῶν ἔργων τῶν ἐντέλλομαι λείπηται, ἔκπεμπε ἐκ τῆς χώρης. καὶ ταῦτα ποιεῦσα αὐτή τε εὐφρανέαι καὶ τὰ ἐντεταλμένα ποιήσεις." τὸν μὲν δὴ εἰρύσαντα τῶν τόξων τὸ ἕτερον (δύο γὰρ δὴ φορέειν τέως Ἡρακλέα) καὶ τὸν ζωστῆρα προδέξαντα, παραδοῦναι τὸ τόξον τε καὶ τὸν ζωστῆρα ἔχοντα ἐπ᾽ ἄκρης τῆς συμβολῆς φιάλην χρυσέην, δόντα δὲ ἀπαλλάσσεσθαι. τὴν δ᾽, ἐπεὶ οἱ γενομένους τοὺς παῖδας ἀνδρωθῆναι, τοῦτο μὲν σφι οὐνόματα θέσθαι, τῷ μὲν Ἀγάθυρσον αὐτῶν, τῷ δ᾽ ἑπομένῳ Γελωνόν, Σκύθην δὲ τῷ νεωτάτῳ, τοῦτο δὲ τῆς ἐπιστολῆς μεμνημένην αὐτὴν ποιῆσαι τά ἐντεταλμένα. καὶ δὴ δύο μὲν οἱ τῶν παίδων, τόν τε Ἀγάθυρσον καὶ τὸν Γελωνόν, οὐκ οἵους τε γενομένους ἐξικέσθαι πρὸς τὸν προκείμενον ἄεθλον, οἴχεσθαι ἐκ τῆς χώρης ἐκβληθέντας ὑπὸ τῆς γειναμένης, τὸν δὲ νεώτατον αὐτῶν Σκύθην ἐπιτελέσαντα καταμεῖναι ἐν τῇ χῴη. καὶ ἀπὸ μὲν Σκύθεω τοῦ Ἡρακλέος γενέσθαι τοὺς αἰεὶ βασιλέας γινομένους Σκυθέων, ἀπὸ δὲ τῆς φιάλης ἔτι καὶ ἐς τόδε φιάλας ἐκ τῶν ζωστήρων φορέειν Σκύθας· τὸ δὴ μοῦνον μηχανήσασθαι τὴν μητέρα Σκύθῃ. ταῦτα δὲ Ἑλλήνων οἱ τὸν Πόντον οἰκέοντες λέγουσι.

21. While discussing Scythian resistance to foreign customs (4.76), Herodotus treats Hylaia as a territory geographically internal to Scythia, but exposed to the risk of Greek influence. Thus, when Anacharsis was making his way through the Hellespont, he stopped at the Greek city of Cyzicus, where he promised the Mother of the Gods that if she granted him a safe return to Scythia, he would establish her worship there. Upon entering Hylaia, he began performing her rites, hidden in the forest. There, however, he was observed by the native Scythian residents and subsequently slain by their king.

22. As discussed by Visintin, "Di Echidna, e di altre femmine anguiformi"; Visintin, "Echidna, Skythes e l'arco di Herakles"; and Ustinova, "Snake-Limbed and Tendril-Limbed Goddesses."

23. Marshall Sahlins, *Islands of History* (Chicago: University of Chicago Press, 1985), esp. 73–103; Sahlins, "The Stranger-King Or Elementary Forms of the Political Life," *Indonesia and the Malay World* 36 (2008): 177–99; Sahlins, "The Alterity of

Power and Vice Versa, with Reflections on Stranger Kings and the Real-Politics of the Marvellous," in Anthony McElligott, Liam Chambers, Clara Breathnach, and Catherine Lawless, eds., *History: From Medieval Ireland to the Post-Modern World,* (Dublin: Irish Academic Press, 2011), 63–101. Greek authors commonly cast Herakles in this role, thereby redefining other peoples as subordinate and somewhat lesser versions of themselves, a move first recognized by Elias J. Bickerman, "Origines Gentium," *Classical Philology* 47 (1952): 65–81.

24. Herodotus 4.9: τούτους, ἐπεὰν γένωνται τρόφιες, ὅ το χρὴ ποιέειν, ἐξηγέο σύ, εἴτε αὐτοῦ κατοικίζω (χώρης γὰρ τῆσδε ἔχω τὸ κράτος αὕτη) εἴτε ἀποπέμπω παρὰ σέ.

25. Herodotus never names Skythes as king, but at 4.6 he does state that the Skythai take their name from their first king, with implicit reference to Skythes (*sympasi de einai ounoma Skolotous, tou basileos epōnymiēn. Skythas de Hellēnes ōnomasan*). Diodorus Siculus 2.43.3 also makes Skythes the eponymous first king of the Skythian people, born of Zeus and an earth-born snake-woman. Hesiod also knew Skythes as primordial ancestor of the Scythians, although he makes no mention of kingship and identifies him as Zeus's, rather than Herakles's, son. Fragment 150 (Merkelbach-West), lines 15–16: *Skythas hippomolgous. / Skythēs men geneth' hyios hypermeneos kroniōnos.*

26. Herodotus 4.48–49 and 4.102 establish the locus of the Agathyrsoi. The first text places them second in the sequence of Scythia's northern neighbors, who are listed from west to east; the second puts them at the headwaters of the Ister (Danube), westernmost of the rivers that flows into Scythian territory. At 4.104, he says of them: "The Agathyrsoi are the most luxurious of men, particularly given to wearing gold. They have promiscuous sexual relations with women . . . and in other customs, they resemble the Thracians." (Ἀγάθυρσοι δὲ ἁβρότατοι ἀνδρῶν εἰσι καὶ χρυσοφόροι τὰ μάλιστα, ἐπίκοινον δὲ τῶν γυναικῶν τὴν μῖξιν ποιεῦνται . . . τὰ δὲ ἄλλα νόμαια Θρήϊξι προσκεχρήκασι.)

27. Herodotus 4.102 places the Gelonoi sixth of eight in the list of the Scythians' northern neighbors, just before the Boudinoi and Sauromatai. Their *nomoi* are described at 4.108–9: εἰσὶ γὰρ οἱ Γελωνοὶ τὸ ἀρχαῖον Ἕλληνες . . . καὶ γλώσσῃ τὰ μὲν Σκυθικῇ, τὰ δε Ἑλληνικῇ χρέωνται. . . . Γελωνοὶ δὲ γῆς τε ἐργάται καὶ σιτοφάγοι καὶ κήπους ἐκτημένοι.

28. Herodotus mentions a *sagaris* four times only, always as the weapon of Scythians (4.5, 4.70, 7.64) or Massagetes (1.215).

29. D. S. Raevskiy, "Skifsky mifologičesky sužet," *Sovietskaja Archeologija* 3 (1970): 90; Raevskiy, *Očerki ideologii skifo-sakskich plemen* (Moscow: Nauka, 1977), 30–36; Raevskiy, *Scythian Mythology* (Sofia: Secor, 1993), 48–54. Raevskiy's interpretation has been widely accepted. See, inter alia, Véronique Schiltz, *Die Skythen und andere Steppenvölker: 8. Jahrhundert v. Chr. bis 1. Jahrhundert nach Chr.* (Munich: C.H. Beck, 1994), 170–78; and Ivantchik, "La légende 'grecque' sur l'origine des scythes," 208–9.

## CHAPTER EIGHT

1. Noteworthy among earlier studies of this text are Wilhelm Backhaus, "Der Hellenen-Barbaren-Gegensatz und die hippokratische Schrift περὶ ἀέρων ὑδάτων

τόπων," *Historia* 25 (1976): 170–85; Claude Calame, "Environnement et nature humaine: Le racisme bien tempéré d'Hippocrate," in *Sciences et racisme* (Lausanne: Payot, 1986), 75–99; Charlotte Triebel-Schubert, "Anthropologie und Norm: Der Skythenabschnitt in der hippokratischen Schrift *Über die Umwelt*," *Medizin-historisches Journal* 25 (1990): 90–103; Juan Antonio López Férez, "Los escritos hipocráticos y el nacimiento de la identidad europea," in H. A. Khan, ed., *The Birth of the European Identity: The Europe-Asia Contrast in Greek Thought* (Nottingham: University of Nottingham, 1994), 90–130; and Stephanie West, "Hippocrates' Scythian Sketches," *Eirene* 35 (1999): 14–32.

2. On this aspect of the text, see Hans Diller, *Wanderarzt und Aitiologe: Studien zur hippokratischen Schrift Περὶ ἀέρων ὑδάτων τόπων*, Philologus Supplement 26.3 (Leipzig: Dieterich'sche verlagsbuchhandlung, 1934).

3. *On Airs, Waters, and Places* 12: Βούλομαι δὲ περὶ τῆς Ἀσίης καὶ τῆς Εὐρώπης δεῖξαι ὁκόσον διαφέρουσιν ἀλλήλων ἐς τὰ πάντα καὶ περὶ τῶν ἐθνέων τῆς μορφῆς, ὅτι διαλλάσσει καὶ μηδὲν ἔοικεν ἀλλήλοισιν.

4. Ibid.: εἰκός τε τὴν χώρην ταύτην τοῦ ἦρος ἐγγύτατα εἶναι κατὰ τὴν φύσιν καὶ τὴν μετριότητα τῶν ὡρέων. τὸ δὲ ἀνδρεῖον καὶ τὸ ταλαίπωρον καὶ τὸ ἔμπονον καὶ τὸ θυμοειδὲς οὐκ ἂν δύναιτο ἐν τοιαύτῃ φύσει ἐγγινεσθαι οὔτε ὁμοφύλου οὔτε ἀλλοφύλου, ἀλλὰ τὴν ἡδονὴν ἀνάγκη κρατεῖν.

More sweeping conclusions of a similar sort, appear in the summary discussion of chapter 24, where the associations with Asia and Europe have previously been so well established that they can here remain implicit.

You will usually find the bodies and temperaments of people adapting to the nature of their land. In places where the earth is rich, soft, and well-watered, where the waters are mostly shallow so they are warm in summer and cold in winter, and where the seasons remain favorable, there the people are fleshy, without well-articulated joints, moist, averse to hard work, and their souls are bad for the most part. One can see laziness and sleepiness in them; as for their arts, they are crude, neither fine, nor keen. And in places where the land is bare, unwatered, and jagged, that are oppressed in winter and scorched by the sun (in summer), there you see people who are hard, dry, and lean, with well-articulated joints, sinewy and hairy. You will find them industrious, quiet, and wakeful in nature. Their temperament and disposition are self-willed and independent, partaking of things wild, rather than tame. With regard to the arts, they are very keen and highly intelligent, and superior to battles.

εὑρήσεις γὰρ ἐπὶ τὸ πλῆθος τῆς χωρῆς τῇ φύσει ἀκολουθέοντα καὶ τὰ εἴδεα τῶν ἀνθρώπων καὶ τοὺς τρόπους. ὅκου μὲν γὰρ ἡ γῆ πίειρα καὶ μαλθακὴ καὶ ἔνυδρος, καὶ τὰ ὕδατα κάρτα μετέωρα, ὥστε θερμὰ εἶναι τοῦ θέρεος καὶ τοῦ χειμῶνος ψυχρά, καὶ τῶν ὡρέων καλῶς κεῖται, ἐνταῦθα καὶ οἱ ἄνθρωποι σαρκώδεές εἰσι καὶ ἄναρθροι καὶ ὑγροὶ καὶ ἀταλαίπωροι καὶ τὴν ψυχὴν κακοὶ ὡς ἐπὶ τὸ πολύ. τό τε ῥάθυμον καὶ τὸ ὑπηρὸν ἔνεστιν ἐν αὐτοῖς ἰδεῖν· ἔς τε τὰς τέχνας παχέες καὶ οὐ λεπτοὶ οὐδ' ὀξέες. ὅκου δ' ἐστὶν ἡ χώρη ψιλή τε καὶ ἄνυδρος καὶ τρηχεῖα καὶ ὑπὸ τοῦ χειμῶνος πιεζομένη καὶ ὑπὸ τοῦ ἡλίου κεκαυμένη, ἐνταῦθα δὲ σκληρούς τε καὶ ἰσχνοὺς καὶ διηρθρωμένους καὶ ἐντόνους καὶ δασέας ἴδοις. τό τε ἐργατικὸν ἐνεὸν ἐν τῇ φύσει τῇ τοιαύτῃ καὶ τὸ ἄγρυπνον, τά τε ἤθεα καὶ τὰς ὀργὰς αὐθάδεας καὶ ἰδιογνώμονας, τοῦ τε ἀγρίου μᾶλλον μετέχοντας ἢ τοῦ ἡμέρου, ἔς τε τὰς τέχνας ὀξυτέρους τε καὶ συνετωτέρους καὶ τὰ πολέμια ἀμείνους εὑρήσεις.

5. Ibid. 16: περὶ δὲ τῆς ἀθυμίης τῶν ἀνθρώπων καὶ τῆς ἀνανδρείης, ὅτι ἀπολεμώτεροί εἰσι τῶν Εὐρωπαίων οἱ Ἀσιηνοὶ καὶ ἡμηρώτεροί τὰ ἤθεα αἱ ὧραι αἴτιαι μάλιστα, οὐ μεγάλας τὰς μεταβολὰς ποιεύμεναι οὔτε ἐπὶ τὸ θερμὸν οὔτε ἐπὶ τὸ ψυχρόν, ἀλλὰ παραπλησίως. οὐ γὰρ γίνονται ἐκπλήξιες τῆς γνώμης οὔτε μετάστασις ἰσχυρὴ τοῦ σώματος, ἀφ' ὅτων εἰκὸς τὴν ὀργὴν ἀγριοῦσθαί τε καὶ τοῦ ἀγνώμονος καὶ θυμοειδέος μετέχειν μᾶλλον ἢ ἐν τῷ αὐτῷ αἰεὶ ἐόντα. αἱ γὰρ μεταβολαί εἰσι τῶν πάντων αἱ ἐπεγείρουσαι τὴν γνώμην τῶν ἀνθρώπων καὶ οὐκ ἐῶσαι ἀτρεμίζειν. διὰ ταύτας ἐμοὶ δοκεῖ τὰς προφάσιας ἄνακες εἶναι τὸ γένος τὸ Ἀσιηνὸν καὶ προσέτι διὰ τοὺς νόμους. τῆς γὰρ Ἀσίης τὰ πολλὰ βασιλεύεται. ὅκου δὲ μὴ αὐτοὶ ἑωυτῶν εἰσι καρτεροὶ οἱ ἄνθωποι μηδὲ αὐτόνομοι, ἀλλὰ δεσπόζονται, οὐ περὶ τούτου αὐτοῖσιν ὁ λόγος ἐστίν, ὅκως τὰ πολέμια ἀσκήσωσιν, ἀλλ' ὅκως μὴ δόξωσι μάχιμοι εἶναι. Cf. ibid. 23.

6. The text consistently defines Asian men in terms of the qualities they lack: masculinity (andreion . . . ouk dynaito . . . enginesthai, ch. 12; anandreiēs, ch. 16; anandreiēn and anandrōthēnai, ch. 22), hardness (talaipōron . . . ouk dynaito . . . enginesthai, ch. 12; atalaipōroi, ch. 24), industriousness (emponon . . . ouk dynaito . . . enginesthai, ch. 12), adventurousness of spirit (thymoeides ouk dynaito . . . enginesthai, ch. 12; athymiēs, ch. 16), bellicosity (apolemōteroi and mē doxōsi makhimoi einai, ch. 16), strength (analkes, ch. 16; asthenees, ch. 21).

7. It is not clear whether the text considers Africa as part of Asia or as a separate continent. Herodotus 4.42 treats the system of three continents as widely but not universally accepted and subject to disputation.

8. Some have suspected that the two sections of the text were originally independent, but the arguments for its unity are persuasive, as developed by Max Pohlenz, "Hippokratesstudien," Nachrichten der Gesellschaft der Wissenschaften zu Göttingen 1/2 (1937): 67–101, esp. 68; and Hermann Grensemann, "Das 24. Kapitel von De aeribus, aquis, locis und die Einheit der Schrift," Hermes 107 (1979): 423–41.

9. On Airs, Waters, and Places 19.

10. Ibid. 20. Treatment involves cauterization of fleshy parts of the body to remove the cold/moist qualities responsible for its flabbiness, weakness, and torpor. As Stephanie West recognized, "Hippocrates' Scythian Sketches," 19–20, by insisting that cauterization gave Scythian warriors the strength they needed, but would otherwise lack, the text was able to account for the well-known prowess of Scythian archers and cavalry, without sacrificing its contention that Scythians are all weak by nature.

11. On Airs, Waters, and Places 19, 21, 22.

12. Ibid. 19. Scythian women are also subject to reproductive disorders due to "the fatness and moistness of their flesh" (21: ἥ τε πιότης τῆς σαρκὸς καὶ ὑγρότης).

13. Ibid. 21: Πολύγονον δὲ οὐχ οἷόν τε εἶναι φύσιν τοιαύτην. οὔτε γὰρ τῷ ἀνδρὶ ἡ ἐπιθυμίη τῆς μείξιος γίνεται πολλὴ διὰ τὴν ὑγρότητα τῆς φύσιος καὶ τῆς κοιλίης τὴν μαλθακότητά τε καὶ τὸν ψυχρότητα, ἀφ' ὅτων ἥκιστα εἰκὸς ἄνδρα οἷόν τε λαγνεύειν.

14. Ibid. 21: "Constantly being jounced by their horses, they come to lack the strength for sex." καὶ ἔτι ὑπὸ τῶν ἵππων αἰεὶ κοπτόμενοι ἀσθενέες γίνονται ἐς τὴν μεῖξειν. The argument is expanded at chapter 22.

These things are common among the Scythians, and they are the most eunuch-like of people for these reasons: the trousers they always wear, the fact that they are on horses most of the time so that they do not masturbate, and because of the cold and of weariness, they forget about desire and sex and before they can get aroused, they are unmanned.

ταῦτα δὲ τοῖσι Σκύθῃσι πρόσεστι, καὶ εὐνουχοειδέστατοί εἰσιν ἀνθρώπων διὰ ταύτας τε τὰς προφάσιας καὶ ὅτι ἀναξυρίδας ἔχουσιν αἰεὶ καί εἰσιν ἐπὶ τῶν ἵππων τὸ πλεῖστον τοῦ χρόνου, ὥστε μήτε χειρὶ ἅπτεσθαι τοῦ αἰδοίου, ὑπό τε τοῦ ψύχεος καὶ τοῦ κόπου ἐπιλήθεσθαι τοῦ ἱμέρου καὶ τῆς μείξιος, καὶ μηδὲν παρακινεῖν πρότερον ἢ ἀνανδρωθῆναι.

The association with the upper class, based on mistaken analogy to the Greek equestrian nobility, figures earlier in this same chapter.

The rich Scythians suffer this, not those who are lowest, but the best-born and those who have acquired most strength. It comes through their horse-riding, and ordinary laborers have it less, because they do not ride.

Τοῦτο δὲ πάσχουσι Σκυθέων οἱ πλούσιοι, οὐχ οἱ κάκιστοι ἀλλ' οἱ εὐγενέστατοι καὶ ἰσχὺν πλείστην κεκτημένοι, διὰ τὴν ἱππασίην, οἱ δὲ πένητες ἧσσον· οὐ γὰρ ἱππάζονται.

15. In chapter 17, the text treats another example of how the consistently cold-moist climate of northern Europe produces aberrations in what Greeks take to be the norms of sex and gender: the warlike women of the Sauromatae. As Triebel-Schubert, "Anthropologie und Norm," recognized, these viragos provided a structural counter-part to the Scythian Anarieis to be discussed shortly.

16. Edmond Lévy, "Les origines du mirage scythe," *Ktema* 6 (1981): 57–68.

17. *Iliad* 13.3–7.

18. Fragment 150.14–16 (Merkelbach-West).

19. Fragment 1.59 (Page) = 3.59 (Calame), on which see Askold I. Ivantchik, "Un fragment de l'épopée scythe: 'Le cheval de Colaxaïs' dans un partheneion d'Alcman," *Ktema* 27 (2002): 257–64.

20. For what is known of Hecataeus's treatment of the Scythians and their neighbors, see Marian Plezia, "Hekataios über die Völker am Nordrand des skythischen Schwarzmeergebietes," *Eos* 50 (1959–60): 27–42.

21. Herodotus 4.13–16. See further E. D. Phillips, "The Legend of Aristeas: Fact and Fancy in Early Greek Notions of East Russia, Siberia, and Innder Asia," *Artibus Asiae* 18 (1955): 161–77; C. M. Bowra, "A Fragment of the Arimaspea," *Classical Quarterly* 6 (1956): 1–10; J. D. P. Bolton, *Aristeas of Proconnesus* (Oxford: Clarendon Press, 1962); Luciano Canfora, *Viaggio di Aristea* (Rome: Laterza, 1996); and Eman-

uele Dettori, "Aristea di Proconneso 'sciamano' e 'corvo': Una presentazione (con qualche nota)," *Quaderni di Classiconorroena* 1 (2005): 9–24.

22. Arthur O. Lovejoy and George Boas, *Primitivism and Related Ideas in Antiquity* (Baltimore: Johns Hopkins University Press, 1935), 287–367.

23. Herodotus describes Scythian head-hunting at 4.64–65, blood-drinking at 4.64 and 70, and human sacrifices at 4.62 and 71.

24. This term occurs only three times in the entire Herodotean text, twice as conditions contrary to fact. Thus, it is used for the mistaken impression that the fortress of Sardis was impregnable (1.84) and for the power the Thracians potentially had by virtue of their numbers, but failed to realize, given their disunity (5.3). Only the Scythians are described as actually being unconquerable, and Herodotus pronounces their realization of this state to be the greatest and wisest of human accomplishments (4.46).

One thing—the greatest of all human matters—was determined by the Scythian race in the wisest way of those we know, although we do not admire them in other matters. The greatest thing discovered by them is this: no one who attacks them can flee, and when they do not wish to be discovered, one cannot lay hold of them. For they have neither towns nor walls that have been built, but are all people who carry their houses with them, mounted archers who live not by agriculture, but by their herds, and whose habitations are pulled by yoked animals. How can such people not be unconquerable and impossible to join in battle?

τῷ δὲ Σκυθικῷ γένεϊ ἓν μὲν τὸ μέγιστον τῶν ἀνθρωπηίων πρηγμάτων σοφώτατα πάντων ἐξεύρηται, τῶν ἡμεῖς ἴδμεν, τὰ μέντοι ἄλλα οὐκ ἄγαμαι. τὸ δὲ μέγιστον οὕτω σφι ἀνεύρηται ὥστε ἀποφυγεῖν τε μηδένα ἐπελθόντα ἐπὶ σφέας, μὴ βουλομένους τε ἐξευρεθῆναι καταλαβεῖν μὴ οἷόν τε εἶναι· τοῖσι γὰρ μήτε ἄστεα μήτε τείχεα ᾖ ἐκτισμένα, ἀλλὰ φερέοικοι ἐόντες πάντες ἔωσι ἱπποξόται, ζῶντες μὴ ἀπ' ἀρότου ἀλλὰ ἀπὸ κτηνέων, οἰκήματά τέ σφι ᾖ ἐπὶ ζευγέων, κῶς οὐκ ἂν εἴησαν οὗτοι ἄμαχοί τε καὶ ἄποροι προσμίσγειν.

25. See further Jacques Jouanna, "Les causes de la défaite des barbares chez Eschyle, Hérodote, et Hippocrate," *Ktema* 6 (1981): 3–15.

26. The ailment denoted by this term is quite uncertain. Attempts at interpretation, from antiquity on, include arthritis, rheumatism, sciatica, hemorrhoids, varicose veins, inflammation of the genitals, aneurisms, etc. For a summary, see Donat Magreth, *Skythische Schamanen? Die Nachrichten über Enarees-Anarieis bei Herodot und Hippokrates* (Schaffhausen: Meier & Cie., 1993), 62–65.

27. On *Airs, Waters, and Places* 22: Ἔτι τε πρὸς τούτοισιν εὐνουχίαι γίνονται οἱ πλεῖστοι ἐν Σκύθῃσι καὶ γυναικεῖα ἐργάζονται καὶ ὡς αἱ γυναῖκες διαιτεῦνται διαλέγονταί τε ὁμοίως· καλεῦνταί τε οἱ τοιοῦτοι Ἀναριεῖς. οἱ μὲν οὖν ἐπιχώριοι τὴν αἰτίην προστιθέασι θεῷ καὶ σέβονται τούτους τοὺς ἀνθρώπους καὶ προσκυνέουσι, δεδοικότες περὶ ἑωυτῶν ἕκαστοι. ἐμοὶ δὲ καὶ αὐτῷ δοκεῖ ταῦτα τὰ πάθεα θεῖα εἶναι καὶ τἄλλα πάντα καὶ οὐδὲν ἕτερον ἑτέρου θειότερον οὐδὲ ἀνθρωπινώτερον, ἀλλὰ πάντα ὁμοῖα καὶ πάντα θεῖα. ἕκαστον δὲ αὐτῶν ἔχει φύσιν τὴν ἑωυτοῦ καὶ οὐδὲν ἄνευ φύσιος γίνεται. καὶ τοῦτο τὸ

πάθος ὥς μοι δοκεῖ γίνεσθαι φράσω· ὑπὸ τῆς ἱππασίης αὐτοὺς κέδματα λαμβάνει, ἅτε αἰεὶ κρεμαμένων ἀπὸ τῶν ἵππων τοῖς ποσίν· ἔπειτα ἀποχωλοῦνται καὶ ἑλκοῦνται τὰ ἰσχία, οἳ ἂν σφόδρα νοσήσωσιν. ἰῶνται δὲ σφᾶς αὐτοὺς τρόπῳ τοιῷδε. ὁκόταν γὰρ ἄρχηται ἡ νοῦσος, ὄπισθεν τοῦ ὠτὸς ἑκατέρου φλέβα τάμνουσιν. ὁκόταν δὲ ἀπορρυῇ τὸ αἷμα, ὕπνος ὑπολαμβάνει ὑπὸ ἀσθενείης καὶ καθεύδουσιν. ἔπειτα ἀνεγείρονται, οἱ μέν τινες ὑγιέες ἐόντες, οἱ δ' οὔ. ἐμοὶ μὲν οὖν δοκεῖ ἐν ταύτῃ τῇ ἰήσει διαφθείρεσθαι ὁ γόνος· εἰσὶ γὰρ παρὰ τὰ ὦτα φλέβες, ἃς ἐάν τις ἐπιτάμῃ, ἄγονοι γίνονται οἱ ἐπιτμηθέντες. ταύτας τοίνυν μοι δοκέουσι τὰς φλέβας ἐπιτάμνειν. οἱ δὲ μετὰ ταῦτα ἐπειδὰν ἀφίκωνται παρὰ γυναῖκας καὶ μὴ οἷοί τ' ἔωσι χρῆσθαί σφισιν, τὸ πρῶτον οὐκ ἐνθυμεῦνται, ἀλλ' ἡσυχίην ἔχουσι. ὁκόταν δὲ δὶς καὶ τρὶς καὶ πλεονάκις αὐτοῖσι πειρωμένοισι μηδὲν ἀλλοιότερον ἀποβαίνῃ, νομίσαντές τι ἡμαρτηκέναι τῷ θεῷ, ὃν ἐπαιτιῶνται, ἐνδύονται στολὴν γυναικείην καταγνόντες ἑωυτῶν ἀνανδρείην. γυναικίζουσί τε καὶ ἐργάζονται μετὰ τῶν γυναικῶν ἅ καὶ ἐκεῖναι. Τοῦτο δὲ πάσχουσι Σκυθέων οἱ πλούσιοι, οὐχ οἱ κάκιστοι ἀλλ' οἱ εὐγενέστατοι καὶ ἰσχὺν πλείστην κεκτημένοι, διὰ τὴν ἱππασίην, οἱ δὲ πένητες ἧσσον· οὐ γὰρ ἱππάζονται. . . . καὶ ἡ τοιαύτη νοῦσος ἀπὸ τοιαύτης προφάσιος τοῖς Σκύθῃσι γίνεται οἵην εἴρηκα. ἔχει δὲ καὶ κατὰ τοὺς λοιποὺς ἀνθρώπους ὁμοίους, ὅκου γὰρ ἱππάζονται μάλιστα καὶ πυκνότατα, ἐκεῖ πλεῖστοι ὑπὸ κεδμάτων καὶ ἰσχιάδων καὶ ποδαγριῶν ἁλίσκονται καὶ λαγνεύειν κάκιστοί εἰσι.

28. The argument of this treatise is thus consonant with that of *On the Sacred Disease*, sufficiently so that some have suggested common authorship of the two texts. See further Philippe van der Eijk, "'Airs, Waters, Places' and 'On the Sacred Disease': Two Different Religiosities?," *Hermes* 119 (1991): 168–76.

29. *On Airs, Waters, and Places* 16: περὶ δὲ τῆς ἀθυμίης τῶν ἀνθρώπων καὶ τῆς ἀνανδρείης, ὅτι ἀπολεμώτεροί εἰσι τῶν Εὐρωπαίων οἱ Ἀσιηνοὶ καὶ ἡμηρώτεροι.

30. Ibid. 22: ὅκου γὰρ ἱππάζονται μάλιστα καὶ πυκνότατα, ἐκεῖ πλεῖστοι ὑπὸ κεδμάτων καὶ ἰσχιάδων καὶ ποδαγριῶν ἁλίσκονται καὶ λαγνεύειν κάκιστοί εἰσι.

31. Most relevant is the testimony of the Hippocratic treatise *On Generation* 2.2: "Those who have had surgery on their ears can have intercourse and emit seed, but only a small amount, weak, and incapable of producing offspring. For most of it passes from the head by the ears to the spinal marrow, and the scarred incision obstructs that passage underneath." ὁκόσοι δὲ ἄρ' οὓς τετμημένοι εἰσίν, οὗτοι λαγνεύουσι μὲν καὶ ἀφιᾶσιν, ὀλίγον δὲ καὶ ἀσθενὲς καὶ ἄγονον· χωρεῖ γὰρ τὸ πλεῖστον ἀπὸ τῆς κεφαλῆς παρὰ τὰ οὔατα ἐς τὸν νωτιαῖον μυελόν· αὕτη δὲ ἡ δίοδος ὑπὸ τῆς τομῆς οὐλῆς γενομένης στερεὴ γέγονεν. See further G. E. R. Lloyd, *Magic, Reason, and Experience* (Cambridge: Cambridge University Press, 1979), 15–28; Charles Chiasson, "Scythian Androgyny and Environmental Determinism in Herodotus and the Hippocratic περὶ ἀέρων ὑδάτων τόπων," *Syllecta Classica* 12 (2001): 33–73, at 52, and the literature cited in the latter at note 44.

32. *On Airs, Waters, and Places* 22: ἐνδύονται στολὴν γυναικείην καταγνόντες ἑωυτῶν ἀνανδρείην. γυναικίζουσί τε καὶ ἐργάζονται μετὰ τῶν γυναικῶν ἃ καὶ ἐκεῖναι.

33. Ibid.: Ἔτι τε πρὸς τούτοισιν εὐνουχίαι γίνονται οἱ πλεῖστοι ἐν Σκύθῃσι καὶ γυναικεῖα ἐργάζονται καὶ ὡς αἱ γυναῖκες διαιτεῦνται διαλέγονταί τε ὁμοίως· καλεῦνταί τε οἱ τοιοῦτοι Ἀναριεῖς.

34. Ibid.: Ἔτι τε πρὸς τούτοισιν εὐνουχίαι γίνονται οἱ πλεῖστοι ἐν Σκύθῃσι καὶ γυναικεῖα ἐργάζονται.

35. Ibid.: εὐνουχοειδέστατοί εἰσιν ἀνθρώπων. On the sleight of hand through which the Hippocratic author treats the Anarieis as restricted to the nobility, but simultaneously representative of all Scythian men, see Alain Ballabriga, "Les eunuques scythes et leurs femmes: Stérilité des femmes et impuissance des hommes en Scythie selon le traité hippocratique *des airs*," *Métis* 1 (1986): 121–38, esp. 134–36.

36. Thus already Felix Jacoby, "Hekataios," in *Paulys Realencyclopädie der classischen Altertumswissenschaft*, ed. Georg Wissowa (Munich: Alfred Druckenmüller, 1894–1972), 7: 2680, 2708, and 2717. More recently, see Magreth, *Skythische Schamanen?* 83–88, with summary of earlier discussions. The most detailed and perceptive comparisons of Herodotus and Hippocrates on the Scythians are Magreth; Chiasson, "Scythian Androgyny and Environmental Determinism"; and West, "Hippocrates' Scythian Sketches."

37. Herodotus 1.103–6. On the historicity of this account, see Askold Ivantchik, "The Scythian 'Rule over Asia': The Classical Tradition and the Historical Reality," in Gocha R. Tsetskhladze, ed., *Ancient Greeks West and East* (Leiden: Brill, 1999), 497–520; and Robert Rollinger, "Herodotus and the Intellectual Heritage of the Ancient Near East," in Sanna Aro and R. M. Whiting, eds., *The Heirs of Assyria* (Helsinki: Neo-Assyrian Text Corpus Project, 2000), 65–77, esp. 70–77 ("Ascalon and the Scythian invasion in Asia").

38. Herodotus 1.105: οἱ δέ ἐπείτε ἀναχωρέοντες ὀπίσω ἐγένοντο τῆς Συρίης ἐν Ἀσκάλωνι πόλι, τῶν πλεόνων Σκυθέων παρεξελθόντων ἀσινέων, ὀλίγοι τινὲς αὐτῶν ὑπολειφθέντες ἐσύλησαν τῆς οὐρανίης Ἀφροδίτης τὸ ἰρόν. τοῖσι δὲ τῶν Σκυθέων συλήσασι τὸ ἰρὸν τὸ ἐν Ἀσκάλωνι καὶ τοῖσι τούτων αἰεὶ ἐκγόνοισι ἐνέσκηψε ὁ θεὸς θήλεαν νοῦσον· ὥστε ἅμα λέγουσι τε οἱ Σκύθαι διὰ τοῦτο σφέας νοσέειν, καὶ ὁρᾶν παρ' ἑωυτοῖσι τοὺς ἀπικνεομένους ἐς τὴν Σκυθικὴν χώρην ὡς διακέαται τοὺς καλέουσι Ἐνάρεας οἱ Σκύθαι.

39. Thus, *On Airs, Waters, and Places* 22: "The people of this country attribute the cause to a deity" (οἱ μὲν οὖν ἐπιχώριοι τὴν αἰτίην προστιθέασι θεῷ) and "They blame a deity, whom they believe they have wronged" (νομίσαντές τι ἡμαρτηκέναι τῷ θεῷ, ὃν ἐπαιτιῶνται).

40. Herodotus 4.67: οἱ δὲ Ἐνάριες οἱ ἀνδρόγυνοι τὴν Ἀφροδίτην σφί λέγουσι μαντικὴν δοῦναι· φιλύρης ὦν φλοιῷ μαντεύονται· ἐπεὰν τὴν φιλύρην τρίχα σχίσῃ, διαπλέκων ἐν τοῖσι δακτύλοισι τοῖσι ἑωυτοῦ καὶ διαλύων χρᾷ.

41. Lucian, *The Syrian Goddess* 15, 27, 51. On the castrated priests of this goddess, see M. J. Vermaseren, *Cybele and Attis: The Myth and the Cult* (London: Thames & Hudson, 1977); Britt-Mari Näsström, *The Abhorrence of Love: Studies in Rituals and Mystic Aspects in Catullus' Poem of Attis* (Stockholm: Almqvist & Wiksell, 1989); J. Peter Södergård, "The Ritualized Bodies of Cybele's Galli and the Methodological Problem of the Plurality of Explanations," in Tore Ahlbäck, ed., *The Problem of Ritual* (Stockholm: Almqvist & Wiksell, 1993), 169–93; and Will Roscoe, "Priests of the Goddess: Gender Transgression in Ancient Religion," *History of Religions* 45 (1996): 195–230.

42. "Uranian Aphrodite" is a title Herodotus uses for prominent "fertility goddesses" of various nations, including the Assyrian Mylitta, Arabian Alilat, and the Persian Mitra (1.131, 3.8). At 4.59, he includes this goddess in the Scythian pantheon, within which context she bears the name Argimpasa or Artimpasa (manuscripts vary).

43. Within the enormous recent literature on the nature of the Herodotean project, particularly noteworthy are James Redfield, "Herodotus the Tourist," *Classical Philology* 80 (1985): 97–118; Catherine Darbo-Peschanski, "Les 'Logoi' des autres dans les 'Histoires' d'Hérodote," *Quaderni di Storia* 22 (1985): 105–28; Paul Cartledge, "Herodotus and 'the Other': A Meditation on Empire," *Échos du Monde Classique* 34 (1990): 27–40; Vivienne Gray, "Herodotus and the Rhetoric of Otherness," *American Journal of Philology* 116 (1995): 185–212; Rosalind Thomas, *Herodotus in Context: Ethnography, Science, and the Art of Persuasion* (Cambridge: Cambridge University Press, 2000); Marco Dorati, *Le Storie di Erodoto: Etnografia e racconto* (Pisa: Istituti editoriali e poligrafici internazionali, 2000); Reinhold Bichler, *Herodots Welt: Der Aufbau der Historie am Bild der fremden Länder und Völker, ihrer Zivilisation und ihrer Geschichte* (Berlin: Akademie Verlag, 2000); Rosaria Vignolo Munson, *Telling Wonders: Ethnographic and Political Discourse in the Work of Herodotus* (Ann Arbor: University of Michigan Press, 2001); and Christopher Pelling, "East Is East and West Is West—or Are They? National Stereotypes in Herodotus," *Histos* 1 (1997): 51–66. François Hartog, *Le miroir d'Hérodote: Essai sur la représentation de l'autre* (Paris: Gallimard, 1980) holds particular interest for its analysis of book 4 and the *Skythikos logos* as a key example of proto-orientalist discourse. For reasons I have explained in chapters 6 and 7 and elsewhere, I consider Hartog's book an extremely useful intervention, but a partial truth that ignores important evidence, simplifying a much more complex reality and exaggerating the extent of Herodotus's ignorance, invention, and ethnocentrism. Relevant to this argument are Bruce Lincoln, *Death, War, and Sacrifice: Studies in Ideology and Practice* (Chicago: University of Chicago Press, 1991), 188–97; Lincoln, *"Happiness for Mankind": Achaemenian Religion and the Imperial Project* (Louvain: Peeters, 2012), 271–88.

44. See above, pp. 98–99.

45. Herodotus 1.105: ὀλίγοι τινὲς αὐτῶν ὑπολειφθέντες ἐσύλησαν τῆς οὐρανίης Ἀφροδίτης τὸ ἱρόν.

46. Karl Meuli, "Scythica," in his *Gesammelte Schriften* (Basel: Schwabbe, 1975), 2: 826.

47. Already in Philipp Gabriel Hensler, *Geschichte der Lustseuche; die zu Ende des XV Jahrhundert in Europa ausbrach* (Altona: Gebrüder Herold, 1783); still asserted, inter alia, by K. Kretschmer, "Scythae," in *Paulys Realencyclopädie der classischen Altertumswissenschaft*, vol. IIA.1, p. 938.

48. Elinor Lieber, "The Hippocratic 'Airs, Waters, Places' on Cross-Dressing Eunuchs: 'Natural' yet also 'Divine'," in Renate Wittern and Pierre Pellegrin, eds., *Hippokratische Medizin und antike Philosophie* (Hildesheim: Olms Weidmann, 1996), 451–76.

49. An early attempt was that of Jan Potocki, *Histoire primitive des peuple de la Russie: avec une exposition complète de toutes les notions, nécessaires à l'intelligence du 4me livre d'Hérodote* (St. Petersburg: Imprimerie de l'Académie impériale des sciences, 1802), 174–75, who thought he recognized the Enareis among certain men of Turkey and the Caucasus whom disease had rendered bald and beardless, after which they adopted a female mode of life.

50. Adolphe Reinach, "L'origine des Amazones: À propos d'une explication nouvelle de la légende amazonienne," *Revue de l'Histoire des Religions* 67 (1913): 277–307; Triebel-Schubert, "Anthropologie und Norm."

51. Michael Ivanovitch Rostovtzeff, *Iranians and Greeks in South Russia* (Oxford: Clarendon Press, 1922), 104–5.

52. Joseph Vendryes, "La couvade chez les Scythes," *Comptes Rendus de l'Académie des Inscriptions et Belles Lettres* (1934), 329–39. Note also Georges Dumézil, "Les 'énarées' scythiques et la grossesse de Narte Hamyc," *Latomus* 5 (1946): 249–55; Dumézil, *Romans de Scythie et d'alentour* (Paris: Payot, 1978), 212–18, who compared the Scythian ailment to an Ossetic folktale describing how a goddess deserted her human husband when the latter offended her, saddling him with her pregnancy in the process.

53. William A. Hammond, "The Disease of the Scythians (*morbus feminarum*) and Certain Analogous Conditions," *American Journal of Neurology and Psychiatry* I/3 (1882): 339–55. More recently, Franz Hampl, "Herodot: Ein kritischer Forschungs-bericht nach methodischen Gesichtspunkten," *Grazer Beiträge* 4 (1975): 97–136.

54. William Reginald Halliday, "A Note on the θήλεα νοῦσον of the Scythians," *Annual of the British School at Athens* 17 (1910–11): 95–102.

55. Karl Meuli, "Scythica," reprinted in his *Gesammelte Schriften*, 2: 817–79, esp. 824–34. This article was originally published in *Hermes* 70 (1935): 121–76.

56. Meuli, "Scythica," 2: 826–27:

Es gibt bei den Tschuktschen, wiewohl selten, weibliche Schamanen, die sich als Männer fühlen und benehmen, weit häufiger jedoch männliche, die sich als Frauen fühlen. Die «Verwandlung» setzt gewöhnlich auf das Geheiss eines Geistes in der Zeit beginnender Geschlechtsreife ein, wo auch die ersten Gesichte und Eingebungen dem werdenden Schamanen sich zuzudrängen pflegen. Sie kann sehr verschiedenen Grades sein, sich beispielsweise nur auf die Haartracht, oder, was sehr häufig ist, nur auf die Kleidung erstrecken. Einer der Bogoras bekannt gewordenen Tschuktschen-Schamanen war als junger Mensch durch die Verwandlung eine Krankheit losgeworden und übte dann den Schamanenberuf weiter aus, selbstverständlich in Weiberkleidung; das hinderte ihn aber nicht, zu heiraten und mit seiner Frau vier Kinder zu zeugen. Offenbar liegt hier eine zeitlich beschränkte Störung der normalen Geschlechtsempfindung vor, die von keinerlei körperlicher Veränderung bedingt oder gefolgt ist; die letztere fehlt, nach Bogoras, auch gänzlich beim vollständigsten Grad der «Verwandlung». In diesem gibt der Schamane nicht nur Tracht, Sprechweise und Beschäftigung der Männer gänzlich auf, um sie mit denen des weiblichen Geschlechts zu vertauschen; er empfindet auch vollständig weiblich und kann sogar in den üblichen Formen der Heirat eine dauernde Verbindung mit einem Manne eingehen und einen äusserlich vollkommen normalen Haushalt gründen.

57. Waldemar Bogoras, *The Chukchee*, Memoirs of the American Museum of Natural History 11 (New York: G. E. Stechert, 1907), 449–55.

58. This was already suggested by Ken Dowden, "Deux notes sur les Scythes et les Arimaspes," *Revue des Études Grecques* 92 (1980): 486–92, an article that has received too little attention.

59. Bogoras's chapter "Shamanism" occupies pp. 413–68 of *The Chukchee*. His section on the "soft men," which bears the title "Sexual Perversion and Transformed

Shamans," is found at 448–57. That "soft men" are relatively rare is stated at 450 ("The instances of such practices are by no means frequent").

60. Bogoras, "Shamanism," in *The Chukchee*, 413–68. The classic definition of shamanism by S. M. Shirokogoroff, *Psychomental Complex of the Tungus* (London: Kegan, Paul, Trench, and Trübner, 1935), 269 is also worth citing for the emphasis it places on the acquired capacity to manage relations with spirits: "Persons of both sexes who have mastered spirits, who at their will can introduce these spirits into themselves and use their powers over spirits in their own interests, particularly helping other people, who suffer from the spirits; in such a capacity they may possess a complex of special methods for dealing with the spirits."

61. Bogoras, *The Chukchee*, 414.

62. Ibid., 452.

63. This argument is developed in the last section of his article "Ursprünge der epischen Poesie," in *Gesammelte Schriften*, 2: 865–79.

64. Karl Meuli, *Odysee und Argonautika: Untersuchungen zur griechischen Sagengeschichte und zum Epos* (Berlin: Weidmann, 1921), reprinted in his *Gesammelte Schriften*, 2: 593–676.

65. Karl Meuli, *Kalewala: Altfinnische Volks- und Helderlieder* (Basel: B. Schwabe, 1940), reprinted in *Gesammelte Schriften*, 2: 677–98 as "Kalewala, das Nationalepos der Finnen." Meuli's interest in the *Kalewala* and its relation to shamanism figures prominently in the closing pages of his "Scythica" essay, in *Gesammelte Schriften*, 2: 876–79.

66. E. R. Dodds, *The Greeks and the Irrational* (Berkeley: University of California Press, 1951), esp. ch. 5, "The Greek Shamans and the Origins of Puritanism," 135–78. Dodds summarized his reworking of what he took from Meuli at 149–50:

> We have seen—or I hope we have seen—how contact with shamanistic beliefs and practices might suggest to a thoughtful people like the Greeks the rudiments of such a psychology [sc.: the "Puritan psychology" that characterizes Orphic and early Pythagorean beliefs about the soul]: how the notion of psychic excursion in sleep or trance might sharpen the soul-body antithesis; how the shamanistic "retreat" might provide the model for a deliberate *askēsis*, a conscious training of the psychic powers through abstinence and spiritual exercises; how tales of vanishing and reappearing shamans might encourage the belief in an indestructible magical or daemonic self; and how the migration of the magical power or spirit from dead shamans to living ones might be generalised as a doctrine of reincarnation.

For many years, Dodds's and Meuli's position was widely adopted, sometimes with great enthusiasm and sometimes with notes of caution, as, for instance, by Walter Burkert, *Lore and Science in Ancient Pythagoreanism*, trans. Edwin L. Minar Jr. (Cambridge, MA: Harvard University Press, 1972), 162–65; and "Γόης: Zum griechischen 'Schamanismus'," *Rheinisches Museum* 105 (1962): 36–55. Recently, these theories have been reconsidered in more critical fashion by Jan Bremmer, *The Rise and Fall of the Afterlife* (London: Routledge, 2002), 29–35; Leonid Zhmud, *Pythagoras and the Early Pythagoreans* (Oxford: Oxford University Press, 2012), 212–15; and Geoffrey

Lloyd, "Pythagoras," in Carl Huffman, ed., *A History of Pythagoreanism* (Cambridge: Cambridge University Press, 2014), 24–45.

67. Carlo Ginzburg, *Storia notturna: Una decifrazione del sabba* (Turin: Giulio Einaudi, 1989); English trans. by Raymond Rosenthal, *Ecstasies: Deciphering the Witches' Sabbath* (New York: Pantheon, 1991). On the role attributed to Scythian shamans, see *Ecstasies*, 207–25 and passim. Note in particular, 219n11, where Ginzburg acknowledges the full dependence of his views on Meuli's article.

68. A Google search for "transgender Scythian shamans" on July 16, 2014, yielded 61,500 results of widely varied nature and quality. Although it is often difficult to draw a distinction between semischolarly and nonscholarly websites, my survey of the first 100 hits shows that 22 percent of the total could be called scholarly or semischolarly. This includes the Wikipedia article, two articles published in reputable journals (*Arctic Anthropology* and *History of Religions*), two dissertations (both on transsexuality and gender liminality), notices for and excerpts from several academic books, and articles in media aiming to inform the general public (*Discover Magazine, The Free Library*). New age and neo-pagan websites accounted for 35 percent of the total, including such sites as The Northern Tradition, Freya Lady of the Labyrinth, Witch Plus, Blue Moon Wicca, Talk-Shamanism, Pagan Forum, Atlantis Online, and Very Important Potheads. LGBT sites accounted for another 30 percent, including Lucky Lady Butterfly, The Golden Prince(ss), LGBT Gamer Community, Copper Age Queer, Corina Dragonfly, Male4all, The Encyclopedia of Homosexuality, and Gender Variance Who's Who. An additional 11 percent were either irrelevant or impossible to classify, including Macedoniantruth (devoted to Bulgarian culture) and Whoosh (devoted to research on Xena, Warrior Princess).

69. The etymology was first established by Caspar Zeuss, *Die Deutschen und die Nachbarstämme* (Munich: Ignaz Joseph Lentner, 1837), 294. For the most recent discussions, see Manfred Mayrhofer, *Einiges zu den Skythen, ihrer Sprache, ihrem Nachleben* (Vienna: Verlag der Österreichischen Akademie der Wissenschaften, 2006), 12 and the literature cited therein. Conceivably, Herodotus may have understood the name to mean "unmanly" and termed them *androgynoi* as something of a gloss. On the extent to which he understood (and sometimes misunderstood) some Scythian lexemes, probably with the help of bilingual Greeks in the Black Sea outposts, see Rüdiger Schmitt, "Herodot und iranische Sprachen," in Robert Rollinger, Brigitte Truschnegg, and Reinhold Bichler, eds. *Herodot und das Persische Weltrich/Herodotus and the Persian Empire* (Wiesbaden: Harrassowitz, 2011), 313–41, esp. 316–23; and George Hinge, "Herodot zur skythischen Sprache: Arimaspen, Amazonen und die Entdeckung des Schwarzen Meeres," *Glotta* 81 (2005): 86–115.

70. Hermann Grassmann, *Wörterbuch zum Rig-Veda*, 4th ed. (Wiesbaden: Otto Harrassowitz, 1964), col. 748 gives the following definitions: "1) *Mann* mit dem Gegensatze *nâri* (Weib); 2) *Mann, Mensch* ohne diesen Gegensatz; 3) die beim Gottesdienste thätigen *Männer*, wie Sänger, Opferer, Opfergeber; in diesem Falle auch 4) häufig mit Adjektiven oder adjektivischen Substantiven verbunden, welche sie näher als Sänger u.s.w. bezeichnen; 5) *Kriegsmann, Held;* insbesondere von Göttern, und zwar meist in dem Sinne der *Helden;* 7) auch so dass Götter und Männer als ein Ganzes zusammengefasst werden, und zwar wieder als *Helden.*"

71. Christian Bartholomae, *Altiranisches Wörterbuch*, 2nd ed. (Berlin: Walter de Gruyter, 1961), cols. 1047–49, gives the general definition "I) Mann als der erwachsene (geschlechtsreife) männliche Mensch, within which it distinguishes three major senses: 1) im Gegensatz zu Weib und Kind; 2) praegn. 'wehrhafter Mann, Kriegsmann; kriegerischer Held'; 3) ohne Betonung des Geschlechts sva. Mensch; Person." For a more detailed study of the occurrences in Old Avestan, see Bruce Lincoln, *Death, War, and Sacrifice: Studies in Ideology and Practice* (Chicago: University of Chicago Press, 1991), 150–53.

72. Bartholomae, *Altiranisches Wörterbuch*, cols. 1049–51 lists indeterminate cases of the following sorts: "A) Gegenüber einem attributiven a) Subst., b) Adj. oder c) Pron. tritt nar- vielfach so zurück, dass wir es unübersetzt lassen können; es gilt das insbesondre vom Nominativ Singular nā, der dabei meist in der stellung der Enklitika—hinter dem ersten Hochton des Satz- oder Versteils—auftritt;" and "B) Ohne Attribut steht 'ein Mann' im Sinn von 'einer, Jemand'; insbesondre hat der Nominativ Singular nā in der Stellung der Enklitika häufig die Bedeutung unsres 'man'." Under each of these, more than a hundred instances are listed.

73. Darius, second inscription at Naqš-ī Rustam (DNb) §§9–10: yāumaịniš ami utā dastaịbiyā utā pādaịbiyā; asabāra uvasabāra ami; θanuvaniya uθanuvaniya ami utā pastiš utā asabāra; ṛštika ami uvṛštika utā pastiš utā asabāra. imā ūnarā, tayā Auramazdā upari mām nīyasaya, utādiš atāvayam bartanaị; vašnā Auramazdāhā, tayamaị kṛtam, imaịbiš ūnaraịbiš akunavam, tayā mām Auramazdā upari nīyasaya. Text from Rüdiger Schmitt, *Die altpersischen Inschriften der Achaimeniden* (Wiesbaden: Reichert Verlag, 2009), 109–10.

74. DNb §10: asabāra uvasabāra ami. The ū- prefix becomes uv- before a vowel.

75. DNb §11: utādiš atāvayam bartanaị. At §9, he uses the same verb to describe the nature of his bodily excellence, with specific reference to warfare: "Because my body is strong, as a maker-of-battles I am a good maker-of-battles." (tayamaị tanūš tāvayati, hamaranakara ami ušhamaranakara.)

76. On the rich oral traditions concerning these mythical beings of extraordinary strength, see Georges Dumézil, *Le livre des héros: Légendes sur les Nartes, traduit de l'ossete* (Paris: Gallimard, 1965).

77. Prince N. Trubetzkoy, "Remarques sur quelques mots iraniens empruntés par les langues du Caucase," *Mémoires de la Société de Linguistique de Paris* 22 (1922): 251–52.

78. H. W. Bailey, "Analecta Indoscythica," *Journal of the Royal Asiatic Society* (1953): 114 and the broader discussion of 106–14. Bailey's suggestion is slightly preferable on phonological grounds, and was adopted by Emile Benveniste, *Études sur la langue ossète* (Paris: C. Klincksieck, 1959), 37. For the fullest discussion, see V. I. Abaev, *Istoriko-etimologičeskij slovar' osetinskogo iazyka* (Leningrad: Akademij Nauk SSSR, 1958–89), 2: 158–60; and for broader Indo-European comparisons, Thomas V. Gamkrelidze and Vjačeslav V. Ivanov, *Indo-European and the Indo-Europeans* (Berlin: Mouton de Gruyter, 1995), 703.

79. Distinctions that are commonly made between priests and warriors among ancient Indic and Iranian peoples are summarized and rendered explicit in a text like *Dēnkart* 3.42.

The greatness and superiority of the priesthood over warriorhood and herdsmanship is evident from many reasons.

One reason is that warriorhood smites the lie that is spiritual by priestly means
and herdsmanship makes sacrifice to the gods by priestly means. Both of these
are very strongly within the priesthood. And the proper teaching that lets them
bring such deeds to fulfillment comes from the priesthood.

Another is that knowing whatever is obligatory to do comes from the priesthood, like recognizing the Creator, or the many meritorious deeds and sins, things
that are essential and fundamental in all action exist within their own limits [i.e.,
those established by priests].

Another is the priority of the priesthood in the reckoning of its greatness
through the [relative] placement of the emblems of priesthood, warriorhood,
and herdsmanship.

Another is taken from the human body, where the head is the sign of the
priesthood, the hand of warriorhood, the belly of herdsmanship, and the feet of
the artisanry. Guidance is the prerogative of the head, whose greatness is reflected
in the superiority of the priesthood, whose sign is the head, over warriorhood,
whose sign is the hand, and herdsmanship, whose sign is the belly, and artisanry,
whose sign is the feet.

The primacy of the priesthood lies also in its relation to the soul, which is also
expressed in names, as that of the priesthood (asrōnīh), which means "eternal
guide of souls" (asar-ruwānīh nimūdār).

Revelation from the Good Religion shows that the priesthood occupies the
most special place of the Wise Lord, as reliably attested by the greatness of the
priesthood over warriorhood and herdsmanship.

hēt mahīh ud frāzīh ī asrōnīh az artēštārīh wāstaryōšīh ī az was cim paydāg
ud aziš ēk ēn kū artēštārīh pad asrōnīg druz ī mēnōg zadan ud wastaryōšīh ī
pad asrōnīg yazdān yazišn saxt harw dō andar asrōnīh saxwan xwēš ōyīg be-šān
ān hamōg kunišn pad rasišn ī az asrōnīh. ēk ēn kū dānistan kardan ī kadār-
iz-ē ī mardōm frēzwānīg ciyōn šnāxtan ī dādār ud was kirbag wināh az asrōnīh
awēšān-iz pēš ud mādagwar az harw kār ī-šān andar xwēš wimand. ēk az fradomīh
ī asrōnīh pad ham ōšmārišn mehīh ī pad-iz gāh ī daxšag ī asrōnīh artēštārīh ud
wāstaryōšīh. ud ēk az-iz tan ī mardōm mehīh sar asrōnīh abar dast ī artēštārīh ud
aškamb ī wāstaryōšīh ud pāy hutuxšīh nišān nimudārīh sar ud mehīh ī abartarīh
ī asrōnīg abar sar abar artēštārīh ī abar dast ud wāstaryōšīh ī abar aškamb ud
hutuxšīh ī abar pāy nišān. nazdistārīh ī asrōnīh ī ō ruwān ī-š abar kē ka-iz ī nām
pad ān ī asrōnīh kē ka asar ruwānīh nimūdār. paydāgīh ī az wēh-dēn asrōnīh pad
+waspuhragāntom gāh ī Ohrmazd wābar gugāyīh ī mehīh ī asrōnīh az artēštārīh
ud wāstaryōšīh.

Concerning the hierarchic distinction Indo-Iranian society drew between priests
and warriors, see Bruce Lincoln, *Priests, Warriors, and Cattle: A Study in the Ecology
of Religions* (Berkeley: University of California Press, 1981).

80. Herodotus 4.23: τούτους οὐδεὶς ἀδικέει ἀνθρώπων (ἱροὶ γὰρ λέγονται ἔιναι),

οὐδέ τι ἀρήιον ὅπλον ἐκτέαται. καὶ τοῦτο μὲν τοῖσι περιοικέουσι οὗτοι εἰσὶ οἱ τὰς διαφορὰς διαιρέοντες, τοῦτο δὲ, ὃς ἂν φεύγων καταφύγῃ ἐς τούτους, ὑπ᾽ οὐδενὸς ἀδικέεται· οὔνομα δέ σφι ἐστὶ Ἀργιππαῖοι. The name of this group also appears in this form in four manuscripts, but others have variants including Ὀργιμπαῖοι, Ὀργεμπαῖοι, and Ὀργιεμπαῖοι. Regrettably, the only serious discussion of which I am aware is E. D. Phillips, "The Argippaei of Herodotus," *Artibus Asiae* 23 (1960): 124–28. On the name Argippaioi, see Rüdiger Schmitt, "Griechische Umdeutung eines 'skythischen' Ethnonyms," *Historische Sprachforschung* 119 (2006): 186–89; on its relation to the ethnonym Argimpasa (or Artimpasa), see Mayrhofer, *Einiges zu den Skythen*, 9–10 and 11; Helmut Humbach and Klaus Faiss, *Herodotus's Scythians and Ptolemy's Central Asia: Semasiological and Onomasiological Studies* (Wiesbaden: Ludwig Reichert, 2012), 7–8 and 9. The longest scholarly treatment of Argimpasa is that of Yulia Ustinova, *The Supreme Gods of the Bosporan Kingdom: Celestial Aphrodite and the Most High God* (Leiden: E.J. Brill, 1999), 75–87, but all sources—primary and secondary—are treated in such credulous fashion to produce an unusable syncretistic muddle.

81. I would, however, hold open the possibility that the *A-naryas *were* the Argippaioi. If the name of the latter (noting the manuscript variations listed in the preceding note) is derived from that of the goddess Argimpasa (whom Herodotus identified with "Uranian Aphrodite," 4.59), the following relations might obtain: (1) A group of Scythians committed war atrocities against the temple of Argimpasa; (2) as a result, the goddess barred them from further martial activity and gave them priestly knowledge, power, and status in compensation; (3) two different titles were used for these priests: Argippaioi, which associated them with their patron deity, and *A-narya, which indicated their negative relation to the practice of warfare.

## CHAPTER NINE

1. On the hall as the microcosmic model of a well-ordered society, see Kathryn Hume, "The Concept of the Hall in Old English Poetry," *Anglo-Saxon England* 3 (1974): 63–74; and Paul Beekman Taylor, "Heorot, Earth, and Asgard: Christian Poetry and Pagan Myth," *Tennessee Studies in Literature* 11 (1966): 119–30.

2. Christine Rauer, *Beowulf and the Dragon: Parallels and Analogues* (Cambridge: D.S. Brewer, 2000), 195–96 includes a list of comparanda that includes dragons from the Völsung legend (Fafnir), the Ragnar legend, the legends of Frotho and Friðleif (from Saxo Grammaticus), and about a dozen others. See also Friedrich Wild, "Drachen im Beowulf und andere Drachen," *Sitzungsberichte der österreichische Akademie der Wissenschaften, Philosophich-Historische Klasse* 238 (1962); Joyce Tally Lionarons, *The Medieval Dragon: The Nature of the Beast in Germanic Literature* (Middlesex: Hisarlik Press, 1998).

3. Maxims II from the Cotton gnomes: *Draca sceal on hlaewe, frod, fraetwum wlanc.* Text in Elliott Dobbie, *Anglo-Saxon Poetic Records*, vol. 6 (New York: Columbia University Press, 1942), 56. Cf. the description of Beowulf's dragon as "glorying in its precious treasure" (*māðm-ǣhta wlonc*), line 2833.

4. *Hordweard* is used of the dragon at lines 2293, 2302, 2554, and 2593; *beorges hyrde* at 2304; *goldweard* at 3081; and *frætwa hyrde* at 3133.

5. *Beowulf* 2233–41:

| | |
|---|---|
| swā hȳ on geār-dagum | gumena nāt-hwylc, |
| eormen-lāfe | æþelan cynnes, |
| þanc-hycgende | þær gehȳdde, |
| dēore māðmas. | Ealle hīe dēað fornam |
| ǣrran mǣlum, | ond sē ān ðā gēn |
| lēoda duguðe, | sē ðǣr lengest hwearf. |
| weard wine-geōmer, | wēnde þæs ylcan |
| þæt hē lȳtel fæc | long-gestrēona |
| brūcan mōste. | Beorh eallgearo |
| wunode on wonge | wæterȳðum nēah, |
| nīwe be næsse, | nearocræftum fæst; |
| þær on innan bær | eorlgestrēona. |

Text here and elsewhere from Friedrich Klaeber, ed., *Beowulf and the Fight at Finnsburg*, 3rd ed. (Lexington, MA: D.C. Heath, 1950).

6. *Beowulf* 3168. The same term occurs only in one other passage, where Hrothgar's gift-hall is said to have become "idle and useless" (*idel ond unnyt*) when Grendel's predations caused it to be abandoned (line 413). In both cases, the word describes something that ought play a crucial role in the circulation of wealth, but has ceased to do so.

7. On hoards as wealth turned stagnant, thus antithetical to its own proper nature, see Martin Stevens, "The Progress of *Beowulf*: From Gold-Hoard to Word-Hoard," *Philological Quarterly* 47 (1968): 219–38, esp. 226–29; Stanley B. Greenfield, "*Gifstol* and Goldhoard in *Beowulf*," in Robert B. Burlin and Edward B. Irving, Jr., eds., *Old English Studies in Honour of John C. Pope* (Toronto: University of Toronto Press, 1974), 107–17, esp. 113; Elisabeth Vestergaard, "Gift-Giving, Hoarding, and Outdoings," in Ross Samson, ed., *Social Approaches to Viking Studies* (Glasgow: Cruithne Press, 1991), 97–104, esp. 102; and Joseph E. Marshall, "*Goldgyfan* or *goldwlance*: A Christian Apology for Beowulf and Treasure," *Studies in Philology* 107 (2010): 1–24, esp. 13–22. Marshall errs, however, in arguing that both Grendel and the dragon are stigmatized for their greed. While both show an unhealthy relation to wealth and the good things of life, Grendel's attitude is one of resentful envy from a position of deprivation; the dragon's, of possessive greed from a position of surplus.

8. It is difficult to capture the nuances of Anglo-Saxon *ðēod-sceaða* in an English translation. The first member of the compound denotes the nation or people as a solidary community, while the second member conjures up one who stands not only outside and against the group, but outside all morality, threating the people with grievous harm. Within Anglo-Saxon literature, this same term (*sceaða* or *sceaþa*) is frequently used of Satan, devils, and Antichrist. See further Joseph Bosworth and T. Northcote Toller, *An Anglo-Saxon Dictionary* (Oxford: Oxford University Press, 1898), 826 and 1049.

9. *Beowulf* 2270–81 Hord-wynne fond

| | |
|---|---|
| eald ūht-sceaða | opene standan. |
| . . . | þǣr hē hǣðen gold |
| waráð wintrum frōd; | ne bȳð him wihte ðȳ sēl. |
| Swā se ðēod-sceaða | þrēo hund wintra |
| hēold on hrūsan | hord-ǣrna sum |
| ēacen-cræftig, | oððæt hyne ān ābealch |
| mon on mōde. | |

10. The text's choice of object is significant, for elsewhere cups appear chiefly in the context of banquets, where noblewomen use cups to distribute drink, honor, sociability, and festivity among the assembled company. To hoard a cup thus removes a prime instrument of social-formation-through-circulation from the process it supports. See further Helen Damico, *Beowulf's Wealhtheow and the Valkyrie Tradition* (Madison: University of Wisconsin Press, 1984).

11. As regards the identity of the cup-taker, most scholars have accepted Friedrich Klaeber's restoration of the damaged text at line 2223 to read *þ(ēow)*, "servant, slave" (Klaeber, *Beowulf and the Fight at Finnsburg*, 83 and 208). Although others have proposed different restorations (most plausibly *þ(ēof)*, "thief," as advocated by Theodore Andersson, "The Thief in *Beowulf*," *Speculum* 59 [1984]: 493–508), the desperate nature of the man's circumstances are established by mention of the *þrēa-nēdla* ("sad necessity, needy affliction") that prompted him to enter the dragon's barrow. The relevant passage reads as follows (lines 2221–26).

| | |
|---|---|
| Not of his own accord | did he break into the serpent's hoard, |
| Nor of his own will, | he who sorely harmed the beast. |
| Rather, out of bitter need | a certain servant [or "thief"] |
| Fled hostile blows | from warriors' sons. |
| Needing shelter, | that guilty man |
| Reached inside there. | |

| | |
|---|---|
| Nealles mid gewealdum | wyrmhord ābræc, |
| sylfes willum, | sē ðe him sāre gesceōd, |
| ac for þrēanēdlan | þ(ēow) nāthwylces |
| hæleða bearna | heteswengeas flēah, |
| (ærnes) þearfa, | ond ðǣr inne fealh, |
| secg synbysig. | |

12. On this point, see the discussion of Marshall, "*Goldgyfan* or *goldwlance*," 14–15.

13. Marcel Mauss, "Essai sur le don, forme archaïque de l'échange" (1925); English trans. by Ian Cunnison, *The Gift: Forms and Functions of Exchange in Archaic Societies* (New York: W.W. Norton, 1967). Good discussions of the role of gifts in the political economy described in *Beowulf* include Michael D. Cherniss, "The Progress of the Hoard in *Beowulf*," *Philological Quarterly* 47 (1967): 473–86; Cherniss, *Ingeld and*

*Christ: Heroic Concepts and Values in Old English Christian Poetry* (The Hague: Mouton, 1972), 79–101; Patricia Silber, "Gold and Its Significance in *Beowulf*," *Annuale Mediaevale* 18 (1977): 5–19; Thomas L. Keller, "The Dragon in *Beowulf* Revisited," *Aevum* 55 (1981): 218–28; Jos Bazelmans, *By Weapons Made Worthy: Lords, Retainers, and Their Relationship in "Beowulf"* (Amsterdam: Amsterdam University Press, 1999), esp. 94–103; Marshall, "*Goldgyfan* or *goldwlance*"; and Peter S. Baker, *Honour, Exchange, and Violence in Beowulf* (Cambridge: D.S. Brewer, 2013).

14. Ernst Leisi, "Gold und Manneswert im *Beowulf*," *Anglia* 71 (1952–53): 259–60, who cites the following terms in support of his point: *ēadig* ("happy, blessed, fortunate, prosperous, rich, perfect"), *sǣlig* ("blessed, fortunate"), *wlanc* ("proud, high-spirited, bold; splendid, great, high, august, magnificent, rich"), *rīce* ("powerful, mighty, great"; only thereafter "rich" in the modern sense), *blǣd* ("enjoyment, prosperity, abundance, success, blessedness, gift, reward, benefit, glory, honor"), *ār* ("honor, glory, rank, dignity, magnificence, respect, reverence; property, possessions, an estate, land"), *spēd* ("speed, success, prosperous issue; means, substance, abundance, wealth"), *duguð* ("good, virtuous, honorable; liberal, munificent"). Also relevant are *ǣht* ("possessions, property, lands, goods, riches, cattle; possession, power"), *god* ("good, good thing, good deed, benefit, goodness, welfare"), and *weorð* ("worth, value"). Definitions taken from Bosworth and Toller, *Anglo-Saxon Dictionary*, ad loc. The fullest discussion of the lexicography of wealth is Paul Beekman Taylor, "The Traditional Language of Treasure in *Beowulf*," *Journal of English and Germanic Philology* 85 (1986): 191–205.

15. On God as the ultimate donor, see Bliss, "*Beowulf*, Lines 3074–3075," 57–63; Edward B. Irving Jr., *A Reading of "Beowulf"* (New Haven, CT: Yale University Press, 1985), 150–52; Silber, "Gold and Its Significance in *Beowulf*," 6–7; Bazelmans, *By Weapons Made Worthy*, 145–47 and 168.

16. *Beowulf* 67–72 (emphasis added):

|  | Him on mōd bearn, |
|---|---|
| þæt healreced | hātan wolde, |
| medoærn micel | men gewyrcean |
| þon[n]e yldo bearn | æfre gefrūnon |
| ond þær on innan | eall gedǣlan. |
| geongum ond ealdum, | *swylc him God sealde* . . . |

17. *Beowulf* 1748–57 (emphasis added):

| þinceð him tō lȳtel, | þæt hē lange hēold, |
|---|---|
| gȳtsað gromhȳdig, | nallas on gylp seleð |
| fætte bēagas, | ond hē þā forðgesceaft |
| forgyteð ond forgȳmeð, | *þæs þe him ǣr God sealde,* |
| *wuldres Waldend,* | weorðmynda dǣl. |
| Hit on endestæf | eft gelimpeð, |
| þæt se līchoma | lǣne gedrēoseð, |
| fǣge gefealleð; | fēhð ōþer tō, |
| sē þe unmurnlīce | mādmas dǣleþ, |
| eorles ǣrgestrēon, | egesan ne gȳmeð. |

Cf. Hrothgar's description of Heremod, whom he presents as the antithesis of proper kingship, lines 1709–22. Heremod's stinginess in giving gifts is treated at 1719–20, immediately after it has been said that his wealth and power were given him by Almighty God, 1716–18.

18. *Bēag-gyfa* occurs at line 1102; *beaga bryttan* at 35, 352, and 1487; *gold-wine gumena* at 1602, 1171, and 1476. *Gold-wine Geata* ("gold-friend to the Geats") at 2419 and 2584; *sinces brytta* at 607, 1170, 1922, and 2071; *sinc-gifa* at 1012, 1342, and 2311; *wil-geofa* at 2900.

19. Most fully on the way exchange economies function through ongoing recon-version of economic to social capital and vice versa, see Pierre Bourdieu, *Outline of a Theory of Practice* (Cambridge: Cambridge University Press, 1977), esp. 171–97; Bourdieu, *Practical Reason: On the Theory of Action* (Stanford, CA: Stanford University Press, 1998), 92–123.

20. *Beowulf* 20–24:

| | |
|---|---|
| Swā sceal geong guma | gōde gewyrcean, |
| fromum feoh-giftum | on fæder bearme, |
| þæt hine on ylde | eft gewunigen |
| wil-gesīþas, | þonne wīg cume, |
| lēode gelǣsten. | |

I have translated the Anglo-Saxon substantive *gód* in line 20 as "goods and goodness" to preserve its full semantic range. Rendering it by one of these options only would unduly restrict and impoverish all it conveys in the present context.

21. *Beowulf* 2606: *Gemunde ðā ðā āre / þe hē him ǣr forgeaf.* Also relevant is Wiglaf's rebuke of the retainers who dared not face the dragon, whom he faulted not just for cowardice, but more precisely for having failed to honor the debt they owed their lord and patron, lines 2633–41.

| | |
|---|---|
| I remember that time | when we partook of mead |
| and we pledged | in the beer hall |
| to our lord, | who gave us these rings, |
| that we would repay | him for the battle-gear, |
| helmets and hard swords, | should some distress |
| come to him. | He chose us from the army |
| of his own will | for this expedition. |
| He judged us worthy of glories | and he gave me these treasures, |
| For he reckoned us | good spear-fighters. |

| | |
|---|---|
| Ic ðæt mǣl geman, | þǣr wē medu þēgun. |
| þonne wē gehēton | ūssum hlāforde |
| in bīor-sele, | ðe ūs ðās bēagas geaf, |
| þæt wē him ðā gūð-getāwa | gyldan woldon, |
| gif him þyslicu | þearf gelumpe, |
| helmas ond heard sweord. | Ðē hē ūsic on herge gecēas |

tō ðyssum sīð-fate            sylfes willum,
onmunde ūsic mǽrða,          ond mē þās māðmas geaf,
þē hē ūsic gār-wīgend        gōde tealde.

22. The position of (royal) generosity in relation to envy and greed can be sche-
matized as in table 9.1.

23. *Selections of Zādspram* presents the story of Āz at 1.29–30, 34.32–45, and
35.35–36. Some scholars, most notably R. C. Zaehner, *Zurvan: A Zoroastrian Dilemma*
(Oxford: Oxford University Press, 1955), 166–83 and passim; Zaehner, *The Dawn and
Twilight of Zoroastrianism* (New York: G.P. Putnam, 1961), 223–29, 253–55, 311–15,
have taken this to be an isolated narrative reflecting heretical doctrines. Such an
interpretation seems extreme, as it fails to take account of the variants found in the
*Greater Bundahišn* 34.2 and 34.28–30, *Pahlavi Rivāyat accompanying the Dādēstān ī
Dēnīg* 48.90–94, and *Mēnōg ī Xrad* 8.13–16. *Zand ī Wahman Yasn* 4.12, 4.41, and 8.2
is also relevant. Further, as has been demonstrated by Hanns-Peter Schmidt, "Vom
awestischen Dämon Āzi zur manichäischen Āz, der Mutter aller Dämonen," in Ronald E. Emmerick, Werner Sundermann, and Peter Zieme, eds., *Studia Manicahaica: IV
internationaler Kongress zum* Manichäismus (Berlin: Akademie Verlag, 2000), 517–27,
the Middle Persian Āz is no extraneous anomaly, but develops quite naturally and logically from an older demon, Āzi, attested in several verses of the Avesta. See further
George C. O. Haas, "The Zoroastrian Demon Āz in the Manichaean Fragments from
Turfan," in *Indo-Iranian Studies* (London: Kegan, Paul, Trench, & Trübner, 1925),
193–96; Marijan Molé, "Un ascétisme moral dans les livres pehlevis?," *Revue de
l'Histoire des Religions* 155 (1959): 145–90, esp. 162–67; Werner Sundermann, "The
Zoroastrian and the Manichaean Demon Āz," in Siamak Adhami, ed., *Paitimāna:
Essays in Iranian, Indo-European, and Indian Studies in Honor of Hanns-Peter Schmidt*
(Costa Mesa, CA: Mazda Publishers, 2003), 328–38; Jes P. Asmussen, "Āz, Iranian
Demon Known from Zoroastrian, Zurvanite, and, especially, Manichaean Sources," in
*Encyclopaedia Iranica*, 3: 168–69; and Jalil Doostkhah, "Āz and Niyāz, Two Powerful
and Haughty Demons in Persian Mythology and Epics," *Sydney Studies in Religion* 11
(2008): 67–70.

24. Thus D. N. MacKenzie, *A Concise Pahlavi Dictionary* (London: Oxford University Press, 1971), 15: "greed, lust." Cf. Henrik Samuel Nyberg, *A Manual of Pahlavi*
(Wiesbaden: Otto Harrassowitz, 1964–74), 2: 41: "avidity, covetousness"; and Christian Bartholomae, *Altiranische Wörterbuch* (Berlin: Walter de Gruyter, 1961), 343:
"Gier, Begierde." Others have favored "concupiscence" (R. C. Zaehner) and "convoi-
tise" (Jean de Menasce). The noun is derived from a verbal root āz-, "to strive for,
long after" (Bartholomae, *Altiranische Wörterbuch*, 342). Alternatively, Hans Schmeja,
"Awestisch āzi- 'Habgier' = altindisch āji- 'Wettkampf'?," *Klagenfurter Beiträge zur
Sprachwissenschaft* 2 (1976): 101–7.

25. This passage has been discussed by Zaehner, *Zurvan*, 176–77; Molé, "Un
ascétisme moral," 146–47; and Schmidt, "Vom awestischen Dämon Āzi zur manichäischen Āz," 521–22. On the *Selections of Zādspram* in general, see Philippe
Gignoux, "Un témoin du syncrétisme mazdéen tardif, le traité pehlevi des 'Sélections
de Zādspram,'" in *Transition Periods in Iranian History* = *Studia Iranica* 5 (1987):

59–72; and Carlo G. Cereti, *La letteratura Pahlavi: Introduzione ai testi con riferimenti alla storia degli studi e alla tradizione manoscritta* (Milan: Mimesis, 2001), 107–18.

26. *Selections of Zādspram* 34.36–37: ud Āz ēk cihrīhā nē tuwān būd ahōgēnīd tā dāmān pargandag bawēd. ān-iš zōrān pad jomā rawāg būdan ī andar dām rāy ō 3 baxt ī ast cihrīg be ⁺cihrīg ud bērōn az cihr. cihrīg ān kā andar xwardārīh kē-š gyān awiš bastag. be-cihrīg kāmagōmandīh ī abar gumēzišn kē xwad waran xwanīhēd kē pad wēnišn ī ō bē ān ī andarōn hangēzīhēd ud cihr ī tan awištābīhēd. berōn az cihr ārzōg ī ō kadār-iz-ē nēkīh ī wēnēd ayāb ašnawēd. harw tōf-ē ō 2 baxt ān ī cihrīg ast suy <ud> tišn, ān ī be cihrīg ast rēzag ud ⁺padirāg ān ī berōn az cihr ast āzwarīhā handōxtan ud penīhā be nē dādan (numbers added). Text here and elsewhere from Philippe Gignoux and Ahmad Tafazzoli, eds. and trans., *Anthologie de Zādspram* (Paris: Association pour l'avancement des études iraniennes, 1993). Cf. *Greater Bundahišn* 27.34–37.

27. *Greater Bundahišn* 14.18–19:

Then for thirty days, they wandered in the wilderness. They came to a white-haired goat, and it squirted milk from its udders into their mouths. When they had consumed the milk, Māšya ("Mortal") said: "I had peace when I had not eaten. That liquid milk, from that there is greater creation of peace. But now, when I have eaten, there is evil in my body."

⁺wiškar frāz ud ō buz-ē(w) spēd-mōy mad hēnd. u-šān pad dahān pēm az pestān mēzid. ka-šān pēm xward būd Mašē guft kū āštīh ī man az ān ka-m nē xward ān ī šuhr pēm u-m ⁺āštīh-dādārtar az ān ast. nūn ka xward ā-m pad tan wad.

28. Ibid. 14.21: "After a second thirty days and nights, they came to a beneficent animal with one dark and one white cheek, and they killed it." (pas pad sīhrōz-šabān ī dudīgar ō gōspand-ē(w) mad hēnd dabr ī spēd ērwārag u-šān ud be kušt.)

29. Ibid. 14.28–30:

For fifty years they had no desire for intercourse, and as there was no intercourse, there were no offspring. On the completion of fifty years, first Mašya ("Mortal") and then Māšyānīg ("Mortaless") thought to desire a son. For this reason, Mašya then said to Māšyānīg: "When I see your vagina, my (penis) rises up big." Then Māšyānīg said: "Brother Mašya, when I see your big penis, my vagina trembles." Then they were carried off together by desire. As they fulfilled their desire, they thought thus: "We should have been doing this for the last fifty years!" In nine months, they gave birth to a male-and-female couple.

u-šān awēšān har(w) dō ēdōn hušk-kun be kard kū-šān panjāh sāl kāmag ī pad ham-gūmēzišnīh nē būd ud ka-iz-šān ham-gūmēzišnīh kard ⁺hād eg-šān frazand nē būd hād. pad bowandagīh ī panjāh sāl ā-šān pus-xwāhišn frāz menīd nazdist Mašē ud pas Māšāni čē-š guft Mašē ō Māšānē kū ka ēd ī tō aškamb wenēm eg ān ī man meh ul āxēzēd. pas Māšānē guft kū brād Mašē ka ān ⁺kēr ī tō meh wenēm ān ī man aškamb drafšēd. pas awēšān kāmag ō ham burdud andar kāmag-wizārišnīh ī-šān kard ēdōn abar menīd kū-mān-īz panjāh sāl kār ēn abāyēd būd. az awēšān zād pad nō māh juxt-ē(w) zan ud mard.

30. The narrative makes the acquisition of goods gradual and piecemeal, incidental to the main action, and does not comment on it in any explicit fashion. Having been born out of vegetation (*Greater Bundahišn* 14.6 and 10), Mašya and Mašyānīg begin their lives clothed in leaves (14.17), after which they acquire firewood to cook the animal they killed (14.21), clothes from the animal's skin (14.22), then clothes of hemp (14.22), and iron for cutting tools (14.23), with which they made wooden bowls (14.23).

31. Most thoroughly on the distinction of spiritual and material existence in Zoroastrianism, see Shaul Shaked, "The Notions *Mēnōg* and *Gētīg* in the Pahlavi Texts and Their Relation to Eschatology," *Acta Orientalia* 33 (1971): 59–107. Specific discussions in which this distinction is used to theorize the nature of demons include *Dādēstān ī Dēnīg* 36.51; *Dēnkart* 3.105, 3.271, 3.401, and 5.7.2.

32. On the relation of mortality to appetite, see Molé, "Un ascétisme moral," 147–54.

33. Pahlavi literature advocates a number of methods for keeping Appetite in check before it can be absolutely defeated at the end of the current world-age. These include contentment (*hunsandīh*, *Cidarg Handarz ī Pōryōtkēšān* 38), "the desire and taste for milk, which holds hunger and thirst at bay" (especially effective in infants and children, according to *Dēnkart* 3.374), reflection on "the transience of the body and material things" (*frasāwandīh ī tan ud xīr ī gētīg*, *Dēnkart* 6.198), or the "frustration of nature" (*anābišn ī cihr*), i.e., of the bodily demands that come as a result of mortality (*Dēnkart* 3.316).

34. *Selections of Zādspram* 34.32: "Then he chose a commander in chief, who is Appetite herself." (u-š pas wizīd spāhbed sālār ī xwad ast Āz.) Previous discussions of Zādspram's eschatology include Zaehner, *Zurvan*, 175–80 and 343–54; Molé, "Un ascétisme moral," 162–71; and Schmidt, "Vom awestischen Dämon Āzi zur manichäischen Āz," 522–24.

35. Ibid. 34.34: "At the Renovation, a remedy for Appetite is the first thing to be sought, because she is commander in chief of the other Lies and the Evil Spirit derives increased force from her." (pad Frašegird fradōm cār ī Āz xwāhīhēd {ast} ēd rāy cē spāhbed sālār ast <ī>abārīgān-iz druzān Ahreman <ī> dušdēn nērōg az ōy wēš.)

36. Ibid. 34.38: ēd ast kē-š wattarīh andar parwand ud {abdom} paydāg kū abdom ⁺cāraggarīh ī Āz rāy Ašwahišt pad ham zōrīh ī ⁺Ērman frēstag be ō zamīg āyēd ud ō dāmān abar garan wināhīhā gōspand sardagān ⁺zadan <ud> kam sūdīh ī u-š ⁺nimāyēd. ēn-iz framāyēd kū mard hēd ma ēdōn gōspand be kušidār bawēd ciyōn-itān pēš frāz pad kušišn kušīd. Cf. *Dēnkart* 7.10.8–9; *Greater Bundahišn* 34.2; *Dādēstān ī Dēnīg* 34.3; *Pahalavi Rivāyat accompanying the Dādēstān ī Dēnīg* 48.20–22.

37. Cf. *Greater Bundahišn* 34.1–3:

It says in the religion: "Just as when Mašya and Mašyānāg emerged from the earth, they first consumed water, then plants, then milk, and then meat, so too people when they are dying first cease to eat meat, then milk, then bread and consume water only until they die." So too in the millennium of Ušēdarmāh [i.e., just before the end-time], the power of appetite decreases so that with one meal every three days and nights, a person continues to be satisfied. Then they cease from meat-consumption, consuming plants and the milk of beneficent animals. Then they cease from milk-consumption also, and then they cease from plant-consumption and become exclusively water-consuming. For the ten years before [the eschatological hero] Sōšyans comes they continue in non-consumption and they do not die. Then Sōšyans causes the dead to rise up.

gōwēd pad dēn kū az ān čiyōn Mašē ud Mašānē ka az zamīg abar rust hēnd nazdist āb ud pas urwar pas šīr ud pas gōšt xward hēnd mardōm-iz ka-šān murdan nazdist <az> gōšt ud šīr ud pas az nān xwardan-iz be estēnd ud ēwāz tā be murdan āb xwarēnd. ēdōn-iz pad hazārag ī Ušēdarmāh nērōg ī āz ēdōn be kāhēd kū mardōm pad ēk pih-xwarišnīh se šab ud rōz pad sagrīh estēnd. pas az ān az gōšt-xwarišnīh be estēnd ud urwar ud pēm ī gōspandān xwarēnd. pas az ān pēm-xwarišnīh-iz abāz estēnd ud pas az urwar-xwarišnīh-iz estēnd ud āb-xwarišn bawēnd. pēš pad dah sāl ka Sōšyans āyēd ō a-xwarišnīh estēnd ud nē mīrēnd. pas Sōšyans rist ul hangēzēnēd.

38. *Greater Bundahišn* 7.10 contains an alternate account of how people came to be carnivorous. Here, Ahreman began his assault on the first human (Gayōmard) by afflicting him with hunger. To defend against this, Ohrmazd gave him meat and butter, which strengthened his life-force and permitted him to resist death a bit longer. In both narratives, meat is opposed to death on the one hand, but to immortality on the other. In the state of primordial perfection, there is no need to eat, least of all to kill animals for one's nourishment, but once mortality has become part of the human condition, carnivorous behavior becomes both sinful and salutary. Also relevant is *Pahlavi Rivāyat accompanying the Dādēstān ī Dēnīg* 14.1–5, where Ohrmazd asks animals to permit humans to benefit from eating their flesh, but promises, by way of compensation, that the weight of the animals' sins will be transferred to those who eat them. On the role of dietary renunciation in the final battle against Ahreman, see Shaul Shaked, *Dualism in Transformation: Varieties of Religion in Sasanian Iran* (London: School of Oriental and African Studies, 1994), 43–44.

39. *Selections of Zādspram* 34.39:

When the accomplishment of the Renovation is near, the hearers of truth desist from the sin of killing animals and eating meat, and the power of Appetite will diminish by one-quarter. (As a result), the stench that is in one's body is expunged, darkness and gloom are partially killed, the spiritual condition is arrayed more fully in substance, and clearer knowledge is acquired.

ka nazd ō Frašegird-kardārīh bawēd nīyōxšīdārān ī Ašwahišt framān az gōspand zadārīh ud gōšt ud xwarišnīh be wardēnd ud 4 ēk ⁺nērōg ī Āz be kāhēd ud ⁺gandagīh ī andar tan ī ⁺ōy ast be ānābīhēd tom-iz tār bahrīhā ⁺zanīhēd mēnōgīgīh ō cihr abērtar paymōzīhēd <ud> dānišnān rōšntar ayābīhēd.

40. Ibid. 34.40:

Appetite is weaker in the bodies of the children whom they bear. Their bodies are less foul and closer to the nature of the gods. By instruction from the gods, they turn away from milk foods, and the power of Appetite diminishes by half.

frazandān ī az awēšān zāyēnd Āz andar tan +abādyāwandtar ud tan kam-gandagtar <ud> ō yazdān +cihr hampaywandtar pad hammōxtārīh ī yazdān az pēm xwarišnīh +wardēnd nēmag nērōg ī Āz be kāhēd.

41. Schmidt, "Vom awestischen Dämon Āzi zur manichäischen Āz," 521 and 524, argued that Zoroastrian constructions of Āz generally focused on hunger alone, while those that included sexual desire did so as a result of Manichaean influence, a view that Sundermann, "The Zoroastrian and the Manichaean Demon Āz," also supported. Such an interpretation mistakes a set of logical priorities establishing different types and degrees of Appetite for a stratigraphic sequence bearing evidence of intrusive elements.

42. *Selections of Zādspram* 34.41 (emphasis added): "And their children, because of their non-consumption of food and drink, become fragrant, less dark, spiritual in nature, *and no longer subject to giving birth.*" (awēšān-iz zāyišnān axwarišnīh rāy hubōy kam-tārīg mēnōg cihr ud a-zāyišnōmand bawēnd.) Cf. *Dādēstān ī Dēnīg* 34.3.

43. Cf. *Greater Bundahišn* 34.24: "[At the Resurrection,] they give everyone their wife and children, and with their wives they have something like sex as it now is in material existence, but no birth of progeny occurs." (ud har(w) kas zan ud frazand dahēnd ud abāg zan māyišn owōn kunēnd čiyōn nūn andar gētīg bē frazand-zāyišnīh nē bawēd.)

Also of interest is the eschatological discussion of *Pahlavi Rivāyat accompanying the Dādēstān ī Dēnīg* 48.105–6, which combines the issue of meat-eating with that of sexual reproduction.

After that, meat eating is not necessary because the pleasure of the taste of all meat is always in people's mouths. . . . And there is desire of man and wife for one another. They direct this and act on it, but there is no birth from them.

pad harw zamān mizag xwašīh ī hamāg gōšt andar dahān estēd. . . . ud mard ud zan ēk abāg did kāmag bawēd ud rāyēnēnd ud kunēnd bē-šān zāyišn nē bawēd.

44. Numerous texts emphasize the insatiable nature of Appetite, including *Dēnkart* 3.61: "Appetite . . . wishes to devour the world in a single bite" (Āz ka-š gēhān pad ēk āsumbišn andar ōbārdan) and *Greater Bundahišn* 27.33: "When all the wealth of the material world has been given to it, still [Appetite] does not become filled and sated" (ka-š hamāg xwāstag ī gētīg be dād [nē] +ōbārēd ud sagr nē bawēd).

45. *Selections of Zādspram* 34.38–45:

Finally, the demon Appetite, because she can obtain no power from the Wise Lord's creatures, quarrels with the Evil Spirit, by whom she was made commander in chief, saying: "Make me sated and well sustained, since I can no longer obtain the energy of food from the Wise Lord's creatures." At the Evil Spirit's order, she then will devour the lesser demons and finally the four commanders. Then, there will remain only two: the Evil Spirit and Appetite. The Wise Lord and the Evil Spirit, Obedience and Appetite then all come to earth. The Wise Lord smites the Evil Spirit. Since the Wise Lord is creator of light and the Evil Spirit of darkness, they are adversaries. Since Obedience is moderate, i.e., spiritual moderation, and Appetite is excess and deficiency, they are paired adversaries in battle. As long as Appetite was allied with the Evil Spirit, one could not find a remedy for that combination. But when Appetite is no longer allied with the Evil Spirit, the Evil Spirit will find himself isolated against three opponents. Two of these are opposed to him in nature (i.e., the Wise Lord and Obedience), one is similar in nature (Appetite, who is more his ally). Since his helper will turn hostile, his adversaries will be victorious.

ka nazd ō Frašegird-kardārīh bawēd nīyōxšīdārān ī Ašwahišt framān az gōspand zadārīh ud gōšt ud xwarišnīh be wardēnd ud 4 ēk ⁺nērōg ī Āz be kāhēd . . . frazan-dān ī az awēšān zāyēnd Āz andar tan ⁺abādyāwandtar ud tan kam-gandagtar < ud > ō yazdān ⁺cihr hampaywandtar pad hammōxtārīh ī yazdān az pēm xwarišnīh ⁺wardēnd nēmag nērōg ī Āz be kāhēd. awēšān-iz zāyišnān axwarišnīh rāy hubōy kam-tārīg mēnōg cihr ud azāyišnōmand bawēnd. ud pas Āz ⁺dēw nē ⁺ayāftan ī nērōg az Ohrmazd dāmān < rāy > be ō Ahreman kē-š pad spāhbedān sālār paydāgēnēd ud rōzīgīhā andar ō dāmān rad ⁺pahikārēd kū-m sagr < ud > huburd kunē cē nē ⁺ayābēm az Ohrmazd dāmān xwarišn zōrān. pad framān ī Ahreman dēw ī xwurdag be abesīhēnēd. abdom ān {ī} 4 spāhbedān frāz mānēnd ud ⁺any 2 ī Ahreman < ud > Āz. frāz ō zamīg āyēnd Ohrmazd < ud > Ahreman Srōš < ud > Āz < ud > {ō} Ohrmazd Ahreman zanēd tā ⁺baxtīg būd Āz abāz Ahreman cār nē ayābēd ān-iz rāy ka Ohrmazd wisp dādār ī rōšnīh u-š tārigīh ī Ahreman petyārag ⁺Srōšahlāy ī paymānīg ast mēnōg paymān u-š frehbūd ud ⁺abēbūd ī Āz petyārag < ud > hambarīhā hēnd pad kōxšišn. be ciyōn Āz abāz < Ahreman > baxtīg < nē > bawēd. Ahreman ēwtāg u-š ⁺hamēmāl ī jud gōhr ī ast Ohrmazd < ud > Srōš ud ēk ī hamgōhr ī ast Āz baxtīgtar. ka-š ayārbe ō hamēmālīh ⁺wašt hambadīg perōzīhēd.

Cf. *Selections of Zādspram* 1.30 and 34.35; *Greater Bundahišn* 34.28–30; *Pahlavi Rivāyat accompanying the Dādēstān ī Dēnīg* 48.90–94. Most fully on Sraoša, see Philip G. Kreyenbroek, *Sraoša in the Zoroastrian Tradition* (Leiden: E.J. Brill, 1985), with discussion of this deity's opposition to Āz at 140–41.

46. Accounts of eschatological perfection include *Greater Bundahišn* 3.26–27, 26.98, 34.22–25; *Dādēstan ī Dēnīg* 31.11, 35.6–7, 36.85–86, 36.99–101; *Dēnkart* 7.8.50; *Pahlavi Rivāyat accompanying the Dādēstān ī Dēnīg* 48.101–7; *Selections of Zādspram* 35.1–3; and Plutarch, *Isis and Osiris* 370b-c (where Appetite appears as *limos*, "hunger, famine," alongside *loimos*, "plague" [= Pahlavi *Niyāz*, "need, want, misery"?] as the last two Ahremanian powers to be overcome). Cf. *Dēnkart* 3.381.

Now, one achieves the perfect contentment of humanity when everything good comes into being for them. At the head of good things are three, which are the absence of need (*abē-niyāzīh*), immortality, and the fulfillment of desire. The absence of need is the removal of Need (*ōgārdan ī Niyāz*), when one achieves the things that are necessary for him. Even in adversity, some need is removed to the extent that one achieves things for people. But Appetite, which gives birth to need (*Āz ī niyāzānag*), and Need, who is spawn of Appetite, grows even more in them (*Niyāz ī Āz hunušak*).

hād bowandag ī šnāyēnīdārīh ī mardōm pad abarbarēd ī harw nēkīh awēšān bawēd. ud nēkīhān sar se ī hast abē-niyāzīh ud amargīh ud kāmag-hanjāmīh. ud abē-niyāzīh pad ōgārdan ī Niyāz frāz barēd xīrān ī abāyišnīg awiš bawēd. andar petyāragōmandīh-iz cand az frāz barēd xīrān ō mardōm niyāz ōgārīhēd frāy-iz az ān abzāyēd padišān Āz ī niyāzānag ud Niyāz ī Āz hunušak.

47. Karl Mannheim, *Ideology and Utopia: An Introduction to the Sociology of Knowledge* (New York: Harcourt, Brace, 1949).

## CHAPTER TEN

1. Aun does not appear in the first or second edition of Frazer´s *Golden Bough* (1890 and 1900, respectively), but shows up repeatedly in the third edition, *The Golden Bough: A Study in Magic and Religion* (London: Macmillan, 1911–15), 4: 57–58, 160–61, 188, and 6: 220. A full discussion also appears in the abridged one-volume edition of 1923. Apparently, Frazer become aware of this datum and recognized its utility for his theories when he read H. S. Chadwick, *The Cult of Othin: An Essay on the Ancient Religion of the North* (London: C.J. Clay & Son, 1899), 3–5 and 27.

2. Thus, inter alia, Gudbrand Vigfusson and F. York Powell, *Corpus Poeticum Boreale: The Poetry of the Old Northern Tongue*, vol. 1, *Eddic Poetry* (Oxford: Clarendon Press, 1883), 409–11; P. D. Chantepie de la Saussaye, *Religion of the Teutons*, trans. Bert Vos (Boston: Ginn, 1902), 371–73; Eugen Mogk, "Die Menschenopfer bei den Germanen," *Abhandlungen der königlichen Gesellschaft der Wissenschaften in Leipzig, Philologisch-historische Klasse* 57 (1909): 601–43; Mogk, "Ein Nachwort zu den Menschenopfern bei den Germanen," *Archiv für Religionswissenschaft* 15 (1912): 422–34; Bernhard Kummer, *Midgards Untergang: Germanische Kult und Glaube in den letzten heidnischen Jahrhunderten* (Leipzig: E. Pfeiffer, 1927), 105–18; Paul Herrmann, *Altdeutsche Kultgebräuche* (Jena: Eugen Diederichs, 1928) 30 ff.; Carl Clemen, *Altgermanische Religionsgeschichte* (Bonn: L. Röhrscheid, 1934), 95–102; E. O. G. Turville-Petre, *Myth and Religion of the North* (London: Weidenfeld & Nicolson, 1964), 46–48; Inga Beck, "Studien zur Erscheinungsform des heidnischen Opfers nach altnordischen Quellen" (PhD diss., Ludwig Maximillians Universität, 1967), 96–101; Jan de Vries, *Altgermanische Religionsgeschichte* (Berlin: Walter de Gruyter, 1970), 408–14, 420–22, and 455–56; Anders Hultgård, "Menschenopfer," in *Reallexikon der Germanischen Altertumskunde*, vol. 19 (Berlin: de Gruyter, 2001), 533–46. Somewhat surprisingly, King Aun does not figure in the discussion of Heinrich Beck, "Germanische Menschenopfer in der literarischen Überlieferung,"

*Abhandlungen der Akademie der Wissenschaften in Göttingen, Philologisch-historische Klasse* 74 (1970): 240–58, nor in that of Rudolf Simek, *Religion und Mythologie der Germanen* (Darmstadt: Wissenschaftliche Buchgesellschaft, 2003), 58–64.

3. The others are the stories of King Vikarr from *Gautrek's Saga* 7, that of Earl Hakón Sigurðarson from the *Saga of Olaf Tryggvason* 42, and that of King Dómaldi from *Ynglingasaga* 15.

4. In addition to the literature cited in note 2, see also Hermann Schneider, *Die Götter der Germanen* (Tübingen: J.C.B. Mohr, 1938), 139; Folke Ström, *Diser, Nornor, Valkyrjor: Fruktbarhetskult och sakralt kungadöme* (Stockholm: Almqvist & Wiksells, 1954), 49–50; Åke V. Ström, "The King God and Sacrifice in Old Norse Religion," in *La regalità sacra / The Sacral Kingship* (Leiden: E.J. Brill, 1959), 711; Hilda Ellis Davidson, *Scandinavian Mythology* (London: Hamlyn, 1969), 36; William Chaney, *The Cult of Kingship in Anglo-Saxon England* (Berkeley: University of California Press, 1970), 40 and 115; Anne Holtsmark, *Norrøn mytologi: Tro og myter i vikingtider* (Oslo: Norske Samlaget, 1970), 143; Lotte Motz, *The King, the Champion, and the Sorceror: A Study in Germanic Myth* (Vienna: Fassbaender, 1996), 78 and 96; Joseph Harris, "Sacrifice and Guilt in Sonatorrek," in Heiko Uecker, ed., *Studien zum Altgermanischen: Festschrift für Heinrich Beck* (Berlin: Walter de Gruyter, 1994), 175–80; Harris, "Homo Necans Borealis: Fatherhood and Sacrifice in Sonatorrek," in Stephen Glosecki, *Myth in Early Northwest Europe* (Tempe: Arizona Center for Medieval and Renaissance Studies, 2007), 162–65.

5. This model of Snorri's authorial activity has been most fully explored by Lars Lönnroth, "Tesen om de två kulturerna: Kritiska studier i den isländska sagaskrivinengens sociala forutsättningar," *Scripta Islandica* 15 (1964): 83–97. An English summary of his position is available in Lars Lönnroth, *European Sources of Icelandic Saga-Writing: An Essay Based on Previous Studies* (Stockholm: Akademisk avhandling, 1965), 14. See also Kolbrún Haraldsdóttir, "Der Historiker Snorri: Autor oder Kompilator?," in Hans Fix, ed., *Snorri Sturluson: Beiträge zu Werk und Rezeption* (Berlin: Walter de Gruyter, 1998), 97–108. The text itself is anonymous, but inferential evidence points strongly to Snorri's authorship. A few scholars have contested this in recent years, but proponents of Snorri's involvement still get the best of the argument, provided one understands his role as having organized and directed a text-producing effort, rather than having written every word himself. In the following discussion, the name "Snorri" denotes whatever agency was responsible for production of *Ynglingasaga* 25. For a summary of the arguments in favor of Snorri's authorship, see Diana Whaley, *Heimskringla: An Introduction* (London: Viking Society for Northern Research, 1991), 13–17; for the skeptical view, Patricia Pires Boulhosa, *Icelanders and the Kings of Norway* (Leiden: E.J. Brill, 2005), 6–21.

6. *Ynglingasaga* 25: Aun eða Áni hét sonr Iǫrundar, er konungr var yfir Svíum eptir fǫður sinn. Hann var vitr maðr ok blótmaðr mikill; engi var hann hermaðr, sat hann at lǫndum. Í þann tíma, er þessir konungar váru at Uppsǫlum, er nú var frá sagt, var yfir Danmǫrku fyrst Danr inn mikilláti; hann varð allgamall; þá sonr hans, Fróði inn mikilláti eða inn friðsami; þá hans synir Hálfdan ok Friðleifr. þeir váru hermenn miklir. Hálfdan var ellri ok fyrir þeim um alt. Hann fór með her sinn til Svíþjóðar á hendr Aun konungi, ok áttu þeir orrostur nǫkkurar, ok hafði Hálfdan iafnan sigr.

Ok at lykðum flýði Aun konungr í Vestra Gautland. Þá hafði hann verit konungr yfir Uppsǫlum xx. vetra; hann var ok í Gautlandi xx. vetra, meðan Hálfdan konungr var at Uppsǫlum. Hálfdan konungr varð sóttdauðr at Uppsǫlum, ok er hann þar heygðr. Eptir þat kom Aun konungr enn til Uppsala; þá var hann lx. þá gerði hann blót mikit ok blét til langlífis sér ok gaf Óðni son sinn ok var honum blótinn. Aun konungr fekk andsvǫr af Óðni, at hann skyldi enn lifa lx. vetra. Aun var þá enn konungr at Uppsǫlum xx. vetra. Þá kom Áli inn frœkni með her sinn til Svíþjóðar, sonr Frilleifs, á hendr Aun konungi, ok áttu þeir orrostur, ok hafði Áli iafnan sigr. þá flýði Aun konungr í annat sinn ríki sitt ok fór í Vestra Gautland. Áli var konungr at Uppsǫlum xx. vetra, áðr Starkaðr inn gamli drap hann.

Eptir fall Ála fór Aun konungr aptr til Uppsala ok réð þá ríkinu enn xx. vetra. Þá gerði hann blót mikit ok blótaði ǫðrum syni sínum. þá sagði Óðinn honum, at hann skyldi æ lifa, meðan hann gæfi Óðni son sinn it tíunda hvert ár, ok þat með, at hann skyldi heiti gefa nǫkkuru heraði í landi sínu eptir tǫlu sona sinna, þeira er hann blótaði til Óðins. En þá er hann hafði blótat vii. sonum sínum, þá lifði hann x. vetr, svá at hann mátti ekki ganga; var hann þá á stóli borinn. þá blótaði hann inum viii. syni sínum, ok lifði hann þá enn x. vetr ok lá þá í kǫr. þá blótaði hann inum ix. syni sínum ok lifði þá enn x. vetr; þá drakk hann horn sem lébarn. Þá átti hann einn son eptir, ok vildi hann þá blóta þeim, ok þá vildi hann gefa Óðni Uppsali ok þau heruð, er þar liggia til, ok láta kalla þat Tíundaland. Svíar bǫnnuðu honum þat, ok varð þá ekki blót. Síðan andaðisk Aun konungr, ok er hann heygðr at Uppsǫlum. Þat er síðan kǫlluð Ánasótt, ef maðr deyr verklauss af elli. Text from Elias Wessén, ed., *Snorri Sturluson, Ynglingasaga* (Copenhagen: Einar Munksgaard, 1952), 27–29.

7. Thus *Landfeðga tal fra Noa til varra konunga*, in Kristian Kålund, ed., *Alfrœdi Íslenzk*, vol. 3 (Copenhagen: S.I. Møller, 1917), 57–58; and the genealogical appendix to Ari the Wise, *Íslendingabók*, in Wolfgang Golther, ed., *Ares Isländerbuch* (Halle: Max Niemeyer, 1892), 25–26.

8. The manuscripts actually read *Auchun, auchim, haqon*, and *aukun*. Editors of the text from Gustav Storm, ed., *Monumenta Historica Norvegiæ* (Christiana [Oslo]: A.W. Brøgger, 1880), 100 to Inger Ekrem and Lars Boje Mortensen, eds., *Historia Norwegie* (Copenhagen: Museum Tusculanum Press, 2003), 76 and 136 have preferred the otherwise unattested form *Auchun*, which is often taken to reflect a scribal error for *\*Authun < \*AuðwinR*.

9. *Historia Norwegiæ* 9.21: Iste genuit Auchun, qui longo uetustatis senio IX annis ante obitum suum dense usum alimonie postponens lac tantum de cornu ut infans suxisse fertur.

10. As an alternate form of the king's name, Áni appears first in *Ynglingasaga* 25, where it provides a folk-etymology for *ána-sótt*, an archaic term of the poetic lexicon that designates peaceful death from extreme old age. Although this word was obsolete in Iceland of the thirteenth century, Snorri encountered it in the *Ynglingatal* account of Aun's death (to be discussed below). Perceiving what he thought to be a deep linguistic connection between the king and the ailment to which he finally succumbed, Snorri invented the name Áni to make that connection apparent, taking *ána-* to be the genitive form of this name. It is, however, more properly understood as the genitive plural of *ái*, "great-grandfather," such that *ánasótt* is "the great-grandfathers' disease." The presence of the name "Áni" in *Ættartala Haralldz fra Odni*

thus reveals its dependence on *Ynglingasaga*. See further Wessén, ed., *Ynglingasaga*, 65, Bjarni Aðalbjarnarson, ed., *Snorri Sturluson, Heimskringla* (Reykjavík: Hið Íslenzka Fornritafélag, 1941), 1:47; Adolf Noreen, *Altnordische Grammatik* (Tübingen: Max Niemeyer Verlag, 1970), 165; and Jan de Vries, *Altnordisches Etymologisches Wörterbuch*, 2nd ed. (Leiden: E.J. Brill, 1977), 9, 18–19, and 20. The pioneer explication of *ána-* was offered by L. Fr. Leffler, "*Ána-sótt*," *Arkiv for Nordiska Filologi* 3 (1886): 188–89. The line of influence and development can be graphed as follows.

|  | *Ynglingatal* (mid-ninth century) | *Ynglingasaga* (between 1220 and 1235) | *Ættartala Haralldz fra Odni* (after *Ynglingasaga*) |
|---|---|---|---|
| King's primary name | Aun | Aun | Áni the Old |
| His cause of death | *ána-sótt* | *ána-sótt* |  |
| King's secondary name |  | Áni (introduced for the pseudo-etymological connection between king and cause of his death) | Aun |

11. *Ættartala Haralldz fra Odni*, in *Flateyjarbók* 1.26: Jorund [var] faudur Ana ens gamla. Er ver kaullum Aun. Er .ix. vetr drack horn fyrir elli sakir aadr hann do.

12. *Landfeðga tal fra Noa til varra konunga*: "Japhet, son of Noah, father of Japhan, father of Zechim, father of Cyprus, father of Celius, father of Saturnus of Crete, father of Jupiter, father of Erichonius, father of Troes, father of Ilus, father of Laomedon, father of Priamus, King of Troy. The next King of Troy was called Mimon or Memmon. He married the daughter of King Priam. Their son was called Tror, whom we call Thor . . ." (Japhet Noa s., faðir Iaphans, f. Zechim, fæður Ciprvs, f. Celivs, f. Satvrnvs I Krit, f. Iupiter, f. Erichonii, f. Troes, f. Ilus, f. Lamedon, f. Priami konungs i Troeo. Mimon eða Memmon het konungr i Troeo, hann atte dottur Priami konungs, þeira svn het Tror . . .)

13. *Ættartala Haralldz fra Odni*: "The king who ruled over Turkey was called Buri. His son was Bur, who was father of Óðinn, King of the Æsir, father of Njörð, father of Freyr . . ." (Burri hefir konungr heitid er reed fyrir Tyrklandi. Hans son var Burs er var fadir Odins Aasakonungs faudur Freyrs faurdur Niardar faudur Freyrs . . .)

14. Appendix to *Íslendingabók*: "These were the names of the ancestors of the Ynglings and Breiðfirðings: (1) Yngvi, King of Turkey, (2) Njörðr, King of Sweden, (3) Freyr . . ." (Þesse ero nomn langfeþga Ynglinga oc Breiþfirþinga: .i. Yngve Tyrkia conungr. .ii. Niorþr Svia conungr. .iii. Frayr . . .) *Historia Norwegiæ* 9.1–3 gives the same sequence, but names Yngvi as the man "who first ruled the kingdom of Sweden" (*quem primum Swethie monarchiam rexisse*) rather than as "King of Turkey."

15. The synoptic table of these genealogies found in Svend Ellehøj, *Studier over den Ældste Norrøne Historieskrivning* (Copenhagen: Einar Munksgaard, 1965), 114–15, is somewhat misleading, since it omits all figures prior to Yngvi or Óðinn. In the most extreme case (that of *Landfeðga tal fra Noa til varra konunga*), this excises the first thirty-two generations of kings.

16. In the Prologue to *Heimskringla*, Snorri announces his sources and principles of method.

Thjodolf the Wise, of Hvin, was a skald of Harald Hairfair. He composed a poem for King Rögnvald the Highly-honored, which is called the Ynglingatal. . . . In that poem thirty of Rögnvald's patrilineal ancestors were named, and it described each of their deaths and burial places. . . . The history of the Ynglings was first written following Thjodolf's report, and then was augmented following the accounts of wise men. . . . But it seems to me that a poem strays least from the source if it is correctly recited and rationally interpreted.

þjóðólfr inn fróði ór Hvini var skáld Haraldz ins hárfagra; hann orti ok um Rǫgnvald konung heiðumhæra kvæði þat, er kallat er Ynglingatal. . . . Í því kvæði eru nefndir xxx. langfeðga hans [sc. Rǫgnvalds] ok sagt frá dauða hvers þeira ok legstað. . . . Eptir þjóðólfs sǫgn er fyrst ritin æfi Ynglinga ok þar við aukit eptir sǫgn fróðra manna. . . . en kvæðin þykkja mér sízt ór stað fœrð, ef þau eru rétt kveðin ok skynsamliga upp tekin.

In addition to *Ynglingatal*, Snorri seems to have relied on the now-lost *Skjǫldunga Saga* for information regarding Aun's battles against the Danish kings Halfdan and Áli. No sources have been identified for his description of Aun's sacrifices, and this is likely to be his own invention.

17. *Ynglingatal* 15–16, cited in *Ynglingasaga* 25:

Knátti endr
at Uppsǫlum
ánasótt
Aun um standa,
ok þrálífr
þiggia skyldi
ióðs alað
ǫðru sinni.

Ok sveiðurs
at sér hverfði
mækis hlut
inn miávara,
er okhreins
áttunga rjóðr
lǫgðis odd
liggjandi drakk.

Máttit hárr
hiarðar mæki
austrkonungr
upp um halda.

18. Thus, inter alia, Henrik Schück, *Studier i Ynglingatal* (Uppsala: Akademiska Boktryckeriet, 1907), 92–93; Mogk, "Die Menschenopfer bei den Germanen," 614–15; Walter Åkerlund, *Studier över Ynglingatal* (Lund: C.W.K. Gleerup, 1939), 137; Bjarni Aðalbjarnarson, ed., *Heimskringla*, 50; Siegfried Beyschlag, *Die Konungasögur: Untersuchungen zur Königssaga bis Snorri* (Copenhagen: Einar Munksgaard, 1950), 30; Folke Ström, *Diser, Nornor, Valkyrjor*, 49; Claus Krag, *Ynglingatal og Ynglingesaga: En studie i historiske kilder* (Oslo: Norges allmenvitenskapelige forskningsråd, 1991), 67–70; Harris, "Sacrifice and Guiklt in Sonatorrek," 176; Hultgård, "Menschenopfer," 541; and Olof Sundqvist, *Freyr's Offspring: Rulers and Religion in Ancient Svea Society* (Uppsala: Acta Universitas Uppsaliensis, Historia Religionum, 2002), 255.

19. That *áttunga rjóðr* cannot mean "sacrificer of his sons" was first recognized by Adolf Noreen, ed. and trans., *Ynglingatal: Text, översättning och kommentar* (Stockholm: Akademiens förlag, 1925), 234–35. Similar reservations have been voiced by Hilda Ellis Davidson, *Myths and Symbols in Pagan Europe* (Syracuse: Syracuse University Press, 1988), 66; and Olof Sundqvist, *Kultledare i fornskandinavisk religion* (Uppsala: Department of Archaeology and Ancient History, Uppsala University, 2007), 83–84.

20. On the word, see Richard Cleasby and Gudbrand Vigfusson, *An Icelandic-English Dictionary*, 2nd ed. (Oxford: Clarendon Press, 1957), 47 and 760; de Vries, *Altnordisches Etymologisches Wörterbuch*, 17 and 682; on the institution, Kirsten Hastrup, *Culture and History in Medieval Iceland* (Oxford: Oxford University Press, 1985), 72–104.

21. Cleasby and Vigfusson, *Icelandic-English Dictionary*, 500. At one time, numerous scholars, including Sveinbjörn Egilsson and Finnur Jónsson, eds., *Lexicon Poeticum Antiquæ Linguæ Septentrionalis: Ordbog over det Norsk-Islanske Skjaldesprog* (Copenhagen: S.L. Møller, 1931), 285, accepted the suggestion of Konrad Gislason, "Nogle Bemærkinger Angående Ynglingatal," *Aarbøger for nordisk Oldkyndighed* (1881): 226–29 that the *Ynglingatal* text should be emended to read *áttunga *hrjóðr*, thereby naming Aun "uprooter, i.e., destroyer of his kinsmen," a move designed to strengthen the sacrificial associations of the phrase. All manuscripts unambiguously read *áttunga rjóðr*, however, and contemporary scholarship is fairly unanimous in rejecting the emendation.

22. Egilsson and Jónsson, *Lexicon Poeticum*, 469: *farve rød, om den af solen frembragte farve*.

23. Sturla Þórðarson 3.14: *unnar fasti rauð rǫnd* ("fire-reddened shield-edge").

24. *Meyjadrápa* 5: *rjóðandi móðir* ("reddened mother"). Cf. Sigvatr Þórðarson 12.3: *gjǫlnar roðnar golli* ("tears of reddened gold").

25. Lilja (Eysteinn) 25: *roðnust rósa* ("reddened roses").

26. *Háttatal* 64: *roðin merki* ("reddened banner").

27. Arnórr Þórðarson 6.15: *hoddum roðnir oddar* ("reddened gold point"). Four of the eleven examples cited under the *Lexicon's* first definition do seem to have bloody associations, however: *Hákonarmál* 8: *roðínn randar himinn* ("reddened war-shields"); *Haraldskvæði* 5: *roðnar randir* ("reddened shield"); *Helgakviða Hundingsbana II* 49: *roðnar brautir* ("roads turning red"); Markús Skeggjason 1.6: *roðínn hauss* ("reddened skull").

28. Egilsson and Jónsson, *Lexicon Poeticum*, 469: *rødfarve i blod*.

29. *Hamðismál* 7: *roðnar . . . bœkr í dreyra* ("linens reddened in blood").

30. *Guðrúnarkviða II* 22: *stafir ristnir ok roðnir* ("runestaves carved and reddened"). Cf. Egill Skallagrímsson, *Lausavísa* 3.

31. Soil: *Reginsmál* 26: *sa er fold ryði* ("he reddened the soil"); cf. *Ynglingatal* 5, *Gráfeldardrápa* 7, *Óttarr svarti* 2.9, and *Rigsþula* 37. Water: Sigvatr þórðarson 2.11: *ruðu . . . skers fold* ("they reddened the soil of the skerry [= sea]"); cf. *Krákumál* 4.

32. Spears at *Hárbarðsljóð* 40 and *Jómsvíkingadrápa* 10; swords at *Krákumál* 28 Arnórr þórðarson 5.10, *Höfuðlausn* 10, *Helgakviða Hjörvarðssonar* 34, Einarr Skúlason 6.48, Egill Skallagrímsson, *Lausavísa* 30, *Fáfnismál* 1, *Ynglingatal* 12 and 17, Holmgöngu-Bersi 13, *Gráfeldardrápa* 4, *Jómsvíkingadrápa* 17, Arnórr þórðarson 3.1, þórmóðr kolbrúnarskáld 1.4, Egill Skallagrímsson, *Lausavísa* 39, *Háttatal* 13, 41 and 57; unspecified blades and weapon-points at *Grottasöngr* 15, *Jómsvíkingadrápa* 7, Sigvatr þórðarson 2.7, Haldórr ókristni 8, *Grípisspá* 50, and *Sigurðakviða en meiri* 5; shields at *Krákumál* 6, Hallfreðr vandræðaskáld, *Lausavísa* 13, *Hákonarmál* 6, Haraldr harðráði 1 and 12, Skáldhallr 2, *Ólafs drápa Tryggvasonar* 13, *Digt om Magnus lagaböter* 3, Kormákr Ögmundarson, *Lausavísa* 53, *Hákonarmál* 8, *Haraldskvœði* 5, *Háttatal* 54; helmets at Gísli Súrsson 27; chain mail at *Háttatal* 7.

33. Óttarr svarti 1.4: *ulfr ryðr kjǫpt* ("wolf reddened in jaw"). Cf. Björn krepphandi 6, Böðvarr balti 3, Sigvatr þórðarson 7.1, þjóðólfr Arnórsson 3.7, þórkell klyppr, Sigvatr þórðarson 1.12, Einarr Skúlason 7.7, *Njála* verse 7, Sigvatr þórðarson 1.1, *Ynglingatal* 17, *Háttatal* 11 and 96.

34. Hallfreðr vandræðaskáld, *Hákonardrápa* 9: *Sǫrla fǫt verða rjóðask í blóði* ("Sörli's foot became reddened in blood").

35. Hallr Snorrason 1: *gramr rauð granar á fenri* ("warrior's mustache reddened by Fenrir"). Cf. Einarr Skúlason 12.8.

36. *Hálfssaga* 15.4: Yðr mun snimma at sverðtogi hauss of höggvinn, en hals roðínn. ("When swords are drawn, I'll soon be hewing off your head and reddening your throat.")

37. The text of *Hyndluljóð* is not preserved in the Codex Regis and Codex Uppsalensis, i.e., the manuscripts in which most eddic poetry has been preserved. Rather, its sole attestation is in Flateyjarbók, a compendium assembled toward the end of the fourteenth century, containing materials of very disparate date, and the poem itself may include verses of disparate origin. See the commentary of Klaus von See et al., *Kommentar zu den Liedern der Edda, 3, Götterlieder* (Heidelberg: Universitätsverlag C. Winter, 2000), 668–89; and Aaron Gurevich, "Édda and Law: Commentary on *Hyndluljóð*," in Gurevich, *Historical Anthropology of the Middle Ages* (Chicago: University of Chicago Press, 1992), 190–99.

38. *Hyndluljóð* 10:

| | |
|---|---|
| Hǫrg hann mér gerði, | hlaðinn steinom, |
| nú er griót þat | at gleri orðit; |
| rauð hann í nýio | nauta blóði, |
| æ trúði Óttarr | á ásynior. |

39. These examples have been assembled and discussed by Åke V. Ström, "Die Hauptriten des Wikingerzeitlichen Nordischen Opfers," in Kurt Rudolph, ed., *Fest-*

*schrift Walter Baetke* (Weimar: Hermann Böhlaus Nachfolger, 1966), 330–42, esp. 331–34. Two examples cited by Ström seem inappropriate, however: *Völuspá* 41, which describes the gods' seat turning red with the violence of Ragnarök, not as the result of sacrifice, and *Eyrbyggjasaga* 4, where the verb *rjóða* does not appear.

40. In eight of the nine passages cited by Ström, the sacrificial blood is taken from an animal victim. The ninth case is that of *Ynglingasaga* 15, which holds special interest for three reasons: (1) the victim in question is human, being King Dómaldi; (2) this view of Dómaldi as sacrificial victim once again rests on Snorri's misreading of the relevant Ynglingatal verse, as Lars Lönnroth has shown, "Dómaldi's Death and the Myth of Sacral Kingship," in John Lindow, Lars Lönnroth, and Gerd Wolfgang Weber, eds., *Structure and Meaning in Old Norse Literature* (Odense: Odense University Press, 1986), 73–93; see also Svante Norr, *To Rede and to Rown: Expressions of Early Scandinavian Kingship in Written Sources* (Uppsala: Dept. of Archaeology and Ancient History, Uppsala University, 1998), 93–95, 3); although the verb *rjóða* does not appear in the *Ynglingatal* discussion of Dómaldi, Snorri introduces it to his retelling of the story, where he treats an insurrectionary regicide as if it were a sacrifice, saying, "[The leaders agreed] to kill Dómaldi and redden the altar with his blood" (*drepa hann ok rjóða stalla með blóði hans*). It is Snorri's view that *rjóða* could be used to describe an act of human sacrifice—something attested in the surviving work of no other author—that permitted him to misread the *Ynglingatal* account of King Aun in the ways detailed above.

41. The objects that are "reddened" include altars (*Saga of Hakon the Good* 14; *Ynglingasaga* 15; *Saga of St. Olaf* 107), temple walls (*Saga of Hakon the Good* 14), cairns (*Hyndluljóð* 10; *Hervarar Saga* 1), rings (*Viga-Glúms Saga* 25; *Hauksbók* 268), and the hillside on which sacrifice was performed (*Hervarar Saga* 20). Anglo-Saxon literature does include one instance where the cognate verb (*reódan*) is used with a human being as its direct object (*Caedmon* 204.2 [ed. Thorpe]: *réodan magan mid mēce*, à propos of Abraham and Isaac), but nothing comparable is found in Old Norse.

42. As first suggested by Noreen, ed., *Ynglingatal*, 234–35.

43. On the way Christian authors systematically misperceived and misdescribed pre-Christian ritual practices associated with sacrifice and what they characterized as "magic," see Walter Baetke, "Christliches Lehngut in der Sagareligion," in Baetke, *Kleine Schriften: Geschichte, Recht und Religion in germanischem Schriftum*, ed. Kurt Rudolph and Ernst Walter (Weimar: Hermann Böhlaus Nachfolger, 1973), 319–50, esp. 334–40,

44. *Ynglingasaga* 25. The near-synonymous phrase *hann var blótmaðr mikill ok fjǫlkunnigr* ("He was a great sacrificer and magically wise") is used at *Egil's Saga* 37, *Saga of Olaf Tryggvasson* 178, and *Heiðarvígasaga* 19 and has been identified by Baetke, "Christliches Lehngut," 338 as a formula used by Christian authors to discredit the pagans described in that fashion.

45. *Ynglingasaga* 2: "He who was chief in the city was called Óðinn. There was a great place for sacrifice. It was the custom there that twelve temple-priests were noblest. They were supposed to rule over sacrifices . . ." (En í borginni var hǫfðingi sá, er Óðinn var kallaðr; þar var blótstaðr mikill. þat var þar siðr, at xii. hofgoðar váru œztir; skyldu þeir ráða fyrir blótum . . .) *Ynglingasaga* 4: "Óðinn made Njörð and Frey sacrificial priests" (Njǫrð ok Frey setti Óðinn blótgoða). *Ynglingasaga* 5:

"Óðínn built a large temple and he sacrificed according to the customs of the Æsir." (Óðinn . . . gerði þar mikit hof ok blót eptir siðvenju Ásann.) *Ynglingasaga* 8: "[Óðinn established that] one should sacrifice at the beginning of winter for the fruitfulness of the year, and in midwinter one should sacrifice for growth. The third time in summer: that was the victory-sacrifice. In all Sweden, people paid tribute to Óðínn, a penny per person, and he was supposed to defend their lands from war and to sacrifice for them for the fruitfulness of the year." (þá skyldi blóta í móti vetri til árs, en at miðjum vetri blóta til gróðrar, it þriðja at sumri, þat var sigrblót. Um alla Svíþjóð guldu menn Óðni skatt, penning fyrir nef hvert, en hann skyldi verja land þeira fyrir ófriði ok blóta þeim til árs.)

46. *Ynglingasaga* 4: "Óðínn took Mimir's head and anointed it with herbs, so that it would not decay, and he spoke incantations over it and worked a spell such that it spoke with him and told him many secret things." (Óðinn tók hǫfuðit ok smurði urtum þeim, er eigi mátti fúna, ok kvað þar yfir galdra ok magnaði svá, at þat mælti við hann ok sagði honum marga leynda hluti.) *Ynglingasaga* 7: "Óðinn had Mímir's head with him and that told him news from other realms, but sometimes he woke dead men up out from the earth or sat himself beneath the hanged." (Óðinn hafði með sér hǫfuð Mímis, ok sagði þat honum tiðendi ór oðrum heimum, en stundum vakði hann upp dauða menn ór jǫrðu eða settisk undir hanga.)

47. *Ynglingasaga* 6: "He knew the magic arts so that he changed appearance in any way that he wished." (hann kunní þær íþróttír, at hann skíptí lítum at líkjum á hverja lund.) *Ynglingasaga* 7: "Óðinn changed his shape. He lay his body down as if sleeping or dead, but he was then a bird or an animal, a fish or a snake, and he went in an instant to distant lands on his errands or those of other men." (Óðinn skipti hǫmum, lá þá búkrinn sem sofinn eða dauðr, en hann var þá fugl eða dýr, fiskr eða ormr, ok fór á einni svipstund á fjarlæg lǫnd at sinum erendum eða annarra manna.)

48. *Ynglingasaga* 5: "Óðinn had foresight and magical wisdom." (Óðinn var forspár ok fjǫlkunnigr.)

49. *Ynglingasaga* 6: "Óðínn knew how to make his enemíes blind, deaf, or terrified in battle, and their weapons bit no more than wands." (Óðínn kunní svá gera, at í orrostu urðu óvínír hans blíndír eða daufír eða óttafullír, en vapn þeíra bítu eígí heldr en vendír.) *Ynglingasaga* 7: "Óðinn knew about ancient buried treasure, where it was hidden, and he knew the song that opens the earth, mountains, stones, and barrows before him. With a single word, he bound those who dwelt there, and he went in and took such as he liked." (Óðinn vissi um alt jarðfé, hvar fólgit var, ok hann kunni þau ljóð, er upp lauksk fyrir honum jorðin ok bjǫrg ok steinar ok haugarnir, ok batt hann með orðum einum þá, er fyrir bjoggu, ok gekk in ok tók þar slíkt, er hann vildi.)

50. *Ynglingasaga* 7: "He knew how to do [the following] with a single word: to extinguish a fire, calm the sea, and change the wind any way he wanted." (þat kunni hann enn at gera með orðum einum at sløkva eld ok kyrra sjá ok snúa vindum, hverja leið er hann vildi.) *Ynglingasaga* 7: "All these magic arts he taught with runes and the songs that are called magic charms." (Allar þessar íþróttir kenndi hann með rúnum ok ljóðum þeim, er galdrar heita.)

51. *Ynglingasaga* 5: "There was much competition between Óðínn and Gylfi in tricks and magic deceptions, and the Æsir were always the stronger." (Mart áttusk þeir Óðinn við ok Gylfi í brǫgðum ok sjónhverfingum, ok urðu Æsir jafnan ríkri.)

52. *Ynglingasaga* 7: "He had two ravens that he had trained with speech. They flew widely over the lands, and they told him much news. From these things he became greatly wise." (Hann átti hrafna .ii., er hann hafði tamit við mál; flugu þeir viða um lǫnd ok sagðu honum mǫrg tiðendi. Af þessum hlutum varð hann stórliga fróðr.)

53. *Ynglingasaga* 7: "Óðinn knew the art called black magic (*seiðr*), which contains most power, and he practiced it himself. As a result of that, he could know the fate of men and the future of things. He could cause men death, bad luck, or disease, and he could also take the wits or strength from men and give them to others. But when this sorcery is performed, it contains so much sexual impropriety (*ergi*) that it does not seem without shame for males to work with it . . ." (Óðinn kunni þá íþrótt, svá at mest máttr fylgði, ok framði sjálfr, er seiðr heitir, en af því mátti hann vita ørlǫg manna ok óorðna hluti, svá ok at gera mǫnnum bana eða óhamingju eða vanheilendi, svá ok at taka frá mǫnnum vit eða afl ok gefa ǫðrum. En þessi fjǫlkyngi, ef framið er, fylgir svá mikil ergi, at eigi þótti karlmǫnnum skammlaust . . .)

54. *Ynglingasaga* 7: hann kendi flestar íþróttir sínar blótgoðunum; váru þeir næst honum um allan fróðleik ok fjǫlkyngi. Margir aðrir námu þó mikit af, ok hefir þadan af dreifzk fjǫlkyngin viða ok haldizk lengi. En Óðin ok þá hǫfðingja xii. blótuðu menn ok kǫlluðu goð sín ok trúðu á lengi síðan. Eptir Óðins nafni var kallaðr Auðun ok hétu menn svá sonu sína.

55. *Ynglingasaga* 25. The other Yngling kings who are described as having practiced sacrifice are Njörð (*Ynglingasaga* 9), Freyr (10), Dómaldi (15), Dag (18), Egil (26), Önund (34), Ingjald (38), and Ólaf (43), but none is "great," and several are deficient in this regard, most notably Dómaldi and Ólaf, who pay for their shortcomings with their lives. One can probably assume sacrifice for all others until the first Christian monarchs (Hákon the Good, Ólaf Tryggvason, and St. Ólaf), although for most of them Snorri takes this for granted, rather than making it explicit.

56. The name *Aun*, attested in all sources save *Historia Norwegiæ* (on which, see above, note 8), reflects an underlying *AuwinR*, with comparanda in *Aovin* (attested in Einhard), the Anglo-Saxon toponyms *Aun-by* and *Auns-by*, Old Swedish *Auni*, runic Norwegian *auni* (attested at Alstad, ca. 900), and Old Irish *Ona*. The extended form *AuðwinR* also yields Anglo-Saxon *Eadwine*, Langobard *Audoin*, and Old Norse *Auðun* (which presumably underlies *Auchun*, the anomalous form cited in *Historia Norwegiae*). See further Noreen, *Altnordische Grammatik*, 165; de Vries, *Altnordisches Etymologisches Wörterbuch*, 18–19 and 20; Erik Henrik Lind, *Norsk-isländska dopnamn ock fingerade namn från medeltiden* (Oslo: J. Dybwad, 1905–15), 105 and 1278.

57. *Ynglingasaga* 7, cited above: Eptir Óðins nafni var kallaðr Auðun ok hétu menn svá sonu sína. The connection of the names Óðinn and Auðun is a learned construct of a folk etymological sort, without philological value. It appears first in this text, and like the ruminations on the names Áni and Tiundaland that are found in the Aun narrative of *Ynglingasaga* 25, it probably originates with Snorri.

58. Vigfusson and Powell, *Corpus Poeticum Boreale: The Poetry of the Old Northern Tongue*, 523; Noreen, ed., *Ynglingatal*, 234–35; Samuel Eitrem, "König Aun in Upsala und Kronos," in *Festskrift til Hjalmar Falk* (Oslo: H. Aschehoug, 1927), 245–61.

59. Georges Dumézil, *Mythes et dieux des Germains* (Paris: Ernest Leroux, 1939), 57–60; Dumézil, *Mythe et épopée*, vol. 2, *Types épiques indo-européens: Un héros, un*

*sorcier, un roi* (Paris: Gallimard, 1971), 264–66; English trans. by Alf Hiltebeitel, *The Destiny of a King* (Chicago: University of Chicago Press, 1973), 20–22.

60. Capt. Downes alluded to this episode in his Preface to *The Tiv Tribe* (Kaduna: The Government Printer, 1933), which begins as follows: "Soon after I was posted to work amongst the Tiv in 1929, various matters came to the surface in connection with their magico-religious beliefs and mental outlook which left us completely at sea." The nature of this episode was recovered from the colonial files some forty years later by David Craig Dorward, "The Development of the British Colonial Administration among the Tiv, 1900–1949," *African Affairs* 68 (1969): 316–33; see esp. 327–28.

61. Downes, *The Tiv Tribe*, esp. 39–48 and 58–59; Downes, *Tiv Religion* (Ibadan: Ibadan University Press, 1971), 26–46, 54–57, 66–69, and passim; Captain R. C. Abraham, *The Tiv People* (Lagos: The Government Printer, 1933), 25–26 and 66–115. Cf. the somewhat defensive account of Akiga Sai, *Akiga's Story: The Tiv Tribe as Seen by One of Its Members*, trans. Rupert East (London: Osford University Press, 1965; 1st ed., 1939), 235–64; and the more restrained discussion of Laura Bohannon and Paul Bohannon, *The Tiv of Central Nigeria* (London: International African Institute, 1953), 84–93. Capt. Abraham did pioneer work on Tiv and other West African languages, but was temperamentally and theoretically ill-equipped for the anthropology of religion and culture. See further the discussion of Frances Harding, "R. C. Abraham and the Tiv People," in Philip J. Jaggar, ed., *Papers in Honour of R. C. Abraham* (London: School of Oriental and African Studies, 1992), 147–61.

62. Abraham, *The Tiv People*, 73, 91–92, 105–6.

63. Ibid., 73: "It has not been possible to prove ritual killing or eating in a single case and this leads us to believe that these ideas are a memory of what was done in the past but has now been abandoned."

64. Above all, see Paul Bohannan, "Extra-Processual Events in Tiv Political Institutions," *American Anthropologist* 60 (1958): 1–12; and Dorward, "Development of the British Colonial Administration among the Tiv."

65. See the discussion in Laura Bohannon, "A Genealogical Charter," *Africa* 22 (1952): 301–15; Bohannon, "Political Aspects of Tiv Social Organisation," in John Middleton and David Tait, eds., *Tribes without Rulers: Studies in African Segmentary Systems* (London: Routledge & Paul, 1958), 33–66; Bohannon and Bohannon, *The Tiv of Central Nigeria*, 15–42.

66. Such autopsies were traditionally practiced, especially when there were suspicions and accusations aimed at the deceased. Cf. Abraham, *The Tiv People*, 26; Sai, *Akiga's Story*, 241; Bohannon, "Extra-Processual Events in Tiv Political Institutions," 3.

67. Regarding the material nature of *tsav* and the capacities ascribed to it, see Abraham, *The Tiv People*, 25–26; Downes, *The Tiv Tribe*, 39, Sai, *Akiga's Story*, 240–41; Bohannon and Bohannon, *The Tiv of Central Nigeria*, 84–85, in connection with 31–37.

68. On disruptive effects of colonial recruitment for such offices as that of district head, see Bohannon, "Extra-Processual Events in Tiv Political Institutions"; Dorward, "Development of the British Colonial Administration among the Tiv"; Dorward, "Ethnography and Administration: A Study of Anglo-Tiv Working Misunderstandings,"

*Journal of African History* 15 (1974): 457–78; Tesemchi Makar, *The History of Political Change among the Tiv in the 19th and 20th Centuries* (Enugu: Fourth Dimension Publishing, 1994), 118–51; and Baver Dzeremo, *Colonialism and the Transformation of Authority in Central Tivland, 1912–1960* (Makurdi: Aboki Publishers, 2002).

69. On these movements, see Sai, *Akiga's Story*, 264–95; Bohannon, "Extra-Processual Events in Tiv Political Institutions"; and Dorward, "Development of the British Colonial Administration among the Tiv." On witch-finding movements in general, see several of the essays in Jean Comaroff and John Comaroff, eds., *Modernity and Its Malcontents: Ritual and Power in Postcolonial Africa* (Chicago: University of Chicago Press, 1993): esp. Ralph A. Austen, "The Moral Economy of Witchcraft: An Essay in Comparative History" (89–110); Andrew Apter, "Atinga Revisited: Yoruba Witchcraft and the Cocoa Economy, 1950–1951" (111–28); Misty L. Bastian, "'Bloodhounds Who Have No Friends': Witchcraft and Locality in the Nigerian Popular Press" (129–66); Mark Auslander, "'Open the Wombs!': The Symbolic Politics of Modern Ngoni Witchfinding" (167–92); and Pamela G. Schmoll, "Black Stomachs, Beautiful Stones: Soul-Eating among Hausa in Niger" (193–220).

70. Downes's account of the Haakaa movement, *Tiv Religion*, 8–16, is instructive in this regard, as is the contrast between Akiga's discussion (Sai, *Akiga's Story*, 240–89, esp. 240–42) and the commentary of his government translator (East, in *Akiga's Story*, 235–40 and 289–95). For an astute treatment of the tensions, misperceptions, and distortions produced by the asymmetric relation of East and Akiga, see Gaurav Gajanan Desai, *Subject to Colonialism: African Self-Fashioning and the Colonial Library* (Durham, NC: Duke University Press, 2001), 117–23.

71. Cristiano Grottanelli, "Ideologie del sacrificio umano: Roma e Cartagine," *Archiv für Religionsgeschichte* 41 (1999): 41–60, quotation from p. 59. With a few additions, much the same text was published as "Ideologie del sacrificio umano," in Stéphane Verger, ed., *Rites et espaces en pays celte et méditerranéen* (Rome: École Française de Rome, 2000), 277–92.

## CHAPTER ELEVEN

1. Mircea Eliade, *The Myth of the Eternal Return*, trans. Willard Trask (New York: Pantheon Books, 1954; French original, 1949). This same line of argument recurred in many of Eliade's works over the course of the next decade as he was achieving international recognition and influence over the nascent discipline of religious studies. Thus, "Le temps et l'éternité dans la pensée indienne," *Eranos Jahrbuch* 20 (1952): 219–52; "Kosmogonische Mythen und magische Heilung," *Paideuma* 6 (1954/58): 194–204; *The Sacred and the Profane* (New York: Harcourt, Brace, 1959; German original, 1957); *Myths, Dreams, and Mysteries* (New York: Harper and Row, 1960; French original, 1957); *Myth and Reality* (New York: Harper & Row, 1963; French original, 1963).

2. Eliade was hardly alone in such views, and he drew freely on such works as Julius Evola, *Rivolta contro il mondo moderno* (Milan: Ulrich Hoepli, 1934); Roger Caillois, *Le mythe et l'homme* (Paris: Gallimard, 1938); Caillois, *L'homme et le sacré* (Paris: Presses Universitaires de France, 1939); Raffaele Pettazzoni, "La verità del

mito," *Studi e Materiali della Storia delle Religioni* 21 (1947–1948): 104–16; Ananda K. Coomaraswamy, *Time and Eternity* (Ascona: Artibus Asiae, 1947); H. Frankfort and H. A. Frankfort, *Before Philosophy: The Intellectual Adventure of Ancient Man* (Chicago: University of Chicago Press, 1949); Henry Corbin, *Le temps cyclique dans mazdéisme et dans l'ismaélisme* (Zürich: Rhein-Verlag, 1952). The continued influence of these ideas is evident, inter alia, in the essays collected in Natale Spineto, *Interrompere il quotidiano: La costruzione del tempo nell' esperienza religiosa* (Milan: Jaca Book, 2005).

3. Just to cite some familiar examples: Eric Hobsbawm and Terence Ranger, eds., *The Invention of Tradition* (Cambridge: Cambridge University Press, 1983); Maurice Bloch, *Ritual, History, and Power: Selected Papers* (London: Athlone Press, 1989); Marshall Sahlins, *How "Natives" Think: About Captain Cook, for Example* (Chicago: University of Chicago Press, 1995); Sahlins, *Islands of History* (Chicago: University of Chicago Press, 1985).

4. Bruce Lincoln, "Der politische Gehalt des Mythos," in Hans Peter Duerr, ed., *Alcheringa, oder die beginnende Zeit: Studien zu Mythologie, Schamanismus, und Religion* (Frankfurt: Qumran Verlag, 1983), 9–25, reprinted in *Psychoanalyse* 4 (1983): 305–18 and translated into Italian as "Concezione del tempo e dimensione politica del mito," *Studi e Materiali di Storia delle Religioni* 7 (1983): 75–86.

5. The literature on José Antonio is largely hagiographic and philo-fascist. For discussions of this sort, see Felipe Jiménez de Sandoval, *José Antonio (biografía apasionada)*, rev. ed. (Madrid: Editorial Bullón, 1963); Julio Gil Pecharromán, *José Antonio Primo de Rivera: Retrato de un visionario* (Madrid: Temas de Hoy, 1996); Francisco M. Fuentes, *José Antonio: La esperanza en el horizonte* (Madrid: F.M. Fuentes, 2003); Jaime Suárez, *Introducción a José Antonio* (Madrid: Plataforma 2003); José A. Baonza, *José Antonio Primo de Rivera: Razón y mito del fascismo español* (Madrid: Editorial Ciencia 3, 2003); Luis Buceta Facotto, Gonzalo Cerezo Barredo, and Eduardo Navarro Álvarez, eds., *Homenaje a José Antonio en su centenario (1903–2003)* (Madrid: Plataforma 2003, 2006). For more critical perspectives, Stanley G. Payne, *Fascism in Spain, 1923–1977* (Madison: University of Wisconsin Press, 1999); César Vidal Manzanares, *José Antonio: La biografía no autorizada* (Madrid: Anaya & M. Muchnik, 1996); Olivier Grimaldi, *Présence de José Antonio, 1936–2006* (Paris: Cercle franco-hispanique, 2006); and Ian Gibson, *En busca de José Antonio* (Madrid: Aguilar, 2008).

6. The speech was made on the occasion of the Falange's merger with other groups of the extreme right. A translation is available in Hugh Thomas, ed., *José Antonio Primo de Rivera: Selected Writings* (New York: Harper & Row, 1972), 88–97 (the passage cited, 96–97). The original Spanish text is available in José Antonio Primo de Rivera, *Obras completas* (Madrid: Vicesecretaría de Educación Popular de F. E. T. Y. de las J. O. N. S., 1945), 27–36, with the passage cited above at 35–36.

Nosotros no aspiramos a nada. No aspiramos si no es, acaso, a ser los primereos en el peligro. Lo que queremos es que España, otra vez, se vuelva a sí misma y, con honor, justicia social, juventud, y entusiasmo patrio, diga lo que esta misma ciudad de Valladolid decía en una carta al emperador Carlos V en 1516:

"Vuestra alteza debe venir a tomar en la una mano aquel yugo que el católico rey vuestro abuelo os dejó, con el cual tantos bravos y soberbios se domaron, y en la otra, las flechas de aquella reina sin par, vuestra abuela doña Isabel, con que puso a los moros tan lejos."

Pues aquí tenéis, en esta misma ciudad de Valladolid, que así lo pedía, el yugo y las flechas; el yugo de la labor y las flechas del poderío. Así, nosotros, bajo el signo del yugo y de las flechas, venimos a devir aquí mismo, en Valladolid: "Castilla, otra vez por España!"

One can also hear part of the speech at http://www.youtube.com/watch?v = WV65GsRrp00.

7. Elsewhere in the speech, José Antonio acknowledged the influence of the other fascisms, while insisting on the originality and authenticity of his own.

They say we are imitators because this movement of ours, this movement of a return to Spain's authentic nature, is a movement that has already emerged elsewhere . . . but just because Italy and Germany have turned inwards and found themselves, should we say that Spain in search of herself is imitating them? Those countries have returned to their own authenticity, and as we do likewise the authenticity we shall find will be our own, not that of either Germany or Italy, and therefore by doing as the Italians or the Germans have done we will be more truly Spaniards than we have ever been. (*Obras completas*, 94)

8. Buenaventura Durruti, quoted from an interview by Pierre van Paasen that appeared in the *Toronto Daily Star*, August 5, 1936, reprinted in Abel Paz, *Durruti: The People Armed* (Montreal: Black Rose Books, 1976), 312–14. A recording of the interview is available at http://www.youtube.com/watch?v = fooZb3NPHJU.

9. Here, it is particularly interesting to find a biblical allusion of apocalyptic import in the discourse of a confirmed atheist and anticlerical militant, when Durruti affirms with confidence, "We are going to inherit the earth," thereby associating the Spanish proletariat with the meek of Matthew 5.5.

10. The fullest discussion of Durruti is Abel Paz, *Durruti in the Spanish Revolution*, trans. Chuck Morse (Oakland, CA: AK Press, 2007; Spanish original, 2004). See also Robert W. Kern, *Red Years, Black Years: A Political History of Spanish Anarchism, 1911–1937* (Philadelphia: Institute for the Study of Human Issues, 1978), 42–43, 152–63, 176–82, 191–95, 200–207, and passim; Jesús Amal, *Yo fui secretario de Durruti: Memórias de un cura aragonés en las filas anarquistas* (Zaragoza: Mira, 1995); Robert J. Alexander, *The Anarchists in the Spanish Civil War* (London: Janus, 1999), 159–71, 202–14, and passim; Julian Casanova, *Anarchism, the Republic, and Civil War in Spain: 1931–1939*, trans. Andrew Dowling (London: Routledge, 2005); and César M. Lorenzo, *Le mouvement anarchiste en Espagne* (Saint-Georges d' Oléron: Les éditions libertaires, 2006), 77–82, 162–66, 327–31, and passim. The novel by Hans Magnus Enzensberger, *Der kurze Sommer der Anarchie* (Frankfurt: Suhrkamp Verlag, 1972) is well researched and worth consulting, as is the film by Jean-Louis Comolli, *Buenaventura Durruti, Anarchiste* (1999), available at https://www.youtube.com /watch?v = rvm7A3L_j9A.

11. This trend was introduced by Norman Cohn, *The Pursuit of the Millennium*

(London: Secker & Warburg, 1957; rev. ed., 1970); E. J. Hobsbawm, *Primitive Rebels: Studies in Archaic Forms of Social Movement in the 19th and 20th Centuries* (New York: W.W. Norton, 1959); and Samuel K. Eddy, *The King Is Dead: Studies in the Near Eastern Resistance to Hellenism* (Lincoln: University of Nebraska Press, 1961). The most recent general work along these lines is Richard Landes, *Heaven on Earth: The Varieties of Millennial Experience* (New York: Oxford University Press, 2011).

12. The classic work on the Ghost Dance is James Mooney, *The Ghost-Dance Religion and the Sioux Outbreak of 1890: Fourteenth Annual Report (Part 2) of the Bureau of Ethnology to the Smithsonian Institution* (Washington, DC: Government Printing Office, 1896), reprinted as *The Ghost Dance Religion and Wounded Knee* (Toronto: Dover Publications, 1973). Studies prior to 1991 are surveyed in Shelley Anne Osterreich, *The American Indian Ghost Dance, 1870 and 1890: An Annotated Bibliography* (Westport, CT: Greenwood Press, 1991). More recent literature includes William S. E. Coleman, *Voices of Wounded Knee* (Lincoln: University of Nebraska Press, 2000); Jeffrey Ostler, *The Plains Sioux and U.S. Colonialism from Lewis and Clark to Wounded Knee* (Cambridge: Cambridge University Press, 2004), 243–360; Alice Beck Kehoe, *The Ghost Dance: Ethnohistory & Revitalization*, 2nd ed. (Long Grove, IL: Waveland Press, 2006); Gregory E. Smoak, *Ghost Dances and Identity: Prophetic Religion and American Indian Ethnogenesis in the Nineteenth Century* (Berkeley: University of California Press, 2006), esp. 152–205; and Rani-Henrik Andersson, *The Lakota Ghost Dance of 1890* (Lincoln: University of Nebraska Press, 2008).

13. Mooney and Ostler both treat this history at length. See also George E. Hyde, *A Sioux Chronicle* (Norman: University of Oklahoma Press, 1956); Robert M. Utley, *The Last Days of the Sioux Nation* (New Haven, CT: Yale University Press, 1963); Edward Lazarus, *Black Hills/White Justice: The Sioux Nation versus the United States, 1775 to the Present* (New York: Harper Collins, 1991); James V. Fenelon, *Culturicide, Resistance, and Survival of the Lakota ("Sioux Nation")* (New York: Garland, 1998); Jill St. Germain, *Broken Treaties: United States and Canadian Relations with the Lakotas and the Plains Cree, 1868–1885* (Lincoln: University of Nebraska Press, 2009); and Paul L. Hedren, *After Custer: Loss and Transformation in Sioux Country* (Norman: University of Oklahoma Press, 2011). On the years most immediately relevant for the Ghost Dance, see Philip S. Hall, *To Have This Land: The Nature of Indian/White Relations, South Dakota, 1888–1891* (Vermillion: University of South Dakota Press, 1991).

14. James McLaughlin, "Report of Standing Rock Agency," in *Annual Report of the Commissioner of Indian Affairs, for the Year 1890* (Washington, DC: Government Printing Office, 1890), 41. McLaughlin's report continues in the same vein.

> The chiefs who live in the past do not appreciate what is being done for the amelioration of the Indian man by a beneficent Government. The young men are beginning to think for themselves, and to do business as individuals, regardless of the interference of tribal relations or chiefs; and the industrial education, coupled with the patient missionary teaching that is now being pushed forward among the rising generation, if continued, insures their christianization, without which there can be no true civilization. Being now in my twentieth year of continuous service among the Sioux I am able to speak from considerable experience, and a

retrospective view shows most wonderful advancement by them in that period, and, having the utmost faith in the good intentions of a large majority of the Sioux people, I feel confident that if properly dealt with their steady advancement will most assuredly continue, each step taken being firmer and more rapid than the preceding one, until they become a happy and prosperous people, factors in the affairs of this, the greatest nation and freest people on the face of the earth.

15. Andersson, *The Lakota Ghost Dance*, 100–27 contains a good discussion of the agents, their views, and their mission. McLaughlin himself opened his memoirs with a telling description of how he understood the job he carried out over his years as an agent among the Lakota (Devil's Lake 1871–81, Standing Rock 1881–95).

When I entered the service the military arm was the only power that appealed to the Indian. To the men of my time was appointed the task of taking the raw and bleeding material which made the hostile strength of the plains Indians, of bringing that material to the mills of the white man, and of transmuting it into a manufactured product that might be absorbed by the nation without interfering with the national digestion.

James McLaughlin, *My Friend the Indian* (Lincoln: University of Nebraska Press, 1989; orig. 1910), p. 3.

16. Having been responsible for the defeat of Custer in 1876, Sitting Bull (ca. 1831–December 15, 1890) was perceived as the most intransigent of all the "non-progressives." As such, he was an object of fear and deep suspicion, continually vilified by McLaughlin and other white authorities. Several biographies are available, including Stanley Vestal, *Sitting Bull: Champion of the Sioux* (Boston: Houghton Mifflin, 1932), Gary Clayton Anderson, *Sitting Bull and the Paradox of Lakota Nationhood* (New York: Harper Collins, 1996), and Robert M. Utley, *Sitting Bull: The Life and Times of an American Patriot* (New York: Henry Holt, 1993).

17. On Wovoka, see Mooney, *The Ghost Dance Religion*, 764–76; Ostler, *The Plains Sioux and U.S. Colonialism*, 243–56; Grace Dauberg, "Wovoka," *Nevada History Quarterly* 11 (1968): 5–53; L. G. Moses, "'The Father Tells Me So!': Wovoka the Ghost Dance Prophet," *American Indian Quarterly* 40 (1985): 335–51; Michael Hittman, *Wovoka and the Ghost Dance* (Yerington, NV: Yerington Paiute Tribe, 1990).

18. Mooney, *The Ghost Dance Religion*, 820, describes the emissaries as having been selected at a council held in fall 1889, being gone all winter, and returning to make their report at Pine Ridge in April 1890. At p. 819, however, he gives a somewhat different chronology and speaks of two different missions, one in fall 1889, the second in 1890, which suggests some confusion in his sources. For more recent discussions, see Ostler, *The Plains Sioux and U.S. Colonialism*, 251–56, and Andersson, *The Lakota Ghost* Dance, 31–38, the latter with attention to the discrepancy in Mooney's dating.

19. On the early activity of Kicking Bear and Short Bull, see Mooney, *Ghost Dance Religion*, 817, 820–21, 843–44; David Humphreys Miller, *Ghost Dance* (Lincoln: Uni-

versity of Nebraska Press, 1959), 48–64, 69, 73, 77–82, 85–86; Andersson, *The Lakota Ghost Dance*, 38–46 and 106.

20. Mooney, *Ghost Dance Religion*, 843, correctly summarized the evidence of official reports: "All the agents are positive in the opinion that at this time, about the middle of June 1890, the Indians had no hostile intentions." As one example, consider McLaughlin's letter of June 18, 1890, to T. J. Morgan, commissioner of Indian affairs, commenting on rumors that Ghost Dance activity was connected to plans for an insurrection.

> SIR: I desire to state that in so far as the Indians of this agency are concerned there is nothing in either their words or actions that would justify the rumor, and I do not believe that such an imprudent step is seriously meditated by any of the Sioux. . . . There are, however, a few malcontents here as at all of the Sioux agencies who cling tenaciously to the old Indian ways and are slow to accept the better order of things, whose influence is exerted in the wrong direction, and this class of Indians are ever ready to circulate idle rumors and sow dissensions to discourage the more progressive; but only a very few of the Sioux could now possibly be united in attempting any overt act against the Government, and the removal from among them of a few individuals (the leaders of disaffection) such as Sitting Bull, Circling Bear, Black Bird, and Circling Hawk of this agency; Spotted Elk (Big Foot) and his lieutenants of Cheyenne River; Crow Dog and Low Dog, of Rosebud, and any of like ilk of Pine Ridge, would end all trouble and uneasiness in the future. By far the larger number of the Sioux are well disposed and there are at this agency some very reliable and trustworthy Indians whose sincerity and truthfulness is of a high order. . . . I have every confidence in the good intentions of the Sioux as a people. They will not be the aggressors in any overt act against white settlers, and if justice is only done them no uneasiness need be entertained. (James McLaughlin, "Report of Standing Rock Agency," in the *Annual Report of the Commissioner of Indian Affairs, for the Year 1891* [Washington, DC: Government Printing Office, 1891], 328)

21. The text is taken from McLaughlin, *My Friend the Indian*, 187–88 (numbers added; I have also replaced McLaughlin's "ghosts" with "spirits" throughout). The full text of Kicking Bear's speech appears at 185–89 and is also available in Rex Alan Smith, *Moon of Popping Trees: The Tragedy at Wounded Knee and the End of the Indian Wars* (Lincoln: University of Nebraska Press, 1975), 103–5; and Andersson, *The Lakota Ghost Dance*, 309–11. Much the same material is included in McLaughlin's letter of October 17, 1890, to Commissioner T. J. Morgan, which Morgan quoted in his *Annual Report of the Commissioner of Indian Affairs, for the Year 1891*, 125. According to McLaughlin, *My Friend the Indian*, 185, this was a near-verbatim reproduction of Kicking Bear's speech, conveyed to him by One Bull, a nephew of Sitting Bull's who served on the Indian police at Standing Rock. Elsewhere, McLaughlin hints that he used One Bull and others to spy on Sitting Bull (ibid., 184). Later in October, McLaughlin charged One Bull with persuading his uncle to come to the agency for consultations, then dismissed One Bull from the force when he failed to do so, appar-

ently fearing that he was loyal to Sitting Bull (Miller, *Ghost Dance*, 107). For One Bull's perspective, see "Interviews and Statements of Chief Henry Oscar One Bull," Box 104, Folder 11, The Walter Stanley Campbell Manuscript Collection, University of Oklahoma Libraries' Western History Collections, http://digital.libraries.ou.edu /cdm/compoundobject/collection/CampbellWS/id/2903/rec/1.

22. The same pattern is attested in the October 31, 1890, speech of Short Bull, quoted by Nelson A. Miles in his "Report of the Major-General Commanding the Army, Dept. of the Missouri," in *Annual Report of the Secretary of War for the Year 1891* (Washington, DC: Government Printing Office, 1892), 142–43 and reproduced by Mooney, *Ghost Dance Religion*, 788–89. Like Kicking Bear, Short Bull anticipated that whites would be placed beneath the earth ("If the soldiers surround you four deep, three of you on whom I put holy shirts will sing a song, which I have taught you, around them, when some of them will drop dead, then the rest will start to run, but their horses will sink into the earth; the riders will jump from their horses, but they will sink into the earth also; then you can do as you desire with them. Now, you must know this, that all the soldiers and that race will be dead; there will be only five thousand of them left living on the earth") and non-dancing Indians in an airy limbo ("Some of my relations have no ears, so I will have them blown away"). Luther Standing Bear, *My People the Sioux*, ed. E. A. Brininstool (Lincoln: University of Nebraska Press, 1975), 218, reports that Short Bull was proclaiming the same doctrine already in spring 1890. Ostler, *The Plains Sioux and U.S. Colonialism*, 295–96, has questioned the authenticity of the Short Bull text, and the circumstances of its first publication (in the *Chicago Tribune*, November 22, 1890, 2, under the title "Hurrying Up the Great Day") are surely suspicious. Its details, however, are sufficiently close to what we know from other sources that I would see this text as originating in an actual address of Short Bull, but subject to modifications—some accidental and some propagandistic—in the process of its translation and transmission. One of these can be attributed to writers at the *Tribune*, who tendentiously modified a phrase in Gen. Miles's version to better serve their alarmist coverage of events unfolding among the Lakota.

> Gen. Miles text: "Now, you must know this, that all the soldiers and that race will be dead."

> *Tribune* version: "Now, you must know this, kill all the soldiers, and that race will be dead."

I am grateful to Prof. Ostler for discussing this problem with me (pers. comm., July 18, 2013).

23. Traditional Lakota cosmology posited a dynamic, but homeostatic relation among humans, animals, and the land. Buffalo were understood to have originated underground and would retreat there when offended by the conduct of humans, Indian or white. Their return was thus to be expected when humans mended their ways. See further Raymond DeMallie, "The Lakota Ghost Dance: An Ethnohistorical Account," *Pacific Historical Review* 51 (1982): 385–405, esp. 390–92.

24. There is, however, a suggestion of supernaturally assisted defensive violence

in a later portion of Kicking Bear's speech, where he is reported to have said the following.

> And while my children are dancing and making ready to join the spirits, they shall have no fear of the white man, for I will take from the whites the secret of making gunpowder, and the powder they now have on hand will not burn when it is directed against the red people, my children, who know the songs and the dances of the spirits; but that powder which my children, the red men, have, will burn and kill when it is directed against the whites and used by those who believe. (McLaughlin, *My Friend the Indian*, 188)

25. McLaughlin to Morgan, October 17, 1890, as cited by Morgan in his *Annual Report of the Commissioner of Indian Affairs, for the Year 1891*, 126.

26. Ibid., 125–26. This episode has been discussed by Mooney, *Ghost Dance Religion*, 847–48; McLaughlin, *My Friend the Indian*, 183–91; Miller, *Ghost Dance*, 97–105; Hyde, *A Sioux Chronicle*, 255–56; Utley, *Last Days of the Sioux Nation*, 97–98; Utley, *Sitting Bull*, 283–85; William T. Hagan, *Indian Police and Judges: Experiments in Acculturation and Control* (New Haven, CT: Yale University Press, 1966), 99; Smith, *Moon of Popping Trees*, 103–6; Coleman, *Voices of Wounded Knee*, 72–75; and Andersson, *The Lakota Ghost Dance*, 65 and 106–9.

27. McLaughlin to Morgan, October 17, 1890, as cited by Morgan in his *Annual Report of the Commissioner of Indian Affairs, for the Year 1891*, 125 (emphasis added).

> It would seem impossible that any person, no matter how ignorant, could be brought to believe such absurd nonsense, but as a matter of fact a great many of the Indians of this agency actually believe it, and since this new doctrine has been engrafted here from the more southern Sioux agencies, the infection has been wonderful, and so pernicious that *it now includes some of the Indians who were formerly numbered with the progressive and more intelligent*, and many of the very best Indians appear dazed and undecided when talking of it, their inherent superstition having been thoroughly aroused.

28. Ibid., 125–26.

> Sitting Bull is high priest and leading apostle of this latest Indian absurdity; in a word he is the chief mischief-maker at this agency, and if he were not here, this craze, so general among the Sioux, would never have gotten a foothold at this agency. . . . I would respectfully recommend the removal from the reservation and confinement in some military prison, some distance from the Sioux country, of Sitting Bull and the parties named in my letter of June 18 last [see above, note 13] some time during the coming winter before next spring opens.

29. Regarding the arrest and murder of Sitting Bull, see Morgan, *Report of the Commissioner of Indian Affairs, for the Year 1891*, 129; McLaughlin, "Report of Standing Rock Agency," ibid., 334–38; Mooney, *The Ghost Dance Religion*, 854–60; Ves-

tal, *Sitting Bull*, 293–315; John M. Carroll, ed., *The Arrest and Killing of Sitting Bull: A Documentary* (Glendale, CA: A.H. Clark, 1986); Utley, *Sitting Bull*, 295–305; Ostler, *The Plains Sioux and U.S. Colonialism*, 320–26; Andersson, *The Lakota Ghost Dance*, 115–18. McLaughlin's description of the two officers commanding the force sent to arrest Sitting Bull is telling.

> Lieut. Bullhead was an excellent man and very progressive . . . as an officer of police [he] could not brook with impatience the indifference with which the magnanimity of the Government was regarded by Sitting Bull and his followers. . . . Bullhead selected as his chief assistant Shave Head, first sergeant of the force, who was as brave as a lion and had the respect of every Indian of the agency—of the progressive and well-disposed through love, and of the evil-doers through fear. (McLaughlin, "Report of Standing Rock Agency," 334)

30. Ostler, *The Plains Sioux and U.S. Colonialism*, 147–48, 205, 212, and passim has stressed that the categorical distinction between "progressives" and "nonprogressives" was a construction of the agents controlling reservations, and further an instrument they used to divide the population subject to them, advance those they favored, and facilitate the accomplishment of their goals, and his point is well taken. Less successful is his attempt to characterize the sharp differences separating the two factions as a dispute over means, not ends, by people who all sought "to ensure the survival of their people under dangerous conditions" (205). By the same token, one could minimize the difference between Republicans and Democrats, since both seek "what is best for America."

31. Andersson, *The Lakota Ghost Dance*, 20–23, 43–48, 80–81, 272–74, 344n158, and passim, stages a sustained argument with scholars who equate dancers with nonprogressives, whom he understands to follow the agents in this misguided assumption. While the evidence he cites is apt and instructive, the case he makes is also misleading. Although agents did begin with the assumption that the dance was a project embraced (primarily) by non-progressives, repeated incidents forced them to realize that things were not so simple. Some of these were the same episodes Andersson cites, and the agents were not blind to their implications; rather, they helped prompt a shift from confident complacency to rapidly mounting concern.

32. Kicking Bear was a distinguished warrior and holy man of the Minneconjou Lakota on the Cheyenne River Reservation, and Short Bull had similar status among the Brulé Lakota at Rosebud. Both had fought with distinction against Custer in 1876 and were among the last of Sitting Bull's followers to surrender in the aftermath to that conflict. Between 1891 and 1915, Short Bull discussed the Ghost Dance and the events culminating in Wounded Knee on five separate occasions. These texts have been conveniently brought together by Sam A. Maddra, *Hostiles? The Lakota Ghost Dance and Buffalo Bill's Wild West* (Norman: University of Oklahoma Press, 2006), 191–218.

33. Vittorio Lanternari, *The Religions of the Oppressed: A Study of Modern Messianic Cults*, trans. Lisa Sergio (New York: Alfred Knopf, 1963; Italian original, 1960).

34. Eddy, *The King Is Dead.*

35. Inter alia, Steven J. Friesen, *Imperial Cults and the Apoicalypse of John: Reading Revelation in the Ruins* (New York: Oxford University Press, 2001); John Dominic Crossan, *God & Empire: Jesus against Rome, Then and Now* (San Francisco: Harper, 2007); Richard A. Horsley, *Revolt of the Scribes: Resistance and Apocalyptic Origins* (Minneapolis: Fortress Press, 2010); Anathea E. Portier-Young, *Apocalypse against Empire: Theologies of Resistance in Early Judaism* (Grand Rapids, MI: William B. Eerdmans, 2011).

36. The fullest study is J. B. Peires, *The Dead Will Arise: Nongqawuse and the Great Xhosa Cattle-Killing Movement of 1856–57* (Bloomington: Indiana University Press, 1989). The episode has also been recently discussed by Landes, *Heaven on Earth*, 91–122.

37. On the broader history, see J. B. Peires, *The House of Phalo: A History of the Xhosa People in the Days of Their Independence* (Berkeley: University of California Press, 1982), esp. 140–69; Peires, *The Dead Will Arise*, 1–77.

38. On Nongqawuse and her prophecies, see Peires, *The Dead Will Arise*, 78–80, 87–94, and passim.

39. Particularly dramatic is an episode told of Chief Mhala's son Smith (who was tellingly named after Sir Harry Smith, British governor in South Africa from 1847–52, as a means of ingratiation). At a public meeting where his father and all others demanded that he sacrifice his herd to help realize Nongqawuse's prophecy, Smith adamantly refused and went on to explain: "They say I am killing my father—so I would kill him before I would kill my cattle." Note that Smith was Mhala's younger son, unlikely to inherit his father's position. His elder brother, Makinana (named after G. MacKinnon, first chief commissioner of British Kaffraria), expressed disbelief in the prophecies, but sacrificed his animals as a show of loyalty to his father. As things turned out, the stance Smith took sufficiently endeared him to the British magistrate, John Cox Gawler, that the latter recognized him as proper chief of the Ndlambe Xhosa. Peires, *The Dead Will Arise*, 171, 189, 194, and 200.

40. On the categories of *amagogotya* and *amathamba*, see Peires, *The Dead Will Arise*, 158–81 and 315–16; on the conflict between them, 203–14, 289–97, and passim.

41. On the elder figure, see Dilwyn F. Ratcliff, *Prelude to Franco: Political Aspects of the Dictatorship of General Miguel Primo de Rivera* (New York: Las Americas Publishing, 1957); Shlomo Ben-Ami, *Fascism from Above: The Dictatorship of Primo de Rivera in Spain, 1923–1930* (Oxford: Clarendon Press, 1983); José Luis Gomez Navarro, *El régimen de Primo de Rivera* (Madrid: Ediciones Cátedra, 1991); Ramón Tamames, *Miguel Primo de Rivera* (Barcelona: Ediciones B, 2004); and Alejandro Quiroga, *Making Spaniards: Primo de Rivera and the Nationalization of the Masses* (Houndmills: Palgrave Macmillan, 2007). On the family in general, Rocio Primo de Rivera, *Los Primo de Rivera: Historia de una familia* (Madrid: La Esfera de los Libros, 2003).

42. Most fully and correctly, he was Don José Antonio Primo de Rivera y Sáenz de Heredia, 1st Duke of Primo de Rivera, 3rd Marquis of Estrella, and Grandee of Spain.

43. For assertions of an eternal Spain, founded on primordial values of unity and a sense of its destined mission, now threatened by fragmentation under foreign

influence, see Thomas, *José Antonio Primo de Rivera*, 44–45, 54, 56, 58, 60, 69, 73–74, 94–95, 127, 132, 139, 146–48, 176, 177, 205, 211–13, 233, 240–41, 263–64.

44. Regarding faction strife and the threat of national dissolution: ibid., 45, 51–53, 58–60, 89–90, 100–101, 105–7, 126, 138–39, 182–83, 233.

45. Denunciations of Rousseau, Marx, liberalism, and Marxism: ibid., 41–44, 47, 49–53, 68–69, 90–93, 98–100, 124–27, 129, 134, 138–39, 143–44, 146, 150–66, 179–81, 205–6, 231–32, 238–40, 242–43, 245–46, 262–63.

46. Announcing and justifying the use of violence: ibid., 46, 56, 65–66, 124–25, 141, 243, 251–53, 258–59, 262, 263–64.

47. On the need to abolish those organizations and tendencies that threaten national unity and grandeur: ibid., 45, 54–55, 61–64, 107, 130, 133.

48. Idealization of Gen. Primo de Rivera's dictatorship: ibid., 35–40, 108–17; for the establishment of a new dictatorship: 47 (disingenuous), 53 (coded with a mythic reference to El Cid), 64–65, 70–72 (Mussolini), 133, 251–52, 260–61.

49. Thomas, ed., *José Antonio Primo de Rivera*, 96 (emphasis added). In the same speech, similar gestures abound, e.g., "eternal values . . . the solidarity of ancestors and descendants" (88), "Castile . . . gives us an idea of what constituted the Spain we no longer possess, and oppresses our hearts with a deep sense of loss" (89), "we are deprived of Spain" (89), "local separatism is a sign of decay" (89), "there is a tendency to forget that the fatherland . . . is a historic mission: a mission of universal dimensions" (89), "prior to the birth of political parties, peoples and individuals knew that above their own reason stood the eternal truth" (90), "to the century which has given us liberalism and with it the parliamentary parties, we owe the legacy of the class struggle" (91), "liberalism produced before our eyes the most inhuman spectacle of all time" (91), "this movement of a return to Spain's authentic nature" (93).

50. Many authors have treated the way Lakota leaders modified the ideas they took from Wovoka, and Thomas W. Overholt, "Short Bull, Black Elk, Sword, and the 'Meaning' of the Ghost Dance," *Religion* 8 (1978): 171–95 paid attention to the variety of interpretations that circulated among the Lakota. While both of these are relevant to my point, I have something broader in mind, i.e., the way a mythic/prophetic/apocalyptic discourse both shapes and is shaped by the previously latent community that it catalyzes.

51. On this process, in which various chiefs sought clarification and reassurance from Nongqawuse, forcing modifications in her pronouncements and prophecies, see Peires, *The Dead Will Arise*, 72–73, 98–108, 121–22, 145–58.

## CHAPTER TWELVE

1. The standard edition of the Old Persian text is Rüdiger Schmitt, ed. and trans., *The Bisitun Inscriptions of Darius the Great: Old Persian Text* (London: School of Oriental and African Studies, 1991). Darius's account of the events whereby he won the throne is found at paragraphs 10–14. Herodotus gives his version of the story at 3.61–88. The relation between the inscription and the Herodotean text has been much discussed, most recently by M. Rahim Shayegan, *Aspects of History and Epic in Ancient Iran: From Gaumāta to Wahnām* (Washington, DC: Center for Hellenic Studies, 2012).

2. Darius, Bisitun inscription, §13: vašnā Auramazdāha adam xšāyaθiya abavam; Auramazdā xšaçam manā frābara.

3. Herodotus 3.80.6: πλῆθος δὲ ἄρχον πρῶτα μὲν οὔνομα πάντων κάλλιστον ἔχει, ἰσονομίην.

4. Ibid. 3.81.3: ἡμεῖς δὲ ἀνδρῶν τῶν ἀρίστων ἐπιλέξαντες ὁμιλίην πούτοισι περιθέωμεν τὸ κράτος· ἐν γὰρ δὴ τούτοισι καὶ αὐτοὶ ἐνεσόμεθα.

5. Ibid. 3.82.1–5, especially 3 (the critique of oligarchy) and 4 (that of democracy).

6. The scene has been much discussed, including in the studies of Jacqueline de Romilly, "Le classement des constitutions d'Hérodote à Aristote," *Revue des Études Grecques* 72 (1959): 81–99; Patrick T. Brannan, "Herodotus and History: The Constitutional Debate preceding Darius' Accession," *Traditio* 19 (1963): 427–38; G. J. D. Aalders, "Het debat over de beste staatsregeling bij Herodotus (3.80–82)," *Lampas* 1 (1968): 45–57; François Lasserre, "Hérodote et Protagoras: Le débat sur les constitutions," *Museum Helveticum* 33 (1976): 65–84; Klaus Bringmann, "Die Verfassungsdebatte bei Herodot 3.80–82 und Dareios' Aufstieg zur Königsherrschaft," *Hermes* 104 (1976): 266–79; J. A. S. Evans, "Notes on the Debate of the Persian Grandees in Herodotus 3.80–82," *Quaderni Urbinati di Cultura Classica* 7 (1981): 79–84; Donald Lateiner, "Herodotean Historiographical Patterning. The Constitutional Debate," *Quaderni di Storia* 10 (1984): 257–84; Christopher Pelling, "Herodotus' Debate on the Constitutions," *Proceedings of the Cambridge Philological Society* 48 (2002): 123–58; and Edmond Lévy, "Les 'Dialogues perses' (Hérodote, III, 80–83) et les débuts de la science politique," *Lalies* 22 (2003): 119–45.

7. The privileges to be enjoyed by the conspirators and their descendants are detailed at 3.84.1–2.

8. Herodotus 3.83.2: ἐγὼ μέν νυν ὑμῖν οὐκ ἐναγωνιεῦμαι· οὔτε γὰρ ἄρχειν οὔτε ἄρχεσθαι ἐθέλω· ἐπὶ τούτῳ δὲ ὑπεξίσταμαι τῆς ἀρχῆς, ἐπ' ᾧ τε ὑπ' οὐδενὸς ὑμέων ἄρξομαι, οὔτε αὐτὸς ἐγὼ οὔτε οἱ ἀπ' ἐμεῦ αἰεὶ γινόμενοι.

9. Ibid. 3.84.1 and 3.

10. Ibid. 3.87.1: οἱ μὲν φασι τὸν Οἰβάρεα ταῦτα μηχανήσασθαι, οἱ δὲ τοιάδε (καὶ γὰρ ἐπ' ἀμφότερα λέγεται ὑπὸ Περσέων). On the Persians from whom Herodotus collected information and oral traditions, including some critical of Darius and other kings, see Rosaria Vignolo Munson, "Who are Herodotus' Persians?," *Classical World* 102 (2009): 457–70.

11. The Greek form of the name reflects Old Persian *Vau-bara- or (more likely) *Vahya-bāra-, which means "bringing good things." The name occurs several times in the Persepolis Fortification Tablets, including one that reports a certain *Vau-bara (Elamite Mauparra) received shipments of grain "for rations of horses" (PF 1665.5: gal ANŠE.KUR.RA.lg-na). For the philological analysis, see J. Tavernier, *Iranica in the Achaemenid Period (ca. 550–330 B.C.): Lexicon of Old Iranian Proper Names and Loanwords, attested in Non-Iranian Texts* (Louvain: Peeters, 2007), 341, or Rüdiger Schmitt, *Iranisches Personennamenbuch*, vol. 5, *Iranische Namen in Nebenüberlieferungen indogermanischer Sprachen* (Vienna: Verlag der Österreichischen Akademie der Wissenschaften, 2011), 272–73, the latter with greater detail.

12. Herodotus 3.87.1: οἱ δὲ τοιάδε . . . ὡς τῆς ἵππου ταύτης τῶν ἄρθρων ἐπιψαύσας

τῇ χειρὶ ἔχοι αὐτὴν κρύψας ἐν τῇσι ἀναξυρίσι· ὡς δὲ ἅμα τῷ ἡλίῳ ἀνιόντι ἀπίεσθαι μέλλειν τοὺς ἵππους, τὸν Οἰβάρεα τοῦτον ἐξείραντα τὴν χεῖρα πρὸς τοῦ Δαρείου ἵππου τοὺς μυκτῆρας προσενεῖκαι, τὸν δὲ αἰσθόμενον φριμάξασθαί τε καὶ χρεμετίσαι.

13. Summarizing the results of the contest Herodotus states (3.88.1): "Thus Darius, son of Hystaspes was appointed king and all those in Asia were subject to him." (Δαρεῖός τε δὴ ὁ Ὑστάσπεος βασιλεὺς ἀπεδέκτο, καὶ οἱ ἦσαν ἐν Ἀσίῃ πάντες κατήκοοι.)

14. The sun is the first of the deities listed after "Zeus" ( = the Iranian Ahura Mazdā) in Herodotus's account of the Persian pantheon (1.131.2). Solar deities are also attested in the Avesta (Hvar, also Ušah, "Dawn"), perhaps also the Persepolis Fortification tablets (Hvarīra, "Sunset," according to Ilya Gershevitch, "Iranian Nouns and Names in Elamite Garb," *Transactions of the Philological Society* 68 [1969]: 173–74).

15. Relevant here is the Zoroastrian idea of x$^v$ar∂nah ("glory"), the solar nimbus that marks a legitimate king and insures his good fortune so long as he lives up to the ideals of the office. Should he fail to do so, however, by telling a lie or other grave failing, the x$^v$ar∂nah departs and he loses his throne. On this complex image and ideology, see Gherardo Gnoli, "*Farr(ah)*," in *Encyclopaedia Iranica* (London: Routledge, 1983), vol. 9, pp. 312–19 and the literature cited therein.

16. Herodotus 3.85–86: Δαρείῳ δέ ἱπποκόμος ἀνὴρ σοφός, τῷ οὔνομα ἦν Οἰβάρης. πρὸς τοῦτον τὸν ἄνδρα, ἐπείτε διελύθησαν, ἔλεξε Δαρεῖος τάδε. Ὄιβαρες, ἡμῖν δέδοκται περὶ τῆς βασιληίης ποιέειν κατὰ τάδε· ὅτευ ἂν ὁ ἵππος πρῶτος φθέγξηται ἅμα τῷ ἡλίῳ ἀνιόντι αὐτῶν ἐπαναβεβηκότων, τοῦτον ἔχειν τὴν βασιληίην. νῦν ὦν εἴ τινα ἔχεις σοφίην, μηχανῶ ὡς ἂν ἡμεῖς σχῶμεν τοῦτο τὸ γέρας καὶ μὴ ἄλλος τις. ἀμείβεται Οἰβάρης τοῖσιδε. ʽεἰ μὲν δὴ ὦ δέσποτα ἐν τούτῳ τοι ἐστὶ ἢ βασιλέα εἶναι ἢ μή, θάρσεε τούτου εἴνεκεν καὶ θυμὸν ἔχε ἀγαθόν, ὡς βασιλεὺς οὐδεὶς ἄλλος πρὸ σεῦ ἔσται· τοιαῦτα ἔχω φάρμακα.ʼ Λέγει Δαρεῖος ʽεἰ τοίνυν τι τοιοῦτον ἔχεις σόφισμα, ὥρη μηχανᾶσθαι καὶ μὴ ἀναβάλλεσθαι, ὡς τῆς ἐπιούσης ἡμέρης ὁ ἀγὼν ἡμῖν ἐστί.ʼ ἀκούσας ταῦτα ὁ Οἰβάρης ποιέει τοιόνδε· ὡς ἐγίνετο ἡ νύξ, τῶν θηλέων ἵππων μίαν, τὴν ὁ Δαρείου ἵππος ἔστεργε μάλιστα, ταύτην ἀγαγὼν ἐς τὸ προάστειον κατέδησε καὶ ἐπήγαγε τὸν Δαρείου ἵππον, καὶ τὰ μὲν πολλὰ περιῆγε ἀγχοῦ τῇ θηλέῃ, τέλος δὲ ἐπῆκε ὀχεῦσαι τὸν ἵππον. ἅμʼ ἡμέρῃ δὲ διαφωσκούσῃ οἱ ἓξ κατὰ συνεθήκαντο παρῆσαν ἐπὶ τῶν ἵππων· διεξελαυνόντων δὲ κατὰ τὸ προάστειον, ὡς κατὰ τοῦτο τὸ χωρίον ἐγίνοντο ἵνα τῆς παροιχομένης νυκτὸς κατεδέδετο ἡ θήλεα ἵππος, ἐνθαῦτα ὁ Δαρείου ἵππος προσδραμὼν ἐχρεμέτισε· ἅμα δὲ τῷ ἵππῳ τοῦτο ποιήσαντι ἀστραπὴ ἐξ αἰθρίης καὶ βροντὴ ἐγένετο. ἐπιγενόμενα δὲ ταῦτα τῷ Δαρείῳ ἐτελέωσέ μιν ὥσπερ ἐκ συνθέτου τευ γενόμενα· οἱ δὲ καταθορόντες ἀπὸ τῶν ἵππων προσεκύνεον τὸν Δαρεῖον. Later texts also allude to the story, including Ctesias, fragment 17 (Lenfant); Justinian 1.10.3–10; Plutarch, *On the Fortune of Alexander* 340b; and Polyaenus 7.10.

17. For different interpretations, see Alexander Hollmann, "The Manipulation of Signs in Herodotos' 'Histories'," *Transactions of the American Philological Association* 135 (2005): 284–85, who sees the thunderbolt as a heavenly wink at Oibares' deception, and Adolf Köhnken, "Die listige Oibares: Dareios' Aufstieg zum Großkönig," *Rheinisches Museum für Philologie* 133 (1990): 129–30, who sees the shorter version as a "fake variant" (*Scheinvariante*) that provides no real alternative to the main version (*die keine echte Alternative zur Hauptversion darstellen*).

18. Köhnken, "Der listige Oibares," 115–37, esp. 131–32.

19. Wolf Aly, *Volksmärchen, Sage und Novelle bei Herodot und seinen Zeitgenossen: Eine Untersuchung über die volkstümblichen Elemente der altgriechischen Prosaerzählung* (Göttingen: Vandenhoeck & Ruprecht, 1921), 78 and 104–5.

20. C. F. Lehmann-Haupt, "Dareios und sein Roß," *Klio* 18 (1923): 59–64; Johannes Friedrich, "Zur Glaubwürdigkeit Herodots: Das angebliche Reiterdenkmal des Dareios und seine urartäische Parallele," *Die Welt als Geschichte* 2 (1936): 107–16.

21. Georges Dumézil, "Hérodote et l'intronisation de Darius," in *L'oubli de l'homme et l'honneur des dieux: Esquisses de mythologie* (Paris: Gallimard, 1985), 246–53, building on the earlier research of Franz Rolf Schröder, "Ein altirischer Krönungsritus und das indogermanische Rossopfer," *Zeitschrift für celtische Philologie* 16 (1927): 310–12.

22. Originally published as Bulletin 135 of the Smithsonian Institution Bureau of American Ethnology, Matthew W. Stirling, *Origin Myth of Acoma and Other Records* (Washington, DC: United States Government Printing Office, 1942); subsequently republished as Edward Proctor Hunt, *The Origin Myth of Acoma Pueblo*, edited with an introduction and notes by Peter Nabokov (New York: Penguin Books, 2015). The story of the two sisters is found at 1–13 in the Stirling edition, 3–30 in the 2015 edition published under Hunt's name.

23. Stirling, 3; Hunt, 8. The process through which the sisters are gradually differentiated from each other is discussed by Lucien Sebag, *L'invention du monde chez les indiens pueblos* (Paris: Maspero, 1971), 70–72.

24. Stirling, 4; Hunt, 12.

25. Ibid.

26. Stirling, 5–6; Hunt, 14.

27. Stirling, 10; Hunt, 22–23.

28. Stirling, 11; Hunt, 25.

29. Fred Eggan, *Social Organization of the Western Pueblos* (Chicago: University of Chicago Press, 1950), 225.

30. Stirling, 12; Hunt, 25–26.

31. When the sisters were asked to choose clans, Nautsiti answered quickly, while Iatiku hesitated, saying "I wish to see the sun, that is the clan I will be" (Stirling, 4; Hunt, 12). Immediately there followed the incident that determined the ethnic identity of the sisters and their descendants.

When the sun appeared it was too bright for Iatiku and it hurt her eyes. She wondered if Nautsiti's eyes hurt her, too, so she put her head down and sideways, letting her hair fall, and looked at Nautsiti. By doing this the light did not strike her squarely in the face and her hair cast a shade. Tsichtinako [the girls' instructor] said, "Iatiku, the sun has not appeared for you. Look at Nautsiti, see how strongly the light is striking her. Notice how white she looks." And although Iatiku turned to the sun, it did not make her as white as Nautsiti, and Iatiku's mind was slowed up while Nautsiti's mind was made fast. (Stirling, 4–5; Hunt, 12)

32. Stirling, 5, 13 and 29; Hunt, 7–9 and 61. Cf. Leslie A. White, "The Acoma Indians," *Forty-Seventh Annual Report of the Bureau of American Ethnology* (Washington, DC: Government Printing Office, 1932), 64, who states, "The sun (*ocatc*) is a great spirit, perhaps the greatest of all supernaturals."

33. Acoma kinship is matrilineal, and traditional residence patterns were matrilateral, although the latter changed somewhat over the course of the twentieth century. See further White, "The Acoma Indians," 34–40; Eggan, *Social Organization,*223–52.

34. Stirling, 11; Hunt, 26.

35. Stirling, 12; Hunt, 27 (slightly modified).

36. Herodotus 3.88.3: πρῶτον μέν νυν τύπον ποιησάμενος λίθον ἔστησε· ζῷον δὲ οἱ ἐνῆν ἀνὴρ ἱππεύς, ἐπέγραψε δὲ γράμματα λέγοντα τάδε· Ἀαρεῖος ὁ Ὑστάσπεος σύν τε τοῦ ἵππου τῇ ἀρετῇ· τὸ οὔνομα λέγων· καὶ Οἰβάρεος τοῦ ἱπποκόμου ἐκτήσατο τὴν Περσέων βασιληίην.'

37. Stirling, 11–12; Hunt, 26.

38. In his most recent writings on the "stranger-king" topos, Marshall Sahlins has come to argue that many peoples theorize power as radically exogenous, entering their society from the ultimate outsiders: the gods themselves, who thus bestow the most absolute form of legitimacy. Thus, Sahlins, "The Stranger-King Or Elementary Forms of the Political Life," *Indonesia and the Malay World* 36 (2008): 177–99; Sahlins, "The Alterity of Power and Vice Versa, with Reflections on Stranger Kings and the Real-Politics of the Marvellous," in Anthony McElligott, Liam Chambers, Clara Breathnach, and Catherine Lawless, eds., *History: From Medieval Ireland to the Post-Modern World* (Dublin: Irish Academic Press, 2011), 63–101; and Marshall Sahlins and David Graeber, *On Kings* (Chicago: Hau Books, 2017). The present essay extends Sahlins's analysis from the political to the social, from kingship to hierarchy.

39. Herodotus 3.83.3 reports that in his day, nearly a hundred years later, the agreement was still intact: "Even now [Otanes's] family is unique among the Persians, as it continues to be free and is ruled only so far as it is willing, while not transgressing the laws of the Persians." (καὶ νῦν αὕτη ἡ οἰκίη διατελέει μούνη ἐλευθέρη ἐοῦσα Περσέων καὶ ἄρχεται τοσαῦτα ὅσα αὐτὴ θέλει, νόμους οὐκ ὑπερβαίνουσα τοὺς Περσέων.)

40. Herodotus describes the privileges at 3.84.2. Darius signals the special status of these men, whom he describes as "my followers" (*anušiyā manā*), and defines their privileges as heritable, in the Bisitun inscription §§68–69.

41. Herodotus 1.138.1 reports that the Persians regarded lying as the most shameful (*aiskhiston*) of all actions, a judgment consistent with Achaemenid royal discourse, which traced all evil to "the Lie" (Old Persian *drauga*) and depicted a lying king as the greatest of dangers to the moral, political, and cosmic order. See further Beate Pongratz-Leisten, "'Lying King' and 'False Prophet': The Intercultural Transfer of a Rhetorical Device within Ancient Near Eastern Ideologies," in A. Panaino and G. Pettinato, eds., *Ideologies as Intercultural Phenomena* (Milan: University of Bologna, 2002), 215–43; Prods Oktor Skjærvø, "Truth and Deception in Ancient Iran," in Carlo G. Cereti and Farrokh Vajifdar, eds., *Ataš-e Dorun: The Fire Within; Jamshid Soroush Sorouschian Commemorative Volume* (N.p.: Mehrborzin Soroushianm 2003), 383–434; and Bruce Lincoln, "The King's Truth," in *"Happiness for Mankind": Achaemenian Religion and the Imperial Project* (Louvain: Peeters, 2012), 20–40.

42. Herodotus 3.118.1–2. On the symbolic importance of the wounds he inflicted, effectively branding the guards as liars, see Lincoln, *"Happiness for Mankind,"* 220–22.

43. Herodotus 3.119.1–7. On this incident, see Carl Werner Müller, "Der Tod des Intaphrenes," *Hyperboreus* 8 (2002): 222–31, esp., 223–26.

44. For convenient summaries of the ancient evidence regarding the six men, see Jack Martin Balcer, *A Prosopographical Study of the Ancient Persians Royal and Noble c. 550–450 B.C.* (Lewiston, ME: Edwin Mellen Press, 1993), ad loc. More extensively, see Josef Wiesehöfer, *Der Aufstand Gaumātas und die Anfänge Dareios I* (Bonn: Rudolf Habelt, 1978), 168–74; Fritz Gschnitzer, *Die sieben Perser und das Königtum des Dareios: Ein Beitrag zur Achaemenidengeschichte und zur Herodotanalyse* (Heidelberg: Carl Winter, 1977); and Pierre Briant, *From Cyrus to Alexander: A History of the Persian Empire*, trans. Peter Daniels (Winona Lake, IN: Eisenbrauns, 2002), 128–37.

45. Several indications suggest that Vindafarnah/Intaphernes held a position of preeminence within the group and thus represented a special challenge to Darius's supremacy. Thus, Darius placed him first in the list of Bisitun §68, while Herodotus's predecessors credited him with killing the usurper (Aeschylus, *Persians* 776 [with the name given as Artaphrenes] and Hellanikos's scholium on line 778 of the same play [with the name given as Daphernes]).

46. Stirling, 12; Hunt, 27.

47. Stirling, 12; Hunt, 27–28. Actually, the story is a bit more complicated, as the Creator (Uchtsiti) never had direct dealings with humans. Rather, he always dealt with the sisters through a mediator, Tschitinako, on whom see Sebag, *L'invention du monde chez les indiens pueblos*, 25–26 and 35; and Jay Miller, "Deified Mind among the Keresan Pueblos," in Mary Key Ritchie and Henry M. Hoenigswald, eds., *General and Amerindian Ethnolinguistics in Remembrance of Stanley Newman* (Berlin: Mouton de Gruyter, 1989), 151–56. It is this latter figure who withdraws, thereby severing not only his relations with humanity, but those between humans and Uchtsiti.

48. Stirling, 13; Hunt, 29 (slightly modified).

49. Stirling, 12; Hunt, 28.

50. Stirling, 14–46 details Iatiku's work as culture hero; Hunt, 31–86.

51. On Tiamuni, see Stirling, 13, 17, 37–40, 47; Hunt, 31, 37, 74–77, 89, 180.

52. Stirling, 13 (emphasis added); Hunt, 29 (slightly modified).

53. On the painful history of the Pueblos relations with Euramericans, see Marc Simmons, "History of Pueblo-Spanish Relations to 1821," in Alfonso Ortiz, ed., *Handbook of North American Indians*, vol. 9, *Southwest* (Washington, DC: Smithsonian Institution, 1979), 178–93; Simmons, "History of the Pueblos since 1821," ibid., 206–23; Steadman Upham, *Polities and Power: An Economic and Political History of the Western Pueblo* (New York: Academic Press, 1982); Joe S. Sandoe, *Pueblo Nations: Eight Centuries of Pueblo Indian History* (Santa Fe: Clear Light, 1992); Andrew Knaut, *The Pueblo Revolt of 1680: Conquest and Resistance in Seventeenth-Century New Mexico* (Norman: University of Oklahoma Press, 1995); and Richard Frost, *The Railroad and the Pueblo Indians: The Impact of the Atchison, Topeka and Santa Fe on the Pueblos of the Rio Grande, 1880–1930* (Salt Lake City: University of Utah Press, 2016); with a focus on Acoma, see Velma Garcia-Mason, "Acoma," in Ortiz, *Handbook of North American Indians*, 450–66; and Ward Alan Minge, *Ácoma: Pueblo in the Sky*, 2nd ed. (Albuquerque: University of New Mexico Press, 1991).

## CHAPTER THIRTEEN

1. C. Daryll Forde, "A Creation Myth from Acoma," *Folklore* 41 (1930): 370. Although Forde went on to an extremely distinguished career, chiefly in African ethnography, his earliest work was in the American Southwest. This is among his first publications.

2. See Matthew W. Stirling, *Origin Myth of Acoma and Other Records* (Washington, DC: United States Government Printing Office, 1942), vii–viii for a brief description of the collaboration. At the moment the Hunt party arrived at the Smithsonian, Stirling was the newly appointed chief of its Bureau of Ethnology, a position he held from 1928 to 1957; Forde was a postdoctoral fellow, Parsons the foremost authority on the pueblos, and White was a recent PhD who had completed much of the research for the Acoma ethnography he published in 1932.

3. Stirling, vii (emphasis added to identify the points of dissonance with Forde's account).

4. Nabokov's work culminated in his publication of Edward Proctor Hunt, *The Origin Myth of Acoma Pueblo*, translated by Henry Wayne Wolf Robe Hunt and Wilbert Edward Blue Sky Eagle Hung, edited by Matthew W. Stirling, Elsie Clews Parsons, Leslie A. White, and Peter Nabokov, introduction by Peter Nabokov (New York: Penguin Books, 2015), xvii–xxii. In the same year, he published a massive biography of Edward Hunt and his family, Peter Nabokov, *How the World Moves: The Odyssey of an American Indian Family* (New York: Viking, 2015).

5. Stirling, vii. Stirling's insertion of the modifier "theoretically" enacts his attempt to maintain some critical distance from Hunt's (tendentiously overstated) claim. Nabokov was a bit (but only a bit) more guarded regarding the source and extent of Hunt's knowledge: "As a medicine man's son, an initiate into the Katsina Society, a candidate for becoming a healer himself, a member of the hunter's society (for killing a bear), and an initiated sacred clown, Edward's exposure to Acoma's esoteric lore was broader than most." "Introduction," in Hunt, *The Origin Myth*, xxi.

6. On the nature of the Duranes School and Hunt's time there, see Nabokov, *How the World Moves*, 109–23. On such institutions in general, the best treatment is David Wallace Adams, *Education for Extinction: American Indians and the Boarding School Experience* (Lawrence: University Press of Kansas, 1995).

7. On Hunt's assumption of his Anglo name, see Nabokov, *How the World Moves*, 130–32.

8. White, "The Acoma Indians," 32. That Hunt was the dreamer is confirmed by Nabokov, *How the World Moves*, 133.

9. Nabokov provides a detailed account of Hunt's life in *How the World Moves* and a convenient summary in his "Introduction," in Hunt, *The Origin Myth*, xvii–xxii.

10. Stirling, vii. Sixteen of these songs were later published by Frances Densmore, "Music of Acoma, Isleta, Cochiti, and Zuñi Pueblos," *Bureau of American Ethnology Bulletin* 165 (Washington, DC: Government Printing Office, 1957), 4–19. Densmore also reported the details of the collaboration between Hunt, Sanchez, and Wilbert Hunt, who translated the contributions of both his father and his stepbrother (4). See further Nabokov, *How the World Moves*, 2–3, 421–25.

11. Forde, "A Creation Myth," 373–74, 375–76, 378; Stirling, 3, 4, 7, 16, 18, 20, 23, 25, 27, 29–30, 32, 34, 35, 36, 38, 39, 40, 41, 43, 49, 57, 59, 60, 62, 65, 80, 87, 88, 89, 91, 103, 104, 108, 111, 113, 114. On the sustaining power present in and activated through the performance of myth and song, see the remarks of Simon Ortiz, himself of Acoma Pueblo: "What We See: A Perspective on Chaco Canyon and Its Ancestry," in Stephen H. Lekson et al., *Chaco Canyon: A Center and Its World* (Santa Fe: Museum of New Mexico Press, 1994), 66. Also useful are the remarks of Miller, "Deified Mind among the Keresan Pueblos," 154–55.

12. Nabokov, *How the World Moves*, 2. Cf. Nabokov, "Introduction" in Hunt, *The Origin Myth*, p. xxxix (emphasis in the original): "By lending incantation, repetition, and vocal range to prayers and blessings, songs brought these mythic events *into the present*, much as they enabled the story's events to take place as they originally had at the dawn of creation."

13. The "creation song" is mentioned twice, but not quoted, by Stirling at 3. The corresponding passages in Hunt, *The Origin Myth*, 7 and 8 are followed by songs (7–8 and 8–9) that help the sisters emerge from the earth and assist the sun in making its first appearance.

14. Hunt, *The Origin Myth*, 8–9, 14, 17–18.

15. Ibid., 29. This phrase does not appear in Forde or Stirling.

16. Ibid., 30.

17. Stirling, 13 (emphasis added); Hunt, *Origin Myth*, 29 (slightly modified).

18. Hunt had previously served as an informant for Edward Curtis, Elsie Clews Parsons, Leslie White, and other researchers, as discussed by Nabokov, *How the World Moves*, 186, 285, 309, 336–38, 377–84, 402, and 407. Cf. 205–38 and passim on his role as a mediator between pueblo Indians and white visitors more generally.

19. Inter alia, see Hamilton A. Tyler, *Pueblo Gods and Myths* (Norman: University of Oklahoma Press, 1964), 104–5; Lucien Sebag, *L'invention du monde chez les Indiens Pueblos* (Paris: Maspero, 1971); Leslie Marmon Silko, *Ceremony* (New York: Viking Books, 1977); Paula Gunn Allen, *The Woman Who Owned the Shadows* (San Francisco: Spinsters Ink, 1983); Allen, *The Sacred Hoop: Recovering the Feminine in American Indian Traditions* (Boston: Beacon, 1986), 13–29; Alfonso Ortiz and Richard Erdoes, eds., *American Indian Myths and Legends* (New York: Pantheon Books, 1984), 97–104; Ramón A. Gutiérrez, *When Jesus Came, the Corn Mothers Went Away: Marriage, Sexuality, and Power in New Mexico, 1500–1846* (Stanford, CA: Stanford University Press, 1991); Karl Kroeber, ed., *Native American Storytelling: A Reader of Myths and Legends* (Malden, MA: Blackwell, 2004).

20. Fred S. Vallo Sr., "New 'Origin' Publication Is Affront to Acoma," *Santa Fe New Mexican*, September 23, 2015, http://www.santafenewmexican.com/opinion/my _view/new-origin-publication-is-affront-to-acoma/article_7d58156b-7d45-5154 -aaec-36a3829b3d30.html.

21. Seven of the pueblos speak mutually comprehensible dialects that are all part of the Keresan language family. Of these, five are classified as "Eastern Keresan" (Cochiti, Santa Ana, Santo Domingo, San Felipe, and Sia), while Acoma and Laguna are "Western." On the social, cultural, and religious commonalities these commu-

nities share, see Leslie A. White, "A Comparative Study of the Keresan Medicine Societies," *Proceedings of the International Congress of Americanists* 23 (1928): 604–19; White, "The World of the Keresan Pueblo Indians," in Stanley Diamond, ed., *Culture in History: Essays in Memory of Paul Radin* (New York: Columbia University Press, 1964), 53–64; Florence Hawley, "Keresan Patterns of Kinship and Social Organization," *American Anthropologist* 52 (1950): 499–512; Charles H. Lange, "The Keresan Component of Southwestern Pueblo Culture," *Southwestern Journal of Anthropology* 14 (1958): 34–50; Robin Fox, *The Keresan Bridge* (London: Athlone Press, 1967); E. Adamson Hoebel, "Keresan Pueblo Law," in Laura Nader, ed., *Law in Culture and Society* (Chicago: Aldine Press, 1968), 92–116; Julius Miller, "The Anthropology of Keres Identity" (PhD diss., Rutgers University, 1972); Anthony Purley, "Keres Pueblo Concepts of Deity," *American Indian Culture and Research Journal* 1 (1974): 29–32; Jay Miller, "Deified Mind among the Keresan Pueblos," in Mary Ritchie Key and Henry M. Hoenigswald, eds., *General and Amerindian Ethnolinguistics in Remembrance of Stanley Newman* (Berlin: Mouton de Gruyter, 1989), 151–56; and Miller, "Keres: Key to the Pueblo Puzzle," *Ethnohistory* 48 (2001): 495–514.

22. White, "The Acoma Indians," 142. Here and elsewhere I have simplified and normalized the orthography of proper names that White and other early ethnographers rendered with philological precision. Cf. the variant collected more recently by Teresa Pijoan, *American Indian Creation Myths* (Santa Fe: Sunstone Press, 2005), 68–72. The many differences between this text and Hunt's were discussed by Sebag, *L'invention du monde chez les indiens pueblos*, 136–42.

23. On Hunt's dealings with White, see Nabokov, *How the World Moves*, 336–38, 377–84, and the "Autobiography of an Acoma Indian" that White obtained from Hunt and published in his "New Material from Acoma," *Bureau of American Ethnology Bulletin* 136, *Anthropological Papers* 32 (Washington, DC: Government Printing Office, 1943), 326–37.

24. White, "The Acoma Indians," 148n52.

25. Ibid., 147–48.

26. Nabokov, *How the World Moves*, 273–74.

27. Nabokov gives no precise date for the meeting, but it seems to have occurred early in Hunt's residence at Santa Ana. As a direct result of what transpired on that occasion, pueblo authorities informed the Hunts that since they did not participate in the ceremonials that sustained the pueblo, they could not make use of its irrigation system, a decision that marked them as outsiders and made their subsistence rather precarious. Three years later, by Hunt's account, they were ordered to leave the pueblo. *How the World Moves*, 274–75.

28. Franz Boas, "Keresan Texts," *Publications of the American Ethnological Society*, vol. 8 (New York: American Ethnological Society, 1928), 221 saw the shifts at Laguna, which involve not only the reversal of name, but transformation of the sisters into a brother and a sister, as the result of Catholic influence.

29. Leslie A. White, "The Pueblo of Sia, New Mexico," *Bureau of American Ethnology Bulletin* 184 (Washington, DC: Government Printing Office, 1962), 120–21.

30. She claims to be "first" in Laguna A; "greater" in Cochiti B; more powerful in

Laguna B and Sia A and B; and entitled to inhabit the favored direction of the south in Cochiti A. Sia B is the sole case where the two decide to compete without either one having claimed primacy.

31. Ruth Benedict, "Tales of the Cochiti Indians," *Bureau of American Ethnology Bulletin* 98 (Washington, DC: Government Printing Office, 1931), 1.

32. Boas, "Keresan Texts," 6; cf. 225.

33. Ibid., 7 and 225.

34. Matilda Coxe Stevenson, "The Sia," *Bureau of Ethnology, Annual Report* 11 (Washington, DC: Government Printing Office, 1894), 34; cf. White, "The Pueblo of Sia," 121; Noël Dumarest, "Notes on Cochiti, New Mexico," *Memoirs of the American Anthropological Association* 27 (Lancaster, PA: American Anthropological Association, 1919), 215; Benedict, "Tales of the Cochiti Indians," 1–2.

35. Stirling, 11; Hunt, *The Origin Myth,* 25 (slightly modified).

36. Dumarest, "Notes on Cochiti, New Mexico," 214–15.

37. White, "The Pueblo of Sia," 121.

38. Stevenson, "The Sia," 33. Pointed contrasts of Nowutset's size and Utset's intelligence are also made earlier in the narrative (29, 31) and help set up the Magpie incident.

39. This is nearly unique. As discussed above, only in Sia A does the Mother of Indians recruit and instruct Magpie, but this is done in a way that defines it as strategic use of intellectual superiority, rather than illicit cheating.

40. Bronislaw Malinowski, *Myth in Primitive Psychology* (London: Kegan Paul, Trench & Trübner, 1926).

41. Marshall Sahlins, *What Kinship Is—and Is Not* (Chicago: University of Chicago Press, 2013), 21.

42. Ibid., 30.

43. For Herodotus's contrast of Greek freedom to slavery under the Persian king, see Kurt von Fritz, "Die griechische ἐλευθερία bei Herodot," *Wiener Studien* 78 (1965): 5–31; Domingo Plácido Suárez, "La *douleía* en Heródoto: Imperialismo persa y relaciones de dependencia," in *Miscelánea en memoria de C. Serrano* (1999): 681–88; Sara Forsdyke, "Athenian Democratic Ideology and Herodotus' *Histories*," *American Journal of Philology* 122 (2001): 329–58, esp. 341–54; and such passages as 1.6.2–3, 1.120.5, 1.169.1–2, 1.170.2, 5.2.1, 5.49.2–3, 5.116.1, 6.11.2, 6.32, 7.8γ.3, 7.19.1, 7.51.2, 7.102–4, 7.135.1–3, 7.139.5, 7.157.1–3, 8.100.3–5, 8.143.1, 9.45.2–3, 9.60.1, 9.90.2, and 9.98.3. On the contrast of qualitative and quantitative advantages (and cultural orientations), see David Konstan, "Persians, Greeks and Empire," *Arethusa* 20 (1987): 59–73.

44. Herodotus 9.122.2: ἐπεὶ Ζεὺς Πέρσῃσι ἡγεμονίην διδοῖ, ἀνδρῶν δὲ σοὶ Κῦρε, κατελὼν Ἀστυάγην, φέρε, γῆν γὰρ ἐκτήμεθα ὀλίγην καὶ ταύτην τρηχέαν, μεταναστάντες ἐκ ταύτης ἄλλην σχῶμεν ἀμείνω. εἰσὶ δὲ πολλαὶ μὲν ἀστυγείτονες πολλαὶ δὲ καὶ ἑκαστέρω, τῶν μίαν σχόντες πλέοσι ἐσόμεθα θωμαστότεροι. οἰκὸς δὲ ἄνδρας ἄρχοντας τοιαῦτα ποιέειν· κότε γὰρ δὴ καὶ παρέξει κάλλιον ἢ ὅτε γε ἀνθρώπων τε πολλῶν ἄρχομεν πάσης τε τῆς Ἀσίης.'

45. Ibid. 9.122.3–4: Κῦρος δὲ ταῦτα ἀκούσας καὶ οὐ θωμάσας τὸν λόγον ἐκέλευε ποιέειν ταῦτα, οὕτω δὲ αὐτοῖσε παραίνεε λεέυων παρασκευάζεσθαι ὡς οὐκέτι ἄρξοντας

ἀλλ᾽ ἀρξομένους· φιλέειν γὰρ ἐκ τῶν μαλακῶν χώρων μαλακοὺς γίνεσθαι· οὐ γάρ τι τῆς αὐτῆς γῆς εἶναι καρπόν τε θωμαστὸν φύειν καὶ ἄνδρας ἀγαθοὺς τὰ πολέμια. ὥστε συγγνόντες Πέρσαι οἴχοντο ἀποστάντες, ἑσσωθέντες τῇ γνώμῃ πρὸς Κύρου, ἄρχειν τε εἵλοντο λυπρὴν οἰκέοντες μᾶλλον ἢ πεδιάδα σπείροντες ἄλλοισι δουλεύειν.

46. There is now a rich literature exploring Herodotus's nuanced views concerning Greek relations to the other. See, inter alia, Paul Cartledge, "Herodotus and 'the Other': A Meditation on Empire," *Échos du Monde Classique* 34 (1990): 27–40; Christopher Pelling, "East Is East and West Is West—or Are They? National Stereotypes in Herodotus," *Histos* 1 (1997): 51–66; Rosaria Vignolo Munson, *Telling Wonders: Ethnographic and Political Discourse in the Work of Herodotus* (Ann Arbor: University of Michigan Press, 2001); Reinhold Bichler, *Herodots Welt* (Berlin: Akademie Verlag, 2001); and Markus Janka, "Der Vater der *Metahistory*: Konstrukte des Eigenen und Fremden in Herodots Historiographie des Vergleichs," *Gymnasium* 117 (2010): 317–44.

47. For Herodotus's critique of kingship, see such passages as 1.11–13, 1.96–100, 1.120.4–6, 1.129.4, 1.210.2, 3.27–33, 3.65.2–7, 5.2.1–2, 6.32, 7.9.1–2, 7.19.1–3, 7.135.1–3, 8.109.3, 8.143.1–3, and 9.116.3. The fullest treatment, that of Kenneth H. Waters, *Herodotos on Tyrants and Despots: A Study in Objectivity* (Wiesbaden: Franz Steiner, 1971) is unfortunately dated in the kinds of questions it raises and analyses it offers. Far preferable are Bernard Laurot, "Idéaux grecs et barbarie chez Hérodote," *Ktema* 6 (1981): 39–48; John G. Gammie, "Herodotus on Kings and Tyrants: Objective Historiography or Conventional Portraiture," *Journal of Near Eastern Studies* 45 (1986): 171–95; Matthew R. Christ, "Herodotean Kings and Historical Inquiry," *Classical Antiquity* 13 (1994): 167–202; Forsdyke, "Athenian Democratic Ideology"; and Carolyn Dewald, "Form and Content: The Question of Tyranny in Herodotus," in Kathryn A. Morgan, ed., *Popular Tyranny: Sovereignty and Its Discontents in Ancient Greece* (Austin: University of Texas Press, 2003), 25–58.

48. Herodotus 3.80.3–6: κῶς δ᾽ ἂν εἴη χρῆμα κατηρτημένον μουναρχίη, τῇ ἔξεστι ἀνευθύνῳ ποιέειν τὰ βούλεται; καὶ γὰρ ἂν τὸν ἄριστον ἀνδρῶν πάντων στάντα ἐς ταύτην ἐκτὸς τῶν ἐωθότων νοημάτων στήσειε. ἐγγίνεται μὲν γάρ οἱ ὕβρις ὑπὸ τῶν παρεόντων ἀγαθῶν, φθόνος δὲ ἀρχῆθεν ἐμφύεται ἀνθρώπῳ.· δύο δ᾽ ἔχων ταῦτα ἔχει πᾶσαν κακότητα· τὰ μὲν γὰρ ὕβρι κεκορημένος ἔρδει πολλὰ καὶ ἀτάσθαλα, τὰ δὲ φθόνῳ. καίτοι ἄνδρα γε τύραννον ἄφθονον ἔδει εἶναι, ἔχοντά γε πάντα τὰ ἀγαθά. τὸ δὲ ὑπεναντίον τούτου ἐς τοὺς πολιήτας πέφυκε· φθονέει γὰρ τοῖσι ἀρίστοισι περιεοῦσί τε καὶ ζώουσι, χαίρει δὲ τοῖσι κακίστοισι τῶν ἀστῶν, διαβολὰς δὲ ἄριστος ἐνδέκεσθαι. ἀναρμοστότατον δὲ πάντων· ἤν τε γὰρ αὐτὸν μετρίως θωμάζῃς, ἄχθεται ὅτι οὐ κάρτα θεραπεύεται, ἤν τε θεραπεύῃ τις κάρτα, ἄχθεται ἅτε θωπί. τὰ δὲ δὴ μέγιστα ἔρχομαι ἐρέων· νόμαιά τε κινέει πάτρια καὶ βιᾶται γυναῖκας κτείνει τε ἀκρίτους. πλῆθος δὲ ἄρχον πρῶτα μὲν οὔνομα πάντων κάλλιστον ἔχει, ἰσονομίην, δεύτερα δὲ τούτων τῶν ὁ μούναρχος ποιέει οὐδέν· πάλῳ μὲν ἀρχὰς ἄρχει, ὑπεύθυνον δὲ ἀρχὴν ἔχει, βουλεύματα δὲ πάντα ἐς τὸ κοινὸν ἀναφέρει. τίθεμαι ὦν γνώμην μετέντας ἡμέας μουναρχίην τὸ πλῆθος ἀέξειν· ἐν γὰρ τῷ πολλῷ ἔνι τὰ πάντα. Note that Otanes labels his presentation a *gnōmē*: not just an opinion, but a considered judgment based on deep and intelligent reflection. This is the same term used to describe the views Cyrus expressed in the passage discussed above (9.122.4). Cf. the fuller explication of the term offered by Pierre Chantraine,

*Dictionnaire étymologique de la langue grecque* (Paris: Klincksieck, 1968–80), 224: "γνώμη 'intelligence, jugement, décision, intention, maxime,' terme plus usuel que γνῶσις et qui implique à la fois l'idée de connaissance et celle d'avis, de décision prise en connaissance de cause."

49. Ibid. 3.80.1: ἐβουλεύοντο οἱ ἐπαναστάντες τοῖσι Μάγοισι περὶ τῶν πάντων πρηγμάτων καὶ ἐλέχθησαν λόγοι ἄπιστοι μὲν ἐνίοισι Ἑλλήνων, ἐλέχθησαν δ' ὦν. At 6.43.3, Herodotus returned to the question, insisting once again on the reality of Otanes's speech.

Sailing along Asia, Mardonius arrived at Ionia, and then I will relate what must be the greatest marvel for those among the Greeks who do not believe that Otanes declared his opinion to the seven noble Persians that it would be right for Persians to have a democracy: having deposed all the tyrants of the Ionians, Mardonius established democracies in their cities.

ὡς δὲ παραπλέων τὴν Ἀσίην ἀπίκετο ὁ Μαρδόνιος ἐς τὴν Ἰωνίην, ἐνθαῦτα μέγιστον θῶμα ἐρέω τοῖσι μὴ ἀποδεκομένοισι Ἑλλήνων Περσέων τοῖσι ἑπτὰ Ὀτάνεα γνώμην ἀποδέξασθαι ὡς χρεὸν εἴη δημοκρατέεσθαι Πέρσας· τοὺς γὰρ τυράννους τῶν Ἰώνων καταπαύσας πάντας ὁ Μαρδόνιος δημοκρατίας κατίστα ἐς τὰς πόλιας.

50. Ibid. 3.68.1: γένεϊ δὲ καὶ χρήμασι ὅμοιος τῷ πρώτῳ Περσέων.

51. Ibid. 3.68.2–69.6.

52. Ibid. 3.70.1–2.

53. Ibid. 3.70.3.

54. Ibid. 3.70.1–4.

55. Ibid. 3.71.5: ἢ ποιέωμεν σήμερον ἢ ἴστε ὑμῖν ὅτι ἢν ὑπερπέσῃ ἡ νῦν ἡμέρη, ὡς οὐκ ἄλλος φθὰς ἐμεῦ κατήγορος ἔσται, ἀλλὰ σφεα αὐτὸς ἐγὼ κατερέω πρὸς τὸν Μάγον.

56. Herodotus 1.136.2 identifies truth as the central principle of Persian morality and at 1.138.1 identifies lying as the most shameful sin. This is consistent with deep principles of Indo-Iranian ethics and cosmology, on which see Prods Oktor Skjærvø, "Truth and Deception in Ancient Iran," in Carlo G. Cereti and Farrokh Vajifdar, eds., *Ataš-e Dorun: The Fire Within; Jamshid Soroush Soroushian Commemorative Volume* (N.p.: Mehrborzin Soroushian, 2003), 383–434.

57. Herodotus 3.72.4–5: ἔνθα γάρ τι δεῖ ψεῦδος λέγεσθαι, λεγέσθω. τοῦ γὰρ αὐτοῦ γλιχόμεθα οἵ τε ψευδόμενοι καὶ οἱ τῇ ἀληθείῃ διαχρεώμενοι. οἱ μέν γε ψεύδονται τότε ἐπεάν τι μέλλωσι τοῖσι ψεύδεσι πείσαντες κερδήσεσθαι, οἱ δ' ἀληθίζονται ἵνα τῇ ἀληθείῃ ἐπισπάσωνται κέρδος καί τι μᾶλλόν σφι ἐπιτράπηται. οὕτω οὐ ταὐτὰ ἀσκέοντες τὠυτοῦ περιεχόμεθα. εἰ δὲ μηδὲν κερδήσεσθαι μέλλοιεν, ὁμοίως ἂν ὅ τε ἀληθιζόμενος ψευδὴς εἴη καὶ ὁ ψευδόμενος ἀληθής. On this scene, which he rightly characterizes as "l'apologie du mensonge," see Pascale Giovannelli-Jouanna, "La ruse et le mensonge dans la représentation du pouvoir chez Hérodote," in Hélène Olivier, Pascale Giovannelli-Jouanna, and François Bérard, eds., *Ruses, secrets et mensonges chez les historiens grecs et latins* (Lyon: Université Jean Moulin, 2006), 65–83, esp. 69–71.

58. Herodotus 3.73.1–3.

59. En route to the palace, Otanes once more attempts to persuade the others to delay and initially enjoys the support of some others who are described as "those around Otanes" (*hoi amphi ton Otanēn*) and contrasted to "those around Darius" (*hoi amphi ton Dareion*). The appearance of a bird omen, however, persuades all the conspirators to make the assault. Herodotus 3.76.2–3.

60. Darius, Bisitun inscription §63:

> Proclaims Darius the King: For this reason the Wise Lord bore me aid, he and the other gods that are: Because I was not vulnerable to deception, I was not a liar, I was not a doer-of-deceit, neither I nor my lineage. I conducted myself according to rectitude. I did deceit neither to the lowly nor to the powerful.

θāti Dārayavauš xšāyaθiya: avahyarādimaị Auramazdā upastām abara utā aniyāha bagāha, tayaị hanti; yaθā naị arīka āham, naị drauujana āham, naị zūrakara āham, naị adam naịmaị taumā. upari r̥štām upariyāyam. naị škauθim naị tunuvantam zūra akunavam.

61. Ibid., §13 (emphasis added): θāti Dārayavauš xšāyaθiya: *naị āha martiya naị Pārsa naị Māda naị amāxam taumāyā kašci,* haya avam Gaumātam tayam magum xšaçam dītam caxriyā. kārašim hacā dr̥šam atr̥sa . . . *kašci naị adr̥šnauš* cišci θanstanaị pari Gaumātam tayam magum, *yātā adam ārsam.* pasāva adam Auramazdām patiyāvanhyaị. Auramazdāmaị upastām abara. Bāgayādaịš māhya 10 raucabiš θakatā āha; avaθā adam *hadā kamnaịbiš martiyaịbiš* avam Gaumātam tayam magum avājanam utā tayaị̆šaị fratamā martiyā anušiyā āhantā.

# BIBLIOGRAPHY

Aalders, G. J. D. 1968. "Het debat over de beste staatsregeling bij Herodotus (3.80–82)." *Lampas* 1: 45–57.

Abaev, V. I. 1956. "Skifskiy byt' i reforma Zoroastra." *Archiv Orientalnì* 24: 23–56.

———. 1958–89. *Istoriko-etimologičeskij slovar' osetinskogo iazyka.* Leningrad: Akademij Nauk SSSR.

———. 1975. "Zoroastr i Skify." In *Monumentum H. S. Nyberg,* 3: 1–12. Leiden: E.J. Brill.

Abraham, Captain R. C. 1933. *The Tiv People.* Lagos: The Government Printer.

Accademici della Crusca. 1741. *Vocabolario degli Accademici della Crusca. Volume Quarto: Q-S.* Venice: Francesco Pitteri.

Aðalbjarnarson, Bjarni, ed. 1941. *Snorri Sturluson, Heimskringla.* Reykjavík: Hið Íslenzka Fornritafélag.

Adams, David Wallace. 1995. *Education for Extinction: American Indians and the Boarding School Experience.* Lawrence: University Press of Kansas.

Åkerlund, Walter. 1939. *Studier över Ynglingatal.* Lund: C.W.K. Gleerup.

Alekseyev, A. Yu. 2005. "Scythian Kings and 'Royal' Burial-Mounds of the Fifth and Fourth Centuries BC." In David Braund, ed., *Scythians and Greeks: Cultural Interactions in Scythia, Athens, and the Early Roman Empire,* 39–55. Exeter: University of Exeter Press.

Alexander, Robert J. 1999. *The Anarchists in the Spanish Civil War.* London: Janus.

Allen, Paula Gunn. 1983. *The Woman Who Owned the Shadows.* San Francisco: Spinsters Ink.

———. 1986. *The Sacred Hoop: Recovering the Feminine in American Indian Traditions.* Boston: Beacon.

Aly, Wolf. 1921. *Volksmärchen, Sage und Novelle bei Herodot und seinen Zeitgenossen: Eine Untersuchung über die volkstümlichen Elemente der altgriechischen Prosaerzählung.* Göttingen: Vandenhoeck & Ruprecht.

Amal, Jesús. 1995. *Yo fui secretario de Durruti: Memórias de un cura aragonés en las filas anarquistas.* Zaragoza: Mira.

Ammon, Laura. 2012. *Work Useful to Religion and the Humanities: A History of the Comparative Method in the Study of Religion from Las Casas to Tylor.* Eugene, OR: Pickwick.

Amouzgar, Jaleh, and Ahmad Tafazzoli, eds. 2000. *Le cinquième livre du Dēnkard*. Paris: Association pour l'avancement des études iraniennes.

Anderson, Gary Clayton. 1996. *Sitting Bull and the Paradox of Lakota Nationhood*. New York: Harper Collins.

Andersson, Rani-Henrik. 2008. *The Lakota Ghost Dance of 1890*. Lincoln: University of Nebraska Press.

Andersson, Theodore. 1984. "The Thief in Beowulf." *Speculum* 59: 493–508.

Anonymous. 1835. "Nothing of a Leader." *London Medical and Surgical Journal* 7 (July 25): 825–26.

Anonymous [μ]. 1838. "Revelations of a 'Clairvoyant'." *New Monthly Magazine and Humorist* 53: 301–9.

Antes, Peter, Armin Geertz, and R. R. Warne, eds. 2004. *New Approaches to the Study of Religion*. Vol. 2, *Textual, Comparative, Sociological, and Cognitive Approaches*. Berlin: W. de Gruyter.

Apter, Andrew. 1993. "Atinga Revisited: Yoruba Witchcraft and the Cocoa Economy, 1950–1951." In Jean Comaroff and John Comaroff, eds., *Modernity and Its Malcontents: Ritual and Power in Postcolonial Africa*, 111–28. Chicago: University of Chicago Press.

Armayor, O. Kimball. 1978. "Did Herodotus Ever Go to the Black Sea?" *Harvard Studies in Classical Philology* 82: 45–62.

Aston, T. H. 1971. "*Past and Present*, Numbers 1–50." *Past and Present* 50: 3.

Asumssen, Jes P. 1974. "Some Remarks on Sasanian Demonology." In *Commémoration Cyrus: Actes du Congrès de Shiraz*, 236–41. Leiden: E.J. Brill.

———. 1987. "*Āz*, Iranian Demon known from Zoroastrian, Zurvanite, and, Especially, Manichaean Sources." In *Encyclopaedia Iranica*, 3: 168–69. London: Routledge.

Auslander, Mark. 1993. "'Open the Wombs!': The Symbolic Politics of Modern Ngoni Witchfinding." In Jean Comaroff and John Comaroff, eds., *Modernity and Its Malcontents: Ritual and Power in Postcolonial Africa*, 167–92. Chicago: University of Chicago Press.

Austen, Ralph A. 1993. "The Moral Economy of Witchcraft: An Essay in Comparative History." In Jean Comaroff and John Comaroff, eds., *Modernity and Its Malcontents: Ritual and Power in Postcolonial Africa*, 89–110. Chicago: University of Chicago Press.

Backhaus, Wilhelm. 1976. "Der Hellenen-Barbaren-Gegensatz und die hippokratische Schrift περὶ ἀέρων ὡδάτων τόπων." *Historia* 25: 170–85.

Bäckman, Louise, and Åke Hultkrantz. 1978. *Studies in Lapp Shamanism*. Stockholm: Almqvist & Wiksell.

Baetke, Walter. 1973. "Christliches Lehngut in der Sagareligion." In Walter Baetke, *Kleine Schriften: Geschichte, Recht und Religion in germanischem Schriftum*, ed. Kurt Rudolph and Ernst Walter, 319–50. Weimar: Hermann Böhlaus Nachfolger.

Baeumler, Alfred. 1934. *Männerbund und Wissenschaft*. Berlin: Junker & Dünnhaupt.

Bailey, H. W. 1953. "Analecta Indoscythica." *Journal of the Royal Asiatic Society*, 95–116.

Baker, Peter S. 2013. *Honour, Exchange, and Violence in "Beowulf."* Cambridge: D.S. Brewer.

Balcer, Jack Martin. 1993. *A Prosopographical Study of the Ancient Persians Royal and Noble, c. 550–450 B.C.* Lewiston, ME: Edwin Mellen Press.

Ballabriga, Alain. 1986. "Les eunuques scythes et leurs femmes: Stérilité des femmes et impuissance des hommes en Scythie selon le traité hippocratique *des airs.*" *Métis* 1: 121–39.

Bandy, Stephen C. 1973. "Cain, Grendel, and the Giants of *Beowulf.*" *Papers on Language and Literature* 9: 235–49.

Baonza, José A. 2003. *José Antonio Primo de Rivera: Razón y Mito del fascismo español.* Madrid: Editorial Ciencia 3.

Barbara, Sébastien. 2011. "Encore sur le mythe de royauté des scythes d'après le *logos skythikos* d'Hérodote (IV, 5–7) et le problème des sources du *scythicos logos* d'Hérodote." In Sébastien Barbara, Michel Mazoyer, and Jain Meurant, *Figures royales des mondes anciens*, 31–57. Paris: Harmattan.

Bartholomae, Christian. 1904. *Altiranische Wörterbuch.* Reprint, Berlin: Walter de Gruyter, 1961.

Bastian, Misty L. 1993. "'Bloodhounds Who Have No Friends': Witchcraft and Locality in the Nigerian Popular Press." In Jean Comaroff and John Comaroff, eds., *Modernity and Its Malcontents: Ritual and Power in Postcolonial Africa*, 129–66. Chicago: University of Chicago Press.

Baumann, Hermann. 1927a. "Die Kunst der afrikanischen Naturvölker." *Übersee- und Kolonialzeitung* 40: 378–79.

———. 1927b. "Die materielle Kultur der Mangbetu und Azande." *Baessler Archiv* 11: 3–129.

———. 1927c. "Vaterrecht und Mutterrecht in Afrika." *Zeitschrift für Ethnologie* 58: 62–161.

———. 1928a. "The Division of Work according to Sex in African Hoe-Culture." *Africa* 1: 289–319.

———. 1928b. "Likundu: Die Sektion der Zauberkraft." *Zeitschrift für Völkerkunde* 60: 75–85.

———. 1929a. "Afrikanisches Kunstgewerbe." In H. T. Bossert, ed., *Geschichte des Kunstgewerbes aller Zeiten und Völker*, 2: 51–148. Berlin: Wasmuth.

———. 1929b. "Die Kunst der Primitiven." In Hermann Gunkel and Leopold Zscharnack, eds., *Die Religion in Geschichte und Gegenwart*, 1383–85. Tübingen: J.C.B. Mohr.

———. 1931a. "Negerbauten." In *Wasmuth's Lexikon der Baukunst* 3: 671–73. Berlin: E. Wasmuth.

———. 1931b. "Ein Volk des Mutterrechts." *Woche* 15: 103–5.

———. 1932a. "Bénin." *Cahiers d'Art* 7: 1–7.

———. 1932b. "Junglingsweihe: Missionare beschneiden ihre Zöglinge." *Die Umschau* 36: 426–29.

———. 1932c. "Die Mannbarkeitsfeiern bei den Tsokwe." *Baessler Archiv* 15: 1–54.

———. 1934a. "Die afrikanischen Kulturkreise." *Africa* 7: 129–39.

——. 1934b. *Vom Grabstock zum Pflug: Frühformen des Bodenbaues.* Berlin: Museum für Völkerkunde.

——. 1936. *Schöpfung und Urzeit des Menschen im Mythus der afrikanischen Völker.* Reprint, Berlin: Dietrich Reimer, 1964.

——, ed. 1941–44. "Koloniale Völkerkunde: In Zusammenarbeit mit der Kolonialwissenschaftlichen Abteilung des Reichsforschungsrates in der deutschen Forschungsgemeinschaft." *Wiener Beiträge zur Kulturgeschichte und Linguistik* 6.

——. 1955. *Das doppelte Geschlecht: Ethnologische Studien zur Bisexualität in Ritus und Mythos.* Reprint, Berlin: Dietrich Reimer, 1986.

Baumann, Hermann, et al. 1943. *Koloniale Völkerkunde, koloniale Sprachforschung, koloniale Rassenforschung: Berichte über die Arbeitstagung im Januar 1943 in Leipzig.* Berlin: Dietrich Reimer.

Baumann, Hermann, Richard Thurnwald, and Diedrich Westermann. 1940. *Völkerkunde von Afrika: Mit besonderer Berücksichtigung der kolonialen Aufgabe.* Essen: Essener Verlangsanstalt.

Bazelmans, Jos. 1999. *By Weapons Made Worthy: Lords, Retainers, and Their Relationship in "Beowulf."* Amsterdam: Amsterdam University Press.

Beck, Heinrich. 1970. "Germanische Menschenopfer in der literarischen Überlieferung." *Abhandlungen der Akademie der Wissenschaften in Göttingen, Philologisch-historische Klasse* 74: 240–58.

Beck, Inga. 1967. "Studien zur Erscheinungsform des heidnischen Opfers nach altnordischen Quellen." PhD diss., Ludwig Maximillians Universität.

Beltrammetti, Anna. 1986. *Erodoto, una storia governata dal discorso: Il racconto morale come una forma di memoria.* Florence: La Nuova Italia.

Ben-Ami, Shlomo. 1983. *Fascism from Above: The Dictatorship of Primo de Rivera in Spain, 1923–1930.* Oxford: Clarendon Press.

Benedict, Ruth. 1931. "Tales of the Cochiti Indians." *Bureau of American Ethnology Bulletin* 98. Washington, DC: Government Printing Office.

Benjamin, Walter. 2003. *Selected Writings.* Vol. 4, *1938–1940.* Ed. Howard Eiland and Michael W. Jennings. Cambridge, MA: Belknap Press of Harvard University Press.

Benveniste, Émile. 1938. "Traditions indo-iraniennes sur les classes sociales." *Journal Asiatique* 230: 530–37.

——. 1959. *Études sur la langue ossète.* Paris: C. Klincksieck.

——. 1964. "Sur la terminologie iranienne du sacrifice." *Journal Asiatique* 252: 45–58.

——. 1969. *Le vocabulaire des institutions indo-européennes.* 2 vols. Paris: Éditions de Minuit.

Berger, Adriana. 1989. "Fascism and Religion in Romania." *Annals of Scholarship* 6: 455–65.

——. 1994. "Mircea Eliade, Romanian Fascism, and the History of Religions in the United States." In Nancy Harrowitz, ed., *Tainted Greatness: Antisemitism and Cultural Heroes,* 51–74. Philadelphia: Temple University Press.

Bernal, Martin. 1987. *Black Athena: The Afroasiatic Roots of Classical Civilization.*

Vol. 1, *The Fabrication of Ancient Greece, 1785–1985*. New Brunswick, NJ: Rutgers University Press.

Beyschlag, Siegfried. 1950. *Die Konungasögur: Untersuchungen zur Königssaga bis Snorri*. Copenhagen: Einar Munksgaard.

Bichler, Reinhold. 2000. *Herodots Welt: Der Aufbau der Historie am Bild der fremden Länder und Völker, ihrer Zivilisation und ihrer Geschichte*. Berlin: Akademie Verlag.

Bickerman, Elias J. 1952. "Origines Gentium." *Classical Philology* 47: 65–81.

Birlinger, Anton. 1888. *Augustin Lercheimer und seine Schrift wider den Hexenwahn*. Strassburg: J.H.E. Heitz.

Blawatsky, W. D., and G.,A. Kochélenko. 1978. "Quelques traits de la religion des scythes." In *Hommages à M. J. Vermaseren*, 1: 60–66. Leiden: E.J. Brill.

Blécourt, Willem de. 2007a. "A Journey to Hell: Reconsidering the Livonian 'Werewolf'." *Magic, Ritual, and Witchcraft* 2: 49–67.

———. 2007b. "The Return of the Sabbat: Mental Archaeologies, Conjectural Histories, or Political Mythologies." In Jonathan Barry and Owen Davies, eds., *Palgrave Advances in Witchcraft Historiography*, 125–45. Houndmills: Palgrave Macmillan.Bloch, Maurice. 1989. *Ritual, History, and Power: Selected Papers*. London: Athlone Press.

Blüher, Hans. 1921. *Die Rolle der Erotik in der männlichen Gesellschaft: Eine Theorie der menschlichen Staatsbildung nach Wesen und Wert*. Jena: Eugen Diederich.

Boas, Franz. 1928. *Keresan Texts*. Publications of the American Ethnological Society, vol. 8. New York: American Ethnological Society.

Bockhorn, Olaf. 1994. "The Battle for the '*Ostmark*': Nazi Folklore in Austria." In James R. Dow and Hannjost Lixfeld, eds., *The Nazification of an Academic Discipline: Folklore in the Third Reich*, 135–55. Bloomington: Indiana University Press.

Boekhoven, Jeroen W. 2011. *Genealogies of Shamanism: Struggles for Power, Charisma, and Authority*. Groningen: Barkhuis.

Bœspflug, François, and Françoise Dunand, eds. 1997. *Le comparatisme en histoire des religions*. Paris: Cerf.

Bogoras, Waldemar. 1907. *The Chukchee*. Memoirs of the American Museum of Natural History 11. New York: G. E. Stechert.

Bohannon, Laura. 1952. "A Genealogical Charter." *Africa* 22: 301–15.

———. 1958. "Political Aspects of Tiv Social Organisation." In John Middleton and David Tait, eds., *Tribes without Rulers: Studies in African Segmentary Systems*, 33–66. London: Routledge & Paul.

Bohannon, Laura, and Paul Bohannon. 1953. *The Tiv of Central Nigeria*. London: International African Institute.

Bohannan, Paul. 1958. "Extra-Processual Events in Tiv Political Institutions." *American Anthropologist* 60: 1–12.

Bolton, J. D. P. 1962. *Aristeas of Proconnesus*. Oxford: Clarendon Press.

Bosworth, Joseph, and T. Northcote Toller. 1898. *An Anglo-Saxon Dictionary*. Oxford: Oxford University Press.

Boulhosa, Patricia Pires. 2005. *Icelanders and the Kings of Norway*. Leiden: E.J. Brill.

Bourdieu, Pierre. 1977. *Outline of a Theory of Practice*. Trans. Richard Nice. Cambridge: Cambridge University Press.

———. 1998. *Practical Reason: On the Theory of Action*. Trans. Richard Nice. Stanford, CA: Stanford University Press.

Bowman, Ronald. 1970. *Aramaic Ritual Texts from Persepolis*. Chicago: Oriental Institute.

Bowra, C. M. 1956. "A Fragment of the Arimaspea." *Classical Quarterly* 6: 1–10.

Boyce, Mary. 1975. *A History of Zoroastrianism*. Vol. 1, *The Early Period*. Leiden: E.J. Brill.

———. 1989. "*Ātaš*." In *Encyclopaedia Iranica*, 3: 1–5. London: Routledge.

Bradley, Henry. 1901. *A New English Dictionary on Historical Principles*. Vol. 4, *F-G*. Ed. James A. H. Murray. Oxford: Clarendon Press.

Brandenstein, Wilhelm. 1953–55. "Die Abstammungssagen der Skythen." *Wiener Zeitschrift für die Kunde des Morgenlands* 52: 183–211.

Brandenstein, Wilhelm, and Manfred Mayrhofer. 1964. *Handbuch des Altpersischen*. Wiesbaden: Otto Harrassowitz.

Brandewie, Ernest. 1990. *When Giants Walked the Earth: The Life and Times of Wilhelm Schmidt, SVD*. Fribourg: University Press.

Brannan, Patrick T. 1963. "Herodotus and History: The Constitutional Debate preceding Darius' Accession." *Traditio* 19: 427–38.

Braun, Jürgen. 1995. *Eine deutsche Karriere: Die Biographie des Ethnologen Hermann Baumann (1902–1972)*. Munich: Akademischer Verlag.

Braund, David, ed. 2005. *Scythians and Greeks: Cultural Interactions in Scythia, Athens, and the Early Roman Empire*. Exeter: University of Exeter Press.

———. 2008. "Royal Scythians and the Slave-Trade in Herodotus' Scythia." *Antichthon* 42: 1–19.

Braund, David, and S. D. Kryzhitskiy, eds. 2007. *Classical Olbia and the Scythian World: From the Sixth Century BC to the Second Century AD*. Oxford: Oxford University Press.

Brelich, Angelo. 1979. *Storia delle religioni: Perchè?* Naples: Liguori Editore.

Bremmer, Jan. 2002. *The Rise and Fall of the Afterlife*. London: Routledge.

Bringmann, Klaus. 1976. "Die Verfassungsdebatte bei Herodot 3.80–82 und Dareios' Aufstieg zur Königsherrschaft." *Hermes* 104: 266–79.

Bruiningk, Hermann von. 1924–28. "Der Werwolf in Livland und das letzte im Wendenschen Landgericht und Dörpischen Hofgericht i. J. 1692 deshalb stattgehabte Strafverfahren." *Mitteilungen aus der livländischen Geschichte* 22: 203–20.

Brunotte, Ulrike. "Mannerbund zwischen Jugend- und Totenkult: Ritual und Communitas am Beginn der Moderne." In Brigitte Luchesi and Kocku von Stuckrad, eds., *Religion im kulturellen Diskurs / Religion in Cultural Discourse: Festschrift für Hans G. Kippenberg*, 401–22. Berlin: Walter de Gruyter, 2014.

Bruns, Claudia. 2008. *Politik des Eros: Der Männerbund in Wissenschaft, Politik und Jugendkultur (1880–1934)*. Vienna: Bohlau.

Bucci, Onorato. 1983. "L'impero achemenide come ordinamento giuridico sovran-

nazionale e *arta* come principio ispiratore di uno *jus commune Persarum (dātā)*."
In *Modes de contacts et processus de transformation dans les sociétés anciennes*,
89–122. Pisa: Scuola Normale Superiore.

Buck, Carl Darling. 1949. *A Dictionary of Selected Synonyms in the Principal Indo-
European Languages*. Chicago: University of Chicago Press.

Burke, Peter. 1985. "Good Witches." *New York Review of Books*, February 28,
32–34.

Burkert, Walter. 1962. "Γόης: Zum griechischen 'Schamanismus'." *Rheinisches
Museum* 105: 36–55.

———. 1972. *Lore and Science in Ancient Pythagoreanism*. Trans. Edwin L. Minar Jr.
Cambridge, MA: Harvard University Press; German original, 1962.

Burkert, Walter, et al., 1990. *Hérodote et les peuples non-grecs*. Geneva: Fondation
Hardt.

Caillois, Roger. 1938. *Le mythe et l'homme*. Paris: Gallimard.

———. 1939. *L'homme et le sacré*. Paris: Presses Universitaires de France.

Calame, Claude. 1986. "Environnement et nature humaine: Le racisme bien
tempéré d'Hippocrate." In *Sciences et racisme*, 75–99. Lausanne: Payot.

Calame, Claude, and Bruce Lincoln, eds. 2012. *Comparer en histoire des religions
antiques: Controverses et propositions*. Liège: Presses Universitaires de Liège.

Canfora, Luciano. 1996. *Viaggio di Aristea*. Rome: Laterza.

Carroll, John M., ed., 1986. *The Arrest and Killing of Sitting Bull: A Documentary*.
Glendale, CA: A.H. Clark.

Cartledge, Paul. 1990. "Herodotus and 'the Other': A Meditation on Empire." *Échos
du Monde Classique* 34: 27–40.

Casanova, Julian. 2005. *Anarchism, the Republic, and Civil War in Spain: 1931–
1939*. Trans. Andrew Dowling. London: Routledge.

Ceausescu, G. 1991. "Un topos de la littérature antique: L'éternelle guerre entre
l'Europe et l'Asie." *Latomus* 50: 327–41.

Ceretti, Carlo. 2001. *La letteratura Pahlavi: Introduzione ai testi con riferimenti alla
storia degli studi e alla tradizione manoscritta*. Milan: Mimesis.

Chadwick, H. S. 1899. *The Cult of Othin: An Essay on the Ancient Religion of the
North*. London: C.J. Clay & Son.

Chaney, William. 1970. *The Cult of Kingship in Anglo-Saxon England*. Berkeley:
University of California Press.

Chantepie de la Saussaye, P. D. 1902. *Religion of the Teutons*. Trans. Bert Vos.
Boston: Ginn; Dutch original, 1900.

Chantraine, Pierre. 1968–80. *Dictionnaire etymologique de la langue grecque*. Paris:
Honoré Champion.

Chase, Colin, ed., 1997. *The Dating of "Beowulf."* Toronto: University of Toronto
Press.

Cherniss, Michael D. 1967. "The Progress of the Hoard in *Beowulf*." *Philological
Quarterly* 47: 473–86.

———. 1972. *Ingeld and Christ: Heroic Concepts and Values in Old English Christian
Poetry*. The Hague: Mouton.

Cheung, Johnny. 2007. *Etymological Dictionary of the Iranian Verb*. Leiden: Brill.

Chiasson, Charles. 2001. "Scythian Androgyny and Environmental Determinism in Herodotus and the Hippocratic πέρι ἀέρων ὑδάτων τόπων" *Syllecta Classica* 12: 33–73.

Chidester, David. 2014. *Empire of Religion: Imperialism and Comparative Religion*. Chicago: University of Chicago Press.

Christ, Matthew R. 1994. "Herodotean Kings and Historical Inquiry." *Classical Antiquity* 13: 167–202.

Christensen, Arthur. 1918–34. *Le premier homme et le premier roi dans l'histoire légendaire des Iraniens*. 2 vols. Uppsala: Appelberg.

Cleasby, Richard, and Gudbrand Vigfusson. 1957. *An Icelandic-English Dictionary*. 2nd ed. Oxford: Clarendon Press.

Clemen, Carl. 1934. *Altgermanische Religionsgeschichte*. Bonn: L. Röhrscheid.

Clemente, Pietro, and Cristiano Grottanelli, eds. 2009. *Comparativa/mente*. Florence: SEID Editori.

Cohn, Norman. 1957. *The Pursuit of the Millennium: Revolutionary Messianism in Medieval and Reformation Europe and Its Bearing on Modern Totalitarian Movements*. London: Secker & Warburg; rev. ed., 1970.

Coleman, William S. E. 2000. *Voices of Wounded Knee*. Lincoln: University of Nebraska Press.

Comaroff, Jean, and John Comaroff, eds. 1993. *Modernity and Its Malcontents: Ritual and Power in Postcolonial Africa*. Chicago: University of Chicago Press.

Comolli, Jean-Louis. 1999. *Buenaventura Durruti, Anarchiste*. Available at https://www.youtube.com/watch?v=rvm7A3L_j9A.

Coomaraswamy, Ananda K. 1947. *Time and Eternity*. Ascona: Artibus Asiae.

Corbin, Henry. 1952. *Le temps cyclique dans mazdéisme et dans l'ismaélisme*. Zurich: Rhein-Verlag.

Cornillot, François. 1981. "De Skythes à Kolaxais." *Studia Iranica* 10: 7–52.

Crossan, John Dominic. 2007. *God & Empire: Jesus against Rome, Then and Now*. San Francisco: Harper.

Czaplicka, M. A. 1914. *Aboriginal Siberia: A Study in Social Anthropology*. Oxford: Clarendon Press.

Damico, Helen. 1984. *Beowulf's Wealhtheow and the Valkyrie Tradition*. Madison: University of Wisconsin Press.

Darbo-Peschanski, Catherine. 1985. "Les 'Logoi' des autres dans les 'Histoires' d'Hérodote." *Quaderni di Storia* 22: 105–28.

——— 1989. "Les barbares à l'épreuve du temps (Hérodote, Thucydide, Xénophon)." *Metis* 4: 233–50.

Dauberg, Grace. 1968. "Wovoka." *Nevada History Quarterly* 11: 5–53.

Davidson, Hilda Ellis. 1969. *Scandinavian Mythology*. London: Hamlyn.

———. 1988. *Myths and Symbols in Pagan Europe*. Syracuse: Syracuse University Press.

Davis, Natalie Zemon. 1975. *Society and Culture in Early Modern France: Eight Essays*. Stanford, CA: Stanford University Press.

DeMallie, Raymond. 1982. "The Lakota Ghost Dance: An Ethnohistorical Account." *Pacific Historical Review* 51: 385–405.

Densmore, Frances. 1957. "Music of Acoma, Isleta, Cochiti, and Zuñi Pueblos." *Bureau of American Ethnology Bulletin* 165. Washington, DC: Government Printing Office.

Desai, Gaurav Gajanan. 2001. *Subject to Colonialism: African Self-Fashioning and the Colonial Library.* Durham, NC: Duke University Press.

Detienne, Marcel. 2000. *Comparer l'incomparable.* Paris: Éditions du Seuil.

Dettori, Emanuele. 2005. "Aristea di Proconneso 'sciamano' e 'corvo': Una presentazione (con qualche nota)." *Quaderni di Classiconorroena* 1: 9–24.

de Vries, Jan. 1970. *Altgermanische Religionsgeschichte.* Berlin: Walter de Gruyter.

———. 1977. *Altnordisches etymologisches Wörterbuch.* 2nd ed. Leiden: E.J. Brill.

Dewald, Carolyn. 2003. "Form and Content: The Question of Tyranny in Herodotus." In Kathryn A. Morgan, ed., *Popular Tyranny: Sovereignty and Its Discontents in Ancient Greece*, 25–58. Austin: University of Texas Press.

Diesner, Hans-Joachim. 1961. "Skythische Religion und Geschichte bei Herodot." *Rheinisches Museum* 104: 202–12.

Diller, Hans. 1934. *Wanderarzt und Aitiologe: Studien zur hippokratischen Schrift Περὶ ἀέρων ὑδάτων τόπων.* Philologus Supplement 26.3. Leipzig: Dieterich'sche verlagsbuchhandlung.

Diószegi, Vilmos. 1996. *Shamanism in Siberia.* Budapest: Akadémiai Kiadó.

Dobbie, Elliott. 1942. *Anglo-Saxon Poetic Records.* Vol. 6. New York: Columbia University Press.

Dodds, E. R. 1951. *The Greeks and the Irrational.* Berkeley: University of California Press.

Donecker, Stefan. 2008. "Konfessionalisierung und religiöse Begegnung im Ostseeraum." In Andrea Komlosy and Hans-Heinrich Nolte, and Imbi Sooman, eds., *Ostsee 700–2000: Gsesellschaft, Wirtschaft, Kultur*, 91–109. Vienna: Promedia.

———. 2009a. "Livland und seine Werwölfe: Ethnizität und Monstrosität an der europäischen Peripherie, 1550–1700." *Jahrbuch des baltischen Deutschtums* 56: 83–98.

———. 2009b. "The Medieval Frontier and Its Aftermath. Historical Discourses in Early Modern Livonia." In Imbi Sooman and Stefan Donecker, eds., *The "Baltic Frontier" Revisited: Power Structures and Cross-Cutural Interactions in the Baltic Sea Region*, 41–62. Vienna: n.p.

———. 2009c. "Werewolves on the Baltic Seashore: Monstrous Frontier of Early Modern Europe, 1550–1700." In Niall Scott, *The Role of the Monster: Myths & Metaphors of Enduring Evil*, 63–75. Oxford: Inter-Disciplinary Press.

———. 2012. "The Werewolves of Livonia: Lycanthropy and Shape-Changing in Scholarly Texts, 1550–1720." *Preternature: Critical and Historical Studies on the Preternatural* 2: 289–322.

Doostkhah, Jalil. 2008. "Āz and Niyāz, Two Powerful and Haughty Demons in Persian Mythology and Epics." *Sydney Studies in Religion* 11: 67–70.

Dorati, Marco. 2000. *Le Storie di Erodoto: Etnografia e racconto.* Pisa: Istituti editoriali e poligrafici internazionali.

Dorward, David Craig. 1969. "The Development of the British Colonial Administration among the Tiv, 1900–1949." *African Affairs* 68: 316–33.

———. 1974. "Ethnography and Administration: A Study of Anglo-Tiv Working Misunderstandings," *Journal of African History* 15: 457–78.

Douglas, Mary. 1966. *Purity and Danger: An Analysis of Concepts of Pollution and Taboo*. London: Routledge & Kegan Paul.

Dowden, Ken. 1980. "Deux notes sur les Scythes et les Arimaspes." *Revue des Études Grecques* 92: 486–92.

Downes, R. M. 1933. *The Tiv Tribe*. Kaduna: The Government Printer.

———. 1971. *Tiv Religion*. Ibadan: Ibadan University Press.

Dubuisson, Daniel. 1993. *Mythologies du XXième siècle*. Lille: Presses universitaires de Lille; 2nd ed., 2008.

———. 2005. *Impostures et pseudo-science: L'oeuvre de Mircea Eliade*. Villeneuve d'Asq: Presses universitaires du Septentrion.

Duchesne-Guillemin, Jacques. 1962. *La religion de l'Iran ancien*. Paris: Presses Universitaires de France.

Dumarest, Noël. 1919. "Notes on Cochiti, New Mexico." *Memoirs of the American Anthropological Association* 27. Lancaster, PA: American Anthropological Association.

Dumézil, Georges. 1930. *Légendes sur les Nartes, suivies de cinq notes mythologiques*. Paris: Institut d'études slaves.

———. 1938. "Les légendes de 'Fils d'aveugles' au Caucase et autour du Caucase." *Revue de l'Histoire des Religions* 117: 50–74.

———. 1939. *Mythes et dieux des Germains*. Paris: Ernest Leroux.

———. 1946. "Les 'énarées' des Scythes et la grossesse de Narte Hamyc." *Latomus* 5: 249–55.

———. 1958. *L'idéologie tripartie des indo-européens*. Brussels: Collection Latomus.

———. 1960a. "À propos de quelques représentations folkloriques des Ossètes." *Paideuma* 7: 216–24.

———. 1960b. "Les trois 'Trésors des ancêtres' dans l'épopée Narte." *Revue de l'Histoire des Religions* 157: 141–54.

———. 1962. "La société scythique avait-elle des classes fonctionnelles?" *Indo-Iranian Journal* 5: 187–202.

———. 1965. *Le livre des héros: Légendes sur les Nartes, traduit de l'ossete*. Paris: Gallimard.

———. 1968–78. *Mythe et epopée*. 3 vols. Paris: Gallimard.

———. 1970. *The Destiny of the Warrior*. Trans. Alf Hiltebeitel. Chicago: University of Chicago Press.

———. 1971. *Mythe et epopée*. Vol. 2, *Types épiques indo-européens: Un héros, un sorcier, un roi*. Paris: Gallimard.

———. 1973. *The Destiny of a King*. Trans. Alf Hiltebeitel. Chicago: University of Chicago Press.

———. 1978. *Romans de Scythie et d'alentour*. Paris: Payot.

———. 1985a. "Hérodote et l'intronisation de Darius." In *L'oubli de l'homme et l'honneur des dieux: Esquisses de mythologie*, 246–53. Paris: Gallimard.

———. 1985b. "Une idylle de vingt ans." In *L'oubli de l'homme et l'honneur des dieux*, 299–318. Paris: Gallimard.

———. 1985c. "Science et politique: Réponse à Carlo Ginzburg." *Annales ESC* 40: 985–89.

———. 1986. *The Plight of a Sorcerer*. Ed. Jaan Puhvel and David Weeks. Berkeley: University of California Press.

Durkheim, Émile. 1965. *Elementary Forms of the Religious Life*. Trans. Joseph Swain. New York: Free Press; French original, 1912.

Durkheim, Émile, and Marcel Mauss. 1963. *Primitive Classification*. Trans. Rodney Needham. Chicago: University of Chicago Press; French original, 1901–2.

Dzeremo, Baver. 2002. *Colonialism and the Transformation of Authority in Central Tivland, 1912–1960*. Makurdi: Aboki Publishers.

Eddy, Samuel K. 1961. *The King Is Dead: Studies in the Near Eastern Resistance to Hellenism*. Lincoln: University of Nebraska Press.

Eggan, Fred 1950. *Social Organization of the Western Pueblos*. Chicago: University of Chicago Press.

Egilsson, Sveinbjörn, and Finnur Jónsson, eds. 1931. *Lexicon Poeticum Antiquæ Linguæ Septentrionalis: Ordbog over det Norsk-Islanske Skjaldesprog*. Copenhagen: S.L. Møller.

Eijk, Philippe van der. 1991. "'Airs, Waters, Places' and 'On the Sacred Disease': Two Different Religiosities?" *Hermes* 119: 168–76.

Eilers, Wilhelm. 1974. "Herd und Feuerstätte in Iran." In Manfred Mayrhofer et al., eds., *Antiquitates Indogermanicae: Gedenkschrift für Hermann Güntert*, 307–38. Innsbruck: Innsbrucker Beiträge zur Sprachwissenschaft.

Einhorn, Paul. 1627. *Wiederlegunge der Abgötteren*. Riga: Gerhard Schröder.

Eitrem, Samuel. 1927. "König Aun in Upsala und Kronos." In *Festskrift til Hjalmar Falk*. Oslo: H. Aschehoug.

Ekrem, Inger, and Lars Boje Mortensen, eds. 2003. *Historia Norwegie*. Copenhagen: Museum Tusculanum Press.

Elfenbein, Josef. 2001. "Splendour and Fortune." In Maria Gabriela Schmidt and Walter Bisang, eds., *Philologica et Linguistica: Festschrift für Helmut Humbach*, 485–96. Trier: Wissenschaftlicher Verlag.

Eliade, Mircea. 1951. *Le chamanisme et les techniques archaiques de l'extase*. Paris: Payot.

———. 1952. "Le temps et l'éternité dans la pensée indienne." *Eranos Jahrbuch* 20: 219–52.

———. 1954. *The Myth of the Eternal Return, or, Cosmos and History*. Trans. Willard Trask. New York: Pantheon Books, 1954; French original, 1949.

———. 1954/58. "Kosmogonische Mythen und magische Heilung." *Paideuma* 6: 194–204.

———. 1959. *The Sacred and the Profane: The Nature of Religion*. Trans. Willard Trask. New York: Harcourt, Brace; German original, 1957.

———. 1960. *Myths, Dreams, and Mysteries: The Encounter between Contemporary Faiths and Archaic Realities*. Trans. Philip Mairet. New York: Harper and Row; French original, 1957.

———. 1963. *Myth and Reality*. Trans. Willard Trask. New York: Harper & Row; French original, 1963.

———. 1964. *Shamanism: Archaic Techniques of Ecstasy*. Trans. Willard Trask. Princeton, NJ: Princeton University Press; French original, 1951.

———. 1975. "Some Observations on European Witchcraft." *History of Religions* 14: 149–72.

———. 1976. *Occultism, Witchcraft, and Cultural Fashions: Essays in Comparative Religion*. Chicago: University of Chicago Press.

Ellehøj, Svend. 1965. *Studier over den ældste norrøne historieskrivning*. Copenhagen: Einar Munksgaard.

Emerson, Oliver Farrar. 1921. "Grendel's Motive in Attacking Heorot." *Modern Language Review* 16: 113–19.

Engels, Friedrich. 1966. *The Peasant War in Germany*. Trans. M. J. Olgin. New York: International Publishers; German original, 1850.

Enzensberger, Hans Magnus. 1972. *Der kurze Sommer der Anarchie*. Frankfurt: Suhrkamp Verlag.

Eribon, Didier. 1992. *Faut-il brûler Dumézil? Mythologie, science, et politique*. Paris: Flammarion.

Ernout, Alfred, and Antoine Meillet. 1951. *Dictionnaire etymologique de la langue latine*. Paris: C. Klincksieck.

Esser, Albert. 1957. "Ueber ein skythisches Männerleiden." *Gymnasium* 64: 347–53.

Evans, Andrew. 2010. *Anthropology at War: World War I and the Science of Race in Germany*. Chicago: University of Chicago Press.

Evans, J. A. S. 1981. "Notes on the Debate of the Persian Grandees in Herodotus 3.80–82." *Quaderni Urbinati di Cultura Classica* 7: 79–84.

Evola, Julius. 1934. *Rivolta contro il mondo moderno*. Milan: Ulrich Hoepli.

Facotto, Luis Buceta, Gonzalo Cerezo Barredo, and Eduardo Navarro Álvarez, eds. 2006. *Homenaje a José Antonio en su centenario (1903–2003)*. Madrid: Plataforma 2003.

Farelius, Birgitta. 1993. "Where Does the Hamite Belong?" *Nomadic Peoples* 32: 107–18.

Feist, Sigmund. 1939. *Vergleichendes Wörterbuch der gotischen Sprache*. Leiden: E.J. Brill.

Felshi, Rita, and Susan Stanford Friedman, eds. 2013. *Comparison: Theories, Approaches, Uses*. Baltimore: Johns Hopkins University Press.

Fenelon, James V. 1998. *Culturicide, Resistance, and Survival of the Lakota ("Sioux Nation")*. New York: Garland.

Feuchtwang, Stephen. 1984. "Interpreting Religion." In Maurice Bloch, ed., *Marxist Analyses and Social Anthropology*, 61–82. London: Tavistock.

Filoramo, Giovanni. 1991. "Una storia infinita: La *Storia notturna* di Carlo Ginzburg." *Rivista di Storia e Letteratura Religiosa* 27: 283–96.

Fischer, Hans. 1990. *Völkerkunde im Nationalsozialismus: Aspekte der Anpassung, Affinität und Behauptung einer wissenschaftlichen Disziplin*. Berlin: Dietrich Reimer.

———. 2003. *Randfiguren der Ethnologie: Gelehrte und Amateure, Schwindler und Phantasten.* Berlin: Dietrich Reimer.

Flaherty, Gloria. 1992. *Shamanism and the Eighteenth Century.* Princeton, NJ: Princeton University Press.

Florence, Mauro. 2013. *Vita di Leone Ginzburg: Intransigenza e passione civile.* Rome: Donzelli.

Forde, C. Daryll. 1930. "A Creation Myth from Acoma." *Folklore* 41: 370–87.

Forsdyke, Sara. 2001. "Athenian Democratic Ideology and Herodotus' *Histories.*" *American Journal of Philology* 122: 329–58.

Fox, Robin. 1967. *The Keresan Bridge.* London: Athlone Press.

Frankfort, H., and H. A. Frankfort. 1949. *Before Philosophy: The Intellectual Adventure of Ancient Man.* Chicago: University of Chicago Press.

Frazer, Sir James George. 1890. *The Golden Bough: A Study in Comparative Religion.* 1st ed. London: Macmillan.

———. 1911–15. *The Golden Bough: A Study in Magic and Religion.* London: Macmillan.

Friedrich, Johannes. 1936. "Zur Glaubwürdigkeit Herodots: Das angebliche Reiterdenkmal des Dareios und seine urartäische Parallele." *Die Welt als Geschichte* 2: 107–16.

Friesen, Steven J. 2001. *Imperial Cults and the Apocalypse of John: Reading Revelation in the Ruins.* New York: Oxford University Press.

Frisk, Hjalmar. 1936. *"Wahrheit" und "Lüge" in den indogermanischen Sprachen: Einige morphologische Beobachtung.* Göteborg: Eilanders Bogtryckeri.

Fritz, Kurt von. 1965. "Die griechische ἐλευθερία bei Herodot." *Wiener Studien* 78: 5–31.

Frobenius, Leo. 1921. *Paideuma: Umrisse einer Kultur- und Seelenlehre.* Munich: C.H. Beck.

———. 1933. *Kulturgeschichte Afrikas.* Zurich: Phaidon Verlag.

Frost, Richard. 2016. *The Railroad and the Pueblo Indians: The Impact of the Atchison, Topeka and Santa Fe on the Pueblos of the Rio Grande, 1880–1930.* Salt Lake City: University of Utah Press.

Fuentes, Francisco M. 2003. *José Antonio: La esperanza en el horizonte.* Madrid: F.M. Fuentes.

Gajek, Esther. 1997. "Germanenkunde und Nationalsozialismus: Zur Verflechtung von Wissenschaft und Politik am Beispiel Otto Höfler." In Richard Faber, ed., *Politische Religion, religiöse Politik*, 173–204. Würzburg: Königshausen & Neumann.

Gamkrelidze, Tomas V., and Vjaceslav V. Ivanov. 1995. *Indo-European and the Indo-Europeans.* Trans. Johanna Nichols. Berlin: Mouton de Gruyter.

Gammie, John G. 1986. "Herodotus on Kings and Tyrants: Objective Historiography or Conventional Portraiture." *Journal of Near Eastern Studies* 45: 171–95.

Garcia-Mason, Velma. 1979. "Acoma." In Alfonso Ortiz, ed., *Handbook of North American Indians,* vol. 9, *Southwest,* 450–66. Washington, DC: Smithsonian Institution.

Geertz, Clifford. 1973. *The Interpretation of Cultures*. New York: Basic Books.

Georges, Pericles. 1994. *Barbarian Asia and the Greek Experience*. Baltimore: Johns Hopkins University Press.

Gershevitch, Ilya. 1969. "Iranian Nouns and Names in Elamite Garb." *Transactions of the Philological Society* 68: 165–200.

Gibson, Ian. 2008. *En busca de José Antonio*. Madrid: Aguilar.

Gignoux, Philippe. 1987. "Un témoin du syncrétisme mazdéen tardif, le traité pehlevi des 'Sélections de Zādspram'." In *Transition Periods in Iranian History = Studia Iranica* 5: 59–72.

Gignoux, Philippe, and Ahmad Tafazzoli, eds. and trans., 1993. *Anthologie de Zādspram*. Paris: Association pour l'avancement des études iraniennes.

Ginzburg, Carlo. 1966. *I Benandanti: Stregoneria e culti agrari tra cinquecento e seicento*. Turin: Giulio Einaudi.

———. 1976. *Il formaggio e i vermi: Il cosmo di un mugnaio del '500*. Turin: Giulio Einaudi.

———. 1980. *The Cheese and the Worms: The World-View of a 15th-Century Miller*. Trans. John Tedeschi and Anne Tedeschi. Baltimore: Johns Hopkins University Press; Italian original, 1970.

———. 1983. *The Night Battles: Witchcraft and Agrarian Cults in the Sixteenth & Seventeenth Centuries*. Trans. John and Anne Tedeschi. Baltimore: Johns Hopkins University Press.

———. 1984. "Mitologia germanica e Nazismo: Su un vecchio libro di Georges Dumézil." *Quaderni Storici* 19: 857–82.

———. 1989a. *Clues, Myths, and the Historical Method*. Trans. John Alfred Tedeschi. Baltimore: Johns Hopkins University Press; Italian original, 1986.

———. 1989b. *Storia notturna: Una decifrazione del sabba*. Turin: Giulio Einaudi.

———. 1991a. *Ecstasies: Deciphering the Witches' Sabbath*. Trans. Raymond Rosenthal. New York: Pantheon.

———. 1991b. *Il giudice e le storico*. Turin: Giulio Einaudi.

———. 1999. *The Judge and the Historian: Marginal Notes on a Late-Twentieth Century Miscarriage of Justice*. Trans. Antony Shugaar. London and New York: Verso.

———. 2002. "De près, de loin: Des rapports de force en histoire; Entretien avec Carlo Ginzburg." *Vacarme* 18 (January 2). Available at http://www.vacarme.org/article235.html.

———. 2003. "On the Dark Side of History: Carlo Ginzburg Talks to Trygve Riiser Gundersen." *Samtiden*. Available at http://www.eurozine.com/articles/2003–07–11-ginzburg-en.html.

———. 2004. "Carlo Ginzburg, 'L'historien et l'avocat du diable': Suite de l'entretien avec Charles Illouz et Laurent Vidal." *Genèses* 54. Available at http://www.cairn.info/revue-geneses-2004–1-page-112.htm.

———. 2012a. "The Europeans Discover (or Rediscover) the Shamans." In *Threads and Traces: True, False, Fictive*, trans. Anne C. Tedeschi and John Tedeschi, 83–95. Baltimore: Johns Hopkins University Press; Italian original, 2006.

———. 2012b. "Witches and Shamans." In *Threads and Traces: True, False, Fictive*, trans. Anne C. Tedeschi and John Tedeschi, 215–27. Baltimore: Johns Hopkins University Press; Italian original, 2006.

Ginzburg, Natalia. 1963. *Lessico famigliare*. Turin: Einaudi.

Giovannelli-Jouanna, Pascale. 2006. "La ruse et le mensonge dans la représentation du pouvoir chez Hérodote." In Hélène Olivier, Pascale Giovannelli-Jouanna, and François Bérard, eds., *Ruses, secrets et mensonges chez les historiens grecs et latins*, 65–83. Lyon: Université Jean Moulin.

Gislason, Konrad. 1881. "Nogle Bemærkinger Angående Ynglingatal." *Aarbøger for Nordisk Oldkyndighed*, 185–251.

Gluckman, Max. 1966. *Custom and Conflict in Africa*. London: Basil Blackwell.

Gnoli, Gherardo. 1983. *"Farr(ah)."* In *Encyclopaedia Iranica*, 9: 312–19. London: Routledge.

Godelier, Maurice. 1977. *Perspectives in Marxist Anthropology*. Trans. Robert Brain. Cambridge: Cambridge University Press; French original, 1973.

Golther, Wolfgang, ed. 1892. *Ares Isländerbuch*. Halle: Max Niemeyer.

Gomez Navarro, José Luis. 1991. *El régimen de Primo de Rivera*. Madrid: Ediciones Cátedra.

Gothsch, Manfred. 1983. *Die deutsche Völkerkunde und ihr Verhältnis zum Kolonialismus*. Baden-Baden: Nomos.

Graf, Klaus. 1993. "Carlo Ginzburgs 'Hexensabbat': Herausforderung an die Methodendiskussion der Geschichtswissenschaft." *Kea* 5: 1–16.

Granet, Marcel. 1977. *Religion of the Chinese People*. Trans. Maurice Freedman. New York: Harper & Row; French original, 1922.

Grassmann, Hermann. 1964. *Wörterbuch zum Rig-Veda*. 4th ed. Wiesbaden: Otto Harrassowitz; 1st ed., 1873.

Gray, Vivienne. 1995. "Herodotus and the Rhetoric of Otherness." *American Journal of Philology* 116: 185–212.

Greenfield, Stanley B. 1974. *"Gifstol* and Goldhoard in *Beowulf."* In Robert B. Burlin and Edward B. Irving, Jr., eds., *Old English Studies in Honour of John C. Pope*, 107–17. Toronto: University of Toronto Press.

Grensemann, Hermann. 1979. "Das 24. Kapitel von *De aeribus, aquis, locis* und die Einheit der Schrift." *Hermes* 107: 423–41.

Grimal, Pierre, ed., 1963. *Mythologies de la Méditerranée au Gange*. Paris: Larousse.

Grimaldi, Olivier. 2006. *Présence de José Antonio, 1936–2006*. Paris: Cercle franco-hispanique.

Grottanelli, Cristiano. 1993. *Ideologie, miti, massacri: Indoeuropei di Georges Dumézil*. Palermo: Sellerio.

———. 1999. "Ideologie del sacrificio umano: Roma e Cartagine." *Archiv für Religionsgeschichte* 41: 41–60.

———. 2000. "Ideologie del sacrificio umano." In Stéphane Verger, ed., *Rites et espaces en pays celte et méditerranéen*, 277–92. Rome: École Française de Rome.

Gschnitzer, Fritz. 1977. *Die sieben Perser und das Königtum des Dareios: Ein Beitrag zur Achaemenidengeschichte und zur Herodotanalyse*. Heidelberg: Carl Winter.

Gurevich, Aaron. 1992. *Historical Anthropology of the Middle Ages*. Chicago: University of Chicago Press.

Gutiérrez, Ramón A. 1991. *When Jesus Came, the Corn Mothers Went Away: Marriage, Sexuality, and Power in New Mexico, 1500–1846*. Stanford, CA: Stanford University Press.

Haas, George C. O. 1925. "The Zoroastrian Demon Āz in the Manichaean Fragments from Turfan." In *Indo-Iranian Studies*, 193–96. London: Kegan, Paul, Trench, & Trübner.

Hagan, William T. 1966. *Indian Police and Judges: Experiments in Acculturation and Control*. New Haven, CT: Yale University Press.

Hall, Edith. 1989. *Inventing the Barbarian: Greek Self-Definition through Tragedy*. Oxford: Clarendon Press.

Hall, Philip S. 1991. *To Have This Land: The Nature of Indian/White Relations, South Dakota, 1888–1891*. Vermillion: University of South Dakota Press.

Halliday, William Reginald. 1910–11. "A Note on the θήλεα νοῦσον of the Scythians." *Annual of the British School at Athens* 17: 95–102.

Hammond, William A. 1882. "The Disease of the Scythians (*morbus feminarum*) and Certain Analogous Conditions." *American Journal of Neurology and Psychiatry* 1/3: 339–55.

Hampl, Franz. 1975. "Herodot: Ein kritischer Forschungsbericht nach methodischen Gesichtspunkten." *Grazer Beiträge* 4: 97–136.

Haraldsdóttir, Kolbrún. 1998. "Der Historiker Snorri: Autor oder Kompilator?" In Hans Fix, ed., *Snorri Sturluson: Beiträge zu Werk und Rezeption*, 97–108. Berlin: Walter de Gruyter.

Harding, Frances. 1992. "R. C. Abraham and the Tiv People." In Philip J. Jaggar, ed., *Papers in Honour of R. C. Abraham*, 147–61. London: School of Oriental and African Studies.

Harris, Joseph. 1994. "Sacrifice and Guilt in Sonatorrek." In Heiko Uecker, ed., *Studien zum Altgermanischen: Festschrift für Heinrich Beck*, 175–80. Berlin: Walter de Gruyter.

———. 2007. "Homo Necans Borealis: Fatherhood and Sacrifice in Sonatorrek." In Stephen Glosecki, *Myth in Early Northwest Europe*, 162–65. Tempe: Arizona Center for Medieval and Renaissance Studies.

Hartland, Edwin Sidney. 1908. "The High Gods of Australia." *Folk-Lore* 9: 290–329.

Hartog, François. 1979a. "Le boeuf autocuiseur et les boissons d'Ares." In Marcel Detienne and Jean-Pierre Vernant, eds., *La cuisine du sacrifice en pays grec*, 251–69. Paris: Gallimard.

———. 1979b. "La question du nomadisme: Les Scythes d' Hérodote." *Acta Antiqua Academiae Scientiarum Hungaricae* 27: 135–48.

———. 1979c. "Les Scythes imaginaires: Espace et nomadisme." *Annales ESC* 34: 1137–74.

———. 1980. *Le miroir d'Hérodote: Essai sur la représentation de l'autre*. Paris: Gallimard.

———. 1988. *The Mirror of Herodotus: The Representation of the Other in the Writing of History*. Trans. Janet Lloyd. Berkeley: University of California Press.

Hastrup, Kirsten. 1985. *Culture and History in Medieval Iceland*. Oxford: Oxford University Press.

Hauer, Jakob Wilhelm. 1923. *Die Religionen: Ihr Werden, ihr Sinn, ihre Wahrheit.* Berlin: W. Kohlhammer.

Hauschild, Thomas, ed. 1995. *Lebenslust und Fremdenfurcht: Ethnologie im Dritten Reich.* Frankfurt: Suhrkamp.

Hawley, Florence. 1950. "Keresan Patterns of Kinship and Social Organization." *American Anthropologist* 52: 499–512.

Hedren, Paul L. 2011. *After Custer: Loss and Transformation in Sioux Country.* Norman: University of Oklahoma Press.

Heiler, Friedrich. 1959. "The History of Religions as a Preparation for the Cooperation of Religions." In Mircea Eliade and Joseph Kitagawa, eds., *The History of Religions: Essays in Methodology,* 132–60. Chicago: University of Chicago Press.

Helder, Willem. 1987. "The Song of Creation in *Beowulf* and the Interpretation of Heorot." *English Studies in Canada* 13: 243–55.

Hensler, Philipp Gabriel. 1783. *Geschichte der Lustseuche; die zu Ende des XV Jahrhundert in Europa ausbrach.* Altona: Gebrüder Herold.

Herrenschmidt, Clarisse. 1977. "Les créations d'Ahuramazda." *Studia Iranica* 6: 17–58.

Herrmann, Paul. 1928. *Altdeutsche Kultgebräuche.* Jena: Eugen Diederichs.

Hertz, Robert. 1960. *Death and the Right Hand.* Trans. Rodney Needham. Glencoe, IL: Free Press.

Hill, Christopher. 1972. *The World Turned Upside Down: Radical Ideas during the English Revolution.* New York: Viking.

Hinge, George. 2003. "Herodots skythiske nomader." In Tønnes Bekker-Nielsen and George Hinge, eds., *På ronden af det ukendte,* 13–33. Aarhus: Aarhus Universitetsforlag.

———. 2004. "Sjælevandring Skythien tur-retur." In Pia Guldager Bilde and Jakob Munk Højte, eds., *Mennesker og guder ved Sortehavets Kyster,* 11–27. Aarhus: Aarhus Universitetsforlag.

———. 2005. "Herodot zur skythischen Sprache: Arimaspen, Amazonen und die Entdeckung des Schwarzen Meeres." *Glotta* 81: 86–115.

Hintze, Almut. 1994. *Der Zamyād-Yašt: Edition, Übersetzung, Kommentar.* Wiesbaden: Ludwig Reichert.

Hittman, Michael. 1990. *Wovoka and the Ghost Dance.* Yerington, NV: Yerington Paiute Tribe.

Hobsbawm, Eric. 1959. *Primitive Rebels: Studies in Archaic Forms of Social Movement in the 19th and 20th Centuries.* Manchester: University of Manchester Press.

Hobsbawm, Eric, and Terence Ranger, eds. 1983. *The Invention of Tradition.* Cambridge: Cambridge University Press.

Hochegger, Hermann. 1994. *Mythes d'origine: Variantes zairoises de 1905 à 1994.* Bandundu, Zaire: Ceeba Publications.

Hodgson, Marshall. 1974–77. *The Venture of Islam: Conscience and History in a World Civilization.* 3 vols. Chicago: University of Chicago Press.

Hoebel, E. Adamson. 1968. "Keresan Pueblo Law." In Laura Nader, ed., *Law in Culture and Society,* 92–116. Chicago: Aldine Press.

Höfler, Otto. 1934. *Kultische Geheimbünde der Germanen.* Frankfurt: Moritz Diester-weg.

———. 1936a. "Der germanische Totenkult und die Sagen vom Wilden Heer." *Oberdeutsche Zeitschrift für Volkskünde* 1: 33–49.

———. 1936b. "Über germanische Verwandlungskulte." *Zeitschrift für deutsches Altertum* 73: 109–15.

———. 1938. "Die politische Leistung der Völkerwanderungszeit." *Kiele Blätter: Veröffentlichung der Wissenschaftlichen Akademie des NSD-Dozentenbundes der Christian Albrechts Universität* 4: 282–97.

———. 1952. *Germanische Sakralkönigtum.* Tübingen: Max Niemeyer.

———. 1973. *Verwandlungskulte, Volkssagen und Mythen.* Vienna: Verlag der öster-reichischen Akademie der Wissenschaften.

———. 1974. "Zwei Grundkräfte im Wodankult." In Manfred Mayrhofer et al., eds., *Antiquitates Indogermanicae: Gedenkschrift für Herman Güntert,* 133–44. Innsbruck: Innsbrucker Beiträge zur Sprachwissenschaft.

———. 1976. "Staatsheiligkeit und Staatsvergottung." In Adolf Fink, ed., *Rechts-geschichte als Kulturgeschichte: Festschrift für Adalbert Erler,* 109–33. Aalen: Scientia Verlag.

Hollmann, Alexander. 2005. "The Manipulation of Signs in Herodotos' 'Histories'." *Transactions of the American Philological Association* 135: 279–327.

Holtsmark, Anne. 1970. *Norrøn mytologi: Tro og myter i vikingtider.* Oslo: Norske Samlaget.

Horsley, Richard A. 2010. *Revolt of the Scribes: Resistance and Apocalyptic Origins.* Minneapolis: Fortress Press.

Hubert, Henri, and Marcel Mauss, 1964. *Sacrifice: Its Nature and Function.* Trans. W. D. Halls. Chicago: University of Chicago Press; French original, 1902.

Hultgård, Anders. 2001. "Menschenopfer." In *Reallexikon der Germanischen Alter-tumskunde,* 19: 533–46. Berlin: de Gruyter.

Humbach, Helmut, and Klaus Faiss. 2012. *Herodotus's Scythians and Ptolemy's Central Asia: Semasiological and Onomasiological Studies.* Wiesbaden: Ludwig Reichert.

Humbach, Helmut, and Pallan R. Ichaporia, eds. and trans. 1998. *Zamyād Yasht: Text, Translation, Commentary.* Wiesbaden: Harrassowitz.

Hume, Kathryn. 1974. "The Concept of the Hall in Old English Poetry." *Anglo-Saxon England* 3: 63–74.

Hunt, Edward Proctor. 2015. *The Origin Myth of Acoma Pueblo.* Edited with an introduction and notes by Peter Nabokov. New York: Penguin Books.

Huyse, Philippe. 1998. "Gab es eine Lautentwicklyng /k/ → /x/ im 'Skytho-Sarmatischen?" *Hyperboreus* 4: 167–90.

Hyde, George E. 1956. *A Sioux Chronicle.* Norman: University of Oklahoma Press.

Idinopulos, Thomas, Brian Wilson, and James Hanges, eds. 2006. *Comparing Reli-gions: Possibilities and Perils?* Leiden: E.J. Brill.

Irving, Edward B. Jr. 1985. *A Reading of "Beowulf."* New Haven, CT: Yale Univer-sity Press.

Ivanoff, Hélène, Jean-Louis Georget, and Richard Kuba, eds. 2015. *Kulturkreise—Leo Frobenius und seine Zeitgenossen.* Berlin: Dietrich Reimer.

Ivantchik, Askold. 1993. "Les guerriers-chiens: Loups-garous et invasions scythes en Asie Mineure." *Revue de l'Histoire des Religions* 210: 305–29.

———. 1999a. "Une légende sur l'origine des Scythes (Hdt. IV 5–7)." *Revue des Études Grecques* 112: 141–92.

———. 1999b. "The Scythian 'Rule over Asia': The Classical Tradition and the Historical Reality." In Gocha R. Tsetskhladze, ed., *Ancient Greeks West and East*, 497–520. Leiden: Brill.

———. 2001. "La légende 'grecque' sur l'origine des Scythes (Hérodote 4.8–10)." In Valérie Fromentin and Sophie Gotteland, eds., *Origines Gentium*, 207–20. Paris: de Boccard.

———. 2002. "Un fragment de l'épopée scythe: 'Le cheval de Colaxaïs' dans un partheneion d'Alcman." *Ktema* 27: 257–64.

Jaafari-Dehaghi, Mahmoud, ed. 1998. *Dādestān ī Dēnīg*. Part 1, *Transcription, Translation, and Commentary*. Paris: Association pour l'avancement des études iraniennes.

Jacobeit, Wolfgang, et al. 1994. *Völkische Wissenschaft: Gestalten und Tendenzen der deutschen und österreichischen Volkskunde in der ersten Hälfte des 20. Jahrhunderts*. Vienna: Böhlau.

Jacques-Lefèvre, Nicole. 2002. "Such an Impure, Cruel, and Savage Beast: Images of the Werewolf in Demonological Works." In Kathryn A. Edwards, ed., *Werewolves, Witches, and Wandering Spirits: Traditional Belief and Folklore in Early Modern Europe*, 181–97. Kirksville, MO: Truman State University Press.

Janka, Markus. 2010. "Der Vater der *Metahistory*: Konstrukte des Eigenen und Fremden in Herodots Historiographie des Vergleichs." *Gymnasium* 117: 317–44.

Jiménez de Sandoval, Felipe. 1963. *José Antonio (biografía apasionada)*. Rev. ed. Madrid: Editorial Bullón.

Johansen, Paul. 1963. "Nationale Vorurteile und Minderwertigkeitsgefühle als sozialer Faktor im mittelalterlichen Livland." In *Alteuropa und die moderne Gesellschaft: Festschrift für Otto Brünner*, 88–115. Göttingen: Vandenhoeck & Ruprecht.

Johansen, Paul, and Heinz von zur Mühlen. 1973. *Deutsch und Undeutsch im mittelalterlichen und frühneuzeitlichen Reval*. Cologne and Vienna: Böhlau.

Jouanna, Jacques. 1981. "Les causes de la défaite des Barbares chez Eschyle, Hérodote et Hippocrate." *Ktema* 6: 3–15.

Kålund, Kristian, ed. 1917. *Alfrœði Íslenzk*. Vol. 3. Copenhagen: S.I. Møller.

Kaske, R. E. 1971. "*Beowulf* and the Book of Enoch." *Speculum* 46: 421–31.

Kehoe, Alice Beck. 2006. *The Ghost Dance: Ethnohistory & Revitalization*. 2nd ed. Long Grove, IL: Waveland Press.

Kellens, Jean. 1996. "*Druj-*." In *Encyclopaedia Iranica*, 7: 562–63. London: Routledge.

Keller, Thomas L. 1981. "The Dragon in *Beowulf* Revisited." *Aevum* 55: 218–28.

Kent, Roland. 1953. *Old Persian: Grammar, Texts, Lexicon*. New Haven, CT: American Oriental Society.

Kern, Robert W. 1978. *Red Years, Black Years: A Political History of Spanish Anarchism, 1911–1937*. Philadelphia: Institute for the Study of Human Issues.

Kippenberg, Hans. 2006. *Discovering Religious History in the Modern Age.* Princeton, NJ: Princeton University Press.

Klaeber, Friedrich, ed. 1950. *Beowulf and the Fight at Finnsburg.* 3rd ed. Lexington, MA: D.C. Heath.

Klaniczay, Gábor. 1990. *The Uses of Supernatural Power: The Transformation of Popular Religion in Medieval and Early-Modern Europe.* Trans. Susan Singerman. Princeton, NJ: Princeton University Press.

———. 2006. "Shamanism and Witchcraft." *Magic, Ritual, and Witchcraft* 1: 214–21.

Knauer, Elfriede R. 2001. "Observations on the Barbarian Custom of Suspending the Heads of Vanquished Enemies from the Neck of Horses." *Archäologische Mitteilungen aus Iran und Turan* 33: 283–332.

Knaut, Andrew. 1995. *The Pueblo Revolt of 1680: Conquest and Resistance in Seventeenth-Century New Mexico.* Norman: University of Oklahoma Press.

Köhnken, Adolf. 1990. "Die listige Oibares: Dareios' Aufstieg zum Großkönig." *Rheinisches Museum für Philologie* 133: 115–37.

Konstan, David. 1987. "Persians, Greeks, and Empire." *Arethusa* 20: 59–73.

Koppers, Wilhelm, ed. 1936. "Die Indogermanen- und Germanenfrage." *Wiener Beiträge zur Kulturgeschichte und Linguistik* 4.

Kotwal, Dastur Firoze M., and James W. Boyd 1991. *A Persian Offering: The Yasna; A Zoroastrian High Liturgy.* Paris: Association pour l'avancement des études iraniennes.

Krag, Claus. 1991. *Ynglingatal og Ynglingesaga: En studie i historiske kilder.* Oslo: Norges allmenvitenskapelige forskningsråd.

Kreyenbroek, Philip G. 1985. *Sraoša in the Zoroastrian Tradition.* Leiden: E.J. Brill.

Kroeber, Karl, ed. 2004. *Native American Storytelling: A Reader of Myths and Legends.* Malden, MA: Blackwell.

Kubysev, A. I. 1991. "Der Bratoljybovka-Kurgan: Die Grabanlage eines skythischen Nomarchen?" *Beiträge zur Archäologie* 18: 131–40.

Kuiper, Yme. 2014. "Witchcraft, Fertility Cults, and Shamanism: Carlo Ginzburg's *I Benandanti* in Retrospect." In Brigitte Luchesi and Kocku von Stuckrad, eds., *Religion im kulturellen Diskurs / Religion in Cultural Discourse: Festschrift für Hans G. Kippenberg,* 33–59. Berlin: Walter de Gruyter.

Kummer, Bernhard. 1927. *Midgards Untergang: Germanische Kult und Glaube in den letzten heidnischen Jahrhunderten.* Leipzig: E. Pfeiffer.

———. 1935. "Männerbundgefahren." *Nordische Stimmen: Zeitschrift für nordisches Wesen und Gewissen* 5: 225–33.

Landes, Richard. 2011. *Heaven on Earth: The Varieties of Millennial Experience.* New York: Oxford University Press.

Lang, Andrew. 1884. *Custom and Myth.* London: Longmans Green.

———. 1898. *The Making of Religion.* London: Longmans Green.

Lange, Charles H. 1958. "The Keresan Component of Southwestern Pueblo Culture." *Southwestern Journal of Anthropology* 14: 34–50.

Lanternari, Vittorio. 1960. *The Religions of the Oppressed: A Study of Modern Messianic Cults.* Trans. Lisa Sergio. New York: Mentor; Italian original, 1960.

———. 1986. "Ripensando a Mircea Eliade." *La Critica Sociologica* 79: 67–82.

Lasserre, François. 1976. "Hérodote et Protagoras: Le débat sur les constitutions." *Museum Helveticum* 33: 65–84.

Lateiner, Donald. 1984. "Herodotean Historiographical Patterning: The Constitutional Debate." *Quaderni di Storia* 10: 257–84.

Laurot, Bernard. 1981. "Idéaux grecs et barbarie chez Hérodote." *Ktema* 6: 39–48.

Lavi, Dr. 1972. "Dosarul Mircea Eliade." *Toladot: Buletinul Institutului Dr. J. Niemirower* 1: 21–26.

Law, Robin. 2009. "The 'Hamitic Hypothesis' in Indigenous West African Historical Thought." *History in Africa* 36: 293–314.

Lazarus, Edward. 1991. *Black Hills/White Justice: The Sioux Nation versus the United States, 1775 to the Present*. New York: Harper Collins.

Leach, Edmund. 1966. "Sermons by a Man on a Ladder." *New York Review of Books*, October 20, 28–31.

Lecoq, Pierre. 1987. "Le mot *farnah* et les Scythes." *Comptes Rendus de l'Académie des Inscriptions et Belles-Lettres*, 671–81.

———. 1995. "Un aspect de la politique religieuse de Gaumāta le mage." In Rika Gyselened, *Au carrefour des religions: Mélanges offerts à Philippe Gignoux*, 183–86. Bures-sur-Yvette: Groupe pour l'étude de la civilisation du Moyen-Orient.

Lee, Alvin A. 1998. *Gold-Hall and Earth-Dragon: "Beowulf" as Metaphor*. Toronto: University of Toronto Press.

Leeuw, Gerardus van der. 1963. *Religion in Essence and Manifestation: A Study in Phenomenology*. Trans. J. E. Turner. New York: Harper and Row; German original, 1933.

Leffler, L. Fr. 1886. "*Ána-sótt*." *Arkiv for Nordiska Filologi* 3: 188–89.

Le Goff, Jacques. 1980. *Time, Work, and Culture in the Middle Ages*. Trans. Arthur Goldhammer. Chicago: University of Chicago Press; French original, 1977.

Lehmann-Haupt, C. F. 1923. "Dareios und sein Roß." *Klio* 18: 59–64.

Leisi, Ernst. 1952–53. "Gold und Manneswert im *Beowulf*." *Anglia* 71: 259–73.

Lenz, Wilhelm. 2004. "*Undeutsch*: Bemerkungen zu einem besonderen Begriff der baltischen Geschichte." In Bernhart Jähnig and Klaus Militzer, eds., *Aus der Geschichte Alt-Livlands: Festschrift für Heinz von zur Mühlen*, 169–84. Münster: Lit Verlag.

Lévi-Strauss, Claude. 1966. *The Savage Mind*. Chicago: University of Chicago Press; French original, 1962.

———. 1969. *The Raw and the Cooked*. Trans. John Weightman and Doreen Weightman. New York: Harper and Row; French original, 1964.

———. 1973. *From Honey to Ashes*. Trans. John Weightman and Doreen Weightman. New York: Harper and Row; French original, 1966.

———. 1978. *The Origin of Table Manners*. Trans. John Weightman and Doreen Weightman. New York: Harper and Row; French original, 1968.

———. 1981. *The Naked Man*. Trans. John Weightman and Doreen Weightman. New York: Harper and Row; French original, 1971.

Lévy, Edmond. 1981. "Les origines du mirage scythe." *Ktema* 6: 57–68.

———. 2003. "Les 'Dialogues perses' (Hérodote, III, 80–83) et les débuts de la science politique." *Lalies* 22: 119–45.

Lewis, Charlton T., and Charles Short. 1879. *A Latin Dictionary*. Oxford: Clarendon Press.

Lieber, Elinor. 1996. "The Hippocratic 'Airs, Waters, Places' on Cross-Dressing Eunuchs: 'Natural' yet also 'Divine'." In Renate Wittern and Pierre Pellegrin, eds., *Hippokratische Medizin und antike Philosophie*, 451–76. Hildesheim: Olms Weidmann.

Lincoln, Bruce. 1981a. *Emerging from the Chrysalis: Studies in Rituals of Women's Initiation*. Cambridge, MA: Harvard University Press.

———. 1981b. *Priests, Warriors, and Cattle: A Study in the Ecology of Religions*. Berkeley: University of California Press.

———. 1983a. "Concezione del tempo e dimensione politica del mito." *Studi e Materiali di Storia delle Religioni* 7 (1983): 75–86.

———. 1983b. "Der politische Gehalt des Mythos." In Hans Peter Duerr, ed., *Alcheringa, oder die beginnende Zeit: Studien zu Mythologie, Schamanismus, und Religion*, 9–25. Frankfurt: Qumran Verlag.

———. 1986a. *Myth, Cosmos, and Society: Indo-European Themes of Creation and Destruction*. Cambridge, MA: Harvard University Press.

———. 1986b. "Shaping the Past and the Future." *Times Literary Supplement*, October 3, 1107–8.

———. 1987. "On the Scythian Royal Burials." In Susan Skomal and Edgar Polomé, eds., *Proto-Indo-European: The Archeology of a Linguistic Problem; Festschrift for Marija Gimbutas*, 267–85. Washington, DC: Journal of Indo-European Studies Monograph Series.

———. 1989. *Discourse and the Construction of Society: Comparative Studies of Myth, Ritual, and Classification*. New York: Oxford University Press; 2nd ed., 2014.

———. 1991. *Death, War, and Sacrifice: Studies in Ideology and Practice*. Chicago: University of Chicago Press.

———. 1999. *Theorizing Myth: Narrative, Ideology, and Scholarship*. Chicago: University of Chicago Press.

———. 2012a. "The Cosmo-logic of Persian Demonology." In *Gods and Demons, Priests and Scholars: Critical Explorations in the History of Religions*, 31–42. Chicago: University of Chicago Press.

———. 2012b. *"Happiness for Mankind": Achaemenian Religion and the Imperial Project*. Louvain: Peeters.

———. 2012c. "The One and the Many in Iranian Creation Myths: Rethinking 'Nostalgia for Paradise'." *Archiv für Religionsgeschiche* 13: 15–30.

———. 2014. "Beginnings of a Friendship." *Mythos* 9 (Special issue in honor of Cristiano Grottanelli): 13–33.

Lind, Erik Henrik. 1905–15. *Norsk-isländska dopnamn ock fingerade namn från medeltiden*. Oslo: J. Dybwad.

Linimayr, Peter. 1994. *Wiener Völkerkunde im Nationalsozialismus: Ansätze zu einer NS-Wissenschaft*. Frankfurt: Peter Lang.

Lionarons, Joyce Tally. 1998. *The Medieval Dragon: The Nature of the Beast in Germanic Literature*. Middlesex: Hisarlik Press.

Lisovy, Igor, and České Budějovice. 2006. "Wenn der skythische König starb . . .

(Die Kulte der Skythen im nördlichen Schwarzmeergebiet)." *Wiener humanistische Blätter* 48: 5–46.

Lloyd, G. E. R. 1979. *Magic, Reason, and Experience.* Cambridge: Cambridge University Press.

———. 2014. "Pythagoras." In Carl Huffman, ed., *A History of Pythagoreanism*, 24–45. Cambridge: Cambridge University Press.

Loma, Aleksander. 2011. "Namenkundliches zur skythischen Abstammungssage." *Studia Etymologica Cracoviensia* 16: 75–92.

Lommel, Herman. 1930. *Die Religion Zarathustras nach dem Awesta dargestellt.* Tübingen: J.C.B. Mohr.

———. 1970. "Die Elemente in Verhältnis zu den Aməša Spəntas." In Bernfried Schlerath, ed., *Zarathuštra*, 377–96. Darmstadt: Wissenschaftliche Gesellschaft.

Lönnroth, Lars. 1964. "Tesen om de två kulturerna: Kritiska studier i den isländska sagaskrivinengens sociala forutsättningar." *Scripta Islandica* 15: 83–97.

———. 1965. *European Sources of Icelandic Saga-Writing: An Essay Based on Previous Studies.* Stockholm: Akademisk avhandling.

———. 1986. "Dómaldi's Death and the Myth of Sacral Kingship." In John Lindow, Lars Lönnroth, and Gerd Wolfgang Weber, eds., *Structure and Meaning in Old Norse Literature*, 73–93. Odense: Odense University Press.

López Férez, Juan Antonio. 1994. "Los escritos hipocráticos y el nacimiento de la identidad europea." In H. A. Khan, ed., *The Birth of the European Identity: The Europe-Asia Contrast in Greek Thought*, 90–130. Nottingham: University of Nottingham.

Lorenzo, César M. 2006. *Le mouvement anarchiste en Espagne.* Saint-Georges d' Oléron: Les éditions libertaires.

Lovejoy, Arthur O., and George Boas. 1935. *Primitivism and Related Ideas in Antiquity.* Baltimore: Johns Hopkins University Press.

Lubotsky, Alexander. 2002. "Scythian Elements in Old Iranian." In Nicholas Sims-Williams, ed, *Indo-Iranian Languages and Peoples*, 191–95. Oxford: The British Academy.

Lüders, Heinrich. 1959. *Varuṇa: II, Varuṇa und das Ṛta.* Göttingen: Vandenhoeck & Ruprecht.

MacKenzie, D. N. 1971. *A Concise Pahlavi Dictionary.* London: Oxford University Press.

Madar, Maia. 1990. "Estonia I: Werewolves and Poisoners." In Bengt Ankarloo and Gustav Henningsen, eds., *Early Modern European Witchcraft: Centres and Peripheries*, 257–72. Oxford: Clarendon Press.

Maddra, Sam A. 2006. *Hostiles? The Lakota Ghost Dance and Buffalo Bill's Wild West.* Norman: University of Oklahoma Press.

Magennis, Hugh. 1996. *Images of Community in Old English Poetry.* Cambridge: Cambridge University Press.

Makar, Tesemchi. 1994. *The History of Political Change among the Tiv in the 19th and 20th Centuries.* Enugu: Fourth Dimension Publishing.

Malinowski, Bronislaw. 1926. *Myth in Primitive Psychology.* London: Kegan Paul, Trench, Trubner.

———. 1954. *Magic, Science, and Religion, and Other Essays*. Garden City, NY: Doubleday.

Mannheim, Karl. 1949. *Ideology and Utopia: An Introduction to the Sociology of Knowledge*. Trans. Louis Wirth and Edward Shils. New York: Harcourt, Brace.

Manzanares, César Vidal. 1996. *José Antonio: La biografía no autorízada*. Madrid: Anaya & M. Muchnik.

Margreth, Donat. 1993. "Skythische Schamanen? Die Nachrichten über Enarees-Anarieis bei Herodot und Hippokrates." PhD diss., Universität Zurich.

Marshall, Joseph E. 2010. "*Goldgyfan* or *goldwlance*: A Christian Apology for Beowulf and Treasure." *Studies in Philology* 107: 1–24.

Marx, Karl, and Friedrich Engels. 1964. *Marx and Engels on Religion*. New York: Schocken Books.

Mauss, Marcel. 1967. *The Gift: Forms and Functions of Exchange in Archaic Societies*. Trans. Ian Cunnison. New York: W.W. Norton; French original, 1925.

Mayrhofer, Manfred. 1973. *Onomastica Persepolitana: Das altiranische Namengut der Persepolis-täfelchen*. Vienna: Österreichischen Akademie der Wissenschaften.

———. 1992–2001. *Etymologisches Wörterbuch des Altindoarischen*. 2 vols. Heidelberg: Carl Winter.

———. 2006. *Einiges zu den Skythen, ihrer Sprache, ihrem Nachleben*. Vienna: Verlag der Österreichischen Akademie der Wissenschaften.

Mayrhofer, Manfred, Wolfgang Meid, Bernfried Schlerath, and Rüdiger Schmitt, eds. 1974. *Antiquitates Indogermanicae: Gedenkschrift für Hermann Güntert*. Innsbruck: Innsbrucker Beiträge zur Sprachwissenschaft.

McLaughlin, James. 1890. "Report of Standing Rock Agency." In *Annual Report of the Commissioner of Indian Affairs, for the Year 1890*. Washington, DC: Government Printing Office.

———. 1891. "Report of Standing Rock Agency." In *Annual Report of the Commissioner of Indian Affairs, for the Year 1891*. Washington, DC: Government Printing Office.

———. 1989. *My Friend the Indian*. Lincoln: University of Nebraska Press; orig. 1910.

Meillet, Antoine, and Émile Benveniste, 1931. *Grammaire du Vieux Perse*. Paris: Honoré Champion.

Mellinkoff, Ruth. 1979. "Cain's Monstrous Progeny in *Beowulf*: Part I, Noachic Tradition." *Anglo-Saxon England* 8: 143–97.

———. 1981. "Cain's Monstrous Progeny in *Beowulf*: Part II, Post-diluvian Survival." *Anglo-Saxon England* 9: 183–97.

Metsvahi, Merili. 2001. "Werwolfprozesse in Estland und Livland im 17. Jahrhundert: Zusammenstöße zwischen der Realität von Richtern und von Bauern." In Jürgen Beyer and Reet Hiiemäe, eds., *Folklore als Tatsachenbericht*, 175–84. Tartu: Sektion für Folkloristik des Estnischen Literaturmuseums.

Meuli, Karl. 1921. *Odysee und Argonautika: Untersuchungen zur griechischen Sagengeschichte und zum Epos*. Berlin: Weidmann.

———. 1933. *Die deutschen Masken*. Berlin: de Gruyter.

———. 1935. "Scythica." *Hermes* 70: 121–76.

———. 1940. *Kalewala: Altfinnische Volks- und Helderlieder*. Basel: B. Schwabe.

———. 1946. "Griechische Opferbräuche." In Olof Gigon et al., eds., *Phyllobolia für Peter von der Mühll*, 185–288. Basel: B. Schwabe.

———. 1975. *Gesammelte Schriften*. Basel: Schwabe.

Miles, Nelson A. 1892. "Report of the Major-General Commanding the Army, Dept. of the Missouri." In *Annual Report of the Secretary of War for the Year 1891*. Washington, DC: Government Printing Office.

Miller, David Humphreys. 1959. *Ghost Dance*. Lincoln: University of Nebraska Press.

Miller, Jay. 1989. "Deified Mind among the Keresan Pueblos." In Mary Key Ritchie and Henry M. Hoenigswald, eds., *General and Amerindian Ethnolinguistics in Remembrance of Stanley Newman*, 151–56. Berlin: Mouton de Gruyter.

———. 2001. "Keres: Key to the Pueblo Puzzle." *Ethnohistory* 48: 495–514.

Miller, Julius. 1972. "The Anthropology of Keres Identity." PhD diss., Rutgers University.

Minge, Ward Alan. 1991. *Ácoma: Pueblo in the Sky*. 2nd ed. Albuquerque: University of New Mexico Press.

Minns, E. H. 1913. *Scythians and Greeks*. Cambridge: Cambridge University Press.

Modi, Jivanji Jamshedji. 1922. *The Religious Ceremonies and Customs of the Parsees*. Bombay: British India Press.

Mogk, Eugen. 1909. "Die Menschenopfer bei den Germanen." *Abhandlungen der königlichen Gesellschaft der Wissenschaften in Leipzig, Philologisch-historische Klasse* 57: 601–43.

———. 1912. "Ein Nachwort zu den Menschenopfern bei den Germanen." *Archiv für Religionswissenschaft* 15: 422–34.

Molé, Marijan. 1952. "Le partage du monde dans la tradition iranienne." *Journal Asiatique* 240: 455–63.

———. 1959. "Un ascétisme moral dans les livres pehlevis?" *Revue de l'Histoire des Religions* 155: 145–90.

———. 1960. "Daēnā, le pont Činvat et l'initiation dans le mazdéisme." *Revue de l'Histoire des Religions* 157: 155–85.

———. 1963. *Culte, mythe et cosmologie dans l'Iran ancien*. Paris: Presses Universitaires de France.

Molho, Tony. 2004. "Carlo Ginzburg: Reflections on the Intellectual Cosmos of a 20th-Century Historian." *History of European Ideas* 30: 121–48.

Momigliano, Arnaldo. 1983. "Premesse per una discussione su Georges Dumézil." *Opus* 2: 329–42.

Monter, E. William. 1969. *European Witchcraft*. New York: Wiley.

———. 1972. "The Historiography of European Witchcraft: Progress and Prospects." *Journal of Interdisciplinary History* 2: 435–51.

Mooney, James. 1896. *The Ghost-Dance Religion and the Sioux Outbreak of 1890: Fourteenth Annual Report (Part 2) of the Bureau of Ethnology to the Smithsonian Institution*. Washington, DC: Government Printing Office.

———. 1973. *The Ghost Dance Religion and Wounded Knee*. Toronto: Dover Publications.

Moses, L. G. 1985. "'The Father Tells Me So!': Wovoka the Ghost Dance Prophet." *American Indian Quarterly* 40: 335–51.

Motz, Lotte. 1996. *The King, the Champion, and the Sorceror: A Study in Germanic Myth.* Vienna: Fassbaender.

Mühlenstein, Hugo. 1986. "Kirschmus und Kahlköpfe." In *O-o-pe-ro-si: Festschrift für Ernst Risch,* 561–64. Berlin: Walter de Gruyter.

Müller, Carl Werner. 2002. "Der Tod des Intaphrenes." *Hyperboreus* 8: 222–31.

Müller-Limberg, Wolfgang. 1991. *Pater Wilhelm Schmidt und die Entwicklung der Wiener Schule der Ethnologie.* Cologne: Philosophische Fakultät der Universität zu Köln.

Munson, Rosaria Vignolo. 2001. *Telling Wonders: Ethnographic and Political Discourse in the Work of Herodotus.* Ann Arbor: University of Michigan Press.

———. 2009. "Who are Herodotus' Persians?" *Classical World* 102: 457–70.

Murphy, Eileen M. 2004. "Herodotus and the Amazons Meet the Cyclops: Philology, Osteoarchaeology, and the Eurasian Iron Age." In Eberhard W. Sauer, ed., *Archaeology and Ancient History: Breaking Down the Boundaries,* 169–84. New York: Routledge.

Murphy, Eileen, Ilia Gokhman, Yuri Chistov, and Ludmila Barkova. 2002. "Prehistoric Old World Scalping: New Cases from the Cemetery of Aymyrlyg, South Siberia." *American Journal of Archaeology* 106: 1–10.

Murphy, Eileen, and James P. Mallory. 2000. "Herodotus and the Cannibals." *Antiquity* 74: 388–94.

Mutti, Claudio. 1989. *Mircea Eliade e la Guardia di Ferro.* Parma: Edizioni all' Insegna del Veltro.

Nabokov, Peter. 2015. *How the World Moves: The Odyssey of an American Indian Family.* New York: Viking.

Narten, Johanna. 1982. *Die Aməša Spəntas im Avesta.* Wiesbaden: Otto Harrassowitz.

Näsström, Britt-Mari. 1989. *The Abhorrence of Love: Studies in Rituals and Mystic Aspects in Catullus' Poem of Attis.* Stockholm: Almqvist & Wiksell.

Needham, Joseph. 1954–82. *Science and Civilization in China.* 5 vols. Cambridge: Cambridge University Press.

Niitemaa, Vilho. 1949. *Die undeutsche Frage in der Politik der livländischen Städte im Mittelalter.* Helsinki: Annales Academiae Scientiarum Fennicae.

Nioradze, Georgii. 1925. *Der Schamanismus bei den sibirischen Völkern.* Stuttgart: Strecker und Schröder.

Nola, Alfonso di. 1977. "Mircea Eliade e l'antisemitismo." *La Rassegna Mensile di Israel* 43 (Jan.–March): 12–15.

Noreen, Adolf, ed. and trans. 1925. *Ynglingatal: Text, översättning och kommentar.* Stockholm: Akademiens förlag.

———. 1970. *Altnordische Grammatik.* Tübingen: Max Niemeyer Verlag.

Norr, Svante. 1998. *To Rede and to Rown: Expressions of Early Scandinavian Kingship in Written Sources.* Uppsala: Dept. of Archaeology and Ancient History, Uppsala University.

Nyberg, Henrik Samuel. 1964–74. *A Manual of Pahlavi.* Wiesbaden: Otto Harrassowitz.

Olaus Magnus. 1555. *Historia de Gentibus Septentrionalibus*. Rome: J.M. de Viottis.

Olympius, Johann Ernest. 1720. *Promptuarium Juris Canonici, Reudalis, Civilis, et Criminalis*. Vienna: Georg Lehmann.

One Bull, Henry Oscar. N.d. "Interviews and Statements of Chief Henry Oscar One Bull." The Walter Stanley Campbell Manuscript Collection, University of Oklahoma Libraries' Western History Collections, Box 104, Folder 11. http:// digital.libraries.ou.edu/cdm/compoundobject/collection/CampbellWS/id/2903 /rec/1.

Ortiz, Alfonso, and Richard Erdoes, eds. 1984. *American Indian Myths and Legends*. New York: Pantheon Books.

Ortiz, Simon. 1994. "What We See: A Perspective on Chaco Canyon and Its Ancestry." In Stephen H. Lekson et al., *Chaco Canyon: A Center and Its World*, 65–72. Santa Fe: Museum of New Mexico Press.

Osterreich, Shelley Anne. 1991. *The American Indian Ghost Dance, 1870 and 1890: An Annotated Bibliography*. Westport, CT: Greenwood Press.

Ostler, Jeffrey. 2004. *The Plains Sioux and U.S. Colonialism from Lewis and Clark to Wounded Knee*. Cambridge: Cambridge University Press.

Otto, Rudolf. 1958. *The Idea of the Holy: An Inquiry into the Non-rational Factor in the Idea of the Divine and Its Relation to the Rational*. Trans. John Harvey. London: Oxford University Press; German original, 1917.

Overholt, Thomas W. 1978. "Short Bull, Black Elk, Sword, and the 'Meaning' of the Ghost Dance." *Religion* 8: 171–95.

Pakzad, Fazlollah, ed. 2005. *Bundahišn: Zoroastrische Kosmogonie und Kosmologie*. Vol. 1, *Kritische Edition*. Tehran: Centre for the Great Islamic Encyclopaedia.

Panaino, Antonio. 2001. "A Few Remarks on the Zoroastrian Conception of the Status of Angra Mainyu and of the Daēvas." *Res Orientales* 13: 99–107.

———. 2013. "Il culto del fuoco nello Zoroastrismo." In *Il fuoco nell' Alto Medioevo*, 65–93. Spoleto: Centro Italiano di Studi sull' Alto Medioevo.

Parsons, Elsie Clews. 1920. "Notes on Ceremonialism at Laguna." *Anthropological Papers of the American Museum of Natural History* 19/4: 85–131.

Patton, Kimberley, and Benjamin Ray, eds. 2000. *A Magic Still Dwells: Comparative Religion in the Postmodern Age*. Berkeley: University of California Press.

Payne, Stanley G. 1999. *Fascism in Spain, 1923–1977*. Madison: University of Wisconsin Press.

Paz, Abel. 1976. *Durruti: The People Armed*. Trans. Nancy MacDonald. Montreal: Black Rose Books.

———. 2007. *Durruti in the Spanish Revolution*. Trans. Chuck Morse. Oakland, CA: AK Press; Spanish original, 2004.

Pecharromán, Julio Gil. 1996. *José Antonio Primo de Rivera: Retrato de un visionario*. Madrid: Temas de Hoy.

Peires, J. B. 1982. *The House of Phalo: A History of the Xhosa People in the Days of Their Independence*. Berkeley: University of California Press.

———. 1989. *The Dead Will Arise: Nongqawuse and the Great Xhosa Cattle-Killing Movement of 1856–57*. Bloomington: Indiana University Press.

Pelling, Christopher. 2002. "Herodotus' Debate on the Constitutions." *Proceedings of the Cambridge Philological Society* 48: 123–58.

———. 2013. "East Is East and West Is West—or Are They? National Stereotypes in Herodotus." First published in *Histos* 1 (1997): 51–66.

Pettazzoni, Raffaele. 1929. *La confessione dei peccati*. Bologna: Nicola Zanichelli.

———. 1947–48. "La verità del mito." *Studi e Materiali della Storia delle Religioni* 21: 104–16.

———. 1956. *The All-Knowing God: Researches into Early Religion and Culture*. Trans. H. J. Rose. London: Methuen; Italian original, 1957.

———. 1967. "History and Phenomenology in the Science of Religion." In *Essays in the History of Religions*, trans. H. J. Rose, 215–19. Leiden: E. J. Brill.

Peucer, Kaspar. 1560. *Commentarius de præcipuis generibus divinationum*. Wittenberg: I. Crato.

Phillips, E. D. 1955. "The Legend of Aristeas: Fact and Fancy in Early Greek Notions of East Russia, Siberia, and Innder Asia." *Artibus Asiae* 18: 161–77.

———. 1960. "The *Argippaei* of Herodotus." *Artibus Asiae* 23: 124–28.

Pijoan, Teresa. 2005. *American Indian Creation Myths*. Santa Fe: Sunstone Press.

Pirart, Eric. 1992. *Kayān Yasn (Yasht 19.9–96): L'origine avestique des dynasties mythiques d'Iran*. Barcelona: Aula Orientalis.

Piras, Andrea. 2000. "Le tre lance del giusto Wirāz e la freccia di Abaris: Ordalia e volo estatico tra iranismo e ellenismo." *Studi Orientali e Linguistici* 7: 95–109.

Plakans, Andrejs. 2000. "Witches and Werewolves in Early Modern Livonia: An Unfinished Project." In Lars M. Andersson, Anna Jansdotter, Badil E. B. Persson, and Charlotte Tornbjer, eds., *Rätten: En Festskrift till Bengt Ankerll*, 255–71. Lund: Nordic Academic Press.

Plezia, Marian. 1959–60. "Hekataios über die Völker am Nordrand des skythischen Schwarzmeergebietes." *Eos* 50: 27–42.

Pócs, Éva. 1989. "Hungarian *Táltos* and His European Parallels." In Mihály Hoppál and Juha Pentikäinen, eds., *Uralic Mythology and Folklore*, 251–74. Budapest: Ethnographic Institute of the Hungarian Academy of Sciences.

———. 1993. "Le sabbat et les mythologies indo-européennes." In Nicole Jacques-Chaquin and Maxime Préaud, eds., *Le sabbat des sorciers VXe-XVIIIe siècles*, 23–31. Grenoble: J. Million.

———. 2011. "Nature and Culture—'The Raw and the Cooked': Shape-Shifting and Double Beings in Central and Eastern European Folklore." In Willem de Blécourt and Christa Agnes Tuczay, eds., *Tierverwandlungen: Codierungen und Diskurse*, 99–134. Tübingen: Francke.

Pócs, Éva, and Gábor Klaniczay, eds. 2008. *Witchcraft Mythologies and Persecutions*. Budapest: Central European University Press.

Pohlenz, Max. 1937. "Hippokratesstudien." *Nachrichten der Gesellschaft der Wissenschaften zu Göttingen* 1/2: 67–101.

Pokorny, Julius. 1959. *Indogermanisches etymologisches Wörterbuch*. Bern: Francke Verlag.

Pongratz-Leisten, Beate. 2002. "'Lying King' and 'False Prophet': The Intercultural Transfer of a Rhetorical Device within Ancient Near Eastern Ideologies." In A. Panaino and G. Pettinato, eds., *Ideologies as Intercultural Phenomena*, 215–43. Milan: University of Bologna.

Portier-Young, Anathea E. 2011. *Apocalypse against Empire: Theologies of Resistance in Early Judaism.* Grand Rapids, MI: William B. Eerdmans.

Potocki, Jan. 1802. *Histoire primitive des peuple de la Russie: avec une exposition complète de toutes les notions, nécessaires à l'intelligence du 4me livre d'Hérodote.* St. Petersburg: Imprimerie de l'Académie impériale des sciences.

Powell, J. Enoch. 1938. *A Lexicon to Herodotus.* Reprint, Cambridge: Cambridge University Press, 2004.

Primo de Rivera, José Antonio. 1945. *Obras completas.* Madrid: Vicesecretaría de Educación Popular de F. E. T. Y. de las J. O. N. S.

Primo de Rivera, Rocio. 2003. *Los Primo de Rivera: Historia de una familia.* Madrid: La Esfera de los Libros.

Purley, Anthony. 1974. "Keres Pueblo Concepts of Deity." *American Indian Culture and Research Journal* 1: 29–32.

Quiroga, Alejandro. 2007. *Making Spaniards: Primo de Rivera and the Nationalization of the Masses.* Houndmills: Palgrave Macmillan.

Raevskiy, Dmitriy. 1970. "Skifsky mifologičesky sužet." *Sovietskaja Archeologija* 3: 90–101.

———. 1977. *Očerki ideologii skifo-sakskich plemen.* Moscow: Nauka.

———. 1993. *Scythian Mythology.* Sofia: Secor Publishers.

Ratcliff, Dilwyn F. 1957. *Prelude to Franco: Political Aspects of the Dictatorship of General Miguel Primo de Rivera.* New York: Las Americas Publishing.

Rauer, Christine. 2000. *Beowulf and the Dragon: Parallels and Analogues.* Cambridge: D.S. Brewer.

Redfield, James. 1985. "Herodotus the Tourist." *Classical Philology* 80: 97–118.

Reinach, Adolphe. 1913. "L'origine des Amazones: À propos d'une explication nouvelle de la légende amazonienne." *Revue de l'Histoire des Religions* 67: 277–307.

Reulecke, Jürgen. 1990. "Das Jahr 1902 und die Ursprünge der Männerbund-Ideologie in Deutschland." In Gisela Völger and Karin von Welck, eds., *Männerbande, Männerbünde: Zur Rolle des Mannes im Kulturvergleich,* 1: 3–10. Cologne: Ethnologica.

Ricketts, Mac Linscott. 1988. *Mircea Eliade: The Romanian Roots, 1907–1945.* Boulder, CO: East European Monographs.

Riedlberger, Peter. 1996. "Skalpieren bei den Skythen: Zu Herodot IV 64." *Klio* 78: 53–60.

Rohrbacher, Peter. 2002. *Die Geschichte des Hamiten-Mythos.* Vienna: Afro-Pub.

Rollinger, Robert. 2000. "Herodotus and the Intellectual Heritage of the Ancient Near East." In Sanna Aro and R. M. Whiting, eds., *The Heirs of Assyria,* 65–77. Helsinki: Neo-Assyrian Text Corpus Project.

Romilly, Jacqueline de. 1959. "Le classement des constitutions d'Hérodote à Aristote." *Revue des Études Grecques* 72: 81–99.

Roscoe, Will. 1996. "Priests of the Goddess: Gender Transgression in Ancient Religion." *History of Religions* 45: 195–230.

Rostovtzeff, Mikhail Ivanovitch. 1922. *Iranians and Greeks in South Russia.* Oxford: Clarendon Press.

———. 1993. *Skythien und der Bosporus.* Vol. 2, *Wiederentdeckte Kapitel und Verwandtes,* ed. Heinz Heinen. Berlin: H. Schoetz.

Sahlins, Marshall. 1985. *Islands of History.* Chicago: University of Chicago Press.

———. 1995. *How "Natives" Think: About Captain Cook, for Example.* Chicago: University of Chicago Press.

———. 2008. "The Stranger-King Or Elementary Forms of the Political Life." *Indonesia and the Malay World* 36: 177–99.

———. 2011. "The Alterity of Power and Vice Versa, with Reflections on Stranger Kings and the Real-Politics of the Marvellous." In Anthony McElligott, Liam Chambers, Clara Breathnach, and Catherine Lawless, eds., *History: From Medieval Ireland to the Post-Modern World,* 63–101. Dublin: Irish Academic Press.

———. 2013. *What Kinship Is—and Is Not.* Chicago: University of Chicago Press.

Sahlins, Marshall, and David Graeber. 2017. *On Kings.* Chicago: Hau Books.

Sai, Akiga. 1965. *Akiga's Story: The Tiv Tribe as Seen by One of Its Members.* Trans. Rupert East. London: Oxford University Press; 1st ed., 1939.

Said, Edward. 1978. *Orientalism.* New York: Vintage Books.

———. 1980. *L'orientalisme: L'orient créé par l'occident.* Trans. Catherine Malamoud. Paris: Éditions du Seuil.

St. Germain, Jill. 2009. *Broken Treaties: United States and Canadian Relations with the Lakotas and the Plains Cree, 1868–1885.* Lincoln: University of Nebraska Press.

Sanders, Edith. 1969. "The Hamitic Hypothesis: Its Origin and Functions in Time Perspective." *Journal of African History* 10: 521–32.

Sandoe, Joe S. 1992. *Pueblo Nations: Eight Centuries of Pueblo Indian History.* Santa Fe: Clear Light.

Schiltz, Véronique. 1994. *Die Skythen und andere Steppenvölker: 8. Jahrhundert v. Chr. bis 1. Jahrhundert nach Chr.* Munich: C.H. Beck.

Schlerath, Bernfried, and P. O. Skjærvø. 1987. "*Aša.*" In *Encyclopaedia Iranica,* 2: 694–96. London: Routledge.

Schlieper, Herbert. 1931. *Die kosmogonischen Mythen der Urvölker.* Bonn: Universitäts-Buchdruckerei.

Schmeja, Hans. 1976. "Awestisch *āzi*- 'Habgier' = altindisch *āji*- 'Wettkampf'?" *Klagenfurter Beiträge zur Sprachwissenschaft* 2: 101–7.

Schmidt, Hanns-Peter. 1996. "The Non-Existence of Ahreman and the Mixture (*gumēzišn*) of Good and Evil." In *K.R. Cama Oriental Institute: Second International Congress Proceedings,* 79–95. Bombay: K.R. Cama Oriental Institute.

———. 2000. "Vom awestischen Dämon Āzi zur manichäischen Āz, der Mutter aller Dämonen." In Ronald E. Emmerick, Werner Sundermann, and Peter Zieme, eds., *Studia Manicahaica: IV internationaler Kongress zum* Manichäismus, 517–27. Berlin: Akademie Verlag.

Schmidt, Wilhelm. 1939. *Primitive Revelation.* Trans. Joseph Bayerl. St. Louis and London: Herder; German original, 1910.

Schmitt, Rüdiger, ed. and trans. 1991. *The Bisitun Inscriptions of Darius the Great: Old Persian Text.* London: School of Oriental and African Studies.

———. 2003. "Die skythischen Personennamen bei Herodot." *Annali del Istituto Orientale di Napoli* 63: 1–31.

———. 2006. "Griechische Umdeutung eines 'skythischen' Ethnonyms." *Historische Sprachforschung* 119: 186–89.

———. 2011a. "Herodot und iranische Sprachen." in Robert Rollinger, Brigitte Truschnegg, and Reinhold Bichler, eds. *Herodot und das Persische Weltrich/ Herodotus and the Persian Empire* (Wiesbaden: Harrassowitz), 313–41.

———. 2011b. *Iranisches Personennamenbuch.* Vol. 5, *Iranische Namen in Neben-überlieferungen indogermanischer Sprachen.* Vienna: Verlag der Österreichischen Akademie der Wissenschaften.

Schmoll, Pamela G. 1993. "Black Stomachs, Beautiful Stones: Soul-Eating among Hausa in Niger." In Jean Comaroff and John Comaroff, eds., *Modernity and Its Malcontents: Ritual and Power in Postcolonial Africa*, 193–220. Chicago: University of Chicago Press.

Schneider, Hermann. 1938. *Die Götter der Germanen.* Tübingen: J.C.B. Mohr.

Schnurbein, Stefanie von. 1990. "Geheime kultische Männerbünde bei den Germanen—Eine Theorie im Spannungsfeld zwischen Wissenschaft und Ideologie." In Gisela Völger and Karin von Welck, eds., *Männerbande, Männerbünde: Zur Rolle des Mannes im Kulturvergleich*, 2: 97–102. Cologne: Ethnologica.

Schröder, Franz Rolf. 1927. "Ein altirischer Krönungsritus und das indogermanische Rossopfer." *Zeitschrift für celtische Philologie* 16: 310–12.

Schück, Henrik. 1907. *Studier i Ynglingatal.* Uppsala: Akademiska Boktryckeriet.

Schurtz, Heinrich. 1902. *Altersklassen und Männerbund: Eine Darstellung der Grundformen der Gesellschaft.* Berlin: G. Reimer.

Schutte, Anne Jacobson. 1976. "Carlo Ginzburg." *Journal of Modern History* 48: 296–315.

Sebag, Lucien. 1971. *L'invention du monde chez les Indiens Pueblos.* Paris: Maspero.

See, Klaus von. 1990. "Politische Männerbund-Ideologie von der wilhelminischen Zeit bis zum Nationalsozialismus." In Gisela Völger and Karin von Welck, eds., *Männerbande, Männerbünde: Zur Rolle des Mannes im Kulturvergleich*, 1: 93–102. Cologne: Ethnologica.

See, Klaus von, et al. 2000. *Kommentar zu den Liedern der Edda.* Vol. 3, *Götterlieder.* Heidelberg: Carl Winter.

Shaked, Shaul. 1967. "Some Notes on Ahreman, the Evil Spirit, and His Creation." In E. E. Urbach et al., eds., *Studies in Mysticism and Religion presented to Gershom G. Scholem*, 227–34. Jerusalem: Magnes Press.

———. 1971. "The Notions *Mēnōg* and *Gētīg* in the Pahlavi Texts and Their Relation to Eschatology." *Acta Orientalia* 33: 59–107.

———. 1994. *Dualism in Transformation: Varieties of Religion in Sasanian Iran.* London: School of Oriental and African Studies.

Sharma, Arvind. 2005. *Religious Studies and Comparative Methodology: The Case for Reciprocal Illumination.* Albany: State University of New York Press,.

Shayegan, M. Rahim. 2012. *Aspects of History and Epic in Ancient Iran: From Gaumāta to Wahnām.* Washington, DC: Center for Hellenic Studies.

Shirokogoroff, S. M. 1935. *Psychomental Complex of the Tungus.* London: Kegan, Paul, Trench, and Trübner.

Silber, Patricia. 1977. "Gold and Its Significance in *Beowulf.*" *Annuale Mediaevale* 18: 5–19.

Silko, Leslie Marmon. 1977. *Ceremony.* New York: Viking Books.

Simek, Rudolf. 2003. *Religion und Mythologie der Germanen.* Darmstadt: Wissenschaftliche Buchgesellschaft.

Simmons, Marc. 1979a. "History of Pueblo-Spanish Relations to 1821." In Alfonso Ortiz, ed., *Handbook of North American Indians,* vol. 9, *Southwest,* 178–93. Washington, DC: Smithsonian Institution.

———. 1979b. "History of the Pueblos since 1821." In Alfonso Ortiz, ed., *Handbook of North American Indians,* vol. 9, *Southwest,* 206–23. Washington, DC: Smithsonian Institution.

Simpson, J. A., and E. S. C. Weiner. 1989. *The Oxford English Dictionary.* 2nd ed. Oxford: Clarendon Press.

Sincerus, Theophilius. 1677. *Nord-Schwedische Hexerey, oder Simia Dei, Gottes Affe. Das ist: Auszführliche Beschreibung der schändlichen Verführungen des leidigen Satans.* N.p.

Skjærvø, Prods Oktor. 1983. "*Farnah*: Mot mede en vieux-perse?" *Bulletin de la Société Linguistique* 78: 241–59.

———. 1987. "*Aždahā*: i. In Old and Middle Iranian." In *Encyclopaedia Iranica,* 3: 191–99. London: Routledge.

———. 2002. "Ahura Mazda and Armaiti, Heaven and Earth, in the Old Avesta." *Journal of the American Oriental Society* 122: 399–410.

———. 2003. "Truth and Deception in Ancient Iran." In Carlo G. Cereti and Farrokh Vajifdar, eds., *Ataš-e Dorun: The Fire Within; Jamshid Soroush Soroushian Commemorative Volume,* 383–434. N.p.: Mehrborzin Soroushian.

———. 2008. "Jamšid: i. Myth of Jamšid." In *Encyclopaedia Iranica,* 14: 501–22. London: Routledge.

Smith, Jonathan Z. 1969. "The Glory, Jest, and Riddle: James George Frazer and *The Golden Bough.*" PhD diss., Yale University.

———. 1973. "When the Bough Breaks." *History of Religions* 12: 342–71.

———. 1982. *Imagining Religion: From Babylon to Jonestown.* Chicago: University of Chicago Press.

———. 2004. "When the Chips Are Down." In *Relating Religion: Essays in the Study of Religion,* 1–60. Chicago: University of Chicago Press.

Smith, Rex Alan. 1975. *Moon of Popping Trees: The Tragedy at Wounded Knee and the End of the Indian Wars.* Lincoln: University of Nebraska Press.

Smoak, Gregory E. 2006. *Ghost Dances and Identity: Prophetic Religion and American Indian Ethnogenesis in the Nineteenth Century.* Berkeley: University of California Press.

Söderblom, Nathan. 1933. *The Living God: Basal Forms of Personal Religion.* Trans. Yngve Brilloth. London: Oxford University Press; Swedish original, 1932.

Södergård, J. Peter. 1993. "The Ritualized Bodies of Cybele's Galli and the Methodological Problem of the Plurality of Explanations." In Tore Ahlbäck, ed., *The Problem of Ritual*, 169–93. Stockholm: Almqvist & Wiksell.

Sonderegger, Arno. 2011. "Africa in Austrian and German African Studies." In Wulf D. Huld, Christian Koller, and Moshe Zimmermann, eds., *Racisms Made in Germany*, 123–44. Vienna: Lit Verlag.

Spehr, Harald. 1936. "Waren die Germanen 'Ekstatiker'?" *Rasse: Monatszeitschrift der nordischen Bewegung* 3: 394–400.

Spineto, Natale, ed. 2005. *Interrompere il quotidiano: La costruzione del tempo nell' esperienza religiosa*. Milan: Jaca Book.

Standing Bear, Luther. 1975. *My People the Sioux*. Ed. E. A. Brininstool. Lincoln: University of Nebraska Press.

Staudacher, Willibald. 1942. *Die Trennung von Himmel und Erde: Ein vorgriechischer Schöpfungsmythus bei Hesiod und den Orphikern*. Tübingen: Bölzle; reprint, Darmstadt: Wissenschaftliche Buchgesellschaft, 1968.

Steinfelden, Augustin Lercheimer von. 1585. *Christlich bedencken und erinnerung von zauberey*. Heidelberg: Müller & Auen.

Stevens, Martin. 1968. "The Progress of *Beowulf*: From Gold-Hoard to Word-Hoard." *Philological Quarterly* 47: 219–38.

Stevenson, Matilda Coxe. 1894. "The Sia." *Bureau of Ethnology, Annual Report* 11. Washington, DC: Government Printing Office.

Stirling, Matthew W. 1942. *Origin Myth of Acoma and Other Records*. Washington, DC: United States Government Printing Office.

Storm, Gustav, ed. 1880. *Monumenta Historica Norvegiæ*. Christiana [Oslo]: A.W. Brøgger.

Straubergs, Karlis. 1939. "Vilkaču ideoloğia Latvijā (Werewolf ideology in Latvia)." In Margers Steparmanis and Arveds Švabe, eds., *Latviesu vesturnieku veltijums Profesoram Robertam Viperam*, 98–114. Riga: A. Gulbis.

———. 1955. "Om Varulvarna i Baltikum." In Sigurd Erixon, ed., *Liv och folkkultur*, 107–2. Stockholm: Samfundet för Svensk Folklivsforskning.

———. 1957. "Zur Jenseitstopographie." *Arv* 13: 56–110.

Streck, Bernhard, ed. 2000. *Ethnologie und Nationalsozialismus*. Gehren: Escher.

Strenski, Ivan. 1987. *Four Theories of Myth in Twentieth-Century History*. Iowa City: University of Iowa Press.

Ström, Åke V. 1959. "The King God and Sacrifice in Old Norse Religion." In *La regalità sacra / The Sacral Kingship*, 702–15. Leiden: E.J. Brill.

———. 1966. "Die Hauptriten des Wikingerzeitlichen nordischen Opfers." In Kurt Rudolph, ed., *Festschrift Walter Baetke*, 330–42. Weimar: Hermann Böhlaus Nachfolger.

Ström, Folke. 1954. *Diser, Nornor, Valkyrjor: Fruktbarhetskult och sakralt kungadöme*. Stockholm: Almqvist & Wiksells.

Suárez, Domingo Plácido. 1999. "La *douleía* en Heródoto: Imperialismo persa y relaciones de dependencia." In *Miscelánea en memoria de C. Serrano*, 681–88. Madrid: CSIC.

Suárez, Jaime. 2003. *Introducción a José Antonio*. Madrid: Plataforma.

Sundermann, Werner. 2003. "The Zoroastrian and the Manichaean Demon Āz." In Siamak Adhami, ed., *Paitimāna: Essays in Iranian, Indo-European, and Indian Studies in Honor of Hanns-Peter Schmidt*, 328–38. Costa Mesa, CA: Mazda Publishers.

Sundqvist, Olof. 2002. *Freyr's Offspring: Rulers and Religion in Ancient Svea Society*. Uppsala: Acta Universitas Uppsaliensis, Historia Religionum.

———. 2007. *Kultledare i fornskandinavisk religion*. Uppsala: Department of Archaeology and Ancient History, Uppsala University.

Tamames, Ramón. 2004. *Miguel Primo de Rivera*. Barcelona: Ediciones B.

Tavernier, J. 2007. *Iranica in the Achaemenid Period (ca. 550–330 B.C.): Lexicon of Old Iranian Proper Names and Loanwords, Attested in Non-Iranian Texts*. Louvain: Peeters.

Taylor, Paul Beekman. 1966. "Heorot, Earth, and Asgard: Christian Poetry and Pagan Myth." *Tennessee Studies in Literature* 11: 119–30.

———. 1986. "The Traditional Language of Treasure in *Beowulf*." *Journal of English and Germanic Philology* 85: 191–205.

Thomas, Hugh, ed. 1972. *José Antonio Primo de Rivera: Selected Writings*. New York: Harper & Row.

Thomas, Louis-Vincent, René Luneau, and J. L. Doneux. 1969. *Les religions d'Afrique Noire: Texts et traditions sacrés*. Paris: Fayard.

Thomas, Rosalind. 2000. *Herodotus in Context: Ethnography, Science, and the Art of Persuasion*. Cambridge: Cambridge University Press.

Thordarson, Fridrik. 1988. "The Scythian Funeral Customs: Some Notes on Herodotus IV, 71–75." In *A Green Leaf: Papers in Honour of Professor Jes P. Asmussen*, 539–47. Leiden: E.J. Brill.

———. 1996. "Herodotus and the Iranians: ὄψις, ἀκοή, ψεῦδος." *Symboloe Osloenses* 71: 42–58.

Timus, Mihaela. 2004. "Les 'Haskell Lectures' de Stig Wikander, University of Chicago, 1967." *Archaeus* 8: 265–322.

Toll, Friedrich von. 1839. "Zur Geschichte der Hexenprocesse: Auszug aus dem Protocoll des Wier- und Jerweschen Manngerichts." *Das Inland* 4: 257–63.

Tranfaglia, Nicola, ed. 1996. *L'itinerario di Leone Ginzburg*. Turin: Boringhieri.

Triebel-Schubert, Charlotte. 1990. "Anthropologie und Norm: Der Skythenabschnitt in der hippokratischen Schrift *Über die Umwelt*." *Medizin-historisches Journal* 25: 90–103.

Trubetzkoy, Prince N. S. 1922. "Remarques sur quelques mots iraniens empruntés par les langues du Caucase." *Mémoires de la Société de Linguistique de Paris* 22: 247–52.

Turner, Victor. 1969. *The Ritual Process: Structure and Anti-structure*. Chicago: Aldine.

Turville-Petre, E. O. G. 1964. *Myth and Religion of the North*. London: Weidenfeld & Nicolson.

Tyler, Hamilton A. 1964. *Pueblo Gods and Myths*. Norman: University of Oklahoma Press.

Tzatourian, Audrey. 2012. *Yima: Structure de la pensée religieuse en Iran ancien*. Paris: L'Harmattan.

Upham, Steadman. 1982. *Polities and Power: An Economic and Political History of the Western Pueblo.* New York: Academic Press.

Urban, Hugh. 2000. "Making a Place to Take a Stand: Jonathan Z. Smith and the Politics and Poetics of Comparison." *Method and Theory in the Study of Religion* 12: 339–78.

Ustinova, Yulia. 1999. *The Supreme Gods of the Bosporan Kingdom: Celestial Aphrodite and the Most High God.* Leiden: E.J. Brill.

———. 2002. "Lycanthropy in Sarmatian Warrior Society: The Kobyskovsko Torque." *Ancient West and East* 1: 102–23.

———. 2005. "Snake-Limbed and Tendril-Limbed Goddesses in the Art and Mythology of the Mediterranean and Black Sea." In David Braund, ed., *Scythians and Greeks: Cultural Interactions in Scythia, Athens, and the Early Roman Empire,* 64–79. Exeter: University of Exeter Press.

Utley, Robert M. 1963. *The Last Days of the Sioux Nation.* New Haven, CT: Yale University Press.

———. 1993. *Sitting Bull: The Life and Times of an American Patriot.* New York: Henry Holt.

Vähi, Tiina. 2006. "The Image of Werewolf in Folk Religion and Its Theological and Demonological Interpretations." In Manfried L. G. Dietrich and Tarmo Kulmar, eds., *The Significance of Base Texts for the Religious Identity / Die Bedeutung von Grundtesten für die religiöse Identität,* 213–37. Münster: Ugarit Verlag.

———. 2011. "Werwölfe—Viehdiebe und Räuber im Wolfspelz? Elemente des archaischen Gewohnheitsrechts in estnischen Werwolfvorstellungen." In Willem de Blécourt and Christa Agnes Tuczay, eds., *Tierverwandlungen: Codierungen und Diskurse,* 135–56. Tübingen: Francke.

Valk, Ülo. 2001. *The Black Gentleman: Manifestations of the Devil in Estonian Folk Religion.* Trans. Ülle Männarti. Helsinki: Suomalainen Tiedeakatemia.

———. 2008. "Reflections of Folk Belief and Legends at the Witch Trials of Estonia." In Eszter Csonka-Takacs, Gabor Klaniczay, and Eva Pocs, eds., *Witchcraft Mythologies and Persecutions,* 269–82. Budapest: Central European University Press.

Vallo, Fred S. Sr., 2015. "New 'Origin' Publication Is Affront to Acoma." *Santa Fe New Mexican.* http://www.santafenewmexican.com/opinion/my_view/new -origin-publication-is-affront-to-acoma/article_7d58156b-7d45-5154-aaec-36a3 829b3d30.html.

Vendryes, Joseph. 1934. "La couvade chez les Scythes." *Comptes Rendus de l'Académie des Inscriptions et Belles Lettres,* 329–39.

Vermaseren, M. J. 1977. *Cybele and Attis: The Myth and the Cult.* London: Thames & Hudson.

Vernant, Jean-Pierre. 1980. *Myth and Society in Ancient Greece.* Trans. Janet Lloyd Sussex: Harvester Press; French original, 1974.

———. 1983. "Hestia-Hermes." In *Myth and Thought among the Greeks,* trans. Janet Lloyd, 127–76. London: Routledge & Kegan Paul.

Vestal, Stanley. 1932. *Sitting Bull: Champion of the Sioux.* Boston: Houghton Mifflin.

Vestergaard, Elisabeth. 1991. "Gift-Giving, Hoarding, and Outdoings." In Ross Samson, ed., *Social Approaches to Viking Studies,* 97–104. Glasgow: Cruithne Press.

Vigfusson, Gudbrand, and F. York Powell. 1883. *Corpus Poeticum Boreale: The Poetry of the Old Northern Tongue.* Vol. 1, *Eddic Poetry.* Oxford: Clarendon Press.

Visintin, Monica. 1997. "Di Echidna, e di altre femmine anguiformi." *Métis* 12: 205–21.

———. 2000. "Echidna, Skythes e l'arco di Herakles: Figure della marginalità nella versione greca delle origini degli Sciti, Herodot 4.8–10." *Materiali e Discussioni per l'Analisi dei Testi Classici* 45: 43–81.

Völger, Gisela, and Karin von Welck, eds. 1990. *Männerbande, Männerbünde: Zur Rolle des Mannes im Kulturvergleich.* 2 vols. Cologne: Ethnologica.

Vossius, Gerard Johannes. 1641. *De theologia gentili et physiologia Christiana.* Amsterdam: Ioannes Blaev.

Wach, Joachim. 1958. *The Comparative Study of Religions.* New York: Columbia University Press.

Walde, Alois, and J. B. Hofmann. 1965. *Lateinisches etymologisches Wörterbuch.* 4th ed. Heidelberg: Carl Winter.

Waters, Kenneth H. 1971. *Herodotos on Tyrants and Despots: A Study in Objectivity.* Wiesbaden: Franz Steiner.

Weber, Max. 1964. *Sociology of Religion.* Trans. Ephraim Fischoff. Boston: Beacon Press; German original, 1922.

———. 1976. *The Protestant Ethic and the Spirit of Capitalism.* Trans. Anthony Giddens. New York: Scribner's; German original, 1922–23.

Weiser, Lily. 1927. *Altgermanische Junglingsweihe und Männerbünde.* Bühl-Baden: Konkordia.

West, Stephanie. 1988. "The Scythian Ultimatum." *Journal of Hellenic Studies* 108: 207–11.

———. 1999a. "Hippocrates' Scythian Sketches." *Eirene* 35: 14–32.

———. 1999b. "Introducing the Scythians: Herodotus on Koumiss (4.2)." *Museum Helveticum* 56: 76–86.

———. 2000. "Herodotus in the North? Reflections on a Colossal Cauldron (4.81)." *Scripta Classica Israelica* 19: 15–34.

———. 2004. "Herodotus and Scythia." In Vassos Karageorghis and Ioannis Tai-facos, eds., *The World of Herodotus,* 73–89. Nicosia: Foundation Anastasios G. Leventis.

———. 2007. "Herodotus and Olbia." In David Braund and S. D. Kryzhitskiy, eds., *Classical Olbia and the Scythian World: From the Sixth Century BC to the Second Century AD,* 79–92. Oxford: Oxford University Press.

White, Leslie A. 1928. "A Comparative Study of the Keresan Medicine Societies." *Proceedings of the International Congress of Americanists* 23: 604–19.

———. 1932a. "The Acoma Indians." *Forty-Seventh Annual Report of the Bureau of American Ethnology.* Washington, DC: Government Printing Office.

———. 1932b. "The Pueblo of San Felipe." *Memoirs of the American Anthropological Association* 38. Menasha, WI: American Anthropological Association.

———. 1935. "The Pueblo of Santo Domingo, New Mexico." *Memoirs of the American Anthropological Association* 43. Menasha, WI: American Anthropological Association.

———. 1942. "The Pueblo of Santa Ana, New Mexico." *Memoirs of the American Anthropological Association* 60. Menasha, WI: American Anthropological Association.

———. 1943. "New Material from Acoma." *Bureau of American Ethnology Bulletin* 136, *Anthropological Papers* 32, 303–60. Washington, DC: Government Printing Office.

———. 1962. "The Pueblo of Sia, New Mexico." *Bureau of American Ethnology Bulletin* 184. Washington, DC: Government Printing Office.

———. 1964. "The World of the Keresan Pueblo Indians." In Stanley Diamond, ed., *Culture in History: Essays in Memory of Paul Radin*, 53–64. New York: Columbia University Press.

Widengren, Geo. 1945–55. *King and Saviour*. 5 vols. Uppsala: Uppsala Universitet Arsskrift.

———. 1968. "Le symbolisme du ceinture." *Iranica Antiqua* 8: 133–55.

Wiesehöfer, Josef. 1978. *Der Aufstand Gaumātas und die Anfänge Dareios I*. Bonn: Rudolf Habelt.

Wild, Friedrich. 1962. "Drachen im Beowulf und andere Drachen." *Sitzungsberichte der österreichische Akademie der Wissenschaften, Philosophisch-historische Klasse* 238.

Williams, David. 1982. *Cain and Beowulf: A Study in Secular Allegory*. Toronto: University of Toronto Press.

Witzel, E. J. Michael. 2012. *The Origins of the World's Mythologies*. Oxford and New York: Oxford University Press.

Zaehner, R. C. 1955. *Zurvan: A Zoroastrian Dilemma*. Oxford: Oxford University Press.

———. 1961. *The Dawn and Twilight of Zoroastrianism*. New York: G.P. Putnam.

Zemzaris, Tālivaldis. 1939. "Vilkaču prāvas Vidzemē (Werewolf Trials in Vidzeme)." In Margers Steprmanis, ed., *Latviesu vesturnieku veltijums Profesoram Dr. hist. Roberta Viperam*, 115–41. Riga: Gulbis.

Zeuss, Caspar. 1837. *Die Deutschen und die Nachbarstämme*. Munich: Ignaz Joseph Lentner.

Zhmud, Leonid. 2012. *Pythagoras and the Early Pythagoreans*. Oxford: Oxford University Press.

Zimmermann, Harm-Peer. 1994. "Männerbund und Totenkult: Methodologische und ideologische Grundlinien der Volks und Altertumskunde Otto Höflers 1933–1945." *Kieler Blätter zur Volkskunde* 26: 5–28.

Znamenski, Andrei A. 2007. *The Beauty of the Primitive: Shamanism and Western Imagination*. New York: Oxford University Press.

# INDEX

Page numbers in italics refer to illustrations and tables.

Lightning Source UK Ltd.
Milton Keynes UK
UKHW04f1446101018
330324UK00001B/1/P

9 780226 564074